AF267439

Israel's Struggle with Hezbollah

Other Books by Clifford Sobin

Living in Heaven, Coping with Hell: Israel's Northern Borders

The Pivotal Years: Israel and The Arab World 1966 – 1977

My Jackson Hole Favorites

Maryland Workers' Compensation

Israel's Struggle with Hezbollah

A War Without End

By Clifford Sobin

Copyright © 2023 by Clifford B. Sobin

Lean Forward Publishing 2023
Cover by JD&J Book Cover Design.

All Rights Reserved, including the right to reproduce this book or portions thereof in any form whatsoever, except for brief excerpts as part of critical reviews or other written materials without the express written permission of the author. For permission requests you may contact the author by accessing the author's website at www.CliffordSobin.com. March 8 and May 24, 2023

ISBN: 978-1-960782-00-7 (hardback)
ISBN: 978-0-9986374-8-8 (paperback)
ISBN: 978-0-9986374-9-5 (eBook)
Library of Congress Control Number: 2023901367
Names: Sobin, Clifford, author.

Title: Israel's struggle with Hezbollah: a war without end / Clifford Sobin.
Description: Rockville, MD: Lean Forward Publishing, 2023. | Includes
    bibliographical references.
Identifiers: LCCN 2023901367 (print) | ISBN 978-0-9986374-8-8
    (paperback) | ISBN 978-0-9986374-9-5 (ebook)
Subjects: LCSH: Lebanon--History. | Lebanon War, 2006. | Syria--Civil
    War, 2011---History. | Hizballah (Lebanon)--History. | Israel--Foreign
    relations--Lebanon. | Middle East--History--21st century. | BISAC:
    HISTORY / Wars & Conflicts / General. | HISTORY / Middle East /
    Israel & Palestine. | HISTORY / Middle East / Syria. | HISTORY /
    Middle East / Iran.
Classification: LCC HV6433.I722 S63 2023 (print) | LCC HV6433.I722
    (ebook) | DDC 320--dc23.

This book is dedicated to my wife, Julie,
My three children and their significant others,
My four grandchildren and those to come, and
To Lieutenant Colonel (Res.) Sarit Zehavi, who has added so much
meaning to my life and done so much on behalf of Israel.

Contents

PART THREE

PART FOUR

Maps

The Region

Regional Religious/Political Control of Lebanon

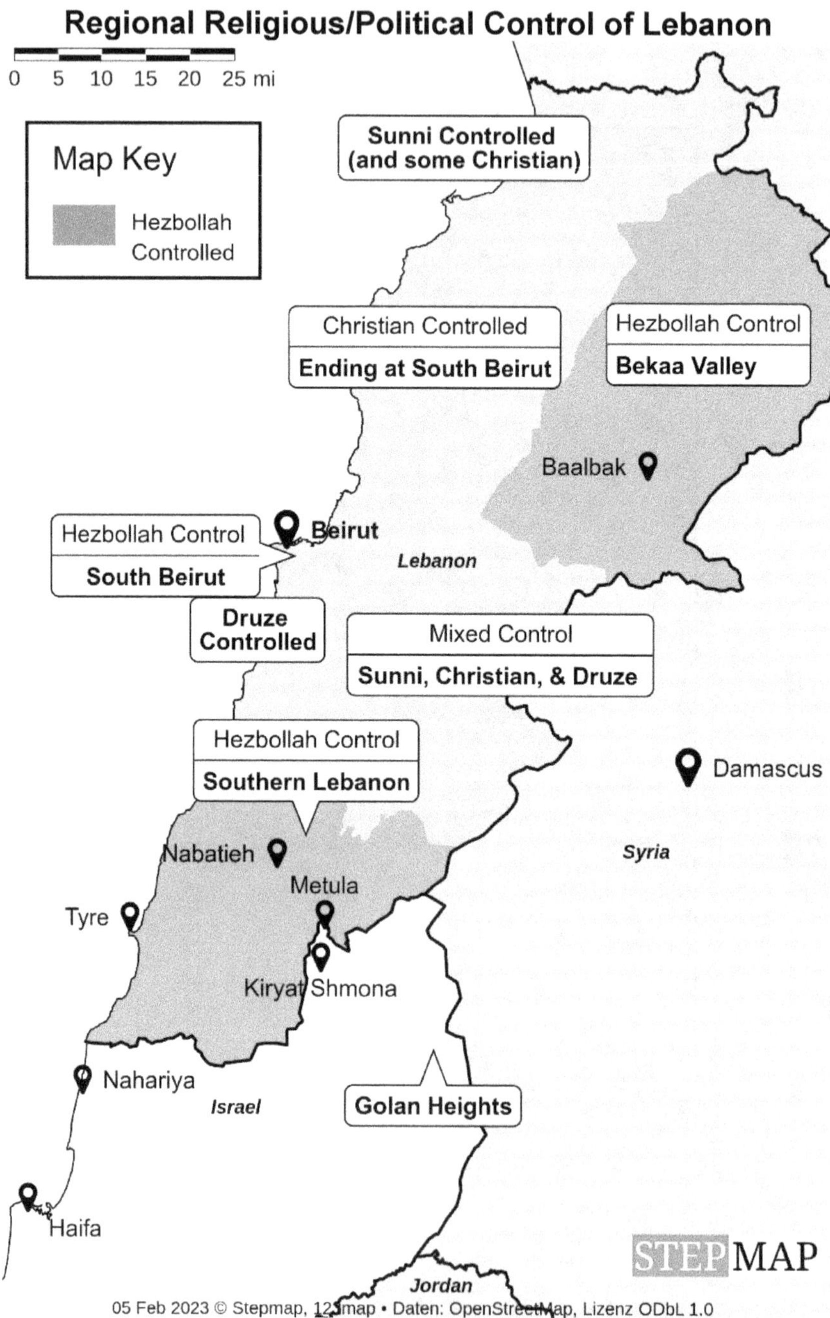

05 Feb 2023 © Stepmap, 123map • Daten: OpenStreetMap, Lizenz ODbL 1.0

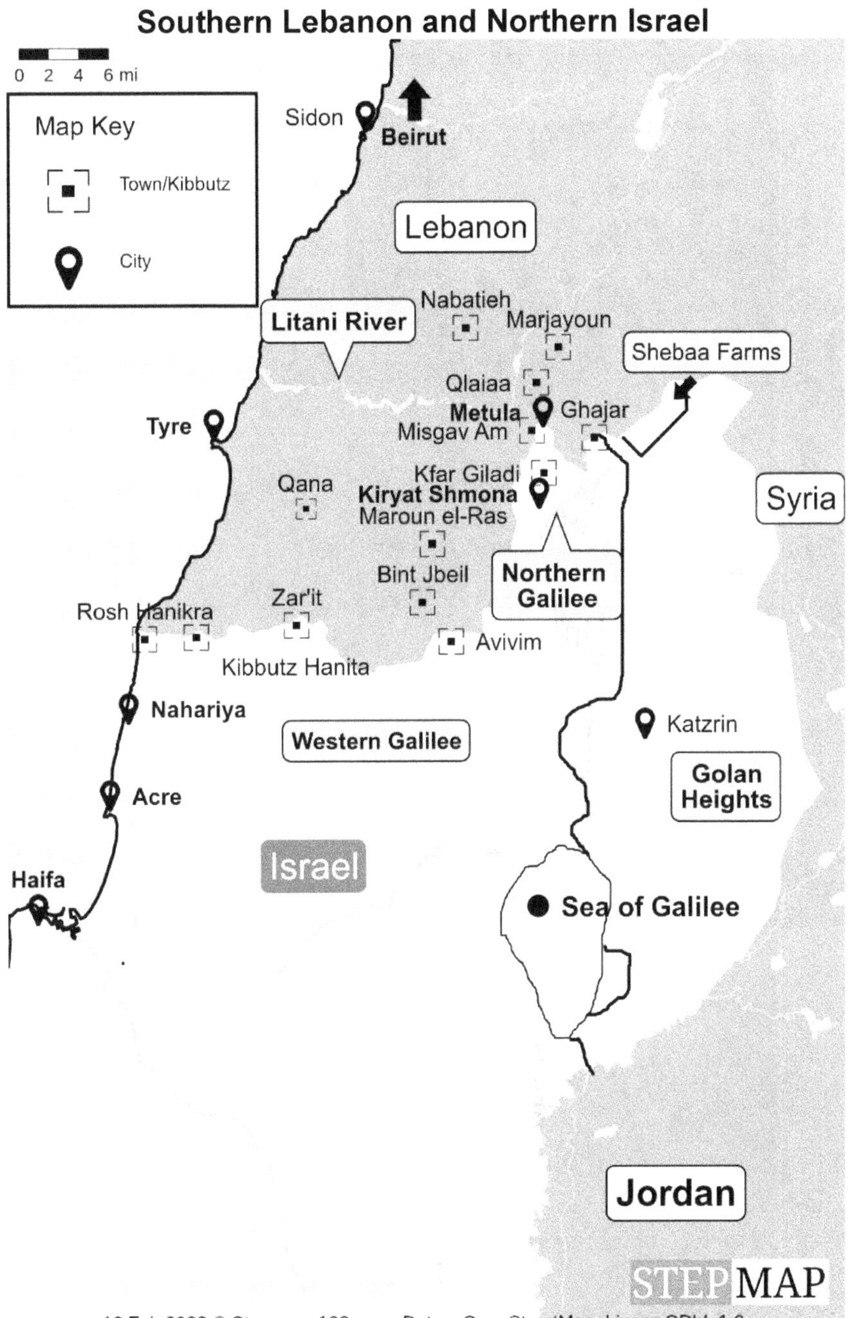

Southern Lebanon and Northern Israel
0 2 4 6 mi
Map Key
Town/Kibbutz
City
Sidon
Beirut
Lebanon
Litani River
Nabatieh
Marjayoun
Shebaa Farms
Qlaiaa
Metula
Ghajar
Tyre
Misgav Am
Syria
Qana
Kfar Giladi
Kiryat Shmona
Maroun el-Ras
Bint Jbeil
Northern Galilee
Rosh Hanikra
Zar'it
Avivim
Kibbutz Hanita
Nahariya
Western Galilee
Katzrin
Acre
Golan Heights
Israel
Haifa
Sea of Galilee
Jordan
STEPMAP
12 Feb 2023 © Stepmap, 123map • Daten: OpenStreetMap, Lizenz ODbL 1.0

Terror Attack Locations

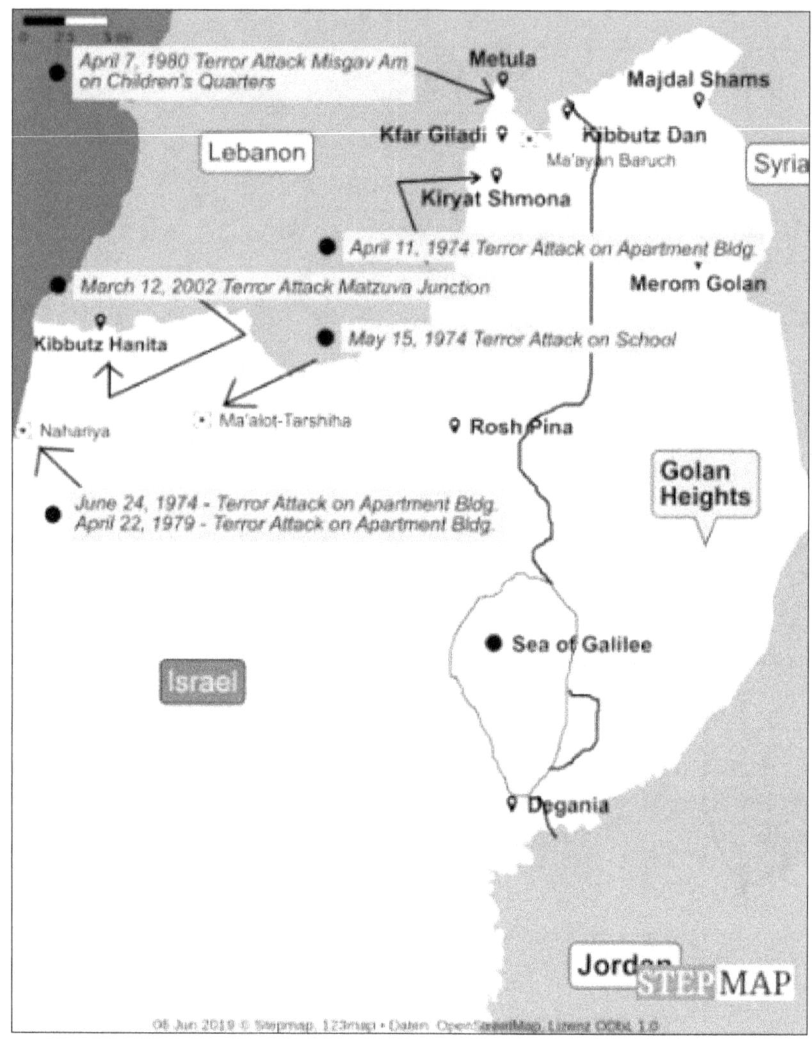

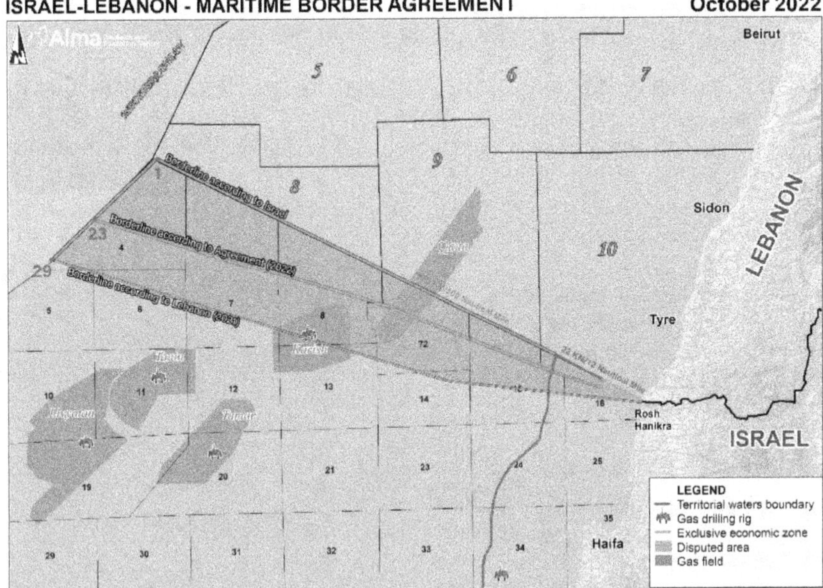
Borderline according to Israel
Borderline according to Agreement (2022)
Borderline according to Lebanon (2021)
Beirut
Sidon
LEBANON
Tyre
Rosh Hanikra
ISRAEL
Haifa
Tanin
Karish
Qana
Leviathan
5
6
7
8
9
10
23
29
1
4
5
6
7
8
10
11
12
13
14
16
19
20
21
23
24
25
29
30
31
32
33
34
35
72
LEGEND
Territorial waters boundary
Gas drilling rig
Exclusive economic zone
Disputed area
Gas field

Locations of Hezbollah Tunnels Extending into Israel

Map Courtesy of the Alma Research and Education Center

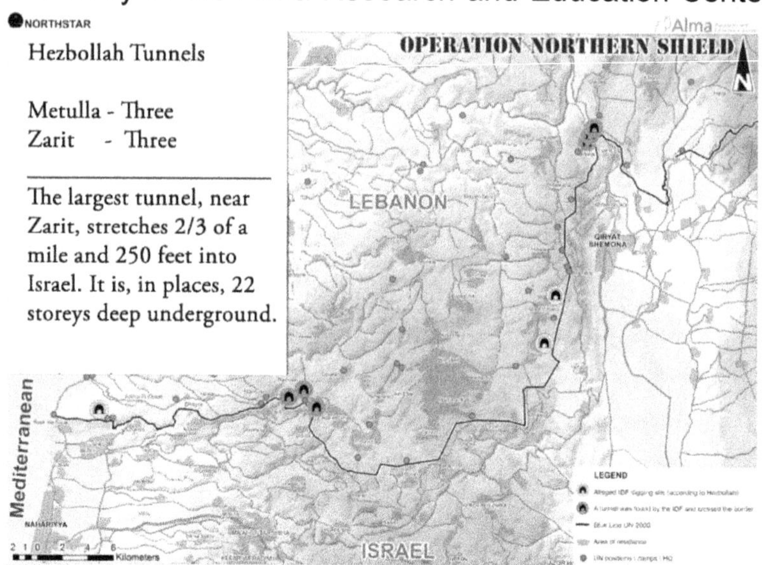

Text rectangle added by the author.

Israel's Struggle with Hezbollah

Introduction

Every morning, on the outskirts of Metula, Israel's northernmost town, the rising sun reveals the network of concertina wire, fencing, and concrete walls that divides Israel and Lebanon. Miles west, on a ridgeline facing north, residents of a venerable kibbutz revel in their tranquil life while also depending on barriers, coupled with a barren, bulldozed mountainside to protect them from terrorists haunting the border region. To the east, on the Golan Heights, rivers of cumulus clouds often rush above Mount Bental, a dormant volcanic cone near the Syrian border, softening the light falling on the pastoral landscape below—and the discordant lines of border fence that cut through the flat terrain.

During those fleeting moments that separate night from day, serenity reigns along Israel's northern borders. I have been there. I have felt it. These quiet moments are precious—even hopeful. But I cannot ignore the hatred. Israel cannot ignore the hatred. For across these borders is Hezbollah, whose evil power grows.

And because of Hezbollah, as well as Iran and Syria, a catastrophic war will likely return to these borders one day.

I wrote this book as a history and a warning. It explores Hezbollah's origins, Israel's response to Hezbollah's growth, and what level of threat exists today. This journey to understanding will travel deep into Lebanon's past to help illuminate its present while examining Iran's and Syria's changing but always malevolent roles in Hezbollah's rise.

And I also wrote this book as a call to action. In it, I discuss what Israel is doing about the threat it faces, what it can and might consider doing to meet that threat, and what we can do to help.

The War that Could Happen: Part One

At first light, Hezbollah operatives were busy readying for an afternoon onslaught. Hours earlier, Iran's Supreme Leader had ordered Hezbollah to attack Israel. Minutes later, fiber-optic lines connecting Shiite villages throughout southern Lebanon, the Bekaa Valley on Lebanon's eastern border with Syria, and South Beirut were humming with activity. Orders flew with rapid succession. Soldiers headed to their posts. Technicians prepared rockets for firing. Flight controllers prepared unmanned aerial vehicles for flight. All according to a predetermined plan to wreak havoc and despair within Israel. All for Iran's benefit.

Just yesterday, Israel was preparing to conduct a snap drill to sharpen its air defenses for a potential battle. Nuclear talks with Iran had ended months ago. A deal had been struck despite Israel's objections. But a deal requires two sides to agree and comply. For this deal, both sides agreed, but only one side complied. Western nations agreed to lift their economic sanctions imposed on Iran in return for Iran's agreement to freeze its nuclear program and to permit independent inspections to ensure its compliance. But Iran did not stop its nuclear program. Instead, it upped the ante. While surreptitiously continuing to develop nuclear weapons and the means to deliver them, it also used the sudden influx of money from sanction relief to supply all its proxies, especially Hezbollah, with more advanced weaponry.

After Israel learned of Iran's perfidy, the time for action drew near. Israel had sworn to prevent Iran from becoming a nuclear power. This was a clear red line. If Iran's leadership were to gain access to nuclear bombs, they would have the tools to bring about Israel's extinction—and would likely use them, in practice or as leverage. Equally concerning was the prospect of Hezbollah possessing thousands more precision-guided rockets, paid for, and provided by Iran. This was another red line Israel could not tolerate being crossed.

And so, realizing the strategic pendulum would soon shift against it, Israel began a countdown for launching a strike against Iran's nuclear program. When was not yet certain. If was hardly in doubt.

Israel's preparation for the drill that morning was open and obvious to those with the technical capability to look. Iran had that capability. Israel's preparations were quickly discovered and reported to Iran's leadership. Was it a drill or was it the precursor for an attack?

Iran had several options. One was absorbing the blow. Another was to reveal Israel's plans to a world unsympathetic to the Jewish state's plight. However, for the Iranians, a third option was most enticing. Strike a blow now so powerful that it would shake Israel to its core before Israel could setback Iran's nuclear program with a targeted strike of its own. Perhaps such a strike would mark the beginning of Israel's demise.

But Iran had no taste for a direct military strike of its own. It did not yet have the means in its own hands to ensure success and even trying would invite a devastating response—perhaps a nuclear one.

However, Iran had the perfect tool—its proxy Hezbollah, with its massive stock of missiles—and its other proxies, also armed with rockets: the Houthis from Yemen, Iraqi Hezbollah from the deserts of Western Iraq, and Hamas and Islamic Jihad from Gaza. Iran's leaders thought a proxy war was ideal. It would give them time to build its first nuclear weapons, and they were certain Israel would be unable to strike their nuclear program during a multi-front war, with thousands of missiles hitting targets inside Israeli territory, nor would Israel risk international condemnation in its time of need. Once Iran's nuclear weapons were built, it would be too late for Israel to do anything about it. Then, facing down Iran's nuclear might, and being devastated by missile strikes from Hezbollah and the other proxies, Israel would be considerably weakened, and the dismantlement of the Jewish State would begin. And so, Iran sent the order to Hezbollah—strike!

What is Hezbollah?

Simply put, Hezbollah is now the ruling power in Lebanon. This is true despite the presence of some individuals who actively oppose it and far more who are cowed into submission. Composed of radicalized Lebanese Shiites determined to see Israel destroyed, it was created and remains controlled in large part by Iran, despite its nominal independence. At its beginning, Hezbollah was an ideological terrorist movement that developed into a guerilla army that follows Shiite ideology. Over the decades, Hezbollah became a state within a state. That is, until now. Today, for all practical purposes, with its ability to shape government policy, Hezbollah is the state of Lebanon.

Since 1982, Iran has sent increasingly advanced weaponry to Hezbollah while also providing training and massive financial support. Hezbollah now possesses approximately 150,000 rockets, many unmanned aerial vehicles (UAVs), huge quantities of other forms of sophisticated advanced weaponry, tens of thousands of battle-hardened reserves, thousands of specialized military forces, and deep financial pockets. In addition, Hezbollah boasts a massive media operation; runs sophisticated criminal operations around the globe that financially augment the hundreds of millions Iran gives it annually; and employs terrorists that strike when it sees fit. All while providing exclusive social services to Shiites within Lebanon and placing its representatives in Lebanon's Parliament, key Cabinet positions, and government ministries.

In short, Hezbollah is a hybrid terrorist entity, taking on the role of a government authority when it wants—providing services to select constituents, inserting its operatives in every village where Shiites predominate, conducting its own foreign policy, and wielding a massive army that doubles as an internal quasi-police presence to protect Hezbollah from forces that might threaten its political power. Hezbollah manages all of this while still acting as a classic terrorist operation, killing innocents for political purposes at home and abroad while engaging in illicit activities that add hundreds of millions of dollars to its coffers.

<u>The War that Could Happen: Part Two</u>

Hezbollah's leadership was not happy about Iran's orders. It knew war with Israel would mean devastation for Lebanon and the Shiites living there. Yet, there was no alternative. At best, refusal would mean an end to the flow of regular money and weapons from Iran, which over time would weaken Hezbollah's grip on power. But more likely, refusal would mean elimination. Either quickly by assassination, or by competition, as hardliners newly emboldened by an angry Iran would take over from within or create new organizations that would strive to usurp Hezbollah. And, of course, if history were a guide, a grateful and newly enriched Iran, flush with money after the sanctions ended, would surely help to rebuild a Lebanon devastated by war. Iran had done so in 2006, even though it had not instigated that war. Surely Iran would do so again.

Therefore, Hezbollah initiated operations.

Many of Hezbollah's targets inside Israel were military—including airfields, mobilization centers, and army bases. Dimona, Israel's nuclear facility, was another obvious one. But these were not the targets whose destruction Iran hoped would shatter Israel's morale. For that, Hezbollah also planned to strike critical economic infrastructure such as power grids, transportation centers, ports, offshore gas facilities, heavy industry, and the like. And, of course, the people of the Israel—their homes and their communities.

At 3 p.m., all was peaceful. The day had proceeded as normal in the northern Galilee. The crisp morning air had given way to heat from the rising sun. Farmers worked in their fields. Many children were still at daycare or attending after-school activities. Tourists swarmed popular attractions. In the major cities, people that commuted to work again after COVID had waned were back in their offices located in the many skyscrapers that dot the Tel Aviv environs.

Then came hell.

Hezbollah had a simple plan: Inundate Israel with thousands of missiles that would destroy its economic infrastructure; use the Radwan, an elite strike force, to capture at least one Israeli town and hold its residents hostage; and kill as many people as it could in an initial strike. Then, bombard Israel's airfields with missiles and swarms of UAVs to impede air operations, while also firing missiles indiscriminately at soft targets such as towns, schools, and buildings to break Israeli civilian morale and complicate mobilization of Israel's Defense Forces (IDF).

Of course, Hezbollah knew that an IDF offensive into Lebanon would be forthcoming. Yet this would also provide an opportunity to counterattack, which Hezbollah had planned for. Tunnels, bunkers, and prepositioned roadside bombs would bleed IDF ground forces entering Lebanon. Inside the country's southern villages, Hezbollah militia units trained for this day would defend their towns. Meanwhile, from inside the homes of villagers and even from inside schools and mosques, both in the south and in other regions of Lebanon, Hezbollah's operatives would continue firing missiles, forcing Israel to choose between ignoring the mayhem the missiles caused and seeking to destroy the homes and other structures storing the missiles, which would cost Lebanese civilian lives. Hezbollah had coldly calculated that Israel inevitably would choose the latter and was eagerly looking forward to that.

Why?

Information warfare is a tool in the arsenal of all armies, but especially so for a hybrid terrorist organization. So, Hezbollah cagily planned that part of its campaign too. Its goal was to garner international sympathy when it did not have the strength to defend itself. Therefore, as part of Hezbollah's battle plan, it embedded operatives from its media outlet in areas where it expected to ambush Israeli ground forces rushing into Lebanon while also readying other film crews to film the damage wrought by Israeli air strikes. And where the damage was not sufficiently sympathetic, Hezbollah planned to manufacture and manipulate facts on the ground and images taken to portray what it wanted. In conjunction with that effort, Hezbollah mobilized its organized foreign correspondent operation to coordinate and transport foreign correspondents, especially friendly ones, to locations where it could best present Israel's supposed war crimes.

But Hezbollah also depended on Iran's assurances that it would not be alone. From the Syrian Golan, both irregular militias and Hezbollah fighters would try to cross into the Golan Heights while more missiles would fly overhead from Syria toward Israel, some fired by Iranian proxies and some by Hezbollah itself. From Western Iraq, as well as Yemen, missiles would fly too. And of course, Hamas and Islamic Jihad in Gaza would join the battle with their rockets, incendiary-laden balloons, and irregular ground forces seeking to penetrate under, over, and through the border fence while specially trained frogmen swam under the ocean's surface north from Gaza and south from Lebanon to complete their terror missions.

From everywhere, missiles would be streaking through the skies, UAVs flying, and terrorists crossing the borders—all with the same goal of murder and mayhem. Meanwhile, with Iran's help, Hezbollah planned to generate further havoc with a massive cyberattack, instigate uprisings in Israeli-Arab communities astride key roads to hinder the IDF's movement and endanger the lives of Jewish civilians in northern Israel. All told, the plan would leave Israel reeling from massive blows coming from all directions, including from within its borders.

Then, Hezbollah planned to hang on. Hang on until the world stopped the fighting and Hezbollah could declare victory. Or hang on until Iran could rush the development of its nuclear arsenal and delivery systems. Then Hezbollah would be shielded by the threat that Iran would deliver those weapons to an already torn and weary Israel. Hezbollah was certain that, with its economy in ruins, thousands dead and the remainder suffering, Israel and its weakened IDF would be restrained by a civilian leadership shocked by the devastation incurred and unwilling to risk suffering more of the same.

*   *   *   *

The scenario I describe above is not fanciful; it is realistic. Such an attack would result in massive civilian loss of life within Israel, quite possibly in the tens of thousands, and property destruction certainly in the billions. Israelis would see power outages of long-standing duration, water shortages, food supply interruptions, and economic devastation on an unprecedented scale. Over the last year, at the time of this writing, we have seen cities in Ukraine torn apart by a Russian army using up to ten thousand missiles coupled with massive artillery bombardments. Hezbollah possesses 150,000 or more rockets capable of carrying payloads, often equal to or more than the systems Russia employs! Iran's proxies have thousands, if not more. It is without doubt within Hezbollah's present capabilities, coupled with Iran's influence over its other proxies to add their firepower, to inflict such havoc on Israeli society that its impact is unknowable. It would certainly destroy the vibrancy and could easily destroy the viability of the Jewish State. As such, the risk Israel faces in a future war with Hezbollah is immense. As is the challenge to minimize it.

How could this be?

The common perception is that Israel has the most powerful army in the Middle East. And that is true. But well-placed blows can fell the most powerful. Ask Goliath about his confrontation with David. Or the many healthy people that succumbed to one of the smallest living organisms—the COVID virus—that replicates and multiplies until it kills its victim.

A nation's power is in large part based on the will of its people. If that will should be broken, the sinews that bind its citizens loosen. What was hard becomes soft. What was resolute becomes hesitant. When confidence dissipates and fear dominates, it is a recipe for a nation's dissolution. That is what Iran hopes to accomplish as part of its long-lasting campaign against Israel. Hezbollah is one of Iran's most important tools for making that happen. It is what Hezbollah has prepared for and what Iran paid for.

This book is based on more than thirty interviews I conducted in Israel and the United States, extensive research, and my knowledge of northern Israel gained by walking the land, meeting its people, and my involvement with *Alma*, a research and education center specializing in Israel's security challenges along its northern borders.

The book is composed of four parts: How Hezbollah came to be; the threat Hezbollah and other Iranian proxy armies pose today; Israel's response; and a call to action regarding how Israel may choose to meet the threat in the future and suggested actions available for concerned readers who wish to weigh in against the rising threat Hezbollah poses. Combined, these sections shine a bright light on the growing darkness.

However, the opinions I personally express, and any errors within, are mine alone.

Chapter One

Lebanon's Creation

The story of Hezbollah should not be separated from the story of Lebanon. And the story of Lebanon is a story of religious strife, cruelty, and dysfunction. There, within a landmass considerably smaller than the American state of Connecticut, stretches a battered nation no more than 135 miles long and fifty miles at its widest. There, four major religious groups have fought for their share of power. But now, one clear winner has emerged from this struggle. It is the Shiite terrorist organization Iran created and still supports, Hezbollah, which translates to the "Party of God."

But this was not always so.

For much of the last century, Christians supported by France controlled Lebanon, Sunni Muslims contested for power, and Druze chafed in their mountain enclaves while pushing for their fair share. Meanwhile, Lebanese Shiites languished in poverty and submission. And, within each religious group, corrupt local chieftains, no more than heads of families, exerted considerable power, demanded allegiance, and brokered favor. The Lebanese word for them is *zuama*. But for our purposes, we will call them family chieftains. Think Mafia Dons.

Still, despite the sectarian divisions and family-led corruption, up until the mid-1970s many outsiders viewed Lebanon as a happy place. In fact, some called the twenty years between 1955 and 1975 the "Golden Age." Wealthy male Arabs from the Persian Gulf and elsewhere would book stays at swanky hotels in Beirut to escape the dreary dictates of their home countries where local religious and legal authorities frowned on drinking, gambling, and womanizing. For them, Beirut, Lebanon's capital, was a place where all things denied at home were possible. Alcohol flowed freely, a large casino catered to gambling pursuits, showgirls glittered, women were available for seduction, and prostitutes serviced. Clubs played loud disco music but also employed belly dancers undulating to Arab music. Fine dining establishments, many serving French cuisine, mixed with shawarma stands. Film festivals, art galleries, and outdoor concerts competed for attention with the many bookstores offering plenty of English and French titles. Western tourists arrived by the hundreds on cruise ships crisscrossing the Mediterranean to enjoy the sights and smells of the city, too. *Life* magazine called Beirut "a kind of Las Vegas-Riviera-St. Moritz flavored with spices of Araby."

The country was awash with money from tourism and business, helped largely by Saudi- and Iraqi-built pipelines that were supposed to terminate in Palestine but after Israel's establishment in 1948 were diverted to Lebanon. Its economy flourished, nourished by wealthy, homegrown Sunni and Christian entrepreneurs, coupled with Muslim businessmen who left Egypt after Gamal Abdel Nasser overthrew King Farouk in 1952. All seemed good, at least for those who shared in the economic wealth and for tourists who didn't venture too far from Beirut.

However, this ostensible paradise, prized by many Christians who also feared losing their privileged position in Lebanese society, left most Shiites in poverty. Nor did its riches extend to the many Sunnis, Palestinians, and Druze who called Lebanon home. Their impoverishment and desperation supplied much combustible material for the explosion brewing. A cauldron that blew up into a murderous civil war in 1975, precipitated by the arrival of Palestinian terrorists that decided to use Lebanon as a base for attacking Israel.

But before delving into the details of Lebanon's civil war, as necessary as they are for understanding Lebanon today, we must first explore a bit of ancient history to provide context. Learning where today's major Lebanese religious sects came from, their memories, and how collectively they formed the imperfect and precarious union that became Lebanon is a crucial prerequisite for wrapping our arms around the phenomenon that is Hezbollah. Only then, after detailing a dash of meddling from Western powers, Iran and Syria's manipulations, and Israel's response to terrorist atrocities will Hezbollah's rise, and longevity, make sense within the context of the mess Lebanon is and has been.

So, let's dive in—one religion, political grouping, event, and individual at a time.

<u>Maronites</u>

For a while, in the middle of the twentieth century, the Maronites were top dog in Lebanon. But that's not how they began, and although still powerful, Hezbollah has now supplanted them. Still, Maronite history is part of Lebanese history, and like them or not, Hezbollah still needs to keep a wary eye on the Maronites today. So too then, I must explain who they are, where they came from, and the role they now play.

At the most basic level, Maronites are Christians with close ties to the Catholic church. They trace their beginnings to Maron, a hermit priest who spent his life outdoors in prayerful solitude, without regard for the elements. Born sometime in the middle of the fourth century, he lived in a mountainous region of Syria near Antioch. By his death in 410 A.D., Maron had established a new order of Catholicism. Later recognized by the Vatican as a saint, he developed a following in a small community in the Orontes River valley in Syria. They called themselves Maronites.

But as the years passed into the sixth and seventh centuries, trouble arrived from the Byzantine Empire that rose from the ruins of the Roman Empire, whose capital was Constantinople (now known as Istanbul). Its citizens viewed Christ differently. Therefore, despite considering themselves Christians, they persecuted the Maronites. Although the Maronites enjoyed some success on the battlefield fending off the Byzantines, the survivors were outnumbered and saw the writing on the wall. Rather than continue the struggle, many Maronites left their homes in Syria to join their brethren who had departed decades earlier to settle in lands now part of Lebanon.

But where would they be safe? They chose the Mount Lebanon mountain range that ran parallel to the Mediterranean coast. With peaks as high as 10,000 feet, the heavily forested mountains ran north and south over more than 100 miles of rough terrain. It worked. The Byzantines did not follow them and when Muslim armies bent on conquest swept through the region during the seventh century, they failed to vanquish the Maronites living in their mountain retreat. Then, rather than continue the fight, an accommodation was made between the Muslim would-be conquerors and the determined inhabitants of Mount Lebanon. For centuries after, Maronite culture thrived in the woods and mountains, their lives somewhat autonomous from the Muslims who now surrounded them on the flatlands below.

Still, things were not perfect. Living in a land dominated by Muslims was difficult. Rules would change and the threat of annihilation was ever-present. That is why the Maronites welcomed the crusaders, many of whom were French, and who first arrived just before the beginning of the twelfth century. Soon, the Maronites' bond with Christianity, and especially the Catholic pope, deepened. The Maronites also forged new cultural and political bonds with France, which was predisposed to help communities that identified with Catholicism. So much so that to this day many Maronites have common French names like Claude, Pierre, and Michel.

By the late 1600s, due to their growing population and propensity to organize and modernize, the Maronites dominated the Mount

Lebanon range as they grew closer to the Roman Catholic Church. During the Crusades, the pope invited the Maronites' leader to visit him in Rome. That visit influenced the Maronites to further align their liturgy with the Catholic Church. Then, in 1521, Pope Leo X called the Maronites "a rose among thorns." Two hundred years later, the Maronites accepted a form of union with the Catholic Church in Rome while retaining much of their own liturgy and independence regarding governance, saints, and holidays.

The Maronites accomplished all this despite having to contend with a new master—the Ottomans, who had invaded the region—and a new nearby enemy, the Druze. We will get to who the Druze are, and who the Ottomans were, in a moment. But suffice it to say, with the Ottomans beginning to lose their grip, the Maronites and the Druze fought three bitter wars in which savagery was the order of the day—1840, 1845, and 1860—the last of which left, depending on the source, up to 20,000 Maronites dead. But because of those wars, with the help of France and other European powers, the Maronites managed to carve out a semblance of autonomy. It was not the total independence they desired, but it was enough to meet Maronite needs for the next sixty years until the Ottoman Empire dissolved. No longer a small number of followers of Maron, the vibrant Maronite population was there to stay.

But the Maronites were not satisfied with just autonomy. Wanting total control of their destiny, Maronites thirsted for their own state. Would they get the opportunity?

Sunnis and Shiites

About the same time the Byzantines and the Maronites clashed, a new religion rose in the East—Islam—started by the Prophet Muhammad based on revelations he reported first receiving in 610 A.D., when he turned forty. Islam spread quickly during the remaining twenty-two years of Prophet Muhammad's life, first through his preaching, and then by conquest and proselytizing. But as is often the case, the death of a revered leader leaves a void to be filled. Prophet Muhammad's followers dealt with the same issue. Who would be the new caliph, or spiritual leader, of Islam?

Four different successors filled Prophet Muhammad's shoes over the next few decades. During that time the Muslim caliphate expanded significantly but infighting continued. Two opposing camps tussled over the succession issue. Most believed new leaders should be chosen by consensus in the tradition of the desert. That group came to be known as Sunni (loosely meaning traditionalists but also defined as "the path" or the "the way" of the Prophet Muhammad). However, others believed the caliph must be a descendant or relative of Prophet Muhammad. The person who best fit those criteria was Fatima, daughter of the prophet. But she was a woman. In those days, that automatically disqualified her. But her husband, Ali, also fit the bill. Not only was he the son-in-law of the Prophet Muhammad, but he also was a first cousin of the prophet. Over time, the group in favor of Ali leading Islam's disciples came to be known as Shiites, meaning "followers of Ali."

Following three others selected by merit not relationship, Ali became Islam's leader forty-five years after Prophet Muhammad passed away. So far, the succession had not unduly divided the Muslim world, though it had not been free of controversy and assassination. But no more. During the fifth year of his reign in 661 AD, former allies of Ali assassinated him. A poisoned sword slash to Ali's head was the chosen method.

Who would be the next leader?

Sunnis supported Muawiya, a powerful and popular individual. But Muawiya was not related to the Prophet Muhammad. Shiites pushed for one of Ali's two sons, Hasan or Hussain. Because Hasan was the eldest son, he got the first shot at it. But he deferred to Muawiya. Ali's second son, Hussain, wasn't so deferential. He wanted the job. Since Hussain was Ali's son, and therefore part of Prophet Muhammad's bloodline, Shiites supported him.

Settlement of this dispute did not end peacefully.

Nineteen years after Ali's death, a battle took place in Karbala, a town in central Iraq, that would have lasting repercussions for Islam and the world at large; and 1,300 years later lead to the birth of Hezbollah. There, Muawiya's son, Yazid, led a large army against Hussain's much smaller band. For ten days, Hussain held out, refusing all requests to surrender. Finally, Yazid's army overran Hussein's small force whereupon a Yazid soldier decapitated Hussain. Later Yazid's Sunni soldiers took Hussain's head to Damascus, a seat of Sunni power in those days.

The Shiites had lost the battle but gained their defining trait—the memory of martyrdom. Imam Hussain's sacrifice became the most recognized symbol of Shiite suffering ever since. Edward Mortimer wrote in *Faith and Power: The Politics of Islam:*

> Sunni Islam is the doctrine of power and achievement. Shi'ism is the doctrine of opposition. The starting point of Shi'ism is defeat: the defeat of Ali and his house....Its primary appeal is therefore to the defeated and oppressed. That is why it has often been the rallying cry for the underdogs in the Muslim world.... Especially the poor and dispossessed.

And so, despite losing his head, Hussain survives in tradition and liturgy.

After the battle at Karbala, the remaining Shiites, vastly outnumbered, sought refuge throughout the Middle East. When Sunni Muslim armies swept into Lebanon in the seventh century, Shiites followed. By the ninth century, some settled in parts of what is now southern Lebanon as well as other parts of what is now Lebanon, frequently near Sunnis and Maronites. However, in the thirteenth and fourteenth centuries, the Sunnis pushed the Shiites into concentrated enclaves in peripheral areas of the north; to the Bekaa

Valley, which lies between the two parallel mountain ranges running north to south; and into southern Lebanon. There, despite constituting a growing percentage of the region's population, most Shiites lived in poverty and obscurity until the late 1970s.

The Sunnis, however, had more economic opportunities. Although poverty still haunted many, others flourished in the entrepreneurial environment that the Maronites and their other Christian allies enjoyed. And, like the Shiites, the Sunni population in Lebanon multiplied—some living in rural areas, while many lived in the cities.

The Druze

Today, there are about a million Druze, most of whom live in Lebanon and Syria, with a smaller concentration in Israel, and others scattered throughout the world. When the Maronites and Muslims came to Lebanon, there were no Druze. That changed in the second millennium.

The Druze faith first appeared sometime around 1010 AD, initially spreading through various parts of Syria. For several years, Sunni Muslims tried to crush this incipient religion that held to tenets different than Islam. Finally, persecution waned, leaving most Druze survivors clinging to life on the slopes of Mount Hermon at the corner where the borders of present-day Syria, Israel, and Lebanon meet, and near present-day Aleppo in Syria.

Pinning down what defines the Druze religion is difficult. Religious leaders wrote its dogma in six books made purposively cryptic so that even if outsiders got hold of the tracts, they still would not understand what the religion is about. That secrecy does not just apply to outsiders. It is for insiders too. The tenets of the faith are kept hidden from most of its adherents. Only a few of each new generation receive the training needed for them to be known as "uqqal" which means enlightened. For most Druze, they accept being "juhal," which means ignorant or non-initiated. They learn a simplified version of their religion that emphasizes moral and ethical behavior.

Nevertheless, despite the significant differences the Druze maintain between their few and many others that surround them, a surprisingly tight-knit community has developed in which interfaith marriage is prohibited, as are conversions since 1043 AD. The Druze are untroubled by these self-imposed limitations to their growth, for they believe that since the number of souls of believers was fixed at the date of creation, the number of living Druze is strictly tied to birth and death. Therefore, according to the Druze, when one member dies and another is born, the soul of the dead person enters the body of the newborn. Their belief in this form of reincarnation doubtless fuels their reputation as fierce, brave fighters and is behind their war cry, "Who wants to sleep in his mother's womb tonight?". Perhaps it also contributes to the closeness of the entire Druze community today, whether they live in Lebanon, Israel, or Syria. Loyal to the country they live in, the Druze nevertheless maintain close ties to other Druze communities, regardless of location or politics.

The Ottoman Empire

No discussion of Lebanon would be complete without addressing the role the Ottomans played in making Lebanon a mess. In their heyday, after sweeping out of what is now Turkey in the thirteenth century, the Ottomans controlled a huge swath of territory that included parts of Europe, Arabia, and North Africa. In 1516, the Ottomans conquered Lebanon (Going forward, I will use the term *Lebanon* to denote the land which became Lebanon, even though it was not yet a country). The Ottoman official religion was Sunni, and the Ottoman sultan (leader) was seen worldwide, other than by Shiites, as the caliph, or leader of the Muslim world. In theory, Ottoman control was problematic for the Maronites, Shiites, and Druze. But since they lived primarily outside of the major cities where Ottoman rule was strongest, they persevered.

Things got rather tense in the region when Muhammad Ali, the ruler of Egypt, occupied Lebanon between 1833 to 1841 (yes—I get the similarity of his name to the famous American fighter but trust me, they were different people), before giving way to the Ottoman reconquest of the region. However, Lebanon's return to Ottoman control did not stop the bloody Maronite versus Druze wars between 1840 and 1860. And France's support of the Maronites, along with Britain's support of the Druze, only exacerbated the situation. Meanwhile, the Shiites remained mired in poverty and bereft of any international aid.

Then came the twentieth century. The Ottomans, already in financial trouble, lost wars as well as territory. In 1914, they made the mistake of allying with Germany in World War I. That decision necessitated something else—their support of Sharif Hussein.

Who was Sharif Hussein?

The Ottoman-appointed emir of Mecca.

What is the emir of Mecca?

The second most powerful Sunni religious authority next to that of the Ottoman sultan. The emir in those days was the steward of Mecca and Medina, Islam's holiest cities. Jerusalem is the third holiest.

Why was Hussein important to the Ottomans?

His support would guarantee that during those tenuous times Arabs in the Middle East would not revolt against Ottoman rule.

But there was somebody else whispering in Hussein's ear—England. The British guaranteed Hussein their support for Arab independence if he would ally with England during the war. The thought of becoming the leader of the Arab world enticed Hussein. In 1915 and 1916, Sir Henry McMahon, the British high commissioner in Egypt, and Hussein engaged in an exchange of proposals known as the Hussein-McMahon correspondence. In it, McMahon promised

British support for an Arab nation that would include Syria. Regarding Lebanon, McMahon pushed back on Hussein's desire to control some of or all that area, too, depending on who's interpreting the correspondence. Hussein, however, doubled down on his request and emphasized that controlling Lebanon was a core demand. But, he suggested, he would wait until after World War One to receive Britain's blessing or acquiescence. McMahon responded with silence. This created an ambiguity as to what Britain's' position on Lebanon would be in the future. Certainly, Hussein thought Britain would be supportive.

Even though McMahon's correspondence did not amount to a contractual treaty, he made quite a sweeping promise on behalf of his government, albeit an ambiguous one. He did so because the British were worried after having suffered a serious reversal of fortune at Gallipoli, where Ottoman soldiers had administered a crushing defeat to British forces. McMahon's focus was on getting the Arabs into the war on the British side. However, the promise created a problem with the French, allies to England in the war.

Why?

England had already made a deal promising much of Lebanon to the French!

Recognizing their difficulty, in May 1916 the British sent Sir Mark Sykes to negotiate with a French representative, Charles Francois Picot. England wanted a zone of influence stretching from the Mediterranean to Iran's border. The French wanted colonial control over Syria, Lebanon, and Palestine. Eventually, they found agreement and used a tri-colored map to memorialize it. Red delineated British ascendancy over Southern Iraq, Transjordan, and the ports of Haifa and Acre in Palestine. Blue, covering Syria and most of adjacent Lebanon, defined areas that the French would control. Brown marked the special case of Palestine. Because Sykes and Picot could not agree, most of Palestine was left for international administration until all the allies could agree on a final resolution.

And then bursting into this mess came the Balfour Declaration. On November 9, 1917, England's foreign minister published a letter sent to Lord Rothschild, the honorary president of the Zionist Federation of Great Britain. In it, England viewed "with favor" a "national home for the Jewish people" in Palestine.

Thus, the British had created quite a problem for themselves. They had signed three different agreements with three different parties that contained three contradicting commitments. How would it resolve that?

England's answer to this conundrum, of course, was another negotiation.

In April 1920, shortly after World War One ended, representatives from Britain, France, and Italy met at San Remo, a port in Italy, to work things out. After six days, the participants decided that England would receive a mandate over Palestine, Transjordan, and Iraq. The French got control over most of Syria and all of Lebanon.

But what about the Arabs and the Jews? Neither was invited to San Remo. And Hussein's son, Faisal, had already taken control of Syria. But not for long. In July 1920, the French defeated Arab forces supporting Faisal and conquered Syria. France was now in control. Hussein's dream to lead a vast Arab nation had been dashed.

And then, Maronites in Lebanon saw an opportunity.

But let me pause for a minute. By now, your head is probably spinning. Don't worry. The last few paragraphs can be summarized in one sentence. The British created a mess that made things crazy in Lebanon and the region. But, as you will see, soon things got crazier. What comes next is important, so try to follow along. But if you get confused, don't worry. I'll summarize things for you at the end.

The Maronites feared that the French would eventually leave Syria, along with Lebanon, to the Arabs. That would leave the Maronites once again under Muslim control and endangered. Creating an independent state under Maronite control was their answer to this problem. Given that Christians then made-up eighty percent of the population in the Mount Lebanon range and Druze the other twenty percent, carving out a Maronite nation in that tiny area along Lebanon's northern coast would have been relatively easy from a demographic perspective. But not from an economic one.

Nations need economic viability. That comes with access to the sea and land for farming. The Maronites saw that was the problem with creating a new nation consisting of just the Mount Lebanon region. To thrive, the new nation would need to include the coastal cities, which were primarily Sunni. It also would need the agricultural areas in the Bekaa Valley and southern Lebanon—even though they contained large Shiite populations. Fortunately for the Maronites, a 1932 census of the entire region they wanted to include in a new Lebanese nation found that 51 percent of the population was Christian (much modern scholarship challenges the accuracy of the census), the majority of whom were Maronites. Sunnis, and to a somewhat lesser degree Shiites, made up most of the remaining population. Trailing in numbers, but significantly larger than other groups, were the Druze.

Negotiations with the French moved slowly. Especially because Muslims in Lebanon preferred a merger with Damascus to create a greater Syria under Muslim rule, which was exactly what the Maronites feared. However, in 1943, the parties finally struck a deal. Christians agreed that Lebanon would be considered an Arab state and Lebanon's Muslims agreed to sever with Syria. But the Maronites received something else important. Per an unwritten agreement known as the National Pact, the president of the country would always be a Maronite Christian and parliament would always have a 6:5 ratio of Christians to Muslims. And even though the National Pact required that the prime minister would always be Sunni and the speaker of Parliament Shiite, it also left the president with the power to approve the choice of prime minister. Therefore, political power would remain in Christian hands. Regarding the army, things were not as clear. The agreement required that its commander must be Maronite, the chief of staff Druze. And as things developed, most of the officer class would be Christian, too, while the lower ranks would be mostly Shiites, Sunni, and Druze. In sectarian Lebanon that was a recipe for impotence. Each of the main religious groups could impair the army's performance.

Now, as promised, comes the summary.

And so, in 1943, tiny Lebanon sprang into being—a new, ostensibly democratic nation controlled by religious affiliation. A new nation whose plan for governance was bound to cause problems, especially if its demographics would change due to birth rates, emigration, and immigration. A nation with the Maronites in control, Sunnis unhappy with their place in governance, Shiites impoverished and sidelined, and the Druze marginalized but in a position to ally with others to the detriment of the religious group in charge. Perhaps not *Game of Thrones*, but certainly a game of religions.

Thirty years later, the games would begin in earnest. But the spark that would light the combustible material that helped create Hezbollah came from an unexpected direction—the Palestinians.

The Palestinians

During and after the 1948 Israel-Arab War for Independence, 100,000 Palestinians fled from Israel to southern Lebanon. As refugees, they were willing to work for less than the impoverished Shiites, whose families had lived there for centuries. And they could not become Lebanese citizens; the government had denied them that.

Why?

Because Arab governments saw the plight of displaced, unsettled Palestinians as a weapon in their propaganda war against Israel. But successive Christian presidents in Lebanon had another motive. The 1932 census had only identified a slim 51 percent majority. Since most Palestinians were Sunni, if they were to receive citizenship, the dubious Christian majority at the time would vanish, along with any leverage their supposed majority provided. Christians would become the new minority and face pressure to give up their political control.

Then, in the early 1970s, Palestinian terrorists hijacked three planes and landed them at desolate Dawson's Field in Jordan. This terrorist act jump-started a confrontation with Jordan's King Hussein that had already been brewing, and which ended with the Palestinian Liberation Organization (PLO), led by Yasser Arafat, fleeing Jordan for Lebanon. Soon thousands more Palestinians, including large numbers of militants, settled in Lebanon.

What does that have to do with Hezbollah? Quite a bit.

When the PLO arrived in Lebanon, it was already experienced in creating a state within a state, having attempted to do the same in Jordan. That's why Jordan's king had evicted them. But only because he had the strength to do it—barely. Lebanon, however, lacked both the strength and the will to execute a similar feat; therefore the PLO's move to create its own fiefdom in southern Lebanon succeeded. The government's failure to stop the Palestinians from taking control, as is often the case in Lebanon, was due to religion and politics.

The Palestinians were overwhelmingly Sunni. Many Muslims and Druze at first welcomed them because they thought their presence would put more pressure on the Maronites to change the structure of Lebanon's government. What may have seemed somewhat fair in 1943, appeared quite unfair to Muslims by 1970. The population in Lebanon had shifted. Muslims now outnumbered Christians. Not surprisingly, the new Muslim majority was unhappy with their minority role in government. They wanted representation commensurate with their numbers. Meanwhile, those same demographic trends raised concerns among the Maronites. After all, they had created an independent Lebanon due to fear of Muslim rule from Damascus. They were now facing the specter of Muslim rule once more.

And, to make matters worse, the PLO's ongoing terrorist operations against Israel from Lebanese soil caused Israel to strike back at the PLO inside Lebanon, sowing more turmoil.

At first, Maronite leaders, seeing their communities and hold on power endangered, demanded that the Lebanese government and army confront the PLO as the Jordanian army had. But since the Lebanese army was composed of soldiers from all religions, taking sides against any one religious group was problematic (a dynamic that continues to this day). So, realizing that the PLO was primarily Sunni and that domestic Sunni, and some Druze, supported the PLO, the army refused to cut off the Palestinian tentacles strangling the nation. Therefore, there was nothing the Christian-led government could do. In response, the government's impotence caused the Maronites to form their own militias. The biggest was the Phalange, started by Pierre Gemayel and later commanded by his son Bashar. We will talk more about Bashar later. Another was the Tigers, commanded by then-Christian President Camille Chamoun and later by his son Danny. Seeing the Maronites organizing their armed groups, Muslims and Druze also raised their own militias. Meanwhile, PLO gunmen roamed the streets of Beirut and shook down Shiites in the south for protection money.

In addition, the PLO went about its primary objective—terrorizing Israeli citizens. After the Six-Day War in 1967—during which Israel had vanquished Syria, Jordan, and Egypt—the Lebanese government stood by as the PLO opened its first bases in southern Lebanon. When a different Palestinian terrorist group based in Lebanon attacked an Israeli civilian passenger airplane on December

24, 1968, the Israelis responded by landing special forces two days later at the airport outside of Beirut, Lebanon's capital. There, to send a message that Israel would not accept the Lebanese government's failure to act against terrorists based in Lebanon whose goal was to kill Israelis, Israeli soldiers blew up a dozen planes on the tarmac, eight of them from Lebanon's national airline.

Unfortunately, Israel's show of force did not convince Lebanon's government to act, and PLO terror continued unabated. In April 1969, a short-lived government attempt to rein in the PLO failed. Meanwhile, Syria made matters worse by using what was then called "The Arafat Trail" to ship weapons across its border to the PLO in Lebanon. When the Lebanese army tried to stop that flow of arms, it nearly caused a war with Syria, a crisis that was only averted after President Nasser of Egypt led a negotiation in Cairo. He brokered a deal that effectively gave the PLO the right to create a state within a state in southern Lebanon from which it could attack Israel, maintain training bases, and have continued access to Syrian-supplied armaments. The territory over which they held virtual sovereignty became known as "Fatahland." It stretched from south of the Litani River, several miles north of Israel) and east of Metula, to portions of Mount Hermon and the Syrian border. Soon, the PLO controlled entry to the country by setting up roadblocks in parts of Beirut and southern Lebanon as well as at the international airport. The PLO even established training camps on Lebanese soil for international terrorists such as the IRA, the Baader-Meinhof gang, and the Japanese Red Army. In addition, the PLO used targeted searches at gunpoint to collect money for the Palestinian cause. As a result, some Christians in the south fled to Beirut. The Christian Phalange, sensing war was imminent, redoubled its self-protection effort by strengthening its militia.

The Shiites, despite their numbers now closely matching the Sunnis, did little to prevent their victimhood.

Realizing the PLO would continue sending terrorists into Israel, and that Lebanon lacked the power and will to stop them, Israel strengthened its border defenses and built roads and a base in the Shebaa Farms area of the Golan Heights, adjacent to Fatahland, which Israel had claimed from Syria in the Six-Day War. I know it appears odd that I mentioned Shebaa Farms seemingly out of the blue. But trust me, Shebaa Farms will become quite important later in the story so I may as well bring your attention to this forlorn section of the Golan Heights now.

The PLO's continued terrorism also prompted the IDF to go after the Palestinian terrorists in southern Lebanon. But mixed in with the Palestinians were Shiites, some of whom were friendly with Israelis and even were unofficially permitted to cross the border to work in Metula, Israel's northernmost town. But the fighting between the IDF and the PLO endangered Shiites living in the region. As a result, many fled for the perceived safety of Beirut, creating yet another zone of poverty in the city that still shined for some.

By 1975, the pot the PLO had stirred was boiling. All it needed to explode was a catalyst. But before we explore that, let's introduce one more important personage to the mix. A person who created an awakening in Lebanon's Shiite community that was integral to Hezbollah's eventual rise.

Musa al-Sadr

When we think of the term "civil war," the first thing that often comes to mind is fighting and killing. But civil wars are not always defined by violence. They can be peaceful, non-violent struggles for self-respect, equality, and economic prosperity. Martin Luther King waged that kind of war. So did Mahatma Gandhi. In Lebanon, in the early 1970s, Shiites were still a downtrodden group, now comprising about a third of the country's population, but controlling far less than a third of Lebanon's wealth. Living mostly in the Bekaa Valley, in southern

Lebanon, and the slums of Beirut—they had little to show for their toil. Not even religious independence because the Shiite religious establishment in Lebanon was not independent. It was run, or at least influenced, by Iran. Lebanese clerics received much of their instruction from Iranian institutions, and Iranian clerics assumed many clerical roles for Shiites in Lebanon. Therefore, it was no surprise when the Shiite religious leader in the coastal port city of Tyre, located in southern Lebanon, looked for a young cleric in Iran to replace him when he decided to retire.

He found Musa al-Sadr.

Shiites in Lebanon would never be the same.

Sadr was born in 1928 in Qom, a holy city for Shiites in Iran and the most important site for Shiite theological study in the world. He also had family roots in Lebanon that traced back to the Prophet Muhammad. Except for a brief period spent studying in Iraq, Sadr lived in Iran for most of his early years and attended religious seminaries there. As such, he was a cultural Iranian but Arab by blood.

At first, Sadr was not excited by the offer to replace the Shiite religious leader. At the time, it was dangerous for an Iranian to live in Lebanon. But perhaps the opportunity to lead was too enticing. In 1959, Sadr arrived in Lebanon. There, this well-groomed six-foot, six-inch man with intense eyes and a head of long black curls stretching beyond his turban began to preach.

And what he said was so very different from those who had come before him. Not interested in obscure arguments about theology, he was all about politics and the plight of Shiites in Lebanon. With his magnetic charisma and energetic and riveting oratory, it was not long before Sadr captured the attention of middle-class Shiites. At first, Sadr connected with accomplished Shiites in their thirties and forties who were well-educated, had money, and were predisposed to inserting their ostracized religious group into the morass of Lebanese politics. He then found a middle ground between the Shiite feudal barons who took advantage of their fellow Shiites and the left, which embraced communism and socialism. Not surprisingly, as Sadr's following grew, those feudal leaders began to despise him.

Why?

Until Sadr's arrival, those "clan leaders" maintained their control of the Shiite masses by meeting their basic needs while preventing them from becoming more educated. One story that made the rounds in Lebanon illustrates this mentality and is recounted by Yair Lapid in his book *Window to the Backyard.* Essentially, when some families went to one of those self-styled lords asking for schools for their children, the feudal lord responded:

> Why do you want to abuse your children and cause them suffering and misery in the schools? Don't you think that it's enough that my son Kamel suffers in his studies? For whom do you think my son Kamel went to suffer in schools and college, if not to spare your children from the suffering?

Shiite feudal lords and their families lived well. The Shiite masses did not. They received little help from the government and little help from their leaders, who were happy to maintain the current system.

Sadr wanted change. His message to Shiites was simple. Stop your traditional lamenting and submissive nature and embrace instead "exaltation and rebellion." As the size of his rallies grew, Sadr urged Shiites to stop wallowing in defeat and instead use their history as a sword. He advocated that *Ashura*, the holiday in which Shiites mourn the death of Hussein at the hands of Yazid's army, should be transformed into a symbol of Shiite refusal to submit to injustice. By 1969, Sadr had succeeded in forging a united front composed of Shiites throughout Lebanon. He also had obtained Lebanese citizenship, formed an officially sanctioned Higher Shiite Council that would separate Shiites from Sunni control, and had become president of that council. Sadr's views were clear and emphatic. Upon assuming the council presidency, he said, "Oh rising generations, if our demands are not met, we will set about taking them by force: if this country is not given, it must be taken."

Sadr was all about rescuing Shiites from their plight in Lebanon. This required the masses to forge their own political path since theirs did not fit into the Christian or Sunni one. He was primarily a nationalist who envisioned a homeland for Shiites in Lebanon. And, although sympathetic to Palestinian issues, he was unhappy with their actions that exposed Shiites in southern Lebanon to the Israeli Defense Forces' counter-terrorist operations. Nor was he happy that the Lebanese government provided Shiites with little financial support.

In 1974, Sadr took things a step further when he founded the "Movement of the Deprived." His rhetoric intensified, now attacking the Lebanese government for neglecting Shiites and failing to protect them against what he considered Israeli incursions. His travels took him into Beirut and the Bekaa Valley. Everywhere, his popularity soared as he urged Shiites to demand more from the government. Some began calling him Imam, a huge honor in Shiite theology that recognized him as the savior of Shiites.

In the Bekaa Valley, while speaking at a large rally, Sadr reacted to the IDF entering southern Lebanon to disrupt PLO terrorists based there by saying there was "no alternative for us except revolution and weapons." Sadr then established a militia to operate as the armed wing of the "Movement of the Deprived." I'll mention the militia's name in Arabic, *Afwai Muqawama al-Lubnaiyya*, just so you know where the acronym "Amal" came from when I refer to it in this and future chapters.

Later, a leader of Amal said, "There was a man, and his name was Musa Sadr. It was Imam Sadr that woke up the sleeping giant that is the [Shiites]of Lebanon." No longer would the masses accept the passivity of Shiite clerical and community leaders. And there you have it—Sadr and what he started was a precursor to Hezbollah. Not a precursor to the evilness that stems from that organization, but an important step towards the mobilization of Shiites in Lebanon. The genie was now coming out of the bottle.

The PLO agreed to train Sadr's new militia, but their relationship was strained. This wasn't surprising; the PLO routinely dominated Shiites in southern Lebanon. It would have been quite hypocritical for Sadr to rail against the Lebanese government controlled by Christians for their failure to provide Shiites with their fair share of resources while at the same time supporting a PLO that treated Shiites in southern Lebanon as second-class citizens. The last thing Sadr wanted was for the PLO to create a state within the state that subjugated his people. That might explain why he mostly stayed out of the civil war that broke out after Shiites began to coalesce, and why he supported Syria's incursion into Lebanon to weaken the PLO. But let's not get ahead of ourselves.

Chapter Two

Lebanon's Civil War

Everything changed in Lebanon when a civil war broke out in 1975. The war led to the death of 150,00 people (three percent of Lebanon's population), caused incalculable property and economic damage, and lasted fourteen years. Its memory still impacts Lebanon today.

Like tectonic plates pressing against each other until the inevitable earthquake shakes and destroys, so too the constant irritations caused by shifting demographics and resultant political pressures in Lebanon provoked drastic change. By the 1970s, Christians were no longer the majority in Lebanon. Down to about forty percent, the Shiites were closing the gap at thirty-two percent, followed by the Sunnis at twenty-two percent and the Druze at a distant six percent. And although Shiites were the fastest-rising group, they also were still the poorest—which would have implications in the future.

How did this huge demographic shift happen in only thirty years? Birthrates, emigration, and immigration.

In the early 1970s, the average size of a Shiite family was nine people. Sunni families averaged eight, and Christians six. Mixed in were the mostly Sunni Palestinians that had fled Israel and Jordan.

Although tensions between Phalangists and Palestinians had been rising, things came to a boil on Sunday, April 13, 1975, a beautiful spring day. By then, the PLO had allied itself with the Lebanese Sunnis and some other non-aligned groups. And the Maronites, increasingly frustrated with the government's refusal to even try to excise the growing cancer of the PLO in Lebanon, had been busy preparing for a confrontation. But April 13 was not supposed to be a day devoted to violence. That morning, Pierre Gemayel, leader of the Phalange, went to dedicate a new church in Christian-controlled East Beirut. For security reasons, his detail closed the area around the church to traffic.

During the church service, an altercation occurred outside between PLO fighters in a car and Phalangists. The confrontation resulted in one PLO fighter, the driver, dying from a gunshot wound. Later, after the service concluded, another car raced through the Phalangist's security cordon. Its license plates were covered, but the car had bumper stickers linking it to a PLO faction, the Popular Front for the Liberation of Palestine. As the car neared the church, passengers fired guns toward it in an apparent attempt to kill Pierre Gemayel. During the ensuing fight, three Phalangist bodyguards died along with a fourth person who attended the service. To this day, the identity of the gunmen remains unknown. But the Phalange certainly had an opinion about the gunmen's affiliation. Later that day, in revenge, Phalangists ambushed a bus, killing twenty-seven Palestinians, and wounding nineteen. The next day the PLO, Muslim militias, and Christian militia started fighting in Beirut. The Lebanese army then split across sectarian lines.

Lebanon's destructive civil war had begun.

Claude Ibrahim's Father

The beginning of the war brought little fighting to southern Lebanon. But soon the Palestinians, supported by Muslim and Druze militias, took to ravaging several Christian villages and small towns in various parts of Lebanon. When that extended to southern Lebanon, Israel moved to support the Christian villages there and sent patrols to help secure Israel's borders from the Lebanese side.

Israeli involvement with the inhabitants of southern Lebanon was nothing new. Well before the 1948 Israel-Arab War for Independence, information from Christians and some Shiites living there had saved lives in Jewish settlements in the northern Galilee. And as the decades passed, it was not uncommon to see southern Lebanon residents—Christians and Shiites—working in Metula. It was nothing official, just individuals and communities mutually benefitting.

Until recently, what I knew of that story came from reading history books and articles. But in April 2022, it became personal for me. That is when I met Claude Ibrahim at a memorial in Metula for soldiers who had fought the PLO and later Hezbollah (we will dive further into that story in a future chapter). Claude, forty-nine years old when I met him, was born in Marjayoun. From where we stood, I could easily see it to the north, first Marjayoun on the highest hill, then Qlaiaa to the left and lower, and then another village to the left of Qlaiaa in sort of a curving, descending line. All three villages were mostly Christian. To their east was Fatahland. And surrounding them were Muslim villages, in 1975 under the PLO's control.

Claude's father was a soldier in the Lebanese army based in Marjayoun. When that army unit dissolved after the 1975 civil war began, many of its Sunni and Shiite soldiers went to nearby Muslim towns with their military equipment. Remaining were 360 Christian soldiers to defend the Christian villages, ravaged by the PLO and the like. The threat was real. Using mortars and snipers, PLO members made life hell for Christian civilians living in the towns. Claude, little more than a toddler, was one of them.

One night, to escape the PLO terrorists coming to take Marjayoun, Claude's mother and father bundled him up and took him to the nearby town of Qlaiaa. Realizing that Qlaiaa would be next on the PLO's list, its defenders knew they needed help.

On the morning of March 10, 1976, an IDF soldier found a letter attached to a stone that had been thrown over the border fence, near Metula. The author, self-identified as a member of the Lebanese Armed Forces, asked for a night meeting at that same spot which later became known as Fatima Gate (then it was a barbed wire fence—now there are haunting ruins hinting at a vibrant past all backed by an imposing concrete security wall).

That night, Christian Lebanese soldiers from Qlaiaa met with IDF representatives. They had a harrowing message, explaining that the PLO was coming for them, and that Qlaiaa would soon fall, its citizens left to suffer a terrible fate as was frequently the case in Lebanon when a village fell. They asked for assistance.

After checking with officers at Israel's Northern Command, the next night the IDF representative responded that the IDF would help. At first, that help took the form of artillery support and communication monitoring. Soon, the assistance became more concrete. The Israelis delivered foodstuffs and small arms and later, heavier armaments. The security relationship between Israel and the Christian community in southern Lebanon had begun. Twenty-four years later that assistance ended. It is a sad story we will soon reach. But for now, the Christians in southern Lebanon survived.

Meanwhile, the "Golden Age" was over. Lebanon's economy reeled, its people suffered, and homes and buildings pounded into dust. Rather than having a functioning government, Lebanon divided into cantonments. The PLO and scattered militias allied to it controlled most of southern Lebanon that was not held by Christian militias, Christians held onto the Mount Lebanon region, and Beirut was divided. To the east, Syria held sway in the Bekaa Valley as it did in much of the rest of Lebanon not controlled by the PLO, the Christians, or the Druze.

Syria? What was Syria doing there?

Syria in Lebanon

Syria's role in Lebanon is an important component of Hezbollah's history and therefore important for our story. Without an activist, or at least a permissive Syria, Hezbollah might never have risen (I don't want to confuse things by talking about Iran now—but for those in the know, don't worry, we will get there soon). Then, for three decades after Hezbollah's founding, Syria was one of Hezbollah's main supporters—politically and materially. Therefore, we can't ignore the role Syria played.

So, let's talk about it.

Syria's leaders always viewed Israel (Palestine in their minds) as their land, which Zionists stole. Therefore, Syria sought to control and wield for its own purposes the PLO and other Palestinian groups bent on destroying Israel. Even after Israel decisively beat the Syrians in the Six-Day War, Syria's leaders still dreamed of incorporating Israel into a Greater Syria. But they didn't want to pay an additional price for achieving this. So, rather than allow the Palestinians to use Syria as a base for its attacks, Syria facilitated the PLO's use of Jordan and Lebanon. While doing so, Syria provided the PLO with arms and equipment, strengthening the organization to such a degree that it can be safely said that Syria's support played an important role in triggering Lebanon's civil war.

However, Syria also coveted Lebanon for eventual inclusion in a Greater Syria. Therefore, Syrian President Hafez Assad (father of present-day Syrian leader, Bashar Assad) did not confine himself to supporting only one religious grouping in Lebanon. Given his experience maintaining power in Syria, Assad knew that manipulating and eventually controlling Lebanon would require maintaining influence and control over all its warring groups. Therefore, three months before the civil war started, he took the unusual step of traveling to Lebanon to meet with its Christian president. Upon arrival, the Lebanon's Christian president surprisingly greeted him as a "hero of the Golan in his second homeland, Lebanon." And some said that they signed an agreement for Syria to send troops to train the Lebanese army. Assad also reached out to Druze chief, Kamal Jumblatt, and sent support to Jumblatt's "Lebanese National Movement." Jumblatt will return to our story soon, but only for a fleeting moment.

Having given or offered sugar to three of the major groups involved in the present internal Lebanese dispute (Palestinian Sunnis, Christians, and Druze), and having been born an Alawite, a religious group related to Shiism, Assad felt little need to involve himself further for the first few months of the civil war as the body count spiraled upward and despair mounted. Then, seeing a tilt in favor of the Christians, in January 1976, Assad sent significant Syrian military forces into Lebanon to protect Palestinians from Christian militia attacks. His primary reason was to prevent Israel from exploiting the turmoil to grab a base of operations inside Lebanon from which it could threaten Syria from the flank.

But then things changed.

First, Assad tried in February 1976 to get all sides to agree to a new "constitutional document" that would improve things for the Muslims. The Christians, now feeling the tides of war shifting against them due in part to Syria's military presence, agreed. Muslim leaders did not, believing that Assad was trying to dominate Lebanon and neuter the Palestinians. Not surprisingly, their intransigence displeased Assad.

With the Christians' plight becoming increasingly desperate, and the collapse of Lebanon's army, Assad sent more troops to Lebanon at the request of its president, under the pretext of defending Lebanese sovereignty. But that was cover for a power grab. The PLO had defied him, and here was an opportunity for Assad to tighten his hold on Lebanon while also increasing his control of PLO terrorists, which he could use as leverage against Israel as needed. Therefore, in a whirlwind reversal of policy, Assad's army supported the Christians by inflicting heavy blows on the PLO. It's enough to give you intellectual whiplash. By mid-October, Syria had taken control of much of Lebanon, including the Bekaa Valley, where many Shiites resided.

But Syrian forces did not extend their reach into southern Lebanon. There, in a deal brokered by the United States, in return for allowing the Syrian army to enter the rest of Lebanon, the Israelis drew a red line north of which the Syrians could have a relatively free hand except for the installation of surface-to-air missiles, south of which the Syrians had to stay out. For security reasons, Israel would not countenance a Syrian military presence on its border with Lebanon, which would constitute a second front. Second, the Israelis knew that the PLO would not voluntarily stop its terror campaign against Israel. That meant the IDF might have to strike PLO targets in southern Lebanon to protect Israeli citizens living in northern Israel. Doing so would require Israel to deal with the political and military complications that Syrian troops intermingled with the PLO in south Lebanon would bring—something it wanted to avoid. A sensible concern. But as a result, outside the Christian villages, the PLO retained control of southern Lebanon.

Guess who didn't like that—many of the Shiites living there. Remember, the PLO treated them with disdain.

Assad also muddied the waters with the Druze by assassinating Druze leader, Kamal Jumblatt, for not toeing the Syrian line. Subsequently, Kamal's son, Walid, took over leadership of the Druze and joined Arafat to fight the Christians. That did not sit well with the Israelis who valued the few Christian villages and towns in southern Lebanon that provided a porous bulwark against PLO activity. Therefore, in September 1977 Israel increased the flow of armaments to Christians in southern Lebanon. Then, in the late 1970s, Assad flip-flopped again, shifting his support from the Christians back to the PLO. Following that, the beleaguered Christian leadership requested Israel to help them push Syria out of Lebanon. Israel refused but promised to intervene if Syria used airpower against Christian forces.

Finally, by the end of the decade, although the conflagration still simmered, most of the fighting had stopped. However, another problem arose that continues to affect the region today. Iran underwent a revolution. The Shah of Iran, friendly to Israel, was out, and on February 1, 1979, Shiite ayatollah, Ruhollah Khomeini, was in. What was once a land ruled by a Persian Shah now had become a Shiite Islamic Republic. And now Israel had a new and more powerful enemy.

Three New Guys Enter the Scene

Coming from Iraq was a short, fat Shiite fellow whose last name was Fadlallah. Unlike Sadr, he supported the Palestinians, pushed for unity between all Muslims, and vociferously argued for the destruction of Israel. Why mention Fadlallah? Because of his influence on Imad Mugniyah and Hassan Nasrallah.

Mugniyah's leadership qualities came naturally to him. He was smart, very serious, and grew up in the slums of Beirut. Before studying with Nasrallah, Mugniyah, despite his Shiite religious background, had fought with the PLO. He had even served with the PLO's elite forces and in Yasser Arafat's guard. After signing up with Hezbollah, Mughniyah led a gang in Shiite areas of Beirut that enforced Islamic law, often harshly. You will read much more about his murderous schemes in future chapters.

Nasrallah, as fiendish and deadly as Mugniyah came to be, was the more masterful of the two. In the mid to late 1970s, Nasrallah was skinny, shy, and had thick eyebrows, which he still sports. Born in Lebanon in 1960, he was the oldest of nine Shiite siblings. His father sold fruit and vegetables from a cart. By age ten, Nasrallah began visiting mosques and receiving religious tutelage, which was interrupted during the civil war when his family had to flee before their village fell to Christians. They landed in another town that, while a communist stronghold, had an Islamic college. There, Nasrallah joined a study group. He also joined Amal. Amal, recognizing his capabilities, named him the local Shiite village representative at the age of fifteen. Later, Nasrallah went to Iraq where he studied Shiism, and met his lifelong mentor, Sayyed Abbas Mussawi, who will later play an important role in the story of Hezbollah's development. Nasrallah returned to Lebanon eighteen months later amid Iraq's crackdown on the Shia.

While I hesitate to refer to names that are hard to pronounce, Mugniyah and Nasrallah are worth remembering. Mugniyah for the terror he planned, and Nasrallah for his eventual leadership of Hezbollah that continues to this day. But our story of the rise of Hezbollah is not yet ripe to tell. A few components are missing that will come to the fore in the next chapter—terror, war, and Iranian perfidy. But of critical importance to understanding the world in which Hezbollah thrives is this—the suffering felt by Christians and Sunnis alike during Lebanon's devastating civil war left a deep mark. A mark that rendered them unwilling to fight the next group that would seek control of Lebanon—Hezbollah.

Chapter Three

The First Lebanon War—1982

Thirteen Palestinian terrorists boarded a boat off Lebanon's shore on March 9, 1978, and headed for Israel's coast. Two days later, they switched to a couple of zodiac boats and made for shore. One of the zodiacs capsized, drowning two. The remaining eleven landed on a beach north of Tel Aviv.

By now, Palestinian terrorists leaving Lebanon to murder Israelis was nothing new. Taking innocent lives had become the PLO's choice diplomatic tool. In 1970, at Moshav Avivim, Palestinian terrorists from Lebanon had fired into a crowded school bus nearby, killing twelve, including nine children, and wounding twenty-five others. Four years later, Palestinian terrorists based in Lebanon had killed twenty Jewish students at Ma'alot, taken the lives of eighteen more Jews in Kiryat Shmona, invaded another kibbutz killing three women, and slaughtered four more Israelis in Nahariya. All in one year! The IDF foiled other terrorist attacks but could do nothing to stop rockets arcing over the hills and then landing with deadly effects. All these terrorist acts shared the same characteristic—the fire and mayhem had originated in Lebanon near its border with Israel. It was obvious to all Israelis that the PLO's bases in southern Lebanon posed a constant threat to the safety of Jews living along the border and that the status quo was not acceptable.

But on March 11, 1978, the terrorists who landed on the beach drew an amount of blood that reached a new level of depravity, which had to be addressed.

In fact, the terrorists took their first life just minutes after reaching dry land. By happenstance, a nature photographer was photographing beach scenes near where the eleven landed. She was the niece of an American senator, Abraham Ribicoff. The terrorists asked her where they were and after she responded, fired at least one shot, crumpling her lifeless body to the sand.

She would not be the last innocent to die that day.

Next, after walking several minutes to a nearby highway, the terrorists hijacked a taxi, killed its occupants, and headed for Tel Aviv. Along the way, they hijacked a chartered bus loaded with families on a day outing. Continuing their travels in the newly captured bus, they shot and tossed grenades at passing cars. Then, for good measure, tossed the lifeless body of one of their captives out of the moving bus.

Not satisfied with the first bus, the terrorists stopped a second one and moved their captives into that bus before resuming their travels. When an Israeli family in a station wagon approached, the terrorists fired bullets into the vehicle, severely wounding the father driving the car and killing a child who had been sleeping in the back.

The bus moved on.

When police caught up with it, they refrained from firing for fear of hitting the hostages. Their first roadblock failed when the bus crashed through the hastily built blockade. A second larger roadblock brought the bus to a halt when nails planted on the roadway punctured its tires. A firefight erupted. Because there had been no time to assemble specialized counter-terrorism forces, only police ill-trained for such situations were present. They screamed to the passengers to jump out but when some did, the terrorists shot them. Finally, the leader of a local counter-terrorism unit arrived ahead of his unit. Rather than wait, he charged the bus, killing two of the terrorists. During the fight, the bus burst into flames.

All told, thirty-eight Israeli civilians died that day, thirteen of whom were children. Seventy-one more were wounded.

Israel had to respond. Three days later, it did.

On March 14, 1978, the IDF launched *Operation Litani* with the main goal of destroying PLO bases between the Litani River and the Israeli border. The Litani runs roughly parallel and several miles north of Israel's western border with Lebanon before taking a sharp northern turn above the northernmost Israeli town of Metula.

In addition to destroying the PLO's bases, the IDF planned to link up with Major Haddad's Christian militia in southern Lebanon while avoiding any confrontation with Syrian forces north of the Litani or in the Bekaa Valley. Thought to be a bit of a loose cannon by some, Haddad was a charismatic Christian Lebanese officer appointed by the Lebanese Army in the 1970s to regain control of southern Lebanon from the Palestinians. The area was familiar to him since he had previously lived in Marjayoun. Haddad's forces had already attracted some members of the local Shiite and Druze communities as well as Christians. All had an interest in forging a defense against the PLO and its Sunni supporters infesting the region.

Israel's desire to establish a security belt inside Lebanon to protect Israeli settlements near the border was music to Haddad's ears. Israel had tried lesser forms of the same thing by providing aid to the Christians, but now wanted something more, a permanent security zone. Given that Haddad and Israel shared a common enemy and common interests, it was a reasonable idea.

But the United Nations (UN) did not support a security belt. Apparently, the lives of Israeli citizens and Lebanese civilians caught in the crossfire meant little to the diplomats cloistered in New York carrying out the wishes of their respective governments. Five days after the fighting started, the United Nations Security Council passed

Resolution 425, which called for "strict respect of Lebanon's territorial integrity, sovereignty, and political independence." What a high-minded, nice-sounding phrase.

Except there were problems with the resolution. Big problems.

The resolution failed to mention the PLO's terrorist bases in Lebanon from which they staged their attacks against Israel. It neglected Israel's right to territorial integrity and sovereignty free of terrorist incursions that targeted its citizenry, often its children. Nor was there any mention of the PLO's treatment of innocent Lebanese living in the region. Or exactly who was going to restore Lebanese control of southern Lebanon. I remind you; Lebanon was embroiled in a civil war in 1978. Not surprisingly, its small army, composed of members of the warring factions and religions, had for all practical purposes fallen apart leaving often brutal militias to fight and rule. Nevertheless, the UN demanded that Israel stop its offensive and withdraw.

The UN, however, threw Israel a bone—a rotten bone that has stuck in the craw of Israel ever since. The UN established UNIFIL, an acronym for the United Nations Interim Force in Lebanon. UNIFIL's mission was to oversee Israel's withdrawal and facilitate Lebanon's establishment of its authority in southern Lebanon.

Unfortunately, UNIFIL did nothing to re-establish the Lebanese government's authority. Nor did UNIFIL stop terrorists from re-establishing themselves along Israel's borders. Nor did it team with the Lebanese government to confront the militias. Nor did it effectively resist Palestinian pressure that forced UNIFIL to restrict its movements. And there was nothing *interim* about it. Forty-four years later, as of this writing, it is still there doing little; perhaps a better word to use in its title would have been *ineffective force* rather than *interim force*! I will explore UNIFIL's failures in Chapter Seventeen.

Less than three months after the fighting started in 1978, after 4,000 foreign UNIFIL troops had reached the region and, under mounting international pressure, Israel withdrew.

Mainly because the UN meddled, *Operation Litani* did not accomplish much. Although the PLO lost 300 fighters, its minions filtered back into southern Lebanon soon after the IDF left. Major Haddad's militia, composed of mainly Christian officers and many Shiites at lower levels, remained, but it was too weak on its own to stop the PLO from re-establishing itself. Therefore, Shiites endured, fled, and some, because of their hatred of the PLO or desire to earn a better living, volunteered to work with Haddad's forces. And now the IDF was left to contend with an international force just over Israel's borders that would complicate or restrict its freedom to strike at the PLO while also doing little to prevent terrorists from sneaking into Israel.

Not surprisingly, Palestinian terrorism resumed. Less than a year after the IDF withdrew, Samir Kuntar led a group of four terrorists from Lebanese soil onto a boat that ended its journey a few miles south of the border on a Nahariyah beach. During their murderous rampage, four more Israelis died, two of them young children from the same family. Kuntar killed the four-year-old by crushing her skull on a rock with the butt of his rifle. The two-year-old died at her mother's hand. Out of fear of discovery, when the terrorists entered their apartment, her mother had covered the little girl's mouth to keep her quiet, accidentally smothering her.

Meanwhile, Haddad struggled to maintain control of a narrow strip of Lebanese land running along Israel's border. In April 1979, he declared that the zone would now be known as "Independent Free Lebanon." However, after making that proclamation, and after his forces, pursuing their own intimidation campaign, wounded several UNIFIL soldiers and likely killed one, the Lebanese army, already wary of his loyalty to Israel, dismissed him. Now, more than ever, he was on his own. While not strong enough to ensure the integrity of the strip of land he claimed, he still managed, with Israel's help, to protect his supporters and provide some checks on the movement of Palestinian forces.

Once again, you might be wondering what all this has to do with Hezbollah. After all, Shiites were mostly just trying to stay out of the way and avoid the fighting. And despite their interest in being freed from the Palestinian yoke, they had little to do with the fact that Lebanon was in the middle of a country-wide civil war, that Palestinians were trying to kill Israelis and Christians, that the Druze were fighting too, and that the IDF was doing its best to stop terrorists.

However, because of what was happening in Iran, things would change soon.

Iran's Revolution and the Shiites in Lebanon

Beginning in January 1978, Iran was embroiled in a revolution. It ended fifteen months later, on April 1, 1979, when exiled Ayatollah Khomeini, a preeminent Shiite scholar, returned to his home country three months after the shah of Iran fled. This was an enormous blow to Israel, which had enjoyed friendly relations with the shah. Khomeini declared Iran would now be an Islamic republic guided by Shiite religious values. And, for good measure, he spewed a virulent hatred of Israel.

Syria was the first Arab country to recognize Khomeini's new regime. It was not Syria's first attempt to reach out to Iran, though. Assad had tried to make friends with the shah in 1975 and 1976. When that didn't work, he switched sides (Assad was good at that) and invited Ayatollah Khomeini to take refuge in Syria while also providing training for Khomeini's rebels at bases located in Syria and Lebanon. Then, after Khomeini took control of Iran, Syria and Iran signed a joint communique in April 1980 that bound both nations to friendship, opposition to Egypt's and Israel's historic peace agreement at Camp David, and declared their joint enmity towards the United States, Israel, and Egypt. When Iraq attacked Iran later that year, Syria proved its friendship by providing Iran diplomatic and military support in exchange for oil and Iran's help in turning the Shiite community in Lebanon against Israel. And so, Assad's desire to use the Shiites as leverage set the stage for Iran to influence events in Lebanon—something Khomeini was only too happy to do.

In Lebanon, most Shiites were impoverished. And their poverty was a petri dish for their rising anger. Someone might still become a terrorist if they own a large house, drive a fancy car, can buy nice clothes, and have a full belly but that person has something to lose by doing so. However, when one is mired in all-consuming poverty, lacking education, and with little hope of improving their lot, the motive to work within society to better one's life and that of one's children is not so present. Helplessness, rather than hopefulness, is a recipe for radicalization and violence. For many who leaned towards doing so, it was about "Shiite inferiority. It [was] about for many, many years that they were neglected, that they were not recognized, that they were humiliated." That was the prevalent situation for Shiites in Lebanon when Iran's agents arrived. Sadr had awakened them, but the vast majority had not yet been activated. Now, Iran had the opportunity and inclination to do so.

An Iranian presence in Lebanon was not unique. Historically, Shiites in Iran and Lebanon had co-mingled. However, Iran at the time was not an Islamic Republic, especially one that wanted to transport its ideology to the world. That changed with Iran's revolution.

The impact of Khomeini's fiery rhetoric on Shiites in Lebanon was almost immediate. Impoverished by government policies that marginalized them, primed by Sadr who had mobilized and empowered them, and inflamed by the PLO's control and the IDF's incursions to stem PLO terrorism—Shiites were thirsting for something new. Other Shiite clerics in Iran had already opened a religious divide within Sadr's Amal whose perspective was more secular than religious. Khomeini's words and actions widened the gap. It was a perfect storm of Iranian desire for domination and Shiite hunger for change. Still, at first only words and ideas were exchanged, and little action was taken. And Iran didn't have the money to push for more theological activism in Lebanon's Shiite community. Besides, by September 1980, Khomeini had bigger concerns—Iraq had invaded Iran.

But what did the revered Musa Sadr think? One might guess he opposed Iran's encroachment and proselytizing. After all, Sadr preached more of a nationalistic line than an Islamic one. He only wanted Lebanese Shiites to fight for their fair share and had never advocated for a Shiite state.

So where was Sadr when Khomeini landed in Iran? Where was he when Iranian acolytes infiltrated Lebanon?

Nobody knows!

In August 1978, three years after the civil war started, Sadr flew to Libya for ceremonies commemorating Muammar Qaddafi's successful power grab years before. Several days later, Sadr and his companions disappeared. Libya denied any involvement with his disappearance, saying that he had flown to Italy. But, as is often said, the funny thing about lies is that facts get in the way. Sadr's suitcases were found in his hotel room in Libya. Although it seems clear that Qaddafi killed him, his motive remains unknown. Some think that PLO chairman, Yasser Arafat, asked Qaddafi to murder Sadr because Sadr's Amal challenged the PLO's control of southern Lebanon and because Sadr supported Syria intervening on behalf of the Christians in 1976. Others believe Qaddafi ordered Sadr's death after they had a contentious discussion about religion. Sadr had reportedly spoken to the Israelis, which was another possible motive. Still another theory involves Ayatollah Khomeini and his adherents. Nevertheless, regardless of what happened, after almost twenty years of building a loyal following, Sadr disappeared from the scene and was never heard from again. But in the wake of his absence, there was a roused Shiite populace and a well-trained Amal militia that largely had sat out the Lebanese Civil War.

Two years after Sadr's disappearance, changes were afoot within Amal. Nabih Berri became its leader in 1980. Born in Sierra Leone to parents that had emigrated from southern Lebanon, Berri, then forty-two, was a lawyer who had spent time in the United States. He tried to marginalize the religious zealots in his organization and embrace a more secular philosophy for Amal.

But Berri had a problem. Sadr's death had created a vacuum, a vacuum doctrinaire religious extremists sought to fill. Soon they infiltrated Amal. Some did so at the behest of Iran. Some were homegrown. And some were Shiites escaping Saddam Hussein in Iraq whose operatives had forced high-ranking, Iraqi Shiite cleric, Baqr al-Sadr (cousin of Musa Sadr), to watch the rape and murder of his sister before driving a nail into his head and then burning his body. One of them, whom we have already met, was Hassan Nasrallah, who organized meetings and lectures to promote his brand of Shiite Islam. Together, those extremists indoctrinated Shiites in Lebanon with a visceral hatred of Israel and fostered a group within Amal that supported transforming Lebanon into an Islamic state.

And so, the Shiite pot bubbled. But the Iranians were not the only ones turning up the heat. Israel's thrust into Lebanon in 1978 played a role too. As did Syria's ongoing support of Amal. Assad saw in the organization Sadr started a viable tool for keeping the PLO in check in southern Lebanon. Therefore, he provided Amal members with training in Syria and even equipped them with Syrian-styled uniforms.

Who would win out? On one side were the more secular members of Amal, who were led by Berri and supported by Syria. On the other, the extremists whom Iran favored. For the next two years, that struggle played out beneath the surface of the conflict between Israel, the PLO, the Christians, and Syria that periodically raged.

In April 1981, the Syrian army tried to gain control of Zahle, a mostly Christian town of about 160,000, little more than thirty miles east of Beirut where the Lebanese mountains meet the Bekaa Valley. Syrian shells crashed into residential areas and residents had no electric power and little to eat or drink. Phalangist leader Bashir Gemayel called it "genocide." Israel, seeing an opportunity to build support within the Christian community and block the Syrians, decided to lend a hand and on April 28 shot down two Syrian helicopters supporting the attack. But that led Syria to place surface-to-air missiles (SAMs) in Lebanon and long-range missiles near its border with Lebanon. These moves obliterated the red-line understandings Israel and Syria had reached years earlier.

Then, two months later in mid-July, the PLO fired 1,000 rockets and artillery shells into Israel, pummeling Kiryat Shmona and other communities. Many Israelis had to leave their homes to avoid injury and death. Ostensibly, the attack was in response to an Israeli air strike against a PLO convoy transporting mounted Katyusha rockets to southern Lebanon where they could be used against Israel. But terror was the favorite tool of Palestinian terrorists. The PLO did not need excuses to employ it. The year before, a terror squad had penetrated the border, snuck into Kibbutz Misgav Am, and held children hostage. Two Israelis died during that attack. The IDF had foiled other attempts to infiltrate Israel's border communities. Therefore, Israel was ill-disposed to permit more rockets to be placed within range of its communities.

In response to the wave of missiles coming from Lebanon, the IDF retaliated by bombing PLO targets, mostly in Beirut and southern

Lebanon. While those strikes were ongoing, Israel announced it would continue firing until the PLO stopped launching missiles at Israel. More than 100 Lebanese died and many more were injured. In addition, some infrastructure was destroyed in the new round of fighting, largely because the PLO had located many of its offices and bases close to civilian structures. This was a strategy that Hezbollah would later duplicate to a far greater degree. Thus, it was inevitable that, although they weren't targeted, Lebanese civilians suffered, too. But so did Israeli civilians, several of whom had died. The difference is the PLO targeted civilians while the IDF targeted weapons and terrorists.

On July 24, American special envoy Philip Habib brokered a ceasefire. His objective was to strike a deal in which the PLO would withdraw its heavy weapons from southern Lebanon and Israel would remove any vestige of its physical presence from Major Haddad's narrow strip of territory. Habib failed. Instead, of the ambiguous deal he strove for, Habib only secured, in practice, a promise from the PLO not to attack Israel from Lebanon. Attacking Israel from anywhere else was fair game. Thus, the PLO cancer could enjoy a safe place to grow in Lebanon. From there it could metastasize throughout the world, to strike Israelis wherever they were. However, at least Israeli citizens could then return to their homes in northern Israel to enjoy a semblance of peace.

But the peace was a sham. And the evil within Lebanon's womb only grew more powerful.

The First Lebanon War—1982

Many books detail in great depth the tactics, strategy, and government decision-making regarding Israel's war in Lebanon. I will give short shrift to that, not because it's unimportant, but because I suspect that you, like me, are in a hurry to get to the main subject of this book—

Hezbollah. So, suffice it to say that on June 3, 1982, a Palestinian terrorist group not affiliated with the PLO and based in Iraq attempted to assassinate Israel's ambassador to England. Their bullets left him paralyzed. In retaliation, the IDF struck targets in southern Lebanon, and the PLO responded by firing Katyusha missiles at targets in northern Israel.

But that was not the end of it.

Defense Minister Ariel Sharon had been looking for an excuse to drive the PLO from Lebanon. Therefore, he convinced the Israeli government to approve sending the IDF about twenty-five miles (forty kilometers) into Lebanon to clean out PLO bases there while avoiding conflict with Syria, which had military units in the Bekaa Valley and elsewhere. That, he argued, was necessary for creating a safer environment for Israel's northern communities. However, although this was Sharon's stated plan, it was not his real one. Sharon did not want to stop at twenty-five miles. Instead, he wanted to go farther—to Beirut—and engage PLO fighters in the capital, eject Syria from Lebanon by military maneuver or fire, and thereby create a new political situation in Lebanon. One that would enable Bashir Gemayel, son of Pierre Gemayel and now military leader of the Phalange, to take control of the country and establish a pro-Israel government.

Many writers have speculated whether Menachem Begin, Israel's prime minister, was party to Sharon's subterfuge. But for our purposes, it does not matter. One person I interviewed, however, had an interesting perspective, which I feel is worth relaying. Begin was very much impacted by the Holocaust in which six million Jews died, many from where he grew up. His immediate predecessors, Shimon Peres and Yitzhak Rabin, saw helping the Christians as a necessary policy but had no illusions about their capacity for cruelty. Begin may have had a different view. For him, like Jews in Europe during World

War II, he may have seen the Christians as a persecuted group, now a minority, which faced extermination in Lebanon without Israel's help.

On June 8, 1982, after receiving the Cabinet's approval to go to war and two days after the IDF crossed the border and surged north, Syrian forces counterattacked. Fighting intensified over the next couple of days as the IDF advanced. Meanwhile, Christians in southern Lebanon were happy to see the Israelis move in. So were Shiites living there. Some threw rice at IDF vehicles to indicate their pleasure. At last, Shiites thought, the Israelis would remove the hated PLO from southern Lebanon and then leave.

Days later, IDF units approached the road connecting Beirut and Damascus and besieged Beirut. This led to Syria's retreat, the defeat of the PLO, and an internationally mediated evacuation of PLO fighters from Lebanon. On August 23, Bashir Gemayal was elected Lebanon's new president.

So far so good. Things were proceeding according to Sharon's plan. The PLO was out of Lebanon, Christians were gaining control of the country, and Syria's hold on Lebanon had been weakened. However, within Israel, domestic opposition increased. Detractors argued that Israel had no business fighting this war of choice, especially beyond the twenty-five-mile limitation that had first been portrayed to the Cabinet as the stop line. One army officer protested what was happening by famously refusing to continue commanding his unit, though he was willing to fight on as a foot soldier in service of his country—but not bear responsibility for its policy.

Then all hell broke loose.

On September 14, a Syrian agent assassinated Bashir Gemayel. Two days later, bent on revenge, Maronite militia passed unchecked through IDF units to enter the Sabra and Shatila Palestinian refugee camps. For nearly two days, Maronite militia rampaged through the camps. Depending on whom you believe, they killed as many as a few hundred people or more than three thousand. The IDF did not intend for the massacre to occur and had no actual advance knowledge of Maronite plans. However, its level of responsibility is still an open question and remains controversial. At a minimum, per the Kahan Commission of Inquiry, which Israel's government ordered in the massacre's wake, the IDF was "indirectly responsible" because it did not anticipate such bloodshed following Gemayel's assassination and did not respond to the violence quickly enough. Furthermore, the IDF should have inferred from the reports that something very bad was happening. At the best, it was not the IDF's finest hour.

After word spread about the massacre, Israel was in the world's crosshairs. International pressure mounted for the IDF to withdraw. And within Israel, Israelis were protesting their government's policy on Lebanon. Nevertheless, Begin and his government hoped to achieve more positive results from the voluntary war it had just fought. On May 17, 1983, Israel concluded an agreement with Amin Gemayel, who had been elected to replace his assassinated brother as president of Lebanon. The deal was supposed to end the state of war between Israel and Lebanon, but it was not a peace treaty. Nor did it call for establishing diplomatic relations. It did, however, contain a unique clause that granted the IDF permission to maintain security in southern Lebanon in conjunction with Lebanese forces including those under command of Major Haddad, in return for Israel withdrawing from elsewhere. But another provision was a potential deal breaker. It stated that Lebanon would require and enforce Syria's withdrawal of all its troops from Lebanon.

Obtaining Syria's agreement to leave was a pipe dream; Syria wanted to maintain pressure on Israel to reclaim the Golan Heights. Reducing pressure on Israel without getting anything in return was the last thing that Hafez Assad would agree to. It was also the last thing that Lebanon's weak military could enforce. So, Israel did not get peace, nor did it achieve quiet. And when pressure mounted from within and without, the Lebanese government repudiated the deal in

March 1984. So much for that unofficial diplomatic document that purportedly would end the state of war between Israel and Lebanon.

Still, things seemed peaceful at first, and the PLO was gone. In southern Lebanon, shortly after the fighting had ended, IDF soldiers felt comfortable frequenting local shops and movie theaters and relaxed atop their vehicles. Israeli tourists even visited Lebanon's coastal cities. El Al opened a ticket office in Sidon for its airline. Roads featured signs in both Hebrew and Arabic, and the IDF worked with Major Haddad to expand his area of influence to the Awali River, several miles past the Litani. And for a while, Shiites tolerated and even cooperated with the IDF as hundreds of Shiites joined Haddad's forces in patrolling the area.

But there was a festering problem.

For Shiites, the IDF began to lose its luster. The initial euphoria they felt being freed from the Palestinian yoke gave way to resentment for what they perceived would be a long, intrusive Israeli occupation. On the ground, the IDF built bases and aggressively went after militants and PLO supporters. Suspects were interned and interrogated. This did not sit well with the Shiite population, which felt victimized. Increasingly, they saw the Israelis as new occupiers rather than saviors.

Making things worse, Haddad needed to find sources of income to support his Christian militia. Therefore, he imposed a tax on gas and other items, which irked Shiite villagers in South Lebanon.

All of this created an opportunity. An opportunity that would become Hezbollah.

Iran got the ball rolling. Just two days after the IDF moved into Lebanon, an Iranian delegation went to Damascus to discuss providing military assistance to Syria. Even though Iran was still embroiled in a long, bloody, existential struggle with Iraq, Ayatollah Khomeini had a "nose for opportunity" and wanted to spread his version of theocracy to Lebanon. After reaching an agreement with the Syrians, Iran issued a communique that announced it was sending forces "to engage in face-to-face battle against Israel, the primary enemy of Islam and Muslims."

The first Iranian soldiers to arrive in Syria were 5,000 members of the Islamic Revolutionary Guard Corps (IRGC). The IRGC is a force more ideologically driven than Iran's regular army. It was (and is) charged with protecting Iran's Islamic system; in 2019, the United States officially designated it a terrorist organization. Iran intended for the IRGC to deploy in Lebanon immediately. But by the time it arrived, the 1982 war was over and Assad would not permit 5,000 ideologically driven soldiers to enter Lebanon from Syrian territory for fear of re-starting a fight that could prove costly to Syria. However, he did allow 1,500 to cross the Syrian border into Lebanon for the express purpose of creating a Lebanese movement that would resist Israel. In return, Iran agreed to give Syria nine million tons of oil a year—for free.

The Iranians built a base in Zabadani, a Syrian town close to the Lebanese border that would become a center of fighting thirty years later in the Syrian Civil War. An old smuggler's route originating in Zabadani wound through a narrow valley and a mountain range into the Bekaa Valley in Lebanon. A few hundred IRGC soldiers used the route to enter Baalbek, the largest town in the Bekaa, where they rented homes. One of them was a short man in his late twenties, Mahmoud Ahmadinejad, who many years later became the president of Iran and was particularly reviled in many quarters of the western world. From Baalbek, they traveled unarmed, but in uniform, to nearby villages where they raised religious awareness, expressed the teachings of Khomeini, and built a foundation for hatred of Israel. Hatred—even though for many years before the Israel-Arab War of 1948, Shiite farmers in southern Lebanon had sold their produce in Metula and others even maintained relationships with Israelis after that war ended. So much so that there was a continuous movement of

Shiites and Christians to and from Israel for decades. So much so that, as one retired and well-informed Israeli general told me, after the 1948 War ended three Shiite villages now in Lebanon asked to be incorporated into Israel.

Before the Iranians arrived, Baalbek was a hotbed for tourism. It boasts a large, well-known Roman temple and once hosted a music festival every summer. Things changed when the Iranians arrived. As was the case with other villages in the immediate area, Baalbek grew to resemble a miniature Iran. Huge murals commemorating important Shiite events like the battle of Karbala were hung. They fought for attention with images of Khomeini staring at the Al-Aqsa Mosque in Jerusalem and with Iranian flags festooned with banners saying, "Death to America." Doubling down, Baalbek renamed its main square after Khomeini. Its culture changed, too. Women started wearing full-length black chadors; alcohol was no longer being sold; religious classes proliferated; and films about the Iran-Iraq war were shown.

For Amal, Iran's entry into the region did not portend well. Although some young Shiites had already left its more secular path in favor of Iran's more revolutionary one, Israel's incursion and Iran's subsequent involvement hastened the process. So did Amal's leader's (Berri) decision to join then-Lebanese president, Elias Sarkis, hardliner Bashir Gemayel (before he was elected president and was assassinated), and Druze leader, Walid Jumblatt, to create a Committee of National Salvation. That angered Iran, which now had enough of Berri's secular tendencies. It also moved some Islamists already part of the Amal movement to create a faction called Islamic Amal. Nasrallah joined Islamic Amal as did Mugniyah, who had fought with the PLO against the Israelis.

Perhaps sensing a coming problem with Islamic Amal, Amal's more secular side even talked informally to the Israelis, continuing the history of connection between Shiites and Jews. Evidently, Shiite antipathy for Israel did not outweigh the perceived need of some in Amal to explore options.

Iran shaped Islamic Amal's ideological path and collaborated with it to create its manifesto that I condense into three concepts:

1) Islam holds all the answers and tools for a better life and is the framework for establishment of Islamic Amal.
2) Resisting Israel is the "ultimate confrontation priority" and that requires a Jihad structure.
3) The organization must strictly obey the *Guardian of the Islamic Trust,* which is another name for Iran's supreme religious leader, at that time, Ayatollah Khomeini.

The organization operated under the name Islamic Amal until 1984 when it took a new title for itself based on a quotation from the Koran, "Verily, the part of God shall be victorious."

The new name was "Hezbollah"—the Party of God.

Chapter Four

Hezbollah's Rise

If you think of Iran's and Syria's goals as two circles of a Venn diagram, Hezbollah's rise occupied the middle where the circles intersected. Syria wanted to control events in Lebanon for its own economic and political dreams while also reclaiming the Golan Heights from Israel. Iran wanted to push its ideological Shiite revolution throughout the Middle East. Hezbollah was a useful tool that could help both countries accomplish their goals. Each nation supplied different but necessary ingredients to help promote Hezbollah: Iran employed its oil wealth and spread its Shiite religious ideology. Syria had its border with Lebanon. Thus, Iran provided the nutrients, Syria the feeding tube. And so two nations that both hated Israel found common cause for nurturing Hezbollah's growth.

At first, Hezbollah did not operate under its present name. Thus, there is an academic disagreement as to when Hezbollah came onto the scene. Some view it as 1985 when the organization announced itself, others 1984, and still others 1982 after the IDF moved into Lebanon. Without taking a position on this scholarly debate, I will describe events under the assumption that Hezbollah began in 1982 when it operated under the name Islamic Amal. It was then, shortly after Israeli troops crossed into Lebanon hoping to end the Palestinian terror threat, that radical Shiite clerics coalesced and began receiving Iranian assistance. Their activities radicalized Shiite society and motivated many to hate Israel thereby, at the very least, creating the foundation for Hezbollah to emerge.

Beginning in the late summer of 1982, organized Shiite resistance first confronted the IDF and the Christians—beginning in West Beirut and the mountains nearby, then in southern Lebanon. As resistance increased, more Shiites noticed the ongoing struggle. When some Sunni Muslims joined the fighting, Hezbollah integrated them into its military wing. Fighting also broke out among Shiites in the Bekaa Valley; some had sided with Hezbollah while others chose to stand with the original, more secular, Amal. Meanwhile, like the PLO before it, Hezbollah benefited from a steady flow of arms traveling along dozens of smuggling routes emanating from Syria. Syria supplied some of those weapons, but most came from Iran.

Of course, not everyone involved in arms smuggling was ideologically pure. Many corrupt Syrian officers saw an opportunity to create a diversified source of illicit income for themselves. Like with the ongoing narcotic production in the parts of the Bekaa Valley under Syrian control, they imposed "taxes" on the movement of arms and narcotics alike. Making a buck off killing Israelis, while also supplying drugs to whoever wanted them seemed like a good idea.

To its future regret, Israel missed the significance of this growing cancer. At first, IDF intelligence considered the attacks Hezbollah launched a nuisance. Ronan Bergman in his book *Rise and Kill First*, quoted a senior intelligence officer as saying, "We missed the process. Instead of hooking up with the Shiites, we kept up the link with the Christians, and we made the majority of Lebanese our enemies." Sivan Yichieli, the former mayor of a northern Israeli town and once an officer in an IDF reconnaissance unit corroborated that thought. He told me, "Hezbollah was a small extreme organization, it wasn't a strong organization. Amal was [the] strong Shiite organization." And then, "I remember when I…was commanding a post in Lebanon. The Division commanding officer came in." Rather than indicating concern regarding Hezbollah's capabilities, Yichieli's commander mocked the organization while Sivan briefed him, transforming its name to one with more Yiddish roots, "Hizboli."

Not only did Israel fail to nip the problem in the bud, but it also missed the link between Iran and Lebanese Shiites. However, Israel was not the only one to fall asleep on its watch. Amal was none too concerned either, even as Hezbollah's influence grew in Amal strongholds in Beirut and then southern Lebanon. How dangerous, its leaders thought, could this new group of men sitting around adorned with prayer beads be to Amal's entrenched role as the military organization created by the revered, but now deceased, Musa al-Sadr?

But Hezbollah was a growing danger: to Amal, to Israel, to Lebanon, and to the United States and the world. Like a hungry carnivore that injects poison into its victim, Hezbollah bit into Shiite Lebanon, injected its toxic ideology, and refused to let go. Soon by deed, although not yet by name, Hezbollah made its presence known by employing suicidal attackers and trafficking in kidnapping, ambushes, and roadside bombs.

Imad Mughniyah's Coming Out Party

Less than fourteen miles from Israel sits the coastal city of Tyre. In 1982, it was one of Lebanon's largest cities—although Beirut dwarfed it in size. After major fighting in the 1982 war stopped, the IDF established a military base there to house soldiers, border police, and intelligence personnel. It was also the home of Lebanese civilian authorities managing routine government functions.

At the same time, Hezbollah tasked Imad Mughniyah (remember him—the guy who had grown up in the slums of Beirut) with putting together a terror and sabotage campaign against the Israelis.

Mughniyah looked for a symbolic target and a useful idiot that would give his life to destroy it. He found both. Meanwhile, Israeli intelligence had picked up word of him and knew he was a psychopath but had no idea where he was or what he was up to.

Mughniyah settled on targeting the building housing the IDF's base in Tyre. Ahmad Qassir was the useful idiot, a sixteen-year-old childhood acquaintance willing to blow himself up for Mughniyah's cause. Reconnoitering the building to ensure success, Mugniyah discovered a critical moment that would be ripe for a devastating blow—the period after IDF night patrols would return but before the morning patrols normally left.

Equipped with a Peugeot sedan loaded with explosives, on a wet November 11, 1982, around 7 a.m., Qassir drove to the seven-story building. More Israelis were present than usual because some soldiers sheltering in tents had come inside to avoid the rain. Qassir stepped on the gas when he got close, smashed into the structure, and then set off the blast. The explosion pancaked the building. Seventy-five Israelis died along with twenty-seven Arab prisoners and civilians.

After an investigation, the IDF blamed the explosion on leaking gas inside the building. But immediately afterward, the IDF closed all but one exit from southern Lebanon. That interruption in travel and commerce exacerbated the anger Shiites were already feeling over Israel's continued presence. To this day, although another investigation of its origins commenced in late 2022, the IDF sticks to its story that the explosion was not due to a terrorist attack. But investigative reporter Ronan Bergman and many others disagree. Based on their findings, I agree with them. But whether it was terror or gas, what is important to our story is that Shiites in Lebanon thought the explosion was due to an attack thus glorifying those who opposed Israel. And so, with the IDF not properly recognizing and responding, Hezbollah grew stronger.

The Danger Grows

Also in 1982, Hezbollah initiated a wave of kidnappings, often called the "Lebanon Hostage Crisis." Over the next decade, Hezbollah abducted approximately 100 people, mostly Americans and Western Europeans, often at the behest of Iran. Victims were held for a long time. Many for months or years before their release. Some were tortured and killed in captivity. Some were traded like chattel between terrorist groups. Some were rescued or managed to escape. Many were chained to radiators and held in isolation. All suffered dearly.

David Dodge, president of the American University in Beirut, was Hezbollah's first victim. On July 19, 1982, a month after the IDF marched into Lebanon, Dodge was kidnapped while walking home from the university. After being held in Lebanon for a time, Iranians took Dodge into their custody and moved him to Tehran, where he languished in prison. He was released a year after being kidnapped. Dodge's successor, Malcolm Kerr, father of Chicago Bull and now Golden State Warrior Coach Steve Kerr, fared worse. He was shot in the back of his head in the hallway outside his office. The Islamic Jihad Organization (usually called Islamic Jihad and not to be confused with the equally fanatic Palestinian Islamic Jihad group) claimed responsibility for both operations. Guess who oversaw Islamic Jihad? None other than Imad Mughniyah! Was Islamic Jihad an independent terrorist group? No. It was an arm of Hezbollah created, in part, to take the blame for Hezbollah's more heinous operations.

1983 saw more bombings. In April, a suicide bomber drove a van loaded with explosives into America's embassy compound in Beirut, parked it in front of the building, and then detonated his bomb. The explosion collapsed the central facade of the building. Sixty-three people died. Once again, Islamic Jihad claimed responsibility.

Six months later, Islamic Jihad unleashed a more devastating attack. A suicide bomber crashed his truck through concertina wire separating the parking lot from a building housing a battalion of US marines sent to Lebanon by American President Ronald Reagan to keep the peace. After weaving his way through an open vehicle gate, smashing into a guard shack, and motoring through the entrance, his vehicle came to a halt in the lobby. The driver then detonated the equivalent of 21,000 pounds of TNT. The blast killed 241 marines within the building. It was the largest non-nuclear explosion the earth had seen since World War II. A few miles away, and ten minutes later, another suicide bomber used his vehicle to carry explosives into a building that housed a French military unit also in Lebanon on a peacekeeping mission. Fifty-eight French soldiers lost their lives in that attack.

Then, on November 4, 1983, came another suicide truck attack on another Israeli headquarters. Again, in Tyre. This time, twenty-nine Israelis died along with thirty-two detainees. Again, it was a Hezbollah operation.

All these suicide attacks certainly increased Shiite support for Hezbollah's activist agenda over Amal's more moderate philosophy. None, however, were as influential as the unfortunate incident that happened two weeks before the second bombing in Tyre.

Every year, in the town of Nabatieh, in southern Lebanon, Shiites arrive on a designated date from throughout the region to parade and celebrate a holiday uniquely special to them—Ashura. It marks a date of great significance for Shiites throughout the world. Some Shiite celebrants strike themselves with whips and beat their chests while parading through the streets. They do this to commemorate, with their anguished pain and ritual bleeding, the lost battle of Karbala where Sunnis beheaded Shiite leader Imam Hussain. On October 15, 1983, 60,000 people crowded into Nabatieh's main square and side areas. For them, it was a day of sorrow, dedicated to the memory of Hussain's and his family's martyrdom. As such, the crowded area was a highly charged, emotional environment—the worst place for a deadly incident involving the IDF. And of course, that is exactly what happened.

A lost IDF patrol consisting of several vehicles blundered into town at the least opportune moment. Stuck in the throng, the soldiers panicked as a crowd mobbed them and hurled stones in their direction. Someone then threw a hand grenade, setting an IDF jeep on fire. The frightened soldiers fired their weapons and threw their own hand grenades, killing at least one celebrator and wounding others.

In India, a decade ago, I was in a car attempting to move through a massive crowd of people lamenting the death of a loved one. Thousands were packed into a small open area on both sides of the road. It was frightening even though the people crushed against my car meant no harm. I can't even begin to understand what it must have been like for young Israelis trapped and seeing only one way out—using their weapons to free themselves.

The next day, Major Haddad's Christian militia made things worse when they came to the town looking for those who had attacked the patrol. The IDF knew it had a problem and arrested the patrol commander who had lost his way. That symbol of contrition did not pacify anyone.

A shitstorm ensued. Shiite clerics who had called for restraint previously refused further cooperation with the Israelis. Shiites who had been recruited by the IDF and its Christian allies deserted. Shiite anger intensified.

Those events handed Hezbollah a perfect recruitment tool. And now, as a result, Amal risked losing much more influence with the Shiite masses if it did not strike back at the Israelis. After that day, Amal ordered its members to actively resist. Amal's adherents followed potential collaborators after they left IDF headquarters—then grabbed, hooded, and killed them in public spots where they were left as a warning. Shiite resistance heated up, riled by events, and clerics trained in Iraq and Iran pushed for an end to Shiite passivity. Roadside bombings became more commonplace. The rhetoric of the now-dead

Sadr, inflamed by a more extreme brand of Shiite fundamentalism fomented by Iran through its proxy Hezbollah, and then intensified by Israel's failure to leave expeditiously after its incursion into Lebanon, resonated more and more with the common Shiite.

However, Hezbollah knew that its cadres required training to be more effective. With Iran's help, Hezbollah established a training base slightly north of Beirut and not too far from Baalbek in the Bekaa Valley. Security was tight. At first, volunteers needed to submit a written request for training that included referrals from two Shiite clerics. Hezbollah would sometimes take up to six months to vet the volunteers. Once approved, Hezbollah operatives would pick them up, blindfold them, and take them to the camp. The base consisted of tunnels dug into the mountainsides, complete with running water and generators for electricity. Anti-aircraft guns encircling the tunnels provided some protection against Israeli air attacks.

The first group had 150 recruits. They received military, religious, and fitness training. Hassan Nasrallah, still shy and skinny, taught religious classes there. Iranian instructors schooled the volunteers on advanced military skills. At first, the program took forty-five days to complete. Later, Hezbollah condensed it to a month. Those with interest and capability were sent to Iran for another three months of training. The camp continued to produce trained operatives until the IDF hit it by air on November 16, 1983. But that did not end the training. It just impeded it, and Hezbollah's army continued to grow. So did its use of tunnels, both in open areas and under homes.

In 1984, the rate of kidnappings and ambushes increased. On March 16, Hezbollah kidnapped CIA station chief William Buckley on his way to work. Buckley was savagely tortured before being executed. Hezbollah didn't confine itself to Lebanon, either. On April 12, Islamic Jihad took responsibility for planting a bomb in a restaurant near a U.S. Air Force base in Spain. That blast killed eighteen American servicemen.

January 1984 also saw an important change of command that impacted the fighting: Major Haddad succumbed to cancer. Haddad was no saint, but he was an important Israeli ally and useful tool for stemming PLO incursions and, later, growing Shiite opposition. IDF General Ephraim Sneh, who once commanded the security zone in Lebanon, said of Haddad, "I worked personally with Major Haddad. He was a tough guy, extremely loyal, a genuine patriot of Lebanon, a true friend of Israel, and a man with dignity." Although I sincerely doubt that Haddad's enemies would have said the same of him, the truth is that Israel needed friends where it could find them. Otherwise, more Israeli lives, both IDF and civilian, would have been lost. With his death, Israel lost an often cruel but effective ally. However, his passing did not end Christian efforts to hold the enclave. General Antoine Lahad, appointed by the Lebanese government, replaced Haddad and renamed the forces formerly under Haddad's control as the South Lebanon Army (SLA).

Cumulatively, attacks from Shiites, Sunnis, and others took a toll on the IDF. The constant drip of IDF casualties sapped Israel's morale. So did the fact that many in Israel thought the nation had become embroiled in a war in Lebanon by choice, not necessity. By the end of 1984, 150 IDF soldiers had been disciplined for refusing to serve in Lebanon. The IDF, first caught between internecine warfare between Druze, Christians, and Muslims right after its 1982 invasion, had now become the target of an increasingly virulent Shiite movement it did not yet fully understand. Nor, after a year and a half of conflict with the nascent Shiite organization, was there an end in sight.

Then came the "Open Letter."

On February 16, 1985, at a press conference in a mosque in southern Beirut, Hezbollah revealed itself to the world for the first time and published what amounted to a manifesto, which a spokesperson read aloud. Forty-eight pages long, the spokesperson called it an "open letter addressed by Hezbollah to the downtrodden in Lebanon and the World." The document contained four major themes.

First, and foremost was Hezbollah's clear intent to obliterate Israel. The spokesperson read, "We condemn sternly all the plans for mediation between us and Israel and we consider the mediators a hostile party because their mediation will only serve to acknowledge the legitimacy of the Zionist occupation of Palestine." And then, to make perfectly clear what was already quite apparent, I emphasize what he read next, *Israel's final departure from Lebanon is a prelude to its final obliteration from existence and the liberation of venerable Jerusalem from the talons of occupation.* Thus, Hezbollah's first goal was not only to rid Lebanon of the IDF but also to rid the world of Israel. Not exactly something from which there is any promise of resolving disputes with negotiations or concession.

Second, the document called for the departure of "Imperial Powers" from Lebanon." That meant the United States and France. Hezbollah saw the United States and the Soviet Union as evil enemies of the third world. In fact, Hezbollah had already killed many Lebanese members of the communist party. But Hezbollah, in line with Iran's views, saw the United States and France as its main Western enemies. France because it supported the Maronites. The United States because Hezbollah thought America used Israel to "inflict suffering on Muslims in Lebanon."

Inexplicably, more than a decade passed following that statement before the United States labeled Hezbollah a terrorist group. Even though just months after the "Open Letter," Imad Mughniyah had led another operation, this time hijacking TWA Flight 847 to Beirut. Even though, while the plane was grounded, a Hezbollah operative brutally killed a passenger who was also an American soldier, callously tossing him to the ground. Even though Hezbollah kidnapped dozens of Americans over the next few years and held one person for seven years. And even though Hezbollah kidnapped U.S. Marine William Higgins, the American chief of the UN Truce and Supervision Organization, in 1998, and then tortured and killed him. Sometimes, when it quacks like a duck it needs to be recognized as a duck. Waiting so long to label Hezbollah a terrorist group was wrong.

The third theme of the manifesto focused on Islam. Although Hezbollah did not demand that Lebanon become an Islamic state, it saw no reason it would not. The manifesto called for Lebanon to decide its own future but predicted that, if free to do so, it would choose Islam. Freedom of choice or coercion? Based on Hezbollah's track record over the last forty years, you decide.

And finally, the document emphasized who the real boss was, with Hezbollah confirming its strong allegiance to Iran and its Supreme Leader, Ayatollah Khomeini. Over time it would become increasingly clear that Hezbollah was in fact an Iranian proxy—operating with the assistance of Iran, under the direction of Iran, and with the permission of Iran. Hezbollah's first leader, Subhi Tufayli, confirmed that in 1987 when he said, "When Imam Khomeini speaks, others must keep silent. He orders us to struggle against America, Israel, [Saudi Arabia], and others, and we will obey."

With Hezbollah's coming out party, Israel finally realized it had a serious problem. In 1985, Yitzhak Rabin, who was the defense minister of Israel at the time, said that Israel's move into Lebanon "let the Shiite genie out of the bottle." The future head of Hezbollah, Hassan Nasrallah, agreed, saying later, "After 1985…was when the popular resistance ended and organized armed resistance began." Before that, Nasrallah said "the main effort…went into mustering and attracting young men and setting up military camps where they could be trained and organized into small groups capable of carrying out resistance attacks against the occupying force. There were no institutions like now, no large organizations or specialized departments."

A new era had begun.

Chapter Five

Israel Partially Withdraws: Hezbollah's Power Grows

In January 1985, Israel initiated a three-stage withdrawal from southern Lebanon, except for the several-mile-wide security zone designated in 1978 after Operation Litani. Policymakers had little choice. Retired Colonel Reven Erlich said that during Israel's negotiations with the Lebanese, because of mounting guerrilla attacks that were increasingly effective, "the IDF continued to sink into the Lebanese swamp." With pressure from home and abroad mounting, and the casualty count growing—in 1984, the death toll equaled one casualty every three days—the IDF felt it had to retreat to more defensible lines. Lines that would deflate political pressure from abroad and dissipate domestic pressure from within.

But Israel still had an intractable problem. The devil it knew (the PLO) had morphed into a monster it did not yet well understand (Hezbollah). At stake were the lives and economic well-being of Israelis living near Lebanon's border. Before the 1982 war, nightmares had become reality with disturbing frequency for those living in the border region. Terrorists killed children, rockets crashed through roofs, and hijacking was a precursor to murder. The government knew that a full withdrawal would see terror return and likely increase—making life unbearable and motivating some to move south—leaving the border abandoned. Unrestrained, the terrorists would be emboldened to do more, the scope and range of their devilment increasing. Unrestrained, eventually the existence of Israel would be jeopardized. Israel would not accept that. If you were a citizen of Israel, would you?

Israel's solution for its conundrum was to maintain and strengthen the security zone stretching a few miles from its border. Creating a buffer zone was reasonable. Lebanon's government had never shut down Palestinian terrorism emanating from southern Lebanon and had little desire to do so. Now, with fighting between the IDF and Shiite militants aligned with both Hezbollah and Amal increasing, and with no hope that the Lebanese Army would take control of southern Lebanon, Israel had no choice. It had to ensure that terrorist entities, this time Shiite rather than the PLO, would not establish themselves near Israel's border with southern Lebanon.

By the end of June, the IDF completed its planned withdrawal. It now held territory in Lebanon that had an average depth of six miles from the border with Israel. Those 328 square miles made up about eight percent of Lebanon. But attacks on the IDF continued. In 1984, Hezbollah and Amal struck the IDF on average fifty times per month. During the first two months of 1985, the number of attacks doubled. Israel's decision to withdraw to a security zone had no impact on Hezbollah's motivation because the IDF would still be in Lebanon and Israel would continue to exist. Therefore, Hezbollah would continue to draw blood.

The IDF tried to reduce its casualties by installing a dusk-to-dawn curfew in the area it controlled. After a Hezbollah operative committed a particularly devastating suicide attack yards from Metula that killed many IDF soldiers, the IDF, hoping to eliminate the suicide bomber phenomena, mandated that two people must always be in vehicles operated by Lebanese civilians. In addition, to make surprise attacks and escapes more difficult, the IDF banned citizens from using motorcycles. And the IDF made parking along major roads illegal to minimize the locations where explosives could be hidden and detonated with devastating effects on IDF convoys. Still, the IDF continued to incur casualties.

What's more, wherever the IDF retreated, Hezbollah advanced. Once in control of a predominately Shiite area, Hezbollah organized the region into groups of about twelve villages each. Within each village, Hezbollah installed a form of home front guard that received minimal military training and that would also serve Hezbollah's political purposes by hanging posters and disseminating propaganda. Also, Hezbollah appointed a liaison officer in each village who reported up the chain of command. Short-term, Hezbollah had two agenda items: continue the fight with Israel and recruit Amal members to join Hezbollah.

Meanwhile, Hezbollah focused on creating what it called a "Society of Resistance" in all the areas it controlled. Hezbollah sought to create a culture whose purpose was to fight Israel. Hezbollah's genius was recognizing that if it wanted to enlist larger numbers of Shiites to help further its mission, it had to improve their lives first. With massive financial support from Iran, Hezbollah did so. In southern Beirut, Hezbollah paid to have years' worth of garbage removed from the streets. It also delivered desperately needed water. Year after year, the depth, quantity, and quality of that support for impoverished Shiites increased.

But that assistance incorporated a cynical manipulation stemming from Hezbollah not permitting Lebanon's central government to provide services or help. Therefore, in the eyes of the Shiite citizenry, only Hezbollah cared. The idea was to create a culture in which Shiites depended on Hezbollah's aid. Aid that would bind them to Hezbollah. In addition, Hezbollah enforced a stricter moral code—no alcohol, no games like backgammon, less music, and dress codes that required women to wear scarves. All this while publicizing Hezbollah's successful attacks.

The plan worked. More and more young Shiites responded to the cause even though the price they paid was submitting to Hezbollah's oppressive ideology.

By the middle of 1985, as the IDF withdrew, Hezbollah's minions committed most of the attacks on the IDF. Per UNIFIL sources, between May and September, 248 attacks targeted the IDF. Then, Hezbollah tried human wave attacks against both SLA and IDF positions, hoping to score both propaganda and blood victories by overwhelming them. But those tactics failed. The defensive positions were often circular and surrounded by mines, guarded by bulldozed walls and oil barrels filled with cement and rings of tires, and strategically placed on hills with views of nearby villages. They were too well-built for human waves, sometimes 200-strong that would attack in daylight. LAF and IDF fire decimated them.

Hezbollah needed to find another way.

For a while, Amal wasn't providing Hezbollah with much help thanks to Syria. Syrian President Assad did not want to see the PLO's Fatah forces reconstitute and take control of the Palestinian refugee camps, ostensibly because he feared that, if the PLO returned, Israel might advance further into Lebanon. Therefore, Assad ordered Amal, over which he maintained much influence, to attack the Palestinians in their camps. Much of the fighting took place in the same Sabra and Shatila camps where Christian Phalange forces had killed so many, events for which Israel was vilified by the international community. Thousands of civilians died due to the fighting, far more than during the indiscriminate massacre in 1982 at the hands of the Maronites. Yet nary a peep of an international outcry. So goes the double standard that Israel lives with. But I digress.

More important for our story of Hezbollah's rise was the impact of Amal's actions. Weakened and distracted by fighting the Palestinians in the camps, Amal lost its focus on attacking the IDF in southern Lebanon. Despite the loss of combat power, this inured to

Hezbollah's benefit, which now had a much freer hand to indoctrinate Shiites living there.

Ensconced in their new hilltop fighting positions, those IDF soldiers who remained in Lebanon were the subject of raging political and military debates within Israel. Ehud Barak, then chief of the IDF Military Intelligence Directorate and future chief of staff and prime minister, said at a meeting in March 1985, "The SLA does not have a chance of being an efficient security filter…[and] will turn into a target [for Hezbollah] where we will have to intervene more and more in order to protect what we have already sent inside." And later in the same meeting, he shouted, "I want to be recorded….We don't realize what's going to happen [if we stay in Lebanon]…Lebanon with all its entanglements and complications…we have got to get our forces out of there!"

Yet, Yitzhak Rabin was satisfied with the situation after the withdrawal to the security zone. Three years later he'd said:

> Instead of 15,000 Israeli soldiers in Lebanon, only several hundred are permanently posted there. We are achieving our objective of peace in the Galilee. No Israeli civilian has been killed as the result of terrorist attacks originating from Lebanon. Thirty-four IDF soldiers have fallen while carrying out this mission. This is a far lower number than in the three years which preceded those past three years.

But despite having withdrawn under pressure, Israel still did not fully recognize the threat Hezbollah posed. Instead, Israel was as concerned about Hezbollah as it was about the PLO. Dangerous? Yes. An existential threat? No. One IDF intelligence officer said, "From Hezbollah's inception, the IDF did not understand Hezbollah at all and had major misunderstandings of the nature of the situation in Lebanon." And by relying on a secured buffer zone "the IDF consolidated the necessary conditions for conflict with Hezbollah and gave Hezbollah the best possible political rationale it needed to exist and continue to fight us." Rabin later agreed with that assessment and reversed his earlier views when he said, "The [1982] war in Lebanon did not eliminate the threat of terrorism against Israel from Lebanese territory; it may have even created a terrorist potential that was even worse than before."

As we shall soon see, Rabin's prediction came to pass.

However, for a while, things were tolerable and the IDF maintained its military superiority over Hezbollah's fighters. Human wave attacks, like the one in 1987 against the IDF position at Beaufort Castle, cost Hezbollah too many casualties. And, initially, most suicide attacks targeting IDF convoys were unsuccessful.

But Hezbollah's tactics evolved. Stealthier strikes replaced brute force. Soon, Hezbollah didn't need to be close to IDF soldiers to be successful; instead, they used improvised explosive devices (IEDs) and fired anti-tank missiles at IDF vehicles from considerable distances. However, regarding the SLA, it was a different story. In January 1987, a twelve-man Hezbollah team cut through the barbed wire protecting an SLA position, made it to the wall, and then used handheld rockets to knock out machine gun positions. SLA soldiers scrambled to save their lives by hiding in a concrete bunker behind a door that could be bolted shut from the inside. Hezbollah's fighters then saw an opportunity and drove away with a prize—an SLA tank and armored personnel carrier given to them by Israel. I can only imagine the euphoria those fighters felt, and the glory they garnered, when their exploits became known.

Still, all was not easy for Hezbollah. There still was the problem of Amal. And some work to do with Syria.

The Syrian Connection

In 1988 and 1989, Hezbollah and Amal continued their struggle to control the Shiite masses in Beirut and southern Lebanon. The 1988 round started when an Amal splinter group loyal to Hezbollah kidnapped American marine William Higgins as he traveled on a coastal road south of Tyre to his UN base. Amal's leader, Nabih Berri, was upset because Higgins worked with the United Nations' forces to keep the peace and Amal had agreed to work with UNIFIL. So, Amal had set out to find Higgins. This brought its rivalry with Hezbollah to a breaking point, causing new fighting to break out between the two camps.

Amal held the upper hand at first in southern Lebanon while Hezbollah maintained its hold on South Beirut. However, when Berri asked Syria for help, Assad played it cagily. Rather than agreeing to Amal's request, he met with Hezbollah. Hezbollah told him it did not want to dominate Lebanon. It only wanted to fight with Israel. That was music to Assad's ears. Therefore, Syria sent its troops into Beirut's southern suburbs to stop the fighting there, allowing Hezbollah to concentrate its strength in southern Lebanon to launch attacks against Israel while also dealing with Amal's supporters in South Lebanon. Eventually, Syria kicked Amal out of Beirut and Hezbollah diminished Amal's influence in southern Lebanon. Given Syria's involvement and Hezbollah's ability to train thousands of fighters with Iran's help, that result was not surprising. It was also not surprising because many middle-class Shiites thought Amal was corrupt.

In the summer of 1989, as Lebanon contended with its ongoing, sporadic civil war that continued to tear it apart, Syria offered to mediate the dispute between Shiites, Sunni, Druze, and Christians. That offer brought a philosophical split within Hezbollah to the forefront. Some did not want to work within Lebanon's political system, which gives power to each religious group. They also did not want to accept Syrian dominance. However, Hassan Nasrallah and others thought it best to accommodate Syria. Tufayli, Hezbollah's more ideological leader, disagreed. When he lost out in that struggle,

Abbas Mussawi replaced him (Remember Mussawi? He was Nasrallah's mentor). Changing leadership did not so much represent a different philosophy as it did different means by which Hezbollah could achieve its goals. Soon, hostages were released, Hezbollah opened a press office, and the organization started down the path of becoming a state within a state.

Then, in October 1989, all the relevant parties met in Taif, a mountain town in Saudi Arabia. With Saudi mediation and Syria wielding its influence behind the scenes, a deal was forged that ostensibly would lead to peace within Lebanon for the Lebanese—but not for Israel. A key tenet of the agreement was that all internal militias and groups within Lebanon, other than the Lebanese army, must disarm. The Christians did (except within the security zone near Israel's border); the Druze did, as did the Sunnis. Even Amal disarmed.

Hezbollah did not.

After disingenuously signing onto the Taif Accords along with all the other groups, Hezbollah refused to disarm. It argued that it needed weapons to defend against Israel and the Christian Southern Lebanese Army (SLA). Many Lebanese sympathized with this argument; after all, the IDF was still present in South Lebanon. And so, all the militias gave up their weapons, the Lebanese army—ineffective due to its composition that included members from all faiths—still had its weapons, while Hezbollah held onto its guns and immediately took steps to acquire more. By retaining its firepower, Hezbollah ensured that it would become by far the most powerful force in Lebanon.

But Hezbollah was not the only disingenuous party. The agreement ambiguously called for the withdrawal of Syrian troops after two years, but only by agreement between Lebanon and Syria. Before then, it read, the Syrian forces *"shall thankfully assist the forces of the legitimate Lebanese government to spread the authority of the State of Lebanon ....*" Not surprisingly, after two years passed, Syria continued to "thankfully assist" and did not leave Lebanon.

The Taif Accords also upended the political status quo, making it easier for Hezbollah to gain political control in the future. The agreement reached by the parties called for an increase in the number of parliamentary seats, and that parliament seats be shared equally among Christians and Muslims. Thus, the Christian 6:5 majority guarantee dating back to 1943 was no more. It was now 50:50. The prime minister position, reserved for a Sunni, used to be occupied by a person picked by the Christian president. Now, the president would be required to consult with Parliament on his choice. This amorphous requirement served to further reduce Christian political control. Score another victory for Muslim Lebanon. Also, the Cabinet, which now would consist of an equal split of Muslims and Christians, had to approve proposals for any new laws. The parties also agreed that executive power, which the president once wielded, would now for most issues rest in the hands of the Cabinet, and that the Cabinet would also control the army. Further complicating matters, formation of the Cabinet now required the president to consult with Parliament and obtain the approval of the prime minister. And decisions on major policy issues would require an affirmative two-thirds vote of all total Cabinet seats, not just the number present at the vote. Thus, if more than a third of the Cabinet members chose to stay home, even if all others were prepared to vote unanimously in favor of something, a legally binding decision could not be made. All told, effectively, the presidency had been neutered. And finally, emphasizing the change in power, the parties to the agreement specified that Lebanon was an Arab country.

As a result, Christians lost their political control of Lebanon, and Hezbollah for the first time had an incentive to join the government. Doing so would allow Hezbollah to augment its military capabilities with political power; collectively, this could cow any domestic opposition. It certainly was not a bloodless coup, for many had died over the last fifteen years. But it was a coup, nevertheless. What might seem on the surface more democratic was in fact a recipe for Hezbollah's takeover.

With the agreement signed, Hezbollah now focused on improving its ability to confront the IDF without having to worry about protecting its rear from opposing domestic militias. And due to the Taif agreement, through Hezbollah's allegiance and dependence, Iran now had gained practical control of Lebanon.

Still, Syria's Assad had cards to play because so much depended on whether he would permit Iranian arms and people to flow through his country on their way to Lebanon. And those cards were important to Assad. He still hoped to use Hezbollah to bleed the IDF until ultimately regaining the Golan Heights by negotiation if not war; for that Assad considered dangling cessation of Hezbollah's attacks on the IDF (although it has never been clear that Assad had the power to make that happen). And, of course, Assad was still eager to keep his hand in Lebanon's mix, having never given up his dream of incorporating Lebanon into a Greater Syria.

Therefore, the game of Lebanese thrones was still on, just some of the players had changed, and Israel was still caught in the middle.

The IDF Tries to Slow Hezbollah Down

Realizing that the IDF and its SLA allies could not just sit back and wait to be attacked, the IDF at times went on the offensive. In 1988, the IDF launched a large operation outside of the security zone that killed forty Hezbollah fighters against the loss of three IDF soldiers. Gal Hirsch, then a company commander and later a division commander in the 2006 war, described in his book, *Defensive Shield*, the intensity and ferocity of the battle. But what he said afterward is revelatory for what Hezbollah had done: "We were fighting in ditches and bunkers, and in face-to-face combat inside houses. At some point, the penny finally dropped and we realized what was becoming evident as the battle's chronology unfolded….It used to be a village once, but now it was a fortress, a citadel."

In a different operation, the IDF attacked another Hezbollah stronghold and killed twenty. Israel's air force also struck hard from the air.

But the damage done was just that—damage. It did not deter Hezbollah. Nor did it prevent Hezbollah from becoming increasingly effective. Soon the tolerable would become intolerable as Hezbollah's minions learned and adapted. While the number of attacks did not change from the '80s through the early '90s, their severity did; they became more lethal. Major General Moshe Kaplinsky, commander of the Golani Brigade in Lebanon between 1993 to 1995, said, "We felt that the resistance had ended when the [Lebanese] Civil War ended [in 1989]. Then it started with an attack here and there, but we did not change our attitude. We were too conservative. We slowly realized between 1990-1993 we were facing a guerrilla war. It took us too long to adjust our behavior."

Hezbollah's new leader, Abbas Musawi, was responsible for much of the organization's increasing success. His ascension marked a change in methods but not in goals. Public calls for an Islamic state in Lebanon would be reduced and he recognized the significant support that Syria supplied Hezbollah in addition to that of Iran. Honoring Syria's role, Musawi thought, would ensure Assad's continued support for Hezbollah retaining its military wing while all other militias disarmed.

But Musawi's leadership proved short-lived.

On February 16, 1992, Musawi rode in a black Mercedes with his wife and child toward a village in South Lebanon. The sky was clear and blue. Two IDF Apache helicopters equipped with missiles trailed the vehicle, without Musawi's knowledge. They were conducting an exercise to see if they could track him; killing him then was not the objective. But the temptation was too great. Two days earlier, three Israeli-Arab Palestinian Islamic Jihad terrorists, supported by both Iran and Syria, had crept into an IDF base and killed three sleeping soldiers with knives, axes, and a pitchfork. Whether that played a role in what happened on February 16 is unclear, but it certainly set the mood in Israel.

Many accounts report that a low-level intelligence commander ordered the helicopters to take the shot. However, Ronen Bergman in his book *Rise and Kill First* convincingly refutes those versions with a detailed chronology that points the finger at the highest levels of government. In any event, what is undisputed is that missiles from those helicopters plowed into the Mercedes, killing Musawi and his family.

Unfortunately for Israel, Musawi's death did not solve its problems with Hezbollah. In fact, it may have magnified them. On a tactical level, the assassination revealed Israel's surveillance and precision-guided missile capabilities. On a strategic level, the death of Musawi led to the rise of an even more effective Hezbollah leader—Hassan Nasrallah

Chapter Six

Hassan Nasrallah

The day after Musawi's death, Hezbollah chose Hassan Nasrallah as its new leader. Thirty-one years later, he still holds that position. At Musawi's funeral, Nasrallah said:

> "America will remain the nation's chief enemy and the greatest Satan of all. Israel will always be for us a cancerous growth that needs to be eradicated, and an artificial entity that should be removed….The Islamic Resistance will remain our only option, our constant response, the path we shall not relinquish, and the battle we will pursue even if the entire world surrenders."

For additional proof of his rabid hatred of Israel, you need to look no further than his speech in 1998 regarding Israel's fiftieth anniversary, during which he said that "the grandsons of apes and pigs" created Israel. And that "to the murderers of the prophets, the grandsons of apes and pigs, we say:...death to Israel." And for any who think his loathing does not extend to Jews living outside Israel, he clarified that, too: "If we searched the entire world for a person more cowardly, despicable, weak, and feeble in psyche, mind, ideology, and religion, we would not find anyone like the Jew. Notice, I do not say the Israeli."

This is the guy who still leads Hezbollah today!

But recognizing Nasrallah's depravity should not lead us to disrespect his capabilities and leadership skills. To this day, his deft handling of Hezbollah has proved crucial for its success.

Immediately after assuming control, Nasrallah sought to recalibrate Hezbollah's approach to politics. Many within the organization thought running candidates for Parliament would weaken the purity of its Islamic mission and pull the organization from its founding principles. The basic question Hezbollah wrestled with was this—if it entered the government how it would weigh Hezbollah's interests vs. Lebanon's interests? But Nasrallah looked at the issue far more simply. He saw participation as necessary for protecting and strengthening Hezbollah's future.

How best to break the impasse? Check with Iran, of course.

Nasrallah met with Supreme Leader Ayatollah Ali Khamenei, Iran's Supreme Leader for the past three years. When Ayatollah Khomeini died in June 1989, Hezbollah's leadership swore allegiance to his successor, Khamenei. Not only did Khamenei become the effective head of state in Iran, but he also assumed the role of supreme religious authority—two positions he still holds today. When Khamenei gave the green light for Hezbollah to enter Lebanese politics, opposition within the organization crumbled.

Providently for the Shiites, and beneficial for Nasrallah's plans, Hezbollah and Amal agreed in 1990 to cooperate rather than fight. Now they ran candidates on a combined slate. And on their first try, their representatives were elected to twelve of 128 seats in Parliament.

Hezbollah had crossed the Rubicon—it was officially participating in politics.

However, Nasrallah still felt it necessary to emphasize that Hezbollah had not wavered from its central mission—the destruction of Israel. After the election, he said, "Our participation in the elections and entry into the Parliament do not alter the fact that we are a resistance party; we shall, in fact, work to turn the whole of Lebanon into a country of resistance, and the state into a state of resistance." Doubling down, a Hezbollah campaign poster in 1996 read "They resist with their blood [referring to Hezbollah], resist with your vote." Now, Hezbollah had both a political and a military arm.

Hmm. It sure seems as if Hezbollah was transitioning from being a state within a state to being a part of the state itself—at least as it pertains to destroying Israel. Previously, Israel had launched operations designed, in part, to influence the Lebanese government, even though it was ill-equipped to take on Hezbollah. Now, for the first time, Hezbollah was part of the government.

Nasrallah's leadership also had Hezbollah thinking about the future. This included brainwashing the next generation. After Nasrallah's rise to power, Hezbollah began introducing Shiite children as young as six and seven to its youth movement. Interwoven with play, sports, and school lessons, Hezbollah's youth camps promote a hostile view of Israel and teach basic familiarity with military activity. It is the first steppingstone toward turning children into resistance fighters. Older children go to *Mustafa* schools where they study religion and pray for resistance fighters. Their summer camps have a military feel to them even though the children do not receive formal military training until after turning eighteen. But by then the task is simpler because they already have gained much familiarity with the use of guns.

In addition, by the late 1990s Hezbollah had placed recruiters in each village to teach religion and Shiite culture, including the concept of martyrdom, which traces back to Karbala and Yazid's killing of Hussain. This practice continues today. Although Shiites are not forced to engage in this educational process, many do—not for the small to nonexistent salaries but for the social system that embraces them and tends to their needs. As a result, villagers came to see Hezbollah as one big family.

To learn more about this phenomenon, I traveled to the International Institute for Counterterrorism at Reichman University in Herzliya, Israel, where I met with their Director for Research, Dr. Eitan Azani. Azani is an expert's expert. Having had much counterterrorism operational experience with the IDF, he is a sought-after consultant and prolific researcher who wrote a seminal book regarding Hezbollah entitled, *Hezbollah: The Story of the Party of God—From Revolution to Institutionalization.* Immediately, I understood that Azani is a serious man who expresses his thoughts with conviction buttressed by experience and knowledge.

While sitting behind his desk and sipping tea, Azani patiently explained that Hezbollah is a "hybrid terror organization." That being a term I was unfamiliar with, I asked him to explain.

Azani said, "The Hybrid terror organizations model (published by Professor Boaz Ganor), has three legs. One is the terror leg. The second is the social leg. And third is the political leg because every organization wants to have political power."

He then explained how Hezbollah fits neatly into that definition. During the first decade of its existence, Azani told me that Hezbollah used violence to "alter circumstances in Lebanon." Then, "in 1992, a significant turning point occurred when Hezbollah participated in parliamentary elections with the support of a religious fatwa issued by Iran's Ayatollah Khamenei." Hezbollah's reason for doing so was to both advocate for, and support, the Shiite community which had been marginalized by Lebanon's government and society until then. A third turning point came in 1998 "when Hezbollah began participating in local government through municipality positions." Accompanying these developments, Hezbollah began to provide services to the Shiite community. A process that has further developed over the decades.

And there you have it: Hezbollah now wields terror/military action, social involvement, and political power. Nasrallah was the key.

It was during the first decade of his rule that Hezbollah morphed into a classic hybrid terror organization.

I left Azani fully understanding his classification of Hezbollah. But still, I wondered when a hybrid terrorist organization stops being an organization and becomes a state of its own. The answer to that question has grave implications for Israeli policy. But before we tackle that question, let's go back to what happened on the ground where Israel and Hezbollah increasingly engaged in a war of attrition.

The Struggle

The day after Musawi's assassination, Israel tasted Hezbollah's retribution. Before dawn, many Katyushas hit Kiryat Shmona, forcing its residents into shelters. It was the first large rocket attack on Israel since the 1982 war. Israeli jets struck back, trying to destroy the rocket launchers. But over the three days of fighting that followed the assassination, Hezbollah successfully launched up to 100 Katyushas, a third of which fell inside Israel.

Hezbollah's ability to strike northern Israel forced the IDF to change its targeting policies. No more would targets get a pass when Hezbollah purposely placed its assets near civilian structures. Of course, when the IDF hit those structures that led to Hezbollah firing more Katyushas. Ronen Cohen, once an IDF officer based in Lebanon, said:

> "It was only after our change in policy that Hezbollah started firing rockets into Kiryat Shmona and Nahariya on a wider scale….It was very general but at this time Hezbollah first created the equation where if we hurt their innocents, they will start shooting Katyushas at us."

Another Israeli policy decision, misguided in retrospect, served to improve Hezbollah's relations with the Palestinians. In December 1992, Prime Minister Rabin, again elected to the job after his first go around in the 1970s, deported to Lebanon 415 Palestinians with suspected ties to Hamas and Islamic Jihad, both Palestinian fundamentalist terrorist organizations. Not surprisingly, the Lebanese government did not want them. Nor did the Christians, who were struggling to control the security strip just north of Israel. And in the end, the plight of the newly released Palestinians served to foster ties between Hezbollah and some Palestinian terrorist groups.

But before we go further, additional context is required. Let's take a shallow dive into the ongoing talks between Israel and Syria.

Syria

Syria wanted to recover the Golan Heights. Israel wanted real peace with Syria in return. Syria did not want real peace. Nor was it willing to negotiate unless Israel stated in advance that it would withdraw from the entire Golan and agree that any deal would be linked to an ultimate result in Lebanon and with the Palestinians. Of course, Rabin would not agree to linkage. Otherwise, either Hezbollah or the Palestinians could increase pressure on Israel by refusing to agree to a deal that had already been negotiated by Israel with Syria, thus increasing the price Israel would have to pay.

Assad's solution to the dilemma? Increase pressure on Israel by enlisting Hezbollah. That request, in Syria's view, was a fair price to charge its patron for permitting Iran to transport weapons to Hezbollah through Syrian territory. Hezbollah obliged. Very likely, Syria's request inspired placement of Hezbollah's roadside bombs in Lebanon, which killed seven IDF soldiers, as well as its rockets that once again hit Kiryat Shmona.

But for Israel, killing soldiers was one thing. Seeing its communities bombarded again was something else. Therefore, in July 1993, The IDF launched *Operation Accountability* in response. Its goal was to damage Hezbollah's capabilities and prevent Hezbollah from using southern Lebanon to attack Israeli citizens. To accomplish that, Rabin said:

> We intend to restore security to our northern citizens by hitting Hezbollah as severely as possible.…To do that, Israel will provoke an exodus of inhabitants from southern Lebanon toward the north in order to put pressure on the Lebanese government and to hit those who collaborate with Hezbollah…. This affords freedom of action to fight the terrorists without harming civilians and in the wake of the operation gives an opportunity to the Lebanese government and its outside supports [Syria] to rein in Hezbollah.

The IDF primarily used precision strikes from the air and from its artillery to avoid incurring casualties and dropped warning leaflets to civilians telling them to get out of the way. Hundreds of thousands clogged the roads streaming out of the region. But the operation had little impact on Hezbollah. Like a metastasized cancer, by then Hezbollah had spread too much throughout southern Lebanon for the attacks to have much impact. It is hard to stop from the air, or by stand-off artillery, a few guys installing a hidden bomb along a deserted roadway at night or prevent a couple of technicians from quickly constructing an improvised launcher to shoot a Katyusha. In fact, within weeks after the campaign ended, the IDF in Lebanon found itself the target of a renewed campaign of ambushes and rocket attacks. What's more, the suffering of the civilian population likely helped Hezbollah's recruiting efforts. Meanwhile, the Lebanese government's inaction highlighted its impotency—it could do nothing to eject Hezbollah even if it wanted to.

The operation ended after the United States stepped in to negotiate "a set of verbal understandings" between Israel and Hezbollah: neither party would target civilians in the future; Israel would not attack deep into Lebanon; and if Hezbollah fired on IDF soldiers, the IDF could return fire directed at the source of the shooting, even inside villages. That, however, left Hezbollah with a green light to kill IDF soldiers in Lebanon. And the informal agreement did not adequately address Syria's continued support for that. Three weeks later, two Hezbollah roadside bombs killed nine IDF soldiers.

Hezbollah was happy. Nasrallah later said, "The Katyusha bombardment has led to a new formula based on mutual force displacement, mutual destruction, and equal terror." Syria was happy too. Since assuming power in 1970, Assad had focused on recovering the Golan Heights from Israel, which had captured it in the 1967 Six-Day War. Assad was now thrilled that Hezbollah could continue killing Israelis and was happy to continue supporting that activity as leverage to force Israel to make a deal regarding the Golan.

But the IDF was unhappy. Since Hezbollah continued to seed civilian areas with its military arsenal, the agreement hamstrung any IDF response due to fear of causing Lebanese civilian casualties.

Also unhappy was Lebanon Prime Minister Rafiq al-Hariri, a Sunni. He had hoped to use the negotiations and the aftermath to leverage Syria out of Lebanon and disarm Hezbollah. Neither happened. And, in fact, both strengthened their grip on Lebanon.

In 1994, Hezbollah launched more Katyushas at civilian targets in northern Israel. But before we go further let's make sure we understand what Katyushas are. This is what I wrote about them in my book *Living in Heaven, Coping with Hell*, which is about the settlement of Israel's northern borders:

> The Russians first developed the Katyusha rocket system during World War II. The Soviets used heavy trucks as a platform to launch volleys of as many as forty-eight up to four miles. German soldiers learned to dread their distinctive scream as they descended from the sky to wreak havoc. The Germans called them "Stalin's organs," but their name actually came from a

Russian song about a girl pining away for her lover who is away on military service. Easy to set-up and fire, the missiles lacked accuracy but not lethality. Packed with explosives and layers of serrated steel or small metal spheres—designed to tear into human flesh with devastating impact—anyone standing unprotected near where a Katyusha lands is unlikely to survive.

The thing about Katyushas is that they are ineffective military weapons. They are famously impossible to aim and are the antithesis of a precision-guided weapon. They are, however, the perfect terror weapon for killing and terrorizing civilians. Neither the shooter nor those targeted on the ground know where they are going to land. The best guess is within a radius of hundreds of yards or even miles from where they are aimed. But when they hit, anyone nearby will die. This greatly differs from Israeli weapons and doctrine, then and now, which make every effort to avoid civilian casualties.

So much for the 1993 verbal understandings intended to limit fighting to military forces in Lebanon.

The Mid-1990s

By 1995, Hezbollah's military had grown significantly stronger. So had its propaganda arm. Beginning in 1991, Hezbollah began filming many of its operations for broadcast on Al-Manar TV, a television station owned by Hezbollah. Al-Manar provided news programming, censored movies, shows for children, religious segments, and even talk shows. But it also broadcast one other thing: combat videos featuring successful operations. In his book *Warriors of God,* Nicholas Blanford recounted what the head of Hezbollah's operations had told him: "Al-Manar is an important weapon for us. It's a political weapon, social weapon, and a cultural weapon." In addition, Hezbollah got into the press relations business. Here was a terrorist organization that had a designated press office, which granted interviews to Western journalists to push the concept that Israel was a brutal occupier and Hezbollah nothing more than freedom fighters. Hmm. Perhaps we should look at it through a different lens—as a sophisticated sovereign information war campaign.

Also problematic for Israel was that Hezbollah's training and doctrine were increasingly bearing fruit. By the mid-1990s, the ratio of IDF to Hezbollah's casualties had gone from 5:1 to 1.5:1.

Hezbollah's deadliest tactic had become the roadside ambush, in which directional claymores spewed hundreds of steel ball bearings through thin-skinned vehicles and flesh alike. At first, IDF sniffer dogs found many of the claymores. Then Hezbollah switched to fiberglass casings painted to resemble rocks to avoid detection. When Hezbollah used cell phones to detonate them from a distance, the IDF started jamming the phones' frequencies. This tit-for-tat game of offense and defense was a constant struggle. As was discerning Hezbollah's evolving strategies for employing the bombs. Sometimes there would be two bombs rather than one. The first was a decoy, designed to be found. The second was intended to kill. The second bomb was always better hidden than the first, scheduled to explode several minutes after the first was discharged or discovered. Occasionally, they would catch IDF soldiers crowded together as they were treating the wounded, transporting casualties, or still working to disarm the first weapon.

But the primary weapon Hezbollah used to deter Israeli action remained the Katyusha. The IDF found them difficult to stop because of Hezbollah's doctrine. Two independent teams would manage the launch cycle. The first, which was the brains of the operation, consisted of artillery specialists and engineers. They would position the launcher and aim it. That group would then leave. A second team would launch the rocket. That team used timers to monitor the available window to escape, for IDF radar could pinpoint the precise location from which the rocket was launched. That left them with mere seconds before Israeli artillery shells were whistling their way.

Topography worked in Hezbollah's favor as well. The SLA and IDF widely dispersed their bases, which were separated by deep valleys filled with thick and thorny underbrush that made seeing people passing through difficult. A friend who fought there told me, "It is not jungle, but it's low and tight wood. When you send UAVs (unmanned airborne vehicles), you don't see anything, you see green. Even if the UAV has a thermal [sensor], it's very hard to find [people], to define an animal versus a human being." Therefore, small Hezbollah reconnaissance teams easily moved unseen between those bases. Larger units found it relatively safe to do so, too. And to avoid being targeted, Hezbollah fighters would mingle with Shiite villagers or find the protection of hidden defensive fortifications complete with tunnels and bunkers. Although Hezbollah did not win any large battles, it was winning by not losing.

"Desperate" is not the word, but the IDF was mindful that things were not going well and searched for a way to reverse the flow of events on the ground. In February 1995, the IDF put together a new unit called *Egoz*. In Hebrew, *Egoz* is an acronym for Anti-Guerilla Micro-Warfare. Designed to operate deep within Hezbollah's territory without requiring resupply, the unit became operational in July. Success came quickly, as the unit ambushed the ambushers, while also training the regular army in new techniques. But it was not enough. Still, Hezbollah was not losing.

Operation Grapes of Wrath

In early April 1996, Hezbollah fired tens of Katyushas at Kiryat Shmona, ostensibly in retaliation for the IDF inadvertently killing Lebanese civilians in recent operations. On April 11, Israel launched *Operation Grapes of Wrath* in response to Hezbollah's wanton attacks. But before we talk about the operation and the aftermath, let's dig a bit into what happened and why.

Israel's critics focus on the IDF accidentally killing several Lebanese civilians yet condone Hezbollah firing Katyushas at communities in Israel's north, including Kiryat Shmona, a practice that has resulted in numerous casualties since 1996. But compare the two practices. The IDF had targeted Hezbollah fighters whose goal was to kill IDF soldiers. The civilians died because Hezbollah shamelessly used civilians as shields, behind which they would fire, thus inviting strikes on civilian areas. They did not die because Israel intended to kill innocents. In fact, the IDF tried hard to avoid injuring civilians, despite the callous way Hezbollah used them. But in war, mistakes happen. The unintentional death of those people was due to mistakes consistent with the vagaries of war. Contrast that with firing numerous Katyushas at a populated area with the singular purpose of indiscriminately killing men, women, and children. Hezbollah had no military objective when doing this; it was pure terrorism.

Israel could no longer tolerate this imbalance. It decided to go big.

Beginning on April 12, and continuing for two weeks, the IDF pounded Lebanon. The goal, again, was to influence the Lebanese government to do something about Hezbollah. Again, the IDF warned the inhabitants of southern Lebanon to evacuate. This time, 400,000 fled. The IDF used airplanes, artillery, and helicopter strikes to go after missile launchers, an electric plant, bridges, and other targets. The head of the Israeli Air Force (IAF) at the time said:

> The idea was to go after the infrastructure of Hezbollah, so there was a lot of emphasis to destroy buildings and bunkers…. Extreme precision was required because the apartment buildings [housing Hezbollah operations centers] also housed the families of the Hezbollah fighters. We did not want CNN to broadcast scenes of dead women and children.

But once again, as it had in 1993, Israel's attacks helped to increase Hezbollah's popularity. Perhaps that should not be surprising. People don't like being forced to flee their homes. On the coastal road, vehicles heading north could do so unimpeded. Those trying to head south found themselves targeted by the IDF. Nobody would want to live in those conditions with bombs bursting everywhere. Even though Hezbollah was the true reason for their plight, the remedy was not within the common person's grasp. Individual citizens had no power to fight Hezbollah and the Lebanese government had neither the will nor the capability to do so. Israel hoped Lebanese civilians would push the government, but the opposite happened. Shiites most impacted by the fighting continued to support Hezbollah. It was the easier path.

At first, the diplomatic route showed some promise. Foreign Minister Ehud Barak, no longer in the IDF but climbing the political ladder in Israel, said that Israel wouldn't negotiate until the Lebanese government stopped Hezbollah from firing Katyushas into Israel. The United States called for a nine-month period over which Hezbollah would disarm. Syria, of course, objected. But Israel still had diplomatic room to maneuver. Operations were proceeding pretty much as planned although some in the IDF grumbled that a ground offensive had not accompanied the air attacks. And the international community had not yet exerted significant pressure on Israel to stop its attacks. Hundreds more Katyushas had fallen into northern Israel. Thus, it was widely recognized that a solution that protected Israeli civilians had to be found.

Then came Qana.

Shortly before 2 p.m., Fijian UNIFIL soldiers heard several mortar shells fired from a cemetery about two hundred yards from their base in the center of Qana, a town left of central southern Lebanon, about eight miles north of Israel. Hezbollah soldiers were firing shells to pin down a nearby IDF special forces unit. When one Fiji soldier tried to stop them, according to a UN report, Hezbollah soldiers shot him in the chest.

Immediately after firing their mortars, the Hezbollah operatives ran into the UNIFIL base; they knew the IDF would soon fire artillery shells at their previous location. Inside the base were 800 civilians who thought it safe from the fighting nearby. The Fijians, fearing the IDF's imminent counter-battery fire against the mortar position, herded as many civilians as possible into bomb shelters; others they tucked into rooms. Soon, the predictable tragedy happened. Thirteen IDF artillery shells whistled down from the clouds, hitting the UNIFIL base. More than 100 civilians died.

Accusations flew immediately, and people still argue today over what happened and why. Some say that the IDF acted intentionally. An IDF investigation found that the artillery unit had used an outdated map that was seventy to a hundred yards off and that it had no intention of harming civilians.

Compounding factors were proximity and inaccuracy. There was simply no excuse for Hezbollah fighters to fire their mortar while so close to masses of civilians; they knew the IDF would respond in kind. Yes, the IDF used radar to pinpoint where counter-battery fire would target. But speed was required for effectiveness and the IDF unit on the receiving end of the mortar shells needed relief, the surrounding hills can affect the accuracy of radar, and of course, there was the issue of the map's accuracy. Sometimes, as IDF Major Matan Vilnai said, "There is a limit to what you can get out of a barrel of a gun in terms of accuracy."

I look at things practically as well as technically. The IDF did not stand to benefit by killing civilians. Killing civilians would not benefit the IDF in any way. However, putting civilians at risk did benefit the Hezbollah operatives who fired those mortars. Logically, they likely assumed that the civilians' presence would prevent the IDF from responding in kind. By setting up their mortar so close to civilians and then running to the camp, the Hezbollah shooters sought safety by using human shields. Sadly, their depravity cost those innocent people their lives. And in the end, it was Hezbollah that benefitted and may even have welcomed those deaths, for that provided it with another propaganda victory, which it surely welcomed.

Today, the Qana site is a memorial, which Hezbollah built and now promotes. The site features banners emblazoned with Islamic sayings that call for vengeance. A sign there says, "Qana is the Karbala; it is the land made holy by the Lord Jesus and contaminated by the Zionist Satan." At Qana, Hezbollah's pompous sanctimony is unmistakable; it ranks terroristic propaganda over the lives of innocents.

Don't buy my argument? Look at Hezbollah's subsequent moves. It has doubled and tripled down on hiding its forces and weaponry among civilians. Today, much of its missile strength lies hidden in people's homes, in schools, and in mosques. Villages are loaded with defensive positions and armaments. So much for Hezbollah's regard for human life. It knows that Israel will have no choice but to go after the weapons and fighters where they are. It knows that accidents will happen, and Lebanese civilians will die. But the death of Lebanese civilians suits them.

Why?

Because much of the world only sees dead civilians and points the finger at who shot them without caring about who put them in harm's way. Many Lebanese felt the same about Qana. For them, Israel was the sole guilty party.

Just, of course, what Hezbollah wanted.

After Qana, international pressure on Israel to stop the fighting intensified.

Once again, the United States searched for a solution. Secretary of State Warren Christopher traveled to Syria to see if Assad would work with him to stop the fighting. Instead, he found a brick wall. Eventually, Christopher brokered a deal that Hezbollah would accept, and, due to the international outcry about Qana, Israel had to accept.

The unwritten oral understandings of that deal have come to be called the "Rules of the Game." They were:

1. Hezbollah agreed to not attack or fire into Israel.
2. Israel and its allies (the SLA) agreed to not hurt civilians or hit civilian targets in Lebanon.
3. Both parties agreed to not hurt civilians or launch attacks from civilian or industrial areas.
4. Both parties agreed that without violating the agreement, each had the right to defend themselves.

The Rules of the Game took effect on April 27. A few days later, Warren Christopher wrote a private letter to Shimon Peres, the prime minister of Israel at the time, which included the following:

> With regard to the right of self-defense referred to in the Understandings dated April 26, 1996, the United States understands that if [Hezbollah] or any other group in Lebanon acts inconsistently with the principles of the Understanding or launches attacks on Israeli forces in Lebanon, whether that attack has taken the form of firing, ambushes, suicide attacks, roadside explosives, or any other type of attack, Israel retains the right in response to take appropriate self-defense measures against the armed groups responsible for the attack.
>
> With regard to the prohibitions on the use of certain areas as launching grounds for attacks, the United States understands that the prohibition refers not only to the firing of weapons, but also to the use of these areas by armed groups as bases from which to carry out attacks.

Sounds good? Not really.

The problem with the 1996 unwritten deal, as with the 1993 informal agreement, was that by omission it legitimized Hezbollah's attacks on the IDF within Lebanon but made it difficult for the IDF to respond to them. And now, due to the language of the agreement, Hezbollah was being depicted as an authorized resistor that had a right to kill Israelis if they were in Lebanon. But perhaps the group tasked with monitoring the deal, per the agreement, would at least ensure the participants held up their ends of the bargain.

Did they? No.

The monitoring group was composed of representatives from the United States, France, Syria, and Lebanon. Syria? How did Syria sneak into that? Its goal was parallel to Hezbollah's—bleed the IDF. The idea that Syria had any interest in restraining Hezbollah was fanciful at best.

Operation Grapes of Wrath, like *Operation Accountability,* failed. Hezbollah's popularity within Lebanon increased because it was fighting back, something the Lebanese army did not do. And because perception often matters more than body counts, Hezbollah's survival mattered more than Israel's military successes. Now, more and more Druze, Sunnis, and even some Christians started to support Hezbollah. That development made the Lebanese government even less interested in controlling the organization. And it became evident that Israel was barking up the wrong tree. Syria, not the Lebanese government, was in charge and peace did not serve the interests of Assad. In his book *High* Price, Daniel Byman wrote: "Syria was more than willing to fight to the last Lebanese."

So true.

The Next Three Years

Fighting continued after April 1996, but it skewed more on Hezbollah's terms than Israel's. Even so, IDF casualties decreased because; except for the Egoz unit and some other units conducting targeted raids, the IDF had adopted more of a defensive posture. This mostly left the initiative to Hezbollah, which became more proficient at roadside attacks.

Col. (res.) Shay Shemesh, who served both as an outpost commander in the late 1990s in Lebanon and now as a reserve brigade commander, spoke to me at length regarding what it was like to serve there at that time. He still enjoys a youthful look that belies his forty-some years. Shay was a tough guy, having served in both Egoz and the IDF's famed Golani brigade. But he looks much more like a kind and loving father, someone you would wish to have as a neighbor.

At first, Shay said, the IDF was much more on the offensive. His troops would conduct offensive operations and patrol the region near the Taybeh outpost he commanded. But as time went on orders changed. Rather than take the fight to Hezbollah they hunkered down in their fortifications where "we drowned our outposts with concrete [and] all kinds of electrical protection." And so, the goal shifted from defeating Hezbollah to not losing soldiers.

Dirty work, Shay told me, even during the years the IDF would still leave the outposts, was often performed by the SLA, which sustained many more casualties than the IDF. Therefore, from Shemesh's perspective, the SLA soldiers were worthy partners even though some stole and a few collaborated with Hezbollah. But "they fought for their homes. [And] they worked with us in good cooperation…[even though] they did the more dangerous work that we didn't want to do."

One story he told lingered with me.

Shemesh's soldiers had encountered a Hezbollah unit and killed several of them. However, multiple IEDs were scattered in the valley where the engagement occurred. Shemesh didn't want to put his men at risk dealing with them. So, his unit called in the SLA to handle the IEDs. One detonated, killing their bomb squad leader. Yes, the SLA was sometimes brutal. But its soldiers were also courageous. And they fought, as many have throughout history, for their families' survival.

<u>Support for the War in Lebanon Wanes Within Israel</u>

Hezbollah had become so proficient with its roadside IEDs that the IDF started using helicopters to ferry troops to and from defensive positions. This led to perhaps the worst accident in the IDF's history, one that would initiate a political movement in Israel that would have a lasting impact.

On February 4, 1997, just after 7 p.m., two helicopters cut through the dark, foggy night. Both were carrying troops toward Israel's security zone in Lebanon. One helicopter's destination was a position at Beaufort Castle, an old crusader fort on a hilltop several miles into Lebanon. The other headed to the "Pumpkin" military post, which Matti Friedman covers so eloquently in his haunting book *Pumpkin Flowers: A Soldier's Story*.

In mid-air, over Moshav She'ar Yashuv, the two helicopters collided. Spiraling downward, one crashed into the Moshav; the other hit the ground several hundred yards away in Kibbutz Dafna's fields, where it lay for several hours while exploding ammunition kept rescuers at bay. All seventy-three soldiers and flight crew aboard the two craft perished.

The impact of the disaster was felt throughout Israel. Israel's president, Ezer Weizman, made condolence calls to each of the families that had lost a loved one. Children wrote poems and the "Four Mothers" movement was spawned. Started by the mothers of four of the downed soldiers, the movement challenged the need to remain in Lebanon, their passion driven by the loss of their children. At first marginalized and ridiculed by most Israelis, the movement gained steam as the human and economic cost of the IDF remaining in Lebanon mounted.

Then came another event, this time a failed IDF operation. On September 4, 1997, an IDF special forces unit came ashore in Lebanon at Ansariya, a little less than fifteen miles north of Tyre, far from the IDF's security zone. The sixteen-strong, black-clad unit crossed the coastal road before heading uphill to the north side of the town. Its goal was to kill a particular Hezbollah leader thought to be there. At the top of the hill was a dirt path. When the unit reached an iron gate alongside it, hell burst forth. A hidden Hezbollah ambush unit triggered two IEDs, shredding Israeli soldiers caught in its kill zone. Other Hezbollah operatives opened fire. Within moments, eleven of the sixteen Israelis had died, four others lay wounded, and only one remained unhurt. The living called for help. IDF helicopters quickly arrived, strafed the area, and landed reinforcements that created a perimeter. The rescuers loaded the wounded into the helicopters, which took them away; some soldiers remained. They searched for the body parts of their comrades blown to pieces in the first blasts. No amount of tissue was too small to leave behind. But then mortar shells landed, killing another. More would die if they did not leave. Shortly before dawn, helicopters evacuated the remaining soldiers.

When the sun rose, it revealed the carnage that had occurred hours before. And despite the best efforts of the IDF's relief force, body parts remained strewn throughout the area—including the decapitated head of one soldier.

Then Israeli Prime Minister Benjamin Netanyahu said it was "one of the worst tragedies that has ever occurred to us." In 1998, Hassan Nasrallah said that Hezbollah knew the Israelis were coming. But how? Two years later Hezbollah answered the question when it revealed that they had learned how to read Israeli drone transmissions that till then were not encrypted, and Hezbollah had spotted drones reconnoitering the area before the Israelis came ashore. Whether true or not, Hezbollah found out somehow.

Nor was the ambush at Ansariya the only intelligence failure the Israelis experienced. A month later, Hezbollah learned from a spy within the SLA that high-level IDF officers were coming to a meeting with SLA leaders. Sure enough, a three-vehicle convoy carrying those officers made its way to Markaba, a village close to the border. A Hezbollah team planted and then detonated a roadside bomb as the vehicles passed by. Another attack nearby surprised other IDF officers in civilian vehicles. Two lost their lives, six others were wounded. Hezbollah was on the hunt for IDF officers.

In total, from August through October of 1997, twenty-seven Israeli soldiers lost their lives at the hands of Hezbollah. As a result, Israeli civilian domestic support for keeping soldiers in Lebanon dwindled. Their frustration matched that of the military. General Levin, then northern commander for the IDF and in overall charge of the IDF in Lebanon, said:

> The present situation, in which Hezbollah is causing us to bleed and we are soaking it up, cannot continue. If you give me the means and the freedom to initiate and implement a large number of offensive actions, I would be able to put Amal and Hezbollah on the defensive....We would have to hit them with a blow they would not forget for a long time.

Brigadier General (res) Erez Maisel told me, "The only way to actually hold the security [strip] from 1996 onwards was by enforcing it with more soldiers, but [with] more soldiers, we [would have] had more casualties." And without those soldiers, Hezbollah could get through because "there were not enough troops and not enough surveillance material there to cover everything." Therefore, whenever they wanted, whenever it is best for them, "they can lob shells over the border. They can [attack] our fortifications, [or fight with the SLA]." Maisel's meaning is clear. Hezbollah had gained the initiative.

And both Shemesh and Maisel agreed, that as the IDF became more reluctant to conduct offensive operations, preferring to stay in its defensive positions, the IDF became more predictable. And predictability in war leads to death.

General Levin did not get the resources or the green light to strike. Instead, the IDF stayed on the defensive, trying to avoid casualties rather than cause Hezbollah pain. It was a poor decision.

Soldier's Stories

Boaz Amidror

While sitting comfortably in the lobby of the Renaissance Hotel in Tel Aviv, Colonel (res.) Boaz Amidror spent almost two hours with me recounting his time in Lebanon. Boaz has been a dear friend for years, and we have spent much time together traveling around Israel and meeting for dinner. But this was the first time we spoke in detail about his experiences in Lebanon.

Boaz arrived in Lebanon as an officer cadet in 1987. He was there to fight, but also to train. Sink or swim in the IDF is serious stuff. Make a mistake and you die.

On the first day in-country, he participated in an ambush. While lying in wait, his unit spotted two suspicious guys. They had already placed IEDs and were on their way home. One of his fellow soldiers shouted at them. "They didn't stop, and they hid," Boaz said, "And so, we approached them, and they opened fire." A fellow soldier, beside Boaz, was hit by a bullet in his leg. They were in a field, which Boaz described to me:

> It had wheat there before, but it was burned black, and every bullet…Like in the movies, phish, phish, phish. You don't get scared because you act, you don't have time to be scared. You act. I was with a [heavy machine gun], and then we laid down and we didn't find them. And then they made a mistake. They went to run away and go to the other side of the hill. And when we came that way, we saw them there. We shouted at them. They

went down to the creek, down the hill. And we went directly there, but they ran to the creek [perpendicular to us].

But Boaz and his comrades didn't know where they were. The echoing shots left them disoriented, and it was impossible to discern where the Hezbollah operatives were firing from. According to Boaz, determining the source of gunfire is often difficult even for seasoned soldiers. It's especially challenging for young cadets. Eventually, however, "when they [tried to run away] Boaz's unit spotted, shot, and killed them both. "It was 1987," Boaz told me, and:

> It was the beginning of Hezbollah. They were wearing jeans, some kind of shirt, not a camouflage shirt, they had regular bags, and they had a strap on their heads with red and green, red, and yellow....They looked miserable. Their bag was empty because the IED had been in there. And they had an AK 47 with a few magazines. That was all their equipment. With jeans. They looked like civilians.

However, the reason Boaz shared this memory with me was not to tell an old war story but to emphasize how Hezbollah evolved.

Eleven years later, in 1998, Boaz was a deputy paratrooper battalion commander stationed at an important post in Lebanon, referred to in the IDF as the "Dead Post." One Saturday night, Boaz was in charge, his commander having gone back to Israel earlier in the day. As part of normal operations then, Boaz had sent a reconnaissance company out at night to search for the enemy. As Boaz put it in his sardonic way, the company "had a meeting with one of the Hezbollah. It was night, they couldn't see anything, so Boaz's soldiers threw a grenade." But because it was night, they thought it too dangerous and difficult to investigate whether the grenade had hit anybody. Better to leave it for daylight.

Sure enough, the next morning, Boaz's men found a body. But what highlighted Hezbollah's evolution was what the dead man was wearing and what he'd been carrying. He was decked in camouflage and, Boaz said, "his equipment was better than ours, he had a special gun with nighttime sites, a black mask on his face. Everything was camouflaged. Perfect. Special boots, special uniform. He looked like a warrior from a special unit."

"So," Boaz told me, "From the guy I saw eleven years before who was in jeans. The last one I saw was like a soldier, a very good soldier." Hezbollah had changed from a terrorist organization into a guerrilla force. A force whose equipment and tactics had improved in part because, as Boaz put it, "your best teacher is your enemy."

Erez Maisel said much the same to me, "We were a good enemy. So, they got better. Those who died, died. The ones who survived were the very good. And we trained them. Indirectly we made them much better."

Over the many years he spent in Lebanon with roles that included officer cadet, platoon leader, service in an elite unit, assistant battalion commander, and eventually brigade commander in 2006, Boaz fought an enemy that was actively trying to kill him and his men. Guerrilla forces, he explained, avoid a fight unless it is on their terms. They are not looking to conquer or defeat. "They want to kill." Thus, he and the IDF in Lebanon were not specifically focused on stopping Hezbollah from killing women and children, which was the terrorist organization's future goal, not their present one. Boaz's primary present aim was to foil Hezbollah's guerrilla army attempts to hunt and kill IDF soldiers in Lebanon. However, the experts and pundits might describe the events of those years, Boaz emphasized, "I'm talking from a soldier's point of view." And, he added, "We learned not to admire of course, but to respect them."

Avraham Levine

Avraham is neither large nor imposing. Born in Israel, while still a child he moved with his parents to the United States before his family returned to Israel. Now working for *Alma*, a research and education center in northern Israel, he served in the IDF in Lebanon where he commanded troops as a young officer. Avraham and I sat down to discuss his experiences there.

One of my first questions to him involved the emotions and mindset of being a young man in Lebanon commanding soldiers barely older than himself. Avraham told me:

> It's weird. I'm not a brave person. I don't do adrenaline-filled stuff. That's not me. Looking back. I don't remember being scared going in. I do remember the responsibility is great, and it takes its toll on you.
>
> I remember, I mean, taking a shower once every two weeks, because I didn't want to be unprepared. If something happens, I want to be the first to be ready.
>
> But I don't remember being scared under fire. You're too busy. And I think that coincides with the PTSD question. It's the people without a job that don't know what they're doing there. They're usually more traumatized than the people that had a job, even if it wasn't that important. So, I tell you, as a commander. Give each soldier something to do and do not sit around. That's why the medics supposedly would have the worst time because they see all the worst. [But] they don't necessarily, they're not necessarily the ones that get more traumatized because they're doing something, they're helping the situation. They're not just sitting around. So, we were told, give each soldier a job, count the soldiers, tell everyone to drink, make sure this is that, you know, you're in charge, but give him a job so he doesn't just sit there and let his mind go crazy. And as a commander, you're way too busy [to be scared].

I then asked Avraham if he was worried when patrolling areas with heavy brush and having to walk a different route each time. We both laughed at his answer. "Yeah," he said, "and I'm not great with navigating, so I'm always nervous that I'm…getting lost. That was a scary thought. If I'm going the wrong way."

Since much of the patrolling involved setting up ambush sites. I asked Avraham what that was like. He responded that they would usually stay in place for "two nights, three days, and then come back." While there, they would "see what you can collect in terms of the intelligence or recognize what's going on the trail." And then if shit came their way, "everyone's prepared, we were like, you mean you're ready to shoot, safety off and you are shooting."

Probing more, I asked what it felt like when he returned from a mission.

> I was young. I think, you know, you don't think about your family. I'll tell you an example. The second stint. So that's May, so I'm pretty sure it was that month [we] withdrew. I'm on a stakeout with my soldiers and by coincidence, we are looking south. And around 10 o'clock at night, in the dark, we see far away fireworks because it's Independence Day in Israel and we're looking towards Kiryat Shmona and then you make the connection, that's why we're here. We're here for Metula and Kiryat Shmona.
>
> So that was a great feeling. One of my soldiers brought a few [of] the really small flags that you put on a cake. He started waving them like we were also celebrating Independence Day. Then you get filled with, you feel the accomplishment, like they are celebrating. That's what I'm here for so they can celebrate. I think it is when you go home…when you think about things later on. It is not when you are busy,

Later, Avraham made an interesting contrast. More than a decade after his experiences in Lebanon, Avraham commanded a unit preparing to go into Gaza as part of *Operation Pillar of Defense.* Every night they drilled, thinking they were about to go in. But then they'd be ordered back to base. On Avraham's last night near Gaza, leadership sent his unit to a location very close to the border. To Avraham, it felt like this was it.

> So, on the bus, I was feeling the pressure. Cause maybe now we're going in and I didn't say goodbye to anybody. And I have kids now, already in the family and this and that. That's when, you know, I felt that was a low point that I was feeling like, damn, I'm not prepared. Did I do everything I want? Like, who's going to take care of what and things like that. But as young soldiers in Lebanon, we were excited. We were, let's go again. When are we coming back?

Avraham told me:

> Lebanon was the goal of every soldier in the IDF. You want to prove what you are worth? You go to Lebanon….Anything less, like anywhere in Judea and Samaria or Gaza was like, what are you doing there? Hebron…was like no, that's peanuts. Go for Lebanon. Lebanon was where the action was.

I then asked if Hezbollah's operatives were good soldiers. He said:

> They were really good with specific capabilities. If I compare soldiers now, they had specialists. So, they had a good sniper. Was he a good soldier? No, he was a good sniper, and he knew what he was supposed to do in that post, from that position…. They were amazing with the same weapons that we had, the TOW, they had the same anti-tank missile…and did pretty well [with] improvised, explosives, but that's it, they weren't, they weren't taking over posts, they weren't winning the big battles.

Things were changing and evolving all the time. Each time you went up to Lebanon, there were new tricks that they were using. We had newer technology to deal with it and it kept on moving and evolving. So, for some time the tanks were doing very well because they had night vision and the ability to hit long-range. And then Hezbollah realized how far they have to be from the tank or at what angle, so they don't see them. And then the tanks were no good for that.

Every time it kept evolving.

<u>The SLA</u>

Like the IDF, SLA soldiers fought against Hezbollah. Shay Shemesh told me, "I think they were relatively good soldiers. They fought for their homes. They worked with us in good cooperation." Avraham Levine respected their abilities as well. As did Boaz Amidror, who said that although the SLA's regular soldiers were not so good, its leaders down to its platoon commanders were "warriors," and that "you could do business" with them. However, the SLA and the IDF did not necessarily work together. Avraham said, "It was two parallel efforts supporting each other." And sometimes, the primary reason for constructing an IDF base was more to support the SLA than to protect Israel. Other times, the SLA and the IDF would take turns using a base depending on each other's needs.

Even the weapons each organization used reflected their parallel rather than united structures. The SLA did not use the same rifles and other small arms that the IDF used. Instead, Claude Ibrahim told me, the SLA used Russian weapons Israel had captured during previous wars with Syria and Jordan. That was particularly ironic because Hezbollah sometimes used Israeli weapons that had been given to the Shah's army by Israel and now had been given by the Islamic regime in Iran to Hezbollah. It's a small world!

But of one thing there is no doubt. While the Israelis often operated in a manner designed to minimize casualties, the SLA took a much more aggressive posture—suffering many more losses than the IDF.

The End of the Security Zone Looms Near

Hezbollah's attacks on the IDF in Lebanon increased in 1998, although new defensive measures decreased Israeli causalities. Because most casualties came from roadside bombs, the IDF changed when patrols would venture out on the roads, traveled mostly at night, and used bulldozers to scrape away anything that could cover up bombs for thirty yards on both sides of roads. Units would even count rocks on successive patrols to see if new rocks (camouflaged bombs) had shown up. On a road leading to Beaufort Castle, the IDF put netting over it to prevent Hezbollah's spotters from discovering the presence of vehicles traveling the route.

In 1999, Brigadier General Erez Gerstein commanded the IDF in Lebanon. The Israeli public respected him, and he had a reputation for toughness. When asked in 1998 whether he thought his Mercedes would protect him against a roadside bomb, Gerstein answered, "It's all a matter of luck." Months later, in February 1999, Gerstein drove to a Shebaa Farms village to make a condolence call to the family of a local SLA officer who had died. His armor-plated Mercedes was one of four vehicles in a convoy. As he passed a UNIFIL position an IED exploded, pushing his car off the road, and then hurling it down into a valley. Gerstein did not survive. His luck had run out.

Gerstein's death may well have been the straw that broke the camel's back. The movement that had been picking up steam in the wake of 1997's helicopter tragedy and the Ansariyah debacle now grew after Gerstein's death. One Golani Brigade officer said that his death "was a big shock to society," and that "it had a huge impact on the IDF." Afterward, as support for the war plummeted within Israel, so did the SLA's morale. In no small part because media reports from Israel made their way to the SLA in Lebanon. When your only patron is seriously considering withdrawing, it should be no surprise that many SLA soldiers and their families started considering running for the hills. Nor did the facts on the ground inspire confidence. In May 1999, the SLA moved its forces closer to Israel's border.

Hezbollah was winning.

Chapter Seven

Israel Leaves Lebanon

For much of the 1990s, Israel was not pressured by its citizens to get out of Lebanon. Usually, no more than 1,200 soldiers were in the security zone at any given time along with 900 members of a liaison unit. But eventually, the constant drip of casualties took its toll causing many to consider Lebanon, Israel's Vietnam. They argued that rather than stay and fight a war that had no end, international mediation would do a better job of stopping Katyushas than the security zone, that Hezbollah now only targeted Israeli soldiers in Lebanon, and that leaving would remove a bloody bargaining chip from Syria's hands.

But those who opposed withdrawing felt doing so would boost Hezbollah's morale and that of all other terrorists targeting Israel. They thought that the present desire to end the pain had overcome the need to prevent more anguish in the future. It was a classic example of wishing away a problem that was not going to go away. With Israel out of Lebanon, nothing would prevent Hezbollah from gaining a stronger grip on the country and increasing its ability to gravely damage Israel in the future. Which is precisely what happened.

Yet staying was maddening. Major General Giora Eiland, head of the IDF operations directorate from 1999-2001, said, "It was quite frustrating, because the IDF did allocate more and more resources—more air assets, more elite units, and more intelligence assets—all to fight Hezbollah and the best thing that could be achieved was to keep the situation more or less what we had a year before." But were the assets available, as limited as they were, allocated correctly? Shay Shemesh does not think so. He told me:

> I would [have liked] to be much more offensive even with risking some of my men's and my [own] life, because I think that's [a] more efficient way of protecting yourself and it gives a message to the enemy because when you fight against guerillas in guerrilla warfare, when you're stagnant and when you're [predictable], and you have only routines and you don't initiate anything, eventually they will [win].

Shay's opinion rings true to me. When fighting a guerrilla army, as Boaz called it, you cannot stay tucked in your hole or behind a wall. The only path to victory is to take the fight to the enemy. In the short run, that means more casualties. However, in the long run, that is the only method for achieving victory while incurring overall fewer casualties. But if an army is not willing to take the initiative, then it needs to leave. Otherwise, the enemy will evolve, become far deadlier after learning from its mistakes and cause more casualties. In some sense, it is like the COVID virus we deal with today. By the world not eliminating it, it has evolved into a far more dangerous pathogen than we first faced in 2020. Can we live with COVID as it evolves? Hopefully.

Can Israel live with Hezbollah by staying on the defensive? Unlikely.

The decision whether to stay or leave came to a head in 1999 when Israel elected Ehud Barak as prime minister. Barak had run on a platform that included getting the IDF out of Lebanon (it was the second of three elections for prime minister based on the popular vote before Israel reverted to selecting its prime minister by a majority coalition of all elected ministers). After his election, an adviser suggested that Barak should pull most of the IDF out of Lebanon but leave elite units to bolster the SLA. Sort of like how America used Green Berets in South Vietnam during the early years of that conflict and Special Forces in Afghanistan in the later years of that conflict. The elite forces would advise but not wave the flag. Barak said no.

Now, leaving was no longer a matter of if but when.

However, serving to delay a unilateral decision to pull out, one glimmer of light shined ever so briefly. Negotiations between Syria and Israel over the Golan Heights showed some promise in the fall of 1999, and Syria had hinted that a successful result might produce disarmament of Hezbollah at Syria's behest. Barak was eager to close a deal but did not want to sacrifice a negotiable card. So, the IDF stayed.

But Hezbollah cared little about a Syrian deal. Its primary missions were to consolidate its strength in Lebanon and to destroy Israel. It also had another powerful benefactor—Iran. And a more active Hezbollah would only benefit Syria's negotiating position. So, whether at Syria's direction to prove its power or because Hezbollah wanted to demonstrate its independence, Hezbollah launched a calculated attack against twenty IDF and SLA outposts in mid-December of 1999. The timing of the attacks hinted at the audience they were designed to reach—hours after, Barak sat down for a previously scheduled meeting with the Syrian foreign minister in Washington, D.C. The message was clear to both Israel and Syria. Hezbollah's cooperation could not be taken for granted.

When talks with Syria went nowhere, Barak turned to Lebanon. As part of his campaign, Barak had promised to get the IDF out of Lebanon by July 2000. Would he? Could he? Should he? What happened next set the stage for where we are today.

The Withdrawal

Many in the IDF opposed withdrawing from the security zone. The head of military intelligence research wrote:

> A withdrawal without an agreement [with Syria] leaves no chance for quiet….It is very possible that at first, a few months after the withdrawal, it will be quiet, as Hezbollah settles down and improves its deterrent capabilities, but then we can expect terror attacks. And the terror attacks wouldn't just be on the Lebanese border, but also abroad and deep inside the borders of the State of Israel.

But Barak remained unconvinced. On March 5, because of Barak's unwavering commitment to withdraw, the IDF said it would pull the army out of Lebanon in July with or without a deal with Syria. That was just another example of tipping one's hand to the detriment of obtaining a palatable outcome through negotiations. It's a problem that plagues many politicians—including American ones.

Shortly thereafter, after further discussions, it was evident Israel and Syria would not strike a deal. Assad was not interested in buying the concessions Barak was selling. Barak then put his full energies into engineering a unilateral withdrawal from Lebanon.

Barak hoped to leave Hezbollah without any justification to kill Israelis. That, he now rationalized, would remove an arrow from Assad's quiver and therefore improve Israel's negotiating position vis-a-vis Syria. To accomplish that, he thought, the IDF had to withdraw from all of Lebanon. But the borders were fluid, subject to interpretation. Therefore, Barak needed the United Nations to buy in. With the UN's buy-in, the international community would acknowledge that Israel had fully complied with Security Council Resolution 425, the 1998 measure that called on Israel to withdraw its forces from Lebanon. Barak reasoned that if Hezbollah were to then launch new cross-border terror operations or missile attacks, the international community would vilify the organization and support Israel's response.

The IDF prepared for an orderly withdrawal in July. It was not to be. Pressure to leave immediately was mounting.

Within Israel, nobody wanted their child to be the last to die in Lebanon. Once it was clear that Israel would leave, many wanted the IDF to withdraw without delay. And in Lebanon, not surprisingly, the SLA was collapsing. Its rank and file saw little benefit in giving their lives to a lost cause and many saw Israel's actions as a betrayal. Meanwhile, Hezbollah licked its chops in anticipation. Information reached the Israelis that Hezbollah was preparing to launch massive attacks during the July withdrawal. Just the image Barak did not want—a beaten, bloodied IDF pulling back under pressure.

Barak then secretly moved up the withdrawal date to May 24. Before then, with little notice, the IDF had handed over many of its outposts to the SLA and started moving equipment back to Israel. By May 19, only about 120 Israeli soldiers remained in Lebanon. Israel had hoped that the SLA would hang on without Israel's presence. Everyone I had spoken to who had served in Lebanon spoke highly of the SLA's capabilities, especially its officers. But the SLA found the drumbeat of news detailing Israel's' imminent departure demoralizing. That, coupled with seeing the IDF draw down its forces, had devastated the SLA's morale. Soon it was clear that the SLA's resistance would crumble. Israel recognized it needed to do something for those who had loyally fought on its side. Hezbollah, after all, would not treat them well. So, Israel offered asylum to SLA members and their families—with a caveat. Those who wanted to flee to Israel had to do so before the last Israeli soldier got out. After that, the borders would be sealed.

Time was short. SLA soldiers wanting to escape Lebanon deserted their posts, grabbed their families, and streamed towards Fatima Gate near Metula, where long lines of people waited to cross into Israel and board the buses waiting for them. After loading onto the transports, 7,000 men, women, and children were taken to a camp near the Sea of Galilee for processing before eventually dispersing to new lives throughout Israel. At dawn, the IDF padlocked the gates.

It was over.

<u>Soldier's Stories</u>

"And then one morning it was like that. They say, tomorrow we [are] pulling out." At the time, Shay Shemesh was an outpost commander. He already had been notified they would eventually pull out. Then he was given a heads up: it would happen in a week. But the actual notice? One day.

The plan was to turn the outpost over to the SLA. When Shay's soldiers left for Israel, they left behind a TV, a stove, and food for its new occupants. But the SLA held the fort for less than a day. Twenty-four hours after Shay's unit left for Israel, Hezbollah took command of the post.

At least Shay had a little time to prepare. Avraham Levine had none.

The day before the withdrawal, Avraham commanded a unit tasked with establishing a stakeout in the bush several miles from their assigned outpost. Avraham's unit was supposed to be there for a few days watching and waiting to intercept any Hezbollah operatives who might stray near them. Before leaving on his mission, Avraham had seen vehicles laden with ammunition and other equipment returning to Israel. Also, expensive munitions were fired by IDF soldiers just to get rid of them. It was obvious that a withdrawal was coming. But there was no news regarding exactly when.

While in the field, Avraham's commander called him on the radio. "Can you come back?" he said.

Avraham answered, "It will take me like a couple of hours to get all the gear together and make sure that we don't leave anything behind, get everyone ready for walking, and then come back on a new route so they don't ambush us."

"If you are here in a couple of hours, there is a convoy that will take you home," his commander responded.

"Two hours, I will be there," Avraham replied. "And we practically ran back to the post…then we just climbed onto the truck and left."

After the Withdrawal

As the IDF left and the SLA crumbled, Hezbollah and its supporters streamed south. Vehicles with Hezbollah and Amal flags or pictures of Nasrallah entered southern Lebanon's villages. One day after a Star of David flag was removed, a Hezbollah flag was mounted at the top of Beaufort Castle, whose parapets can be seen throughout much of southern Lebanon and from the northern tip of Israel.

After the IDF exited Lebanon, Barak announced, "From now on, the government of Lebanon is accountable for what takes place within its territory, and the Lebanese and Syrian governments are responsible for preventing acts of terror or aggression against Israel, which is today deployed within its borders."

Two days after the withdrawal, Nasrallah came to Bint Jbeil, near the border, and in a speech that has grown famous in the region, said, "We offer this lofty Lebanese example to our people in Palestine. You do not need tanks, strategic balance, rockets, or cannons to liberate your land: all you need are the martyrs who shook and struck fear in this angry Zionist entity….*I tell you that Israel is weaker than a spider's web.*" I italicized the last part of his speech because the "spider's web" analogy has echoed to this day. We will revisit whether Israel is now weaker than a spider's web later in this book.

In the days following the withdrawal, triumphant and angry Lebanese crowds went to Fatima Gate to throw stones (some of which stuck in the border fence), bottles of burning oil, fireworks, and firebombs, and to shout abuse at Israelis guarding the border and any

Israeli civilians straying close. On weekends, the crowds were larger, and merchants set up stalls selling food and Hezbollah memorabilia. It was a weekly party with hatred as the theme.

UNIFIL wanted to start joint patrols with the Lebanese Armed Forces (LAF) in the region. But the LAF refused to cooperate until Israel's full withdrawal was verified. However, verification required knowing where the border was. The whitewashed stone cairns that had once marked much of it had been gone for a long time. Therefore, for more than three months beginning in early April, UN cartographic experts labored to determine exactly where the border was. Eventually, they recommended using the line that had for decades been recognized as the demarcation between Israel, Lebanon, and Syria for determining whether the IDF had completely withdrawn from Lebanon. It was a line that had defined part of the area of responsibility since 1974 for UNDOF, the UN peacekeeping force that separated Israeli and Syrian forces and the line defining the area of responsibility since 1978 for UNIFIL. Although available maps were imperfect, they provided a basis for negotiating the line and over the decades all three parties had repeatedly approved them for use.

That line came to be known as the Blue Line. It is not a permanent boundary line, but as a UN cartographer put it, "a practical line for the purpose of confirming the Israeli withdrawal." And as noted by the UN, the Blue Line does not prejudice any future negotiations between Lebanon and Israel to determine a permanent boundary. Today, more than twenty years after negotiations to determine the course of the Blue Line ended, it is marked by 272 blue barrels.

One story serves to illustrate how intensely the ground was examined, as well as the contortions the parties made to reach compromises. In Israel, a couple of miles west of Kiryat Shmona, on a hill near Kibbutz Manara, there is a tomb. Lebanese say it contains the remains of Sheikh Abbad, a Shiite cleric famous 500 years ago for, along with his supporters, making reed mats of the highest quality and selling them near the Sea of Galilee. On the other hand, Jews say the tomb is where Rabbi Ashi was put to rest in the fifth century. Rabbi Ashi was the first editor of the Babylonian Talmud. As you can imagine, both Lebanon and Israel felt it important to maintain sovereignty over the burial grounds. Although frankly, leaving religious concerns aside, why should anybody care?

But there was a problem.

The tomb's location was within the several-yard margin of error that the UN cartographers had labored under. Think about it for a minute. Depending on a map's scale, even on a map drawn with a scale of a few hundred yards to the inch, thin lines marking borders cover several yards. Nothing is perfect. Human beings live their lives quite well in a world of imperfection. Recognizing that gave rise to the saying, "Don't let perfect be the enemy of good." But in that region of the world, imperfection brings controversy and opportunity to pursue goals not aligned with peace. Fortunately, in this instance, the UN prodded both parties and they compromised. They agreed to an even split—the UN could draw the Blue Line border straight down the middle of the tomb. Now, half of whoever lies there is in Israel and the other half is in Lebanon! So much for religious concerns.

Finally, in late July, both Israel and Lebanon agreed to accept the UN's designated Blue Line "with reservation." The UN then confirmed that Israel had honored Security Council Resolution 425 and Lebanon moved about 1,000 police officers and soldiers into southern Lebanon. Not enough to enforce peace against an armed Hezbollah, nor was it intended to be. The Lebanese defense minister said that the LAF would never be "border guards for Israel." But at least it indicated that the border dispute was over. And maybe the fighting.

Or was it?

Over the summer, after the IDF withdrew, Hezbollah had a big internal debate. Should the organization focus just on resistance or both resistance and corruption within Lebanon? Nasrallah once again consulted with Hezbollah's spiritual and material benefactor, Iran. Supreme Leader Khamenei gave his blessing to Nasrallah to double down on resistance. But Hezbollah needed an excuse to continue its fight.

So, Nasrallah created one—Shebaa Farms. There, Hezbollah was determined to make perfect the enemy of good. And along the way lay claim to why Lebanon needed Hezbollah.

During the Six-Day War in 1967, the IDF occupied the lower portions of what has come to be known as Shebaa Farms, a two-by-seven-mile stretch of mountainous terrain on the southwestern shoulder of Mount Hermon in the far northern section of the Golan Heights. I know—that was a difficult sentence to follow. But what I want you to take from it is that Shebaa Farms is in the middle of nowhere. In 1970, the IDF occupied the upper area. Very few people lived there and in the words of a UN representative who visited the region, it is "a worthless piece of land [that Nasrallah would say proved the occupation was not over and thereby] use it as a justification for having Hezbollah [continue the] resistance."

However, Shebaa Farms was not worthless to Israel. It is crucial high ground that looms over Israeli villages, kibbutzim, and moshavim. Its only value to Lebanon was that its possession of it would allow Hezbollah to fire rockets, mortars, and even bullets at Jewish citizens within Israel below. Israel valued Shebaa Farms for the opposite reason. Possessing it would not allow Hezbollah to have that opportunity.

Until then, Lebanon had never claimed the region, although there had been some loose talk regarding Shebaa Farms as occupied territory. And maps that Syria gave to the UN in 1974 made clear that Syria at that time considered Shebaa Farms its land. In addition, UN cartographers had reviewed eighty maps from multiple sources that proved it Syrian land. Even the Lebanese 1,000 lira bill had a map of

Lebanon on it that excluded Shebaa Farms, proving the Lebanese thought it was part of Syria too. Especially because the one contraindicating map discovered at the time, with a drafting date on it of 1966, was given to the UN by Lebanese President Lahoud. But experts determined that that map was a forgery created only weeks before the withdrawal, not decades earlier. Therefore, since there was no convincing evidence to the contrary, the UN supported Israel's position by placing Shebaa Farms on the Israel side of the Blue Line—considering it Syrian territory occupied by Israel.

Nor did the Syrians support Hezbollah's claim that it was Lebanese land. Instead, to avoid relinquishing rights to the land they called their own while still stirring the pot, the Syrians straddled the issue by only stating that Shebaa Farms was "occupied Arab land."

But Nasrallah wanted an excuse to continue his fight with Israel. A fight to liberate occupied territory would fit the bill. And the Rules of the Game required Hezbollah to confine its attacks on the IDF to where the IDF occupied Lebanese territory. Falsely stating that Shebaa Farms was occupied Lebanese territory would provide Hezbollah with that opportunity. Therefore, Nasrallah declared Shebaa Farms part of Lebanon. Now Hezbollah had all the justification it needed to remain armed and attack Israelis. Its war with Israel was not over.

Should Israel Have Withdrawn?

I asked several Israelis who fought in Lebanon whether Israel should have withdrawn in May 2000.

*   *   *   *

Shay Shemesh served in Lebanon from 1997 to the withdrawal in 2000. Five years later, he commanded a battalion based inside the Netzarim settlement, the last Jewish settlement in the Gaza Strip that was evacuated in August 2005. He told me that it was a legitimate political decision for Israel to withdraw from both, but especially from southern Lebanon because it was never claimed as part of Israel (as a present-day archaeologist, he said there is at least some argument that the Gaza Strip really is part of Israel, even though he had no interest in Israel staying there because of its dense Palestinian population). But in Lebanon it was clear, the IDF was only in it for security reasons.

However, looking back on his days as a soldier and post commander in Lebanon, Shay had concerns about the timing of the withdrawal. He told me:

> When I was there as a soldier, as a commander, everyone told me, look, we are here for a reason. Look north, you can see Hezbollah, look south, you can see the lights of Kiryat Shmona. You understand you are the protector of the northern border of Israel because these people want to kill us. There is no other way.

> But then one morning they said, okay, we are withdrawing. We were pulling out our troopers. And then I asked, wait a minute, have we killed all the Hezbollah militants? Have we won this war? No.

> Do we have any peace agreement with Lebanon…that assures our security? No. So why are we pulling out? And if we are pulling out, then why in the first place we went in?

> I don't understand the logic.

> I think the way it happened; it looked like we were running away. First, it looks like we lost the war. We didn't do any peaceful Lebanon. We didn't [defeat] Hezbollah. We've been there for nineteen years, and we are pulling out. So, it doesn't make any sense. And we lost an ally because the south Lebanese army felt betrayed because they were our allies, we didn't back them. And I think that all our enemies saw that and understood that if they hurt us enough, we're [retreating]. And I think that's what started

the second Intifada in 2002, and that's what initiated eventually the [operation to clean out entrenched terrorists] in the west bank and that's what initiated escalation in Gaza.

And after it was on in Gaza, and then we withdraw from Gaza the same way, we didn't make peace with anyone, we didn't defeat Hamas. So how come we withdraw from Gaza? Or, if we think we shouldn't have been there in the first place, why did we occupy Gaza and stay there for decades, it doesn't make any sense.

But it does make sense to our enemies that they see even without beating them and even without making a peace process with them, [a] peace agreement with them, we are folding.

So, if they hurt us enough [we leave] and I think [it]was a very, very bad message.

Major General (res.) Gershon Hacohen echoed a similar sentiment while we spoke at his unique, rustic, man-cave-like retreat located in a small moshav named Nimrod high in the Golan Heights. From his home's wooden deck, which he'd built with his own hands, I could see the spine of Shebaa Farms. Gershon served with distinction in the IDF and is held in high regard by many for his intellectualism and curiosity. I was privileged to spend two hours with him discussing a wide range of topics. Regarding the withdrawal and Shebaa Farms, he said:

It was an excuse [for Hezbollah to have a continuous struggle]. The lesson is that it is never over, never-ending. [Hezbollah will] always find an excuse because what they want is a permanent struggle....And the asymmetry here is one of the Israeli problems. Because if we want just to get another day of tranquility and they want to not just get their homeland, but much more than that, they…create a permanent irritancy.

In essence, Gershon told me, Hezbollah creates a problem, and if Israel caves on that, it will create another problem and so on, each time hoping for more concessions leading to death by a thousand bites. It was clear to me he viewed Israel's withdrawal from Lebanon as a concession that, at least in hindsight, only led to more bites.

When I asked Avraham Levine what the attitude of the soldiers was when they were pulled out, he was quick to answer, "We lost. The soldier never likes to go back. We're going backwards." Also, he said, "It wasn't a great plan, very similar to Afghanistan in that way."

He then explained that if he were prime minister, he would never put a date on a withdrawal.

> Once you [announce] a date…the countdown starts, then why would I invest. Why am I risking my soldiers? Why am I doing this? So, if it's next week, then fine….But if it's a year…then time goes by, and everyone knows that's the deadline….Why would I risk them? We're going to leave anyway. Why would I do this?
>
> I'll put it this way….We were winning. If you take the numbers in terms of how many people were killed on both sides. We were beating Hezbollah day in day out, but the support from inside the country, the civilian support and the morale in Israel was we are losing too many soldiers.

Nor was Avraham surprised that the SLA folded when it became clear Israel would withdraw imminently. And, he explained, because SLA positions constituted part of the defensive line, "Once they started folding, we had to leave."

*   *   *   *

But not everyone I interviewed thought Israel should have stayed. Boaz Amidror, who even today in his fifties personifies the term "warrior," told me, "After we looked at it from a perspective of ten years later, it was so stupid to be there, but we didn't think that way. We were sure we did the right things."

Boaz's statement surprised me. It was not at all what I expected. Of course, I had to press him on it. I asked, "Why do you think you were stupid to be there?"

He answered in the emphatic way that he sometimes uses to drive home a point:

> Because you see now that it's better to be outside. Because if you are outside, you are not in a guerilla warfare that the guerilla try, does not succeed, try does not succeed, try [again], does not succeed, try succeed, try don't succeed. And they don't care. [But], the people in Israel do not care how many terrorists are dead. They count how many [IDF] bodies we are bringing home.

Brigadier General Erez Maisel felt pretty much the same as Boaz. When I asked him if he agreed with Barak's decision to withdraw, he said, "[It] was ten years too late. We should have left in 1990. [Any year] after 1989 was a good year to leave....It wasn't going to get any better. It was only going to get worse." Nor did Erez buy the argument that unless Israel maintained the security zone Hezbollah would chase the IDF into the Galilee.

*   *   *   *

In my view, it was a mistake to leave when and how the IDF did in May 2000. Barak's retreat from Lebanon did reduce pressure on the IDF, but it also left Hezbollah with the initiative, able to pick where and when to strike again—which it did. I cannot say Barak was naive in thinking that retreating from Lebanon would improve Israel's position. No person who has performed so well in so many leadership and combat roles during his time in the IDF should ever be called naive. But he made the same mistake that so many make—thinking his opponent would act according to his thinking as opposed to theirs. Hezbollah was dedicated to destroying Israel. That goal did not change after Israel withdrew. Israel's rationality was not Hezbollah's.

Nor should anyone think that if Israel had just retreated from Shebaa Farms that Hezbollah would have accepted Israel's existence. Hezbollah spokesperson Hassan Ezzedin emphasized that to the writer Jeffrey Goldberg, saying: "If they go from Shebaa, we will not stop fighting them. Our goal is to liberate the 1948 borders of Palestine." And any Jews that survive "can go back to Germany, or wherever they came from" unless they lived in Palestine before 1948 in which case they can "live as a minority and they will be cared for by the Muslim authority." But even that dubious life as a minority under Muslim rule was in doubt since Nasrallah said in 2002, "If [Jews] all gather in Israel, it will save us the trouble of going after them worldwide."

For almost twenty years, Israel had suffered from terrorizing Palestinian attacks launched from Lebanon into Israel. As any nation would, Israel responded, sometimes smartly, sometimes less so. As a result, Lebanese civilians suffered, and partly as a result, a new enemy far more dangerous than the last had arisen. Nurtured by Iran, used by Syria, and appreciated by Shiites within Lebanon—Hezbollah emerged.

In essence, Israel's withdrawal created an opportunity for a new beginning. But rather than the hoped-for peace, the new beginning begot a far more dangerous foe. Instead of having to deal with a terrorist organization with some ties to other countries, now Israel had to contend with a hybrid terrorist organization—a state within a state— with two powerful benefactors in Iran and Syria. And so, at the turn of the new century, the Druze had been diminished, Sunni Palestinians vanquished, the Maronites neutered, the SLA eviscerated, and the Shiites empowered. All at the hands of a Hezbollah no longer checked by anyone within Lebanon.

What would then emerge over time is something even worse, not just a state within a state, but a Shiite-controlled state dedicated to Israel's destruction, shielded by Iran and its other proxies.

But in the fall of 2000, Hezbollah was not yet ready to engage in a major war with Israel. In the coming months, Hezbollah would satisfy itself with carrying the fight to the IDF, mostly within Shebaa Farms, while carefully calibrating its operations so as not to give Israel a reason to launch a massive response. To that story is where we now turn.

Chapter Eight

Kidnaps, Katyushas, & Assassination

In July 1989, eleven years before Israel pulled out of Lebanon, IDF commandos captured Sheikh Abdel Karim Obeid. Obeid, a cleric closely tied with Hezbollah, was the commander of Palestinian Islamic Jihad in southern Lebanon. In 1982, he helped capture hostages from western nations. Israel's reason for capturing him remains murky. It may have been to gain knowledge regarding the whereabouts of a missing Israeli airman, Ron Arad, shot down three years before over Lebanon. It may also have been that Israel snatched Obeid at the behest of the United States to obtain information about the missing American, William Higgins, who was kidnapped by Hezbollah in 1988. But the reason is not important. What matters is what Hezbollah did after the IDF left Lebanon.

The First Kidnapping

A mile south of Shebaa Village, in the Sheba Farms region, a gate in the border fence divided Israeli-held territory from Lebanon. Early in the afternoon on October 7, 2000, less than five months after Israel withdrew from Lebanon, an IDF vehicle carrying three soldiers descended a hill on the road passing the gate. Several miles to the west, on the other side of the Galilee, hundreds of Palestinians mustered by Hezbollah demonstrated near the border to support the intifada underway in the West Bank. It was a diversion.

A UNIFIL post, near the gate, was staffed by soldiers from India. That morning a unit from the post patrolled the Blue Line and noticed something strange. Two Hezbollah observation posts near the town of Ghajar, close to Shebaa Farms, were empty. Suspicious, the soldiers reported to their headquarters that something was up.

They were correct.

The Israeli vehicle pulled off the road near the gate in the fence. When two soldiers exited it, ambushers set off two hidden roadside bombs. Simultaneously, other Hezbollah operatives launched a barrage of mortar shells at IDF bases in Shebaa Farms. Then, a Range Rover pulled up to the gate from the Lebanese side of the border. Hezbollah operatives exited the vehicle, blew open the gate, and charged through while others provided cover fire. They grabbed all three IDF soldiers, now wounded or dead, put them into the Range Rover, and took off. The kidnap operation took three and a half minutes. It took the IDF thirty minutes to realize the soldiers were missing.

UNIFIL later found the Range Rover. Inside were bloodstains. Analysts thought one or two of the soldiers had died in the car. It turns out all three had died during the operation, but Hezbollah never disclosed that, believing it could exact a higher price for their return if the Israelis thought at least one soldier was still alive.

Eight days later, in a sting operation, Hezbollah took captive Elhanan Tannenbaum, a fifty-four-year-old officer in the reserves. He had been trying to arrange a shipment of heroin and cocaine from Lebanon to Israel. Clearly, he had attempted to deal with the wrong guys.

Eventually, negotiations were conducted, assisted by Germany's secret service. First, Hezbollah demanded that Israel release Shiekh Obeid or Samir Kuntar, the leader of the group that had committed horrific acts in Nahariya more than two decades before. Israel refused.

Israel countered by demanding information about missing airman Ron Arad. Hezbollah was not forthcoming.

Eventually, a deal was made, and Hezbollah released Tannenbaum in 2004, alive, to Israel, along with the bodies of the other three missing soldiers. In return, Israel released 400 prisoners, most of whom were Lebanese and Palestinian, as well as the remains of some Hezbollah guerrillas.

In the abstract, the deal might appear unfair. The exchange ratio of 400 to one is grossly out of whack. But not necessarily so if you consider the high value Israel places on the lives of its soldiers. Paying such a steep price for Tannenbaum, who allegedly was engaged in criminal activity, was especially hard to swallow. Nor did the return of the bodies of the other three soldiers balance the scales, even more so because there are some reports, which the IDF denies, that those soldiers also were engaged in drug activities and that Hezbollah had lured them to the gate in the border fence to purchase drugs. Nevertheless, the IDF wants its soldiers to know that, if they're captured, the army and the nation will do everything possible to bring them home, whether dead or alive. This passion for preserving the lives of its soldiers and recovering their remains is Israeli society's emotional contract with those willing to give their lives for their country. We will explore this subject more deeply in Chapter Twenty-Three.

However, did Nasrallah see the exchange as further proof of his belief that Israel was "weaker than a spider's web?" Would Israel sacrificing so much for so little embolden him to look for more opportunities to kidnap and kill?

Whichever side of the issue you fall on, know that Israel's government also wrestled with the decision. Especially whether any deal should be made without obtaining information regarding Arad's fate. Israel's Cabinet voted to approve the deal by the slim margin of twelve to eleven.

Worse for Israel's interests was Prime Minister Barak's failure to respond with force to Hezbollah's brazen act. Per its interpretation of the Rules of the Game, Hezbollah viewed its attack on the soldiers and the kidnapping of Tannenbaum as permissible. Hezbollah needed to be disabused of that notion. Otherwise, it would continue to draw blood. But at the time, the Second Intifada was in full swing in the West Bank and Gaza. If Barak would have ordered a violent response, Hezbollah might have responded by firing Katyushas at Israel's northern communities, perhaps necessitating an even stronger IDF counterstrike, which might have led to another war. A war, according to Professor Chuck Freilich, then a member of Israel's newly formed national security council, that Barak did not think Israel could afford to fight while the Intifada was raging.

But when Barak did not respond in kind, Hezbollah believed Israel was tacitly agreeing that the killing of soldiers at Shebaa Farms was acceptable under the terms of their negotiations, made years earlier. And—or, even worse—by not forcefully responding, Hezbollah understood that Israel would be deterred from doing more. As a result, more was to come.

There is also a sideshow that must be addressed before we leave this event. It is the question of UNIFIL's role. It turns out that the UN secretly possessed two videotapes of the kidnapping for nearly a year before confirming their existence. Then, once exposed, the UN refused to give them to the Israelis or even show them to them.

The IDF wanted to see the tapes to help it determine whether any of the soldiers had survived the attack. It took months after their existence became known to Israel for the UN to permit Israeli intelligence to look at unedited copies of the tapes. Regarding the propriety of withholding that information, a chagrined UN issued a statement that read, "Serious errors in judgment were made, in particular, by those who failed to convey information to the Israelis, which would have been helpful in the assessment of the condition of the three abducted soldiers." I go into greater detail about this sordid incident in my book *Living in Heaven, Coping with Hell.*

Aftermath

For the next six years, Shebaa Farms was a battle zone. Intermittently, Sagger missiles and mortar shells made life hell for IDF soldiers stationed there. In October 2001, Hezbollah fired thirty-three anti-tank missiles at targets in the zone. Over the next few years, Hezbollah targeted Israelis in Shebaa Farms with an estimated 1,000 mortar rounds and more than 200 rockets—that's almost 100 explosive munitions for each square mile. The attacks killed or wounded several IDF soldiers. Usually, the IDF did not respond to any great extent. And so, hunting IDF targets in Shebaa Farms became business as usual. Hezbollah called them "reminder operations."

But Hezbollah was not satisfied with just "reminder operations." Nasrallah pocketed Israel's acquiescence and pushed further, less than two years later clearly violating the Rules of the Game.

On March 12, 2002, two Palestinians acting with Hezbollah's permission went on the hunt five miles from the Mediterranean in the Western Galilee on land that was part of Israel. For this story, I borrow from my book about Israel's northern borders, *Living in Heaven, Coping with Hell*:

> This time, two terrorists crossed the border near Kibbutz Hanita. There, the fence laden with technological wizardry designed to detect intrusions failed because the terrorists had used a "trapeze ladder" to "sail" over the fence without touching it. Safely across, wearing IDF uniforms to cloak their true purpose, they made their way to a hillside overlooking the road from the border town of Shlomi to Kibbutz Matzuva. From there, after killing a shepherd tending his flock, they fired weapons and threw hand grenades at civilian vehicles on the road.

Before being killed by IDF security forces, the two terrorists killed an IDF officer and four citizens. Two of the citizens were a mother and her fifteen-year-old daughter that lived in Kibbutz Hanita. Innocently, they had descended the winding road in the family car. Their ride back up that road was to their funeral, attended by hundreds. In a New York Times article written two days later, a young immigrant from Russia said, 'We were used to Katyusha rockets, but terrorists in Shlomi? This is something completely different. Then you knew it was coming from the other side. Now, it's like you've been stabbed in the back.

Another middle-aged woman, Nurit Naaman, said that the aftershock reminded her of her childhood years living on the border, 'There was fear then," she said. "Personal security was close to zero. We felt unprotected. Now there's exactly the same atmosphere, but today it's more personal—the danger is more tangible.'"

Then, in August 2003, shrapnel falling from the sky killed a sixteen-year-old Israeli boy in Shlomi, a border town also in the Western Galilee. The shrapnel came from anti-aircraft shells Hezbollah fired at Israeli planes flying over Lebanon. Apologists say that it was the unfortunate result of Hezbollah defending itself from Israeli overflights that obtained critical intelligence. But Hezbollah knew that the anti-aircraft shells had no hope of hitting the planes. Hezbollah also knew what goes up must come down. It was a perfect opportunity for mayhem, which the terrorist organization grabbed. The shells were aimed to explode over Israeli settlements. Hezbollah had done so before on dozens of occasions, injuring many. This time, they hit pay dirt. How convenient their excuse! Nothing more than a lie excusing the indiscriminate shelling of Israeli civilians.

Other Hezbollah activities violated the Rules of the Game, including an anti-tank shell fired across the border at Za'arit, an Israeli border town, and a Hezbollah sniper killing two IDF soldiers at the western end of Israel's border. Still, Israel did not rise to the bait. But by not doing so, it undercut Israel's deterrence. By the end of 2003, in a span of approximately two-and-a-half years, Hezbollah launched 264 cross-border attacks of one type or another.

Meanwhile, Hezbollah strengthened its defenses and, thanks to a fortuitous event, sharpened its offensive capabilities. Two weeks after Israel pulled out of Lebanon, Hafez Assad died a natural death. His son Bashar, groomed to succeed him, took over. Whereas Hafez had carefully monitored and controlled the quantity of arms reaching Hezbollah through Syrian territory, Bashar let them flood in.

Within six years of Israel leaving Lebanon, by May 2006, Hezbollah had obtained more than 13,000 rockets of several types, some with ranges up to thirty miles. Its technology and tactics for preventing Israel from destroying those missiles improved too. Hezbollah placed launchers for many on the reverse slopes of mountains and hills facing Israel. This made it difficult for the IDF to target them with artillery; firing shells that had to pass over hills and then descend sharply to destroy the launchers on slopes facing away from Israel was a challenging task. In many cases, because of the terrain and the distance, it was not possible.

Hezbollah technicians fixed some missile launchers to platforms that could be raised to fire and then lowered into the ground for protection. Hezbollah placed other launchers, used for long-range rockets, in trucks hidden in garages of buildings and homes. And for the longest-range rockets, whose size demanded a more intricate launch mechanism, Hezbollah placed their launchers on platforms hidden in shipping containers equipped with roofs that could be opened. Those platforms could then be raised to fire missiles placed on the launchers.

Aware that heat signatures might reveal the launchers' locations, Hezbollah had its operatives put thermal blankets over the launchers after firing them; that way, any heat generated by ignited missiles would go undetected by Israeli sensors. This would preserve those launchers for future usage.

Hezbollah's signal technology improved as well. At first, Hezbollah communicated by using walkie-talkies and field phones. But both were susceptible to Israeli eavesdropping. In the 1990s, Hezbollah's communication systems used copper lines buried in cables that were part of Lebanon's internal communications network. Then, Hezbollah replaced the copper in the cables with fiber that permitted more data transfer and was less susceptible to interception and jamming. Beginning in 2000, Iran began training Hezbollah communications personnel. A few years later, in 2005, Iran and Syria began building listening stations to intercept Israeli communications, which could be forwarded to Hezbollah. And, taking a page out of the IDF's book of tricks, Hezbollah placed thermal and regular cameras in its border posts to track IDF movements.

During the years after Israel's withdrawal, Hezbollah also reorganized its ground forces by dividing Lebanese territory held by Hezbollah into four commands. Each command was then divided into sectors of twelve to fifteen villages, which were subdivided once again in the organizational structure for command-and-control purposes into groups of two to three villages. As part of the command structure, each sector had a headquarters charged with constructing defenses that included building fortifications and tunnels.

One command stretched from the border with Israel to the Litani River. There, Hezbollah forces numbered about 1,000 full-time fighters plus 3,000 reservists. Hezbollah charged the Nasr unit, the name of the grouping in that southern Lebanon sector, with defense and when ordered to do so, harassment of Israel with rockets and other weaponry. Units there had range cards and utilized Google Maps to identify and mark the location of targets in Israel. Hezbollah fighters in that region also formed tank-hunting teams, armed with the latest anti-tank missiles, that in the event of an IDF attack were to deploy at choke points along roads that invading IDF tanks would move along. Other defenses included explosives placed in pits where IDF vehicles might travel, sniper teams, and deep bunkers from which supplies could be drawn. The extent of those underground installations was incredible. Some were 120 feet deep and spread over almost a square mile. They contained firing positions, storage for ammunition and food, sleeping and medical facilities, bathrooms, and even hot and cold water. Combatants could live for weeks in them without coming to the surface. And they were built stealthily. One was embarrassingly close to an unsuspecting UNIFIL base.

North of the Litani River was another command. Here the Badr unit held sway. Its main mission was to launch longer-range missiles into Israel, provide reinforcements as needed to the Nasr unit, and stop any IDF penetrations north of the Litani.

A third command covered the Bekaa Valley. Its primary mission was training, storing equipment coming from Syria and transferring that equipment to southern Lebanon.

Hezbollah established the fourth command in Beirut. There, Hezbollah placed its primary command-and-control building that doubled as housing for the organization's top leaders.

In addition, Hezbollah employed a coastal defense command that included an amphibious unit and radar equipment to track the movement of Israeli warships. Given the highly technical and specialized nature of many of the missions, many assigned to the coastal defense command received training in Iran—most likely training that included beach landings and underwater demolition.

Hezbollah also undertook intelligence and propaganda operations during this time that continue in many forms to this day. One part of the propaganda operation was general in nature. Hezbollah's Al-Manar TV station sent video technicians to film whenever Hezbollah launched missiles or engaged in other offensive actions. Often, operations would begin when the sun set in the west to make for the best lighting for camera footage. When striking Shebaa Farms, videotape crews would set up behind a UNIFL base less than a mile from the border. Al-Manar would not only show the attack videos to Lebanese audiences but also beam them worldwide, which meant Israeli audiences could see them too.

Hezbollah also tried, by placing billboards within easy sight of Israeli civilians, to lower the morale of Israelis living along the border (a practice that continues to this day). Some would picture injured and killed Israelis. One included an image of an Israeli soldier's head blown off with a caption underneath that said, "Sharon: Your soldiers are still in Lebanon."

Israeli Arabs engaged with Hezbollah in the drug business often assisted Hezbollah's intelligence operation. They provided Hezbollah with details of border posts and numbers of soldiers. With their assistance, Hezbollah built a target bank for launching missiles into Israel. Frequently, exchanges of drugs, money, and information would happen in Ghajar, a disputed town, two-thirds of which the Lebanese controlled until 2006, that contained a Hezbollah post in an abandoned bomb shelter. In September 2002, Israel broke up a ten-member Arab spy ring working for Hezbollah that included a Bedouin Lieutenant Colonel serving in the IDF who had lost an eye fighting Hezbollah six years before.

Plainly, Hezbollah was evolving once again, now moving from a guerrilla force to something much more akin to a sovereign army. A deadly project facilitated by the IDF's departure from southern Lebanon and Israel's political decision to refrain from retaliating against Hezbollah except when extraordinarily antagonized.

But it is important, also, to recognize that Nasrallah's leadership played a crucial role in Hezbollah's transformation. Major General Amos Malka, IDF intelligence chief in 2001, said of Nasrallah: "I must say that the way in which he leads his organization fascinates me.

He combines strategic thinking, perfect control, tactical work, and use of the psychological element. He is definitely a fascinating figure for any intelligence agent."

Then, in 2005, in a further bid to protect Israeli soldiers and to avoid friction with Hezbollah, the IDF began withdrawing troops from many of its posts along the border, replacing them with cameras and sensors. In effect, Hezbollah had succeeded in pushing the IDF back from the border. Its tactics for accomplishing this included tricking Israeli soldiers, many of them teenagers in their first years of service, to cross the border where the Rules of the Game would permit Hezbollah to kill them! One favored tactic was to plant a visible roadside bomb along the Lebanese side of Israel's border fence but still within Israeli territory. Then hope that IDF soldiers sent to dismantle the bomb would accidentally stray over the border. On one occasion, when the driver of a tractor mistakenly crossed the border, a Hezbollah operator lying in wait fired a missile at him, killing him.

Meanwhile, Hezbollah did not hesitate to send its soldiers to reconnoiter in Israel. On June 29, 2005, a flurry of Hezbollah mortar shells and counterstrikes from Israeli helicopters and planes crisscrossed the border. The fracas started when three Hezbollah operatives infiltrated Israel in the Shebaa Farms region where there then was no border fence. They had come at night with night vision equipment and hidden under netting. Before the IDF discovered them, they used their equipment to videotape a detailed description of the area. But they also relaxed. Captured videos showed two of them resting and chewing gum. It must have been quite a sight, bearded soldiers in camouflage clothing chomping on gum in the middle of an idyllic habitat. Their commander said on the captured recording, "What could be better than this?" Hours later, the three were on the run, chased by IDF soldiers. Two made it back to Lebanon. IDF soldiers killed the third, who was their commander.

The three likely were one of many reconnaissance units sent to prepare for another kidnapping of an IDF soldier.

Over time, the practical impact of the IDF's withdrawal became clear. According to Maj. General Udi Adam, who led the Northern Command between 2005-2006, it meant Israel "was relinquishing Israeli sovereignty on the northern border and giving Hezbollah a freehand…on the border."

That freehand led Hezbollah to plan and employ one of its most dastardly tactics—kidnapping Israeli soldiers to exact exorbitant ransoms and roil Israel's citizenry. It worked in October 2000. Why not again?

On November 21, 2005, Hezbollah made another snatch-and-grab attempt. This time in the divided town of Ghajar. There, Hezbollah attempted to kidnap IDF soldiers with the hope of trading them for far more Hezbollah prisoners and sympathizers being held in Israeli jails. Five years earlier they had achieved a 400 to one ratio. Maybe it could raise the price now?

While Hezbollah's mortar shells and rockets struck positions throughout the region (often a sign that something was up), about twenty specially trained Hezbollah terrorists crossed on foot, motorcycles, and all-terrain vehicles into Israeli-held southern Ghajar.

They hoped to get in and out quickly with captives while the IDF was distracted by the shelling. Fortunately, Israel had learned of the pending attack. A corporal trained as a sniper lying along the route of the attackers killed some of the Hezbollah invaders. The rest withdrew without completing their mission.

Concerning, however, was that the IDF had picked up intelligence regarding the kidnap attempt at least three days before. When Northern Command sought permission to preempt, the IDF's chief of staff refused the request. Hamstrung, Northern Command publicized its special emergency IDF deployment along the border in hopes of intimidating Hezbollah. It did not work. This was a clear sign that Israeli deterrence was in freefall. Afterward, the IDF blew up Hezbollah's base in northern Ghajar, but this tit-for-tat achieved little. Hezbollah would soon try again.

Politics and Propaganda

After Israel withdrew in 2000, Hezbollah knew it had to work to maintain domestic support for its resistance against Israel. To serve that purpose, Hezbollah built memorials of its struggle to throw the IDF out of Lebanon. One was a visitation center at Beaufort Castle, with a clear view of Israel's northern Galilee. Another was the memorial at Qana. The prisoner swap with the Israelis that brought 400 people home, after the kidnapping of the IDF soldiers in October 2000, also helped to promote Hezbollah's strength and value.

Hezbollah propaganda dominated the areas it controlled. Soon after Israel's withdrawal, entering those regions was like passing through a portal to another world. Obvious was the lack of prosperity juxtaposed with numerous green and yellow Hezbollah flags adorned with the images of AK-47s. Hezbollah posters lining roadways and hanging from lamp posts and electric poles depicted portraits of martyrs, including suicide bombers. Portraits of Iranian leaders and Bashar Assad were ubiquitous. And portraits of Musa Sadr were common, too, for Amal was Hezbollah's ally at the time. The same is still true today.

But also, like in the Hezbollah-controlled suburban area immediately south of Beirut called Dahiyeb, there was another truth. There, Lebanon's government had no power or influence. Lebanon's police were forbidden to enter, and before 2006 the army could not enter either. Nor could the government provide basic services to Shiites like picking up trash or operating schools. Hezbollah took over that role and prevented any other government intrusions. Children in these areas grew up on a doctrine of hate carefully nurtured by Hezbollah. It was the only life they knew.

Even driving from the international airport to Beirut proved challenging. Arriving visitors and residents alike had to motor from the airport through Hezbollah territory to get to the city center. Even though the government controlled the road, portraits of Nasrallah and other Iranian and Hezbollah leaders were plainly visible (in the summer of 2022 Hezbollah agreed to remove them to foster tourism. We will see if it does so permanently.). Exiting from the road meant entering another world—Hezbollah's world. In a time when Lebanon still stamped identification cards with the religion of the person, unless you were Shiite, immersing oneself over or on the border of that world always had the potential to end in disaster. Thus, crossing into Hezbollah's world was like crossing the border from one country to another.

By 2006, Hezbollah had built four hospitals and thirty schools and created many foundations to support Shiites in Shiite areas—all with Iranian money. Meanwhile, Hezbollah did not permit the Lebanese government to contribute or embark on its own social programs to assist the Shiites. Now truth be told, the government had not previously invested a proportionate amount in Shiite well-being. Still, the idea was, and still is today, to use welfare and other programs to bind Shiites to Hezbollah. Even if a Shiite was liberal, moderate, or in some other way opposed to Hezbollah, that person had no choice but to engage with Hezbollah. No other alternative existed in their universe. If ever the idea of a state within a state needed an example for explanation, here it was.

Amid this power grab, the other religious groups were hesitant to confront an increasingly powerful Hezbollah. It was a conundrum for a population still reeling from a civil war that had taken 150,000 lives and caused significant displacement and property loss, not to mention damage and loss of life incurred during Israel's struggle with both the PLO and Hezbollah. Nevertheless, after Israel withdrew, domestic support waned for Hezbollah's ongoing resistance against Israel. That concerned Nasrallah.

Further complicating things, with Hezbollah's increasing involvement in government, Nasrallah had to deal with Lebanon's internal political and economic issues too. More and more people with the means to leave Lebanon were doing just that, especially members of the Christian community. Economic issues increasingly took a toll on the middle class and many had no choice but to be subservient to political bosses of one sect or another, making life inside Lebanon intolerable. Those developments threatened the long-term stability of Lebanon and posed a political risk for Hezbollah.

Into that mess, Rafiq al-Hariri returned for his second stint as the Sunni prime minister in 2000. Hariri grew up in a middle-class Sunni household. As an adult, he started a construction business that led to him becoming a billionaire.

During his first term as a prime minister, Hariri tried to get Syria to agree to a deal, without linkage to the Golan Heights, which would both get Israel out of south Lebanon and disarm Hezbollah. Not surprisingly, Hafez Assad refused to go along.

Also, thinking that international grants and loans would be paid back by economic growth, Hariri initiated construction projects in areas Hezbollah didn't control. Within Hezbollah's zones of control, plenty of Iranian money flowed. However, with then-Christian President Lahoud totally in Syria's and Hezbollah's pockets, Hariri gave up and resigned in 1998. Two years later, he was back but resigned again in 2004 after a dispute involving Syria's successful push to extend Lahoud's term in office another three years.

Why do I even bother mentioning Hariri? Because soon he would attempt another return to power and the impact of that would roil the region.

In 2004, the UN Security Council passed Resolution 1559, which called on Syria to withdraw from Lebanon and Hezbollah to disarm.

Neither was willing to do so, and neither would ever do so voluntarily. But the UN resolution did succeed in increasing domestic opposition to both Hezbollah and Syria.

Emboldened, Druze leader Walid Jumblatt told the Syrians that he would not support any Syrian-pushed candidates for Parliament in the upcoming 2005 election. Young Assad would not take that recalcitrance sitting down. Per a *New York Times* article published on March 22, 2005, Syria's representative in Lebanon said to Jumblatt, "You have to think about it, and we have to think about it," which, given that Syrian agents had assassinated Jumblatt's father, was a rather ominous statement.

Meanwhile, despite Syria's and Hezbollah's intimidation tactics towards him, Hariri, seeing the political winds blowing in his favor, decided once again to run for prime minister in the election scheduled for May 2005. He felt confident that both Sunnis and Druze would support him.

On February 14, 2005, Hariri's candidacy ended. A massive car bomb killed him along with twenty-two others. There is little doubt that Syria and Hezbollah were behind it. Tens of thousands attended his funeral.

Hezbollah, sensing the need to take the political high ground in the face of the accusations, organized a pro-Syrian demonstration that went forward on March 8. Hundreds of thousands came carrying Hezbollah flags and pictures of Assad. Most were Shiites.

Pretty impressive. That is until March 14 rolled around.

Six days after Hezbollah's event came the response. Lebanon then was about one-third Christian, a little less than a third Sunni, one-third Shiite, and five percent Druze. Pouring into the streets of Beirut came one million people, a quarter of Lebanon's total population! Present were Christians, Sunnis, and Druze. Signs with the Christian cross mingled with the Muslim crescent. Although many people consider much of the Mideast divided by tribal loyalty, here was the best expression of division by religion. The Shiites on one side and Muslims, Christians, and Druze on the other. If only Hariri had enjoyed such support when alive. And for the region and the world, if only the anti-Hezbollah sentiment displayed that day had remained wholly intact. Still, a powerful political force arose that came to be known as the March 14 alliance. It sprang to life because of the "Cedar Revolution's" many demonstrations which began on March 14.

A month later, Saad Hariri, Rafiq's son, took the lead in his father's movement. Soon after, because of strong suspicions of complicity in Rafiq's death, and under international and domestic pressure, Syrian forces withdrew from Lebanon. This created a void Nasrallah was determined to fill. And, of course, there was that upcoming May election.

With the death of Hariri and Hezbollah's suspected involvement, Nasrallah believed, more than ever, that Hezbollah must increase its involvement in Lebanese politics. He knew there would inevitably be a call to investigate who was behind the assassination. Nasrallah hoped to block that. Therefore, he made a political deal with Maronite Michel Aoun, who hoped to become president one day. Aoun is an interesting character who once commanded the Lebanese army, opposed the Taif agreement, and earned the enmity of Syria, which forced him to flee to France. There he lived for fifteen years, returning after the Syrians withdrew in April. Now, unfortunately, his lust for power outweighed his prior principles.

Unfortunately for the March 14 alliance, despite winning a staggering seventy-two seats in Parliament, it fell just short of enough seats to remove the current president, Lahoud, from the presidency. The March 14 alliance failed because Aoun's political faction received twenty-one seats that allowed him, along with Hezbollah's and Amal's factions, to block the removal of Lahoud. Then, for the first time, because of the ensuing negotiations, Hezbollah was able to seat its first two cabinet members, one of whom received the electricity portfolio.

Now, Hezbollah had a grasp on a part of Lebanon's infrastructure and more than ever was part of Lebanon's government—a concept to remember as future events unfold. And a new name came to the fore— Foud Siniora—who became the Sunni prime minister.

But in addition to Nasrallah's desire to block the formation of a tribunal to investigate Hariri's killing, he had another significant concern—calls for Hezbollah to disarm. In September 2004, UN Resolution 1559 included a provision that particularly annoyed Nasrallah when it called "for the disbanding and disarmament of all Lebanese and non-Lebanese militias." To stop the creation of an investigative body, Hezbollah's Cabinet members, along with its allies in the Cabinet, had walked out of a cabinet meeting. Given their numbers, that blocked the government from taking any action on anything per the Taif Agreement. In other words, stalemate on everything. Stalemates are not the hallmarks of good government. Therefore, in December 2005, Siniora negotiated a deal. Hezbollah consented to the government approving the creation of a mixed Lebanese and international tribunal to perform the investigation of Hariri's assassination. In return, the government agreed never to refer to Hezbollah as a "militia." Instead, they were to be considered a "national resistance group." With that verbal sleight of hand, Nasrallah had extricated Hezbollah from the UN Resolution that only referred to militias.

So, as 2005 rolled into 2006, Hezbollah, despite a shaky start to the year, now had more influence in Lebanon's byzantine political structure, had strengthened its support or at least reliance on it among Shiites, had reduced its risks of being forcibly disarmed, and had built by far the strongest military force in Lebanon. All had been accomplished with the increasing support of its most important patron and ideological parent, Iran.

Still, Nasrallah had some lingering concerns. With Syria gone, Hezbollah would no longer benefit from Syria's supportive military within Lebanon, a Hariri tribunal could cause some future problems, and there still were grumblings within Lebanon about Hezbollah's constant tweaking of the Israelis.

But the coast was relatively clear for Hezbollah. Nasrallah, therefore, saw no reason not to continue his confrontational policies with Israel. And nothing had changed in his worldview, expressed years before in April 2000, when he said:

> The Jews invented the legend of the Nazi atrocities. Anyone who reads [Islamic and certain other] texts cannot think of co-existence with them, of peace, or about accepting their presence, not only in Palestine of 1948 but even in a small [part] of Palestine, because they are a cancer which is likely to spread again at any moment.

So why was it that the Lebanese Shiites came to hate Israel and Jews so much? Remember, they once hailed the IDF as liberators in 1982. The answer leads back to Iran with a nod to Sadr, who had created a combustible environment. Khomeini then made a promise to Shiites, in general, to lead them from poverty to domination. That gave them dignity and respect. After all, it is better to be feared than fearful. That set the stage.

Meanwhile, inside Lebanon, the other main religious groups had outside international supporters—Christians had the French and Sunnis had much of the Arab world. The Shiites, therefore, were all too happy to accept Iran's assistance. Especially because Iran was a rising power. Nasser's Pan-Arab approach had failed, Saddam Hussein's power grab ended in ashes, and even the PLO was at Oslo seeking a deal. Now it was Iran's turn to seek control of the Middle East.

But also part of the Ayatollah's premise and basis for his hold on power was that Israel was evil and a cancer. Dictators love to have a fall guy. Lebanon was a natural partner for the ayatollahs—not only because it had a downtrodden Shiite populace, but because Shiites had come to believe that Israel had stayed too long after kicking the Palestinians out. Therefore, Shiites in Lebanon were low-hanging fruit for Khomeini to collect and inflame with his hatred of Israel.

So, what would Hezbollah do now?

Easy: kidnap more IDF soldiers. Then make more one-sided deals while simultaneously launching attacks against the IDF at times and places of its choosing.

Then, fortune for Hezbollah struck when Israel's prime minister, Ariel Sharon, lapsed into a stroke-induced coma in January 2006. Until then, during the five years he served as prime minister, Sharon forcefully confronted Arafat in the West Bank, dealt with the Second Intifada, and evacuated Jewish settlements from Gaza. While that was going on, he did not want a confrontation with Hezbollah. So, right or wrong, he left them alone. But make no mistake, Sharon was a military man at heart. He was the architect of the 1982 campaign in Lebanon. Before that, he had led troops in all of Israel's wars brilliantly. He never shrank from taking the offensive and taking calculated risks to defeat his opponents. Eventually, when he felt the time was right, he certainly would've had a reckoning with Hezbollah.

But now he was in a coma, which he never came out of.

After Sharon's collapse, Ehud Olmert accepted the mantle of prime minister of Israel. Olmert was a political creature with little military experience other than as a draftee. He had never planned military campaigns nor led soldiers in battle. Meanwhile, the IDF was changing its philosophy and planning to emphasize the use of its airpower rather than ground forces if Hezbollah provoked them. And for the first time, the IDF's chief of staff, its highest military office, was occupied by a former air force commander with no experience leading ground troops. And so, Olmert came to power at exactly the wrong time. A time when Israel would face a military challenge unlike any before it, with a military leader championing a new, untried doctrine.

Nothing good would come of it.

Chapter Nine

The Second Lebanon War—2006

Udi Goldwasser was thirteen when his father moved their family from Israel to South Africa. Udi was not happy about it. In fact, he complained so much that his parents promised that if after three months he still was unhappy they would return to Israel. Three months later his mood had not changed but his parents tried to renege on their pledge. Udi knew he needed to do something dramatic to force his parents to see things his way.

So, he disappeared.

After being dropped off at a Jewish youth movement meeting, he did not show for the pickup. For the next three hours, his parents and much of the Jewish community in Durbin, South Africa frantically searched for him to no avail.

Udi was a determined boy. He wanted to dictate terms.

Dramatically, when his mother stood near a bush, Udi stepped from behind it and said, "Here I am. See, I fooled you. All this time, I have been watching you searching for me. If you don't let me go back to Israel, I will disappear again."

Point made.

Udi's parents arranged for him to stay with relatives in Israel. Eighteen years later, he had made a home in Nahariyya, where he lived with his wife, Karnit. There, long after serving his mandatory military duty, Udi became a deep-sea diving coach and amateur photographer but planned on soon getting a master's degree at Haifa University.

And, as was true of most men his age, Goldwasser served in the IDF's reserves. That service required doffing his civilian attire for an IDF uniform and becoming a soldier for a few weeks every year.

Another young man, named Eldad Regev, was stationed at the same base where Goldwasser had reported for reserve duty. A twenty-six-year-old law student, Regev loved soccer, books, and music. In the regular army, he served in an elite infantry unit. Now, like Goldwasser, he had been called for reserve duty.

On July 12, 2006, Goldwasser and Regev were assigned to the IDF's base at Za'arit along Israel's border with Lebanon. That day, their unit's call-up period was coming to an end, and many were experiencing "end-of-term feeling." After a little more than three weeks of active service, the big topics on the last day of reserve duty were always how long it would take to get home and would the replacement unit arrive on time to ensure there was no delay. Everyone hoped to see their wives, families, or girlfriends by evening. But that rush to get home impacted security. The IDF considered change days dangerous. Hezbollah saw them as an opportunity.

Goldwasser's last duty assignment was to lead a patrol along the border road south of Za'arit. Before starting those patrols, he usually would partake in a mandatory briefing. Not this day. However, he did learn from the unit's patrol commander, who traveled that road during the night, that there had been a "red touch" at 2:20 a.m. near point 105. A "red touch" meant sensors had detected someone, or something, touching the security fence. But the commander had investigated and found nothing amiss. Goldwasser planned to check it out too. However, he was not unduly concerned. Two days before, IDF command had relaxed an alert that had barred free movement in the red areas.

Ever since Hezbollah's kidnap attempt at Ghajar eight months before, IDF's northern command had been on guard for another. Even more so after June 25, 2006. On that date, Hamas terrorists based in the Gaza Strip, more than 100 miles south of Za'arit, had snuck into Israel through a stealthily built tunnel near Kibbutz Kerem Shalom, adjacent to the border.

While others fired Katyushas and mortars at IDF positions, the terrorists emerged from their underground passageway near an IDF tank position, surprising the crew. After killing two and wounding one, they captured Gilad Shilat and hustled him back through the tunnel and into Gaza. In the ensuing confusion with explosions and fighting in multiple locations, it took the IDF some time to realize that Shilat had been taken. By then he was gone.

Although Hamas was a different terrorist organization operating in a different region, Northern Command predicted Hezbollah would employ similar tactics to achieve the same result. Udi Adam, head of Northern Command, and Gal Hirsch, commander of the 91st division charged with defending the region, raised the alert status on June 25 from two to four (on a scale of one to five). Units close to the border had their furloughs canceled. At point 105, and other areas known to be weak spots along the fence line, Egoz special forces units prepared ambushes. But nothing happened.

Hirsch did not have enough soldiers to continue the alert ad infinitum. Especially after the Shilat kidnapping, which had siphoned resources to deal with Gaza and to initiate *Operation Summer Rain* which saw IDF units entering Gaza in hope of both returning Shalit to Israel and suppressing Hamas missile fire. For a short period thereafter, the missiles stopped firing from Gaza, but the operation failed to secure Shalit's release (Hamas exchanged him five years later in return for more than 1,000 Palestinian prisoners who, collectively, were responsible for killing more than 500 Israelis).

Short on soldiers, now fatigued by the drawn-out alert, Hirsch's officers pressured him to ease up. Finally, he relented on July 10, dropping the alert status to level three. At level three, red zones reopened for IDF movement. Hirsch later said that Hezbollah had "simply sat there and waited for us to lower the alert."

Hezbollah had charged Imad Moughniyah with commanding a new kidnapping attempt. It was a smart choice. Till then, Moughniyah's track record had been stellar. He had masterminded the bombing of the IDF base in Tyre in 1982; he was involved in the 1983 bombing of the U.S. Marine base in Beirut and the 1985 hijacking of the TWA airliner during which the American soldier onboard was killed; he had led the successful operation in 2000 that took three IDF soldiers; and he had commanded many other operations that had killed Israelis and kidnapped westerners. Moughniyah picked point 105 for the attempt because the area could not be observed from any fixed IDF position and because the closest IDF position was not always manned. Nor at that time were there any working observation cameras nearby. It's unclear whether Hezbollah sharpshooters had knocked them out at the time of the attack or whether they were never installed. Making matters worse for any hapless IDF soldiers caught in a Hezbollah vise, the terrain in the area muddled radio reception. In short, it was a dead zone. Soldiers driving past point 105 would be on their own, with no hope of a relief force arriving soon.

It was the perfect setting for an ambush.

Goldwasser led his two-hummer vehicle patrol out of Za'arit sometime around 8:45 a.m. Hummers are the modern equivalent of World War II jeeps. Although enclosed, Hummers then were soft-skinned and offered little protection from gunfire, rockets, and explosives. As commander, Goldwasser sat in the lead Humvee to the right of the driver, Razak Mu'adi, a career soldier. In the back sat Eldad Regev and Tomer Weinberg. Three other soldiers manned the second Humvee. Procedure called for the second Hummer to have four soldiers in it, but the patrol had to make do with three.

A little past 9 a.m., Goldwasser's unit came around a bend in the road. His vehicle led. After the second Hummer crested a hill and began to descend, Hezbollah operatives hiding in Lebanon struck the vehicle with machine gun and antitank fire. They planned to disable the second vehicle to prevent it from coming to the aid of Goldwasser's Hummer about 110 yards ahead and partway down the hill. The driver of the second vehicle died in the initial onslaught. The other two in the second Humvee died while exiting the vehicle. That left vehicle one.

A small force that had sneaked into Israel during the night, and likely had set off the "red-touch" alarm, fired into the right side of Goldwasser's Hummer. Weinberg, badly wounded, and Mu'adi, slightly injured, jumped out the left side and hid in the bushes. Regev and Goldwasser, either too stunned or too wounded, remained in the vehicle. Hezbollah operatives appeared seconds later and pulled them from the Hummer. Simultaneously, Hezbollah artillery fired shells at nearby IDF military positions and Za'arit, wounding several citizens and IDF soldiers. Many years later, Hezbollah released a stunning video showing the burning vehicles and Hezbollah's minions crossing the border through a wooded area and racing up the road to Goldwasser's Hummer while others provided covering fire.

Weinberg and Mu'adi could not see the abduction of Goldwasser and Regev from where they hid. And they feared firing back. Wienberg later said he "had already said my goodbyes. Just a few steps and they could have come and taken me too."

In his office in Za'arit, battalion commander Benny Azran heard explosions. "Already," he said, "as I was walking from my office to the command and communications room, I knew we'd had it. I entered the room and there [were] so many reports from so many places. ...I didn't know where to turn my attention to first." Azran announced they had a Hannibal situation—the code word for enemy abduction of IDF soldiers.

After hearing a report of the incident, Ze'ev, a sergeant major in the battalion's support company, called his company commander, Norm Schneider. The report did not include the location of the attack, but Schneider knew that point 105 was a weak spot and immediately headed there along a route that provided more cover than the border road. Meanwhile, all attempts by the battalion to reach Goldwasser's patrol failed. Even though Hezbollah's shelling made communications difficult, the IDF's inability to contact either of Goldwasser's vehicles did not bode well.

Forty-five minutes after the attack, only a locked gate separated the path Schneider took to the border road. He could see smoke rising. A soldier shot open the gate. Then, Schneider's hurriedly gathered small force burst through to the road and the burning vehicles. Mu'adi spotted them and, despite his wounds, jumped out of the bushes. Alongside the second Hummer lay two bodies. Another was still inside. Next to a cut in the border fence was a blood-stained flak jacket belonging to one of the missing soldiers. Schneider's group was too late.

IDF doctrine called for doing everything possible to recover kidnapped soldiers in the first moments after an abduction because opportunity dwindles as more time passes. But Schneider's group totaled eight. And it was not moments after their abduction. It was forty-five minutes later. Pursuit would be futile and dangerous with such a small group and likely they would encounter booby traps along the way. There was nothing they could do. Like Shalit a few weeks before, Goldwasser and Regev were gone.

Schneider's decision proved correct. Civilian jeeps waiting on the Lebanese side of the border fence had raced the captured soldiers to the nearby village of Ayta ash Shab, less than a mile away and visible from Israel. Schneider never would have caught up to them and if he had tried, he and his men probably would have been killed or captured too. Proving the point, more than an hour after the kidnap, an Israeli

Merkava tank crossed the border to attempt a rescue. Racing ahead, the tank's operator had no idea that Hezbollah operatives had buried a massive IED in the dirt beneath the path the tank followed. In the ensuing explosion, all four crewmen died. Another IDF soldier died when Hezbollah fighters shot him while he was extricating the bodies in the tank.

Subsequently, after seeing Goldwasser's damaged Hummer and the blood stains inside the vehicle, analysts concluded that both men had sustained serious injuries, at least one life-threatening, before being pulled out. According to investigative reporter Ronen Bergman, those conclusions were not presented to Prime Minister Olmert until more than a month later—the day before the ensuing war ended. Much would happen before that.

When the dust settled that day, a shocked nation mourned the death of eight soldiers, the injuries of several others including Weinberg and Mu'adi, and the kidnapping of two more. Now, three IDF soldiers had been captured, one in Gaza and two in Lebanon. And perhaps equally as stunning for a nation proud of its prowess, a Merkava tank, a presumed king of the battlefield, had been destroyed by a mine. This open season could not continue. According to the Winograd Commission, which investigated the events at the request of Israel's government, Northern Command had known that "the next abduction attempt was just a matter of time, and it was doubtful if it could be avoided."

Clearly, Israel had lost its ability to deter Hezbollah. The 2000 withdrawal from Lebanon had sent the wrong message. Then, Israel's failure to respond forcefully to the October 2000 abduction, the 2005 attempted abduction at Ghajar, and Hezbollah's many other deadly attempted and successful attacks over the last six years had created an intolerable environment in which Hezbollah felt it could act with impunity. This could not continue. Israel had to respond. But how?

War

It turns out that in 2002, Israel's then chief of staff, Moshe Boogie Yaalon, had planned for a forceful response to Hezbollah's antics. Yaalon's strategy consisted of two prongs: massive application of airpower combined with an immediate army mobilization that could lead to a ground attack days later.

With Israel's air force (IAF), Yaalon wanted to achieve two things on the first day of war: minimize Hezbollah's ability to fire missiles by destroying both missiles and launchers in Hezbollah's possession; and inflict a massive blow on Lebanese infrastructure that supported Hezbollah. Meanwhile, Israel's ground forces would mobilize.

Although the IDF had increased the size and capability of its standing army over the years, a large-scale offensive into Lebanon still required mobilizing tens of thousands of reserves if not more. Also, both standing army and reservist units would need to get to the northern borders from bases scattered throughout Israel. That meant transporting soldiers, tanks, ammunition, and all the other components of war many miles over narrow and often hilly and curvy roads. This would take time, probably a couple of days or more. The same, however, was not true of the IAF, which could inflict the massive blows Yaalon planned for without help from IAF reservists.

If the international community responded to the opening battles by applying effective pressure on Hezbollah to disarm, then fine. That would be the end of things. But if not, Yaalon's plan called for the ground forces now present along the borders to move into Lebanon, first outside of towns and villages to avoid mines and IEDs that would cause unnecessary casualties and then within the built-up areas with overwhelming force. Simultaneously, Yaalon planned to envelop Hezbollah by using helicopters to ferry troops deep into Lebanon.

But in the wake of the ambush and kidnapping, it became apparent that Yaalon's plan was based on an army that was more of an empty shell. Reservist training had been cut for financial reasons and the standing army, preoccupied with the Second Intifada in the West Bank, was not prepared for a war with Hezbollah, which would be far more intense than defeating a popular uprising. Even armored units suffered from a dearth of training. Rather than practice maneuvering tanks, soldiers in armored units were performing guard duty in Palestinian towns. And, making matters worse, Israel's casualty-averse public had come to believe that war could be fought on the cheap, using airpower alone without risking soldiers' lives. Therefore, it was unclear if the IDF was prepared to carry out Yaalon's plan.

Israel's prime minister, Ehud Olmert, met with his Cabinet hours after Hezbollah kidnapped Goldwasser and Regev. In Lebanon, Prime Minister Siniora and many ministers in Lebanon's Parliament were furious with Hezbollah for kidnapping the soldiers because they feared Israel would respond fiercely. His concern was justified. With the approval of his Cabinet, Olmert ordered a massive attack.

Except for one thing.

Olmert did not order the mobilization of Israel's ground forces reserves. Instead, he relied on the advice of his chief of staff, Dan Halutz, who counseled that the war could be won on the cheap with airpower alone, even though the IDF had produced studies that concluded that ground forces would have to invade to complete the mission. Thus, one of Yaalon's prongs, as ill-trained and unprepared as it was, was held back. The ground forces did not mobilize their reserves.

The next day, the IAF struck at the Fajar long-range missiles that Iran had transferred to Hezbollah. It also hit numerous other missile launchers, airport runways, border crossings with Syria, and many other infrastructure targets as Yaalon had planned. And, after dropping leaflets and broadcasting messages that warned civilians to flee the area, the IAF hit Hezbollah's stronghold in southern Beirut.

Once again, hundreds of thousands of Lebanese civilians fled southern Lebanon. That made it easier for the IAF to destroy missile launchers and other sites of military value that Hezbollah had tried to protect by embedding them in civilian areas. In Beirut, Hezbollah's leaders valued self-preservation. They left their headquarters for safer places.

Olmert's goal was to change the Rules of the Game, restore deterrence, and push the international community to press for Hezbollah's disarmament. On that first day, the IAF claimed to have destroyed ninety percent of Hezbollah's long-range missiles. On that first day, even though Hezbollah's Katyushas were falling on northern Israel, things seemed under control. And on that first day, the international community seemed sympathetic. There was simply no excuse for what Hezbollah had done. Still, there was a nagging problem. Would airpower alone accomplish Olmert's strategic goals? And what might Hezbollah have up its sleeve?

The next day, Nasrallah appeared on Al-Manar TV. During his speech, an aide handed him a note. He then turned back to his TV audience and told them to look to the ocean for evidence of Hezbollah's first surprise. There, flames shot skyward from the Hanit, an Israeli missile boat. By mistake, the officer in charge of the vessel had not turned on its missile defenses because he didn't think them necessary. But they were. Hezbollah fired at least two ground-sea anti-ship missiles at the Israeli ship. One struck the Hanit, killing four. By fortune alone, the Hanit did not sink. The other missile missed its intended target. Instead, it hit and sunk a Cambodian merchant ship with a crew of twelve Egyptians, one of whom was hurt seriously. I have scoured all available sources and have not found any condemnation by the UN, or anybody else, for sinking that ship. What a surprise! Imagine the universal disapprobation if the IDF had made that mistake.

On day five, the IDF's planes and artillery were still firing missiles and shells into Lebanon but there were fewer and fewer military targets to find and hit effectively. Hezbollah's forces were too dispersed, too entrenched within civilian centers, and too much underground to easily locate from the air. As a result, Hezbollah still managed to fire more than 100 Katyushas per day at northern Israel, which caused massive disruption, property damage, and many injuries and deaths.

Ground troops were needed to complete the job, but Israel had still not mobilized the reserves! The IDF had not even tried to implement Yaalon's plan with standing forces.

On the fifth day, Olmert spoke to the Israeli public. With no end in sight, he said that Israel's goals were as follows:

1.   Return of the kidnapped soldiers.
2.   A total ceasefire everywhere, meaning Shebaa Farms too.
3.   Removal of Hezbollah from Lebanon's border with Israel.
4.   Hezbollah's disarmament.
5.   Having Lebanon's army move into southern Lebanon to secure the Blue Line.

And, he said, "We will continue to operate in full force until we achieve this." But with what?

Two days later, a small Egoz unit sent on a reconnaissance mission found itself mired in a Hezbollah stronghold. There, in bushy terrain, the Israelis came upon numerous camouflaged bunkers and tunnels of which they'd been unaware. Soon, the Israelis referred to those positions as "nature reserves." One soldier later said, "We expected a tent and three [rifles]—that was the intelligence we were given. Instead, we found a hydraulic steel door leading to a well-equipped network of tunnels." A local IDF commander sent a paratroop unit to rescue the trapped Egoz soldiers, who were pinned down and taking casualties near the Lebanese village of Maroon el-Ras. As the unit moved through the village, Hezbollah forces set upon them from prepared positions, including tunnels. The unit also encountered booby traps and IEDs which riddled the village. Soon, the paratroopers required rescue too. The IDF eventually secured Maroon el-Ras and freed the trapped units but incurred heavy casualties doing so. It was a warning of what would come if the IDF would try to secure the two hundred Shiite villages in southern Lebanon.

A few days later the IDF withdrew from Maroon el-Ras with nothing to show for the blood of its soldiers.

The second week of war saw more of the same. A few days after the morass at Maroon el-Ras, another IDF paratroop unit raided a town nearby called Bint Jbeil, which is visible from elevated spots in Israel. In May 2000, shortly after the IDF had withdrawn, Nasrallah made one of his few public appearances at Bint Jbeil, where he gave his boastful "spider's web" speech; therefore, the IDF command saw taking the town as an important symbolic move. Fighting was fierce, and since the chief of staff refused to commit sufficient force to the fight, and since Hezbollah's defenders had refused to fold, the IDF never fully secured the town.

The fighting at Bint Jbeil and Maroon el-Ras had a searing impact on an IDF determined to minimize casualties. Israel's northern commander refused to send any more soldiers into the "nature reserves." One officer said, "[They] can swallow an entire battalion." But the only real answer to occupying the region and avoiding a bloodbath was to employ overwhelming force. Previously, with the nation's existence at stake, the IDF had achieved numerous victories by concentrating its ground forces on strategic focal points and utilizing rapid movements. Concentration of forces coupled with novel tactics also worked in the West Bank in 2002, especially in the crowded area of the Jenin refugee camp.

It was not to be this time.

During that first week, Dan Halutz, Israel's chief of staff, refused to mobilize reservists for the ground forces. Nor did Olmert order him to do so. Perhaps Olmert could be excused. Arguably, he did not have the military experience to countermand the advice he received.

However, there are plenty of civilian leaders with no military experience who had the wisdom to overrule military advice. Abraham Lincoln, for one.

Halutz, however, had no excuse. Even when he saw that airpower alone was insufficient, he refrained from ordering a massive mobilization. Finally, when he saw that there was no choice, Halutz called up 100,000 reservists. But only a few thousand went to war in Lebanon. Then, rather than following Yaalon's plan of using overwhelming force and dropping ground forces in strategic positions behind Hezbollah's forces to surround them when it was clear that the air force alone could not achieve Israel's objectives, Halutz reluctantly agreed to only permit battalion-sized raids into a few southern Lebanese villages with hopes of capturing key people and achieving symbolic victories. But Israeli symbolic victories meant nothing to Hezbollah. For Hezbollah, the long game was, and still is, everything.

Maj. General Giora Eiland later said, "To damage Hezbollah a lot would have required at least three reserve divisions for a long time to go into Lebanon." Instead, Israel fought the 2006 war with one arm tied behind its back and the other not even present.

Finally, in late July, the IDF began to mobilize substantial portions of its reserve army. By then it was too late.

International support for Israel, already wavering, plummeted when another tragedy accelerated the process. Again, it was in Qana, the same town where more than 100 civilians had lost their lives a decade before when IDF artillery had inadvertently struck a UN compound. Everywhere, including in Qana, Hezbollah used civilian structures to hide Katyusha launchers, which, by July 30, had sent more than 1,500 Katyushas winging towards Israeli civilians in northern Israel. Before unleashing its attack in Qana, the IAF dropped warning leaflets and warned the town's residents that they should evacuate, for the IAF would soon strike buildings in Qana that housed Hezbollah soldiers or armaments. Tragically, sixty people elected to stay, sheltering in a garage underneath a three-story structure. When two bombs hit the building, twenty-eight civilians died.

That unintended consequence fanned the flames of international discontent with Israel's operations. Soon the window to achieve a meaningful victory would close. Under pressure from the United States, Israel agreed to halt air strikes targeting southern Lebanon for forty-eight hours and Olmert belatedly recognized that he had no choice but to move ground forces into Lebanon. However, the reservists now called to duty were not prepared to perform well in Lebanon's cauldron. Over the years, while serving their mandatory few weeks every twelve months, reservists had performed guard duty, patrolled the West Bank, or even, before the IDF's withdrawal, just manned hilltop posts in Lebanon prior to the IDF's withdrawal in 2000. They were not trained, or equipped, to jump immediately into a maelstrom. Whipping them into shape required time. Thus, the IDF waited until August 7 before announcing that, in forty-eight hours, it would launch an offensive whose objective was to take all of southern Lebanon up to the Litani River. Then the IDF delayed the operation for two more days until August 11, the same day the UN Security Council unanimously approved Resolution 1701, which called for a ceasefire. Two days later the ceasefire the UN had demanded took effect—but not until thirty-three more Israeli soldiers died during those last two days of fighting.

On the last day of the war, Hezbollah fired 253 Katyushas at Israel. In all, Hezbollah had launched about 4,000 missiles during the thirty-four-day war, causing half a billion dollars of property losses in Israel and forcing 250,000 people—half of northern Israel's population—to flee south. Also, Hezbollah's ability to further damage Israel's homeland with its thousands of remaining missiles had remained intact, Goldwasser and Regev were still in Hezbollah's hands, and Israel's last-minute plan, *Operation Change of Direction*, had failed to achieve anything meaningful.

The Fighting Stops but the War Continues

As part of the ceasefire, Israel received some tangible things on paper. In return for the IDF again withdrawing behind the Blue Line, Resolution 1701 called for UNIFIL to rein in Hezbollah's activities more aggressively and for the LAF to deploy its forces throughout southern Lebanon. It also demanded the "establishment between the Blue Line and the Litani River of an area free of any armed personnel, assets and weapons other than those of the government of Lebanon and of UNIFIL," and "the disarmament of all armed groups in Lebanon."

But once again, what sounded rather good for Israel was not so in practice.

The clear intent embodied in the resolution was for Hezbollah to disarm and for Lebanon's army to have sole control, in conjunction with UNIFIL, of southern Lebanon. That would ensure that the region would not again become filled with terrorists bent on destroying Israel. And, of course, if no more terror would emanate from southern Lebanon, Israel would have no reason to strike targets there. Thus, leaving the inhabitants of southern Lebanon in peace.

Well, maybe not the intent of some.

After the ceasefire began, Lebanon's defense minister said, "The army is not going to the south to strip Hezbollah of its weapons and do the work that Israel did not." Sadly, as you will soon read, Hezbollah did not disarm, the Lebanese army did not assert control of southern Lebanon, and UNIFIL continued its record of ineffectiveness. Only Israel abided by the terms of the resolution—dutifully once again withdrawing behind the Blue Line.

So much for Israel relying on UN resolutions.

The Propaganda War

Hezbollah is honest about its view of the press. Hassan Ezziedine, once head of Hezbollah's press department, said, "We believe that the media have an important role in the conflict with the Israeli enemy, as important as the military wing."

Over the course of the 2006 war, Hezbollah's military wing fired almost 4,000 rockets into Israel. And distressingly, despite the IAF's notable success hitting Hezbollah's longer-range missiles on the first day of fighting, towards the end of the war, Hezbollah managed to fire a daily average of 200 missiles at Israel, doubling the 100 it averaged each day during the first two weeks. Those missiles intentionally hunted Israeli civilians while Israel hunted Hezbollah operatives, weapons, and infrastructure. But Hezbollah's effective propaganda machine, which co-opted the media to sway international opinion, successfully obscured the reality that Hezbollah, not Israel, hunted, and continues to hunt, civilians.

During the fighting, the Reuters news agency published a photo showing smoke rising over Beirut after a reported Israeli air attack. But there was something funny about the picture. It contained repeating patterns of smoke and duplicated buildings. It was a forgery. A Lebanese photographer employed by Reuters since 1993 had used Photoshop to make the damage appear greater than it was. Reuters dubiously explained that the photographer was "trying to remove dust marks" and had "made mistakes due to the bad lighting conditions."

Other falsified photos appeared. One purportedly showed an Israeli plane firing three missiles at Lebanese civilians. No. It was a defensive flare expelled to trick the guidance systems of missiles targeting the plane. Again, a trickster had employed trusty Photoshop to manipulate the image. And guess what? The pictures came from the same photographer. Even more alarming, the person issuing the disingenuous statement about bad lighting conditions causing an error had a dual loyalty—she worked for Qatar's Al Jazeera as well as Reuters. Hmm.

Eventually, Reuters removed 920 photos shot by that photographer from its database. But the damage had already been done. Some of his pictures had been used by the *New York Times*, *Washington Post*, and others. On the other hand, many publications failed or refused to publish pictures documenting collusion between Hezbollah and the LAF—including in one instance when a Hezbollah missile launcher was photographed on a civilian truck on a LAF base.

Hezbollah used another propaganda tactic to great success—staged scenes. A green-helmeted guy often showed up at locations where fighting had occurred. After the bombing at Qana, the green-helmeted guy held a dead baby in the air, like a trophy to be admired, for cameramen to take what would look to some as a candid shot. But in truth, photographers swarmed several deep to get the shot. All getting a frontal image. All staged. Certainly not candid. The sensational and awful pictures appeared on the front pages of newspapers worldwide. Even worse, a German crew documented that all was not as it seemed. They captured video of workers removing a dead child from the back of an ambulance, wrapped in a blanket. Only after they laid the child on the ground, and after signaling for the photographers to come closer, the green-helmeted guy pulled the blanket from the child. The rest was history—or not? The well-worn phrase "fake news" comes to mind.

It also appears that the green-helmeted guy was experienced at this. Two decades earlier, he had displayed the body of a headless child for maximum effect.

Bryan Denton confirmed "the daily practice of directed shots." He said that in one case "a group of photojournalists was choreographing the unearthing of bodies, directing emergency workers here and there, asking them to position the bodies just so, even removing bodies that had already been put in graves so that they can photograph them in peoples' arms." Along the same lines, another photographer said a "young boy [was] pushed to stand reluctantly next to [an unexploded bomb in a living room] while we get our cameras out and record the scene for posterity." Other staging techniques included perfectly positioning stuffed animals in a manner designed to tug on viewers' emotions.

Staging the dead was bad enough—but on other occasions, actors took fake news to another level.

A Reuter's photograph, taken on July 22, 2006, showed an elderly Arab woman crying in front of what appeared to be her destroyed Beirut apartment. AP then released another picture, taken two weeks later, of the same woman, making the same wailing sound, weeping in front of the same building. Both the Reuters image and the AP image had captions saying that the building had been destroyed the night before. Two weeks later, AP released another picture of the woman. This time she was moving through her purportedly destroyed home far from Beirut in southern Lebanon. And then, several days later another picture of her appeared—this time walking through yet another destroyed home. It turns out Hezbollah had controlled access to bombed areas. Therefore, many journalists depended on Hezbollah to provide buses for them to ride in so they could tour the area. Magically, the woman kept appearing for them to snap a picture of.

She must have been an expert wailer.

The *New York Times* code of ethics requires that photos that "purport to depict reality must be genuine in every way." Obviously, it was a code that some journalists in Lebanon didn't always follow.

Aftermath

Who won?

Lebanon suffered far more destruction than Israel, and Hezbollah incurred many more casualties and material losses than the IDF. But in the end, Hezbollah still stood, and Israel's military reputation had suffered a blow. What's more, Hezbollah received confirmation that

Israel's reluctance to incur casualties hamstrung its use of ground forces.

However, Israel had gained something too—Hezbollah now understood that even if an all-out war with the Jewish state might not include a full land invasion, much of Lebanon's roads, bridges, electrical facilities, and the like would not survive the battle. That could lead to increased political and even physical opposition from angry Christians, Sunnis, Druze, and even some Shiites.

Therefore, in some respects, both sides won. Hezbollah survived, a victory in and of itself, and in the process proved Israel would struggle to stop Hezbollah from firing missiles that would strike and cause damage in Israel. However, Israel's actions succeeded in restoring some measure of deterrence by demonstrating its willingness to wreak so much havoc on Hezbollah's host country that domestic politics might turn the population against Hezbollah.

Weeks later, Nasrallah said that he would not have ordered the kidnapping if he had thought there was even a "one percent" chance that Israel would have reacted as it did. Was that true? Or was that for domestic consumption? Or was it for Iran's consumption since Iran's Ayatollah Khamenei was allegedly peeved that Nasrallah had wasted so much for so little? Likely, we will never know. But Hezbollah has not attempted to kidnap an Israeli since.

Before the war, Hezbollah had worked hard to ensure it would survive a war with Israel. Command and control of its fighting units had been decentralized, giving individual units more autonomy. The "nature reserves" contained an array of bunkers and tunnels in which fighters could remain for weeks at a time, safe from bombardment and well stocked with supplies. Also, vast numbers of defensive positions and bunkers had been constructed within many of the towns in southern Lebanon. Collectively, they protected fighters and allowed them to move securely from one position to another. In addition, Hezbollah managed to preserve its ability to launch Katyushas throughout the war. Many were fired from parking garages and even from the windows of apartments.

But the rapid rate of firing and Hezbollah's decision to entwine itself with civilian structures came at a cost. Most of its weaponry had been used or destroyed and many of the towns in southern Lebanon were filled with rubble. Throughout Lebanon, 125,000 homes and apartments were destroyed in the fighting, and ninety-one bridges were blown up. Estimates of immediate costs to Lebanon's economy, including property damage, were up to five billion dollars, plus fifteen billion more over the next three years due to lost output and tourism. Clearly, Hezbollah needed help. A whole bunch of people desperately needed basic amenities, and needy people can easily become angry people.

Then Iran came to the rescue.

With Iran's financial assistance, (estimates are that Iran's financial assistance totaled roughly 400 million dollars after the war, plus annual supplements in those years averaging more than 200 million dollars) Hezbollah took over running local schools and community centers and distributed medical care and food. Hezbollah supporters (mostly Shiites) received $12,000 for their damaged home if it was in Beirut and $10,000 if their home was in southern Lebanon. Hezbollah also embarked on large construction projects like a new highway intended to create a transportation network between Shiites in western Beirut and the Bekaa Valley. All of that shored up its domestic base.

But Hezbollah wanted something more. It wanted to deter the Israelis from ever entering Lebanon again. Surviving was no longer enough. For that, Nasrallah turned once more to Iran and Syria.

Chapter Ten

Post War Understandings

In previous chapters, I mentioned the term "deterrence," and I will use that term in this and future chapters. So, for now let's use the following definition—it is Israel's and Hezbollah's attempt to discourage the other from doing something by instilling fear of the consequences. In its simplest form that means if you do this, I'm going to do something bad to you. But to deter the other side, the other side must accept the status quo, meaning it is okay as things stand.

What does the status quo mean within the context of the tangled regional conflict we are discussing?

Before Israel's withdrawal in 2000, and even for the subsequent six years, Hezbollah struggled to assert its ideology and become the dominant force in Lebanon. As such, it wanted to bolster its size and power, increasingly challenge Israel, and assume control of the hearts and minds of Shiites in Lebanon. Israel's deterrence did little to rein in Hezbollah's desire to expand its reach and support, which it felt it could only achieve by confronting the IDF in Lebanon. But the 2006 ceasefire heralded a new era. After going toe-to-toe with Israel and surviving, Hezbollah gained credibility and, in some cases, grudging respect. Now, not only would it dominate the Lebanese Shiite population, but it also had gained the capacity to intimidate the Sunni, Christian, and Druze populations in Lebanon. And it had cleverly found and then twisted a manufactured cause that would come to resonate among many Lebanese of all religious backgrounds—the belief that Hezbollah was a necessary and righteous tool for restoring Shebaa Farms to Lebanese sovereignty. That combination of political and military power and purpose left Hezbollah thinking time was on its side. In other words, for now, Hezbollah was fine with the way things were.

Israel's government, despite the perception of many, was also relatively satisfied. Its northern borders were the quietest they'd been in decades; it had taught Hezbollah that Israel would not pull punches if pushed too far; and it had obliterated much of Hezbollah's present ability to strike Israel's interior.

Thus, neither Israel nor Hezbollah liked the status quo, but both accepted it. And since each side retained the ability to significantly damage the other but neither side felt compelled to radically change the present situation, mutual deterrence came into being to a greater extent than before. But like a fault line that stores more and more energy until that energy is suddenly, and violently, released, their mutual deterrence stored Hezbollah's hatred while providing it with an opportunity to increase its strength in anticipation of its next round of war with Israel.

Nasrallah alluded to this phenomenon when he said, "The long-term strategy of the Islamic Resistance is clear and does not require additional explanation. It involves fighting against Israel and liberating Jerusalem... namely, ending Israel as a state." However, he said, "We are not unrealistic. We do not pretend that our military capabilities and the numbers of our Mujahidin would be enough to regain Jerusalem. ...We do, however, believe that the resistance has to finish the job it started."

Soon, Iran provided Hezbollah with a flood of new weapons, much of them advanced infantry and ground-air weaponry. Hezbollah also re-configured its ground forces, organizing larger fighting units that would have greater offensive potential. Most importantly for the organization, Iran replenished Hezbollah's inventory of missiles, and then supplemented that stockpile with many tens of thousands more. Weaponry poured in by land and sea. In fact, Iran sent such vast quantities that Jonathan Davis, an IDF spokesperson at the time, said, "We think of Hezbollah as the Iranian army."

Many of the new weapons ended up in southern Lebanon. So much for any benefit UNIFIL and the LAF were supposed to bring. So much for Resolution 1701's proscription for armed groups, other than the national army, possessing weapons. Rather than promoting peace, UNIFIL now was an impediment complicating any IDF response to the growing threat on Israel's border. Michael Oren, Israel's future ambassador to the United States, said what was obvious at the time and still is now: "UNIFIL has to be a combat force otherwise it is a shield of Hezbollah."

Over four short years after the 2006 war ended, Hezbollah's capability to harm Israel grew immensely. Thanks to Iran and Syria too, Hezbollah received missiles that could carry a half-ton warhead 150 miles and strike within 500 yards of its target. It also received Scud missiles with a 450-mile range. Now, all of Israel was within reach of Hezbollah's rockets. And Hezbollah had learned a lesson from the fighting in Bint Jbeil and Maroon el-Ras and the tragedy in Qana. Now, more than ever before, Hezbollah positioned its missiles and soldiers in villages and towns. More and more bunkers sprouted among buildings, and the tunnels traced underneath their foundations. Cumulatively, the new defensive structures turned built-up areas into horror venues designed to inflict maximum casualties on Israeli forces entering designated kill zones with no regard for the Lebanese civilians who would suffer as a result. Suffering, both real and staged, that Hezbollah would then exploit to maximum effect with international media.

Hezbollah also sought to further improve its communications and electronic warfare capabilities. Soon after the 2006 war ended, it embarked on an ambitious project to install an encrypted cell phone network and to expand fiber-optic lines for connecting most villages in southern Lebanon with Hezbollah's control centers in Beirut and elsewhere. In addition, Iran helped Hezbollah learn how to interfere with IDF ground controllers communicating with their drones.

In short, Hezbollah's capabilities ratcheted higher during the pause that deterrence delivered. No longer a terrorist force, or even a guerrilla one, Hezbollah now fielded an army already much more powerful than that of the state it fed off, and more powerful than that of many nations throughout the world.

Nevertheless, Hezbollah had a political problem to deal with. The March 14 group, which had sent a million strong to protest the 2005 assassination of Hariri, was not happy. Within weeks of the 2006 ceasefire, the group accused Hezbollah of dragging Lebanon into the destructive war and pushed for Hezbollah to disarm, as UN Resolution 1701 demanded. By October, the country was enduring another political crisis. But the March 14 group had a critical problem. Although it had the votes, it lacked the guns.

Hezbollah demanded a national unity government be created, of which it would have a one-third share, so that, per the Taif Accords, it would be able to block any policies it did not like. However, the March 14 group knew what Hezbollah really wanted—the ability to stop the government from approving the creation of an international committee to investigate Hariri's murder. In November, the Cabinet's five Shiite members walked out to block a vote that would have approved the tribunal. In response, Christian President Lahoud refused to stand strong. Instead, he said that since the Taif Agreement required all factions within Lebanon to participate in government, Hezbollah's walk-out prevented the government from endorsing the creation of an international tribunal for investigating Hariri's murder. Then, in early December, Hezbollah staged a massive protest in downtown Beirut and built a tent city to pressure Sunni Prime Minister Siniora.

Regarding Hezbollah, Druze warlord Walid Jumblatt, whose father had been killed by Syria, said, "They control part of Lebanon without the possibility of the Lebanese State to enter it and enforce law and order. That's the situation. The solution is not in Lebanon. The solution is in Tehran."

In January 2007, having successfully cowed leaders of the other religious factions, Hezbollah intensified matters by severing transportation links leading to Beirut. Masked Hezbollah gunmen set ablaze, on many roads, tires mingled with piled rocks. The LAF refused to restore access. In southern Lebanon, Hezbollah set up roadblocks. Angry Sunnis, now feeling the same kind of pressure they had once imposed, with the PLO's help, on Shiites, used sticks, since they did not have guns, to try to break up the barricades. In those instances, the LAF pushed the feuding sides apart. Still, the confrontations resulted in deaths. Finally, motivated by the bloody toll, Hezbollah eased up. The experience of 1975 was still a harsh memory. Hezbollah at the time was unwilling to risk causing another civil war.

That changed the following year.

In the spring of 2008, Jumblatt convinced Hariri and other allies in the Christian parties to work together to disable Hezbollah's parallel communication network. Think about that for a moment. Lebanon had a communications network for the benefit of the populace subject to taxes, regulation, etc. Hezbollah had another one for its own exclusive use.

Jumblatt's group also sought to fire the head of Beirut airport security because he had turned a blind eye to arms shipments arriving at the airport for Hezbollah. In addition, the security chief acquiesced to Hezbollah installing a security camera at the airport that tracked who was coming and going. Imagine the U.S. government permitting a terrorist-owned Facebook or Google to do the same (let's not get bogged down with the metaphor).

So, on May 5, Lebanon's minister of telecommunications announced that the government would no longer tolerate Hezbollah controlling the hundreds of thousands of private communication links it had created in Shiite communities. Nor would the government accept Hezbollah's control of the communication towers it had built in the Bekaa Valley near the border with Syria. He said they were "no longer an issue concerning the security of the resistance, but rather the security of Lebanon and the toppling of its [government]."

Nasrallah would not stand for Lebanon asserting its authority. Fearing the government would soon move to shut down Hezbollah's parallel communications system, he announced a press conference for May 8. Streets in Beirut cleared in anticipation of violence. To reporters at the press conference, Nasrallah declared, "The [government's] decisions are tantamount to a declaration of war, and the start of a war on behalf of the United States and Israel." In his view, Hezbollah's communication network was "the most important weapon in the resistance," and he stated, "We have a right to defend our existence from whoever declares and begins a war on us, even if they are our brothers."

Those were fighting words, and soon the fighting started.

Armed Hezbollah thugs moved into Beirut along with Amal supporters and members of SSNP (a Syrian-supported militant group). These groups murdered citizens and destroyed property, but once again the LAF did nothing. Forty LAF officers resigned in protest of the army's impotence.

Elsewhere, fighting broke out in Tripoli, a majority Sunni city, but a gang there loyal to the government faced down some SSNP terrorists, dragged them outside the building they had entered, and used axes to mutilate them. In Druze territory, Hezbollah forces attacked but made little headway. However, Jumblatt, the Druze's leader, knew he could not win a sustained fight. The Druze had no logistical support, and a long fight would wear them down. The

Christians, by now divided between those who supported Hezbollah in some fashion and those who did not, sat out. Prudently, Hezbollah did not go into Christian areas, knowing that would unite the Christians against it.

By the end of that brutal day, Hezbollah forces had surrounded the homes of many of the March 14 group's leaders. The next day, it was clear to all that Hezbollah was in control. The groups opposing it had not coalesced and lacked the will to carry on the fight. Hezbollah then paused; its point made.

Little more than a week later, on May 21, leaders representing all factions in the dispute met in Qatar to fashion a compromise. Chastened by their weakness, the March 14 group had already backed down regarding the airport. The airport security man the group despised was already back to work. At the meeting, the government agreed to not interfere with Hezbollah's parallel communications network.

But that was not the end of it.

The parties also agreed that candidates Hezbollah supported would now form one-third plus one of the Cabinet. This huge concession gave Hezbollah the ability to block the government from doing almost anything it didn't like. And, making things worse, was the compromise reached regarding the new Christian president. Lahoud's additional three-year term had expired several months before. The new compromise candidate whom all had agreed to install was army commander Michael Suleiman—known to have a soft spot for Hezbollah's ally, Syria.

And so, like an animal ensnared by a python's coils struggling in vain to break free, the March 14 group's fight ended with Hezbollah tightening its grip on Lebanon. Nobody who opposed Hezbollah had the heart to start another civil war. Prime Minister Siniora perhaps best expressed the prevailing view, "Violence is not the way," and "It is not possible for me to start a war against my countrymen in order to disarm them while at the same time they argue that the enemy is occupying a part of my country." Hezbollah's brilliant sham regarding Shebaa Farms had done the job.

Two years after the war ended, Hezbollah returned the bodies of IDF soldiers Goldwasser and Regev in return for Israel releasing the heinous Samir Kuntar and others. Former chief rabbi of the IDF, Yisrael Weiss, said, "If we thought the enemy was cruel to the living and the dead, we were surprised, when we opened the caskets, to discover just how cruel. And I'll leave it at that."

A year later, although Hezbollah's opposition had gained seats in Parliament, Jumblatt declared himself neutral and led his Druze party out of the March 14 coalition. And even though several months later Saad Hariri replaced Siniora as prime minister, the position his father had sought to reclaim before his assassination, the son proved little more than a figurehead. Nasrallah had won. In 2009, Lebanon's Parliament even voted to permit Hezbollah to keep its weapons. That the investigation into Hariri's death had found links between the assassination and Hezbollah did not matter. Nasrallah clearly had become the most powerful person in Lebanon and was in de facto control of its government.

Nasrallah's growing power led to, or perhaps was aided by, Hezbollah's slight change in policy. In an open letter manifesto carefully calibrated between ideology and political need, Hezbollah relaxed some of the religious requirements it formerly imposed on the population under its control, no longer demanded the creation of an Islamic state in Lebanon, spoke against sectarianism, and called for unity while still railing against the United States and Israel (and refusing any compromise with Israel). Rather than crushing Lebanon, Hezbollah's tentacles were absorbing it.

Two years later, in 2011, a leaked IDF map delineated 1,000 Hezbollah bunkers, weapons storage facilities, and other military sites scattered throughout Lebanon, including in the north. It was visual proof that Hezbollah used of all of Lebanon to power its confrontation with Israel. Thus, Israeli Prime Minister Benjamin Netanyahu was right on the mark in 2009 when he said, "It is the Lebanese government that is responsible for upholding the ceasefire, and we view it as responsible for any violations and aggression directed at us from Lebanese territory." Netanyahu's words made clear that another war would bring large-scale destruction to Lebanon whose government was now under Hezbollah's control.

How Israel got to that position comes next.

Evolution of Israel's Strategy for Fighting Hezbollah in a War

Israel's successful use of airpower during the 1982 Lebanon War highlighted how the air force might be utilized in future wars in Lebanon. However, the problems IDF ground forces experienced during that war led IDF reformists to advocate increasing reliance on airpower delivering precision-guided munitions on targets versus taking and holding territory with land forces. That meant less training for land units and more focus on making the IDF "slimmer and smarter."

Dan Shomron, IDF chief of staff from 1987-1991, said, "Quality is the first thing. A large army for us is like Swiss cheese, more holes than cheese." Shomron's comment highlighted the IDF's dilemma. Since it had limited financial resources, it could not do everything at once. Trying to do so would leave holes everywhere. Therefore, it had to make tough decisions that would impact how it would conduct wars in the future.

In a search for quality that incorporated technical superiority, soon the IDF leaned more towards purchasing new equipment for its air force and spent less on training its ground forces to fight the next war. That seemed reasonable. The peace treaty with Egypt that took effect in the early 1980s had taken the largest Arab ground army out of the military equation.

After Shomron, the next IDF chief of staff, Ehud Barak, pushed his predecessor's ideas further. Then, Shaul Mofaz, chief of staff from 1998 to 2002, bought in as well. He shut down logistical units and closed training bases—steps that more and more over time would impact the IDF's ability to fight a land-based war. However, some within the IDF were alarmed by these developments. They argued that Hezbollah's guerrilla forces could not be attacked successfully by air alone, they would have to be destroyed by ground forces. But their voices did not prevail. Especially because of a new political development—the Oslo Accords, signed in 1993 by Israel and the Palestinians. The false hopes surrounding those accords led to both domestic and international pressure to avoid making waves on the northern front while peace with the Palestinians was in the offing. This political impetus pushed hard against using ground forces for offensive operations in Lebanon.

Still, some viewed things differently and proceeded accordingly. General Amiram Levin, head of Northern Command between 1994 to 1998, was one of those people, and he had an opportunity to act accordingly when he commanded Egoz. When the government changed its classification of Hezbollah in 1992 from a guerrilla organization to a terrorist group, Levin had the opening he needed to create the Egoz reconnaissance battalion, which received specialized training on tactics required to defeat Hezbollah. With that training, and experience gained in the field, Levin had hoped that the Egoz unit would then teach the rest of the army how to effectively confront Hezbollah's fighters. The IDF, he said, must "start fighting it the way a modern army fights guerrillas," and that "our goal is to win every battle and inflict as many casualties as possible." Levin's strategy was to accumulate numerous tactical wins with ground forces that would eventually add up to a strategic victory.

The Egoz unit trained to fight in the bushy, forested, and mountainous terrain in southern Lebanon. It mastered concealment, intelligence collection, and surveillance techniques. The men in the unit also specialized in close-in fighting. And because success often required remaining in the field for weeks at a time, the unit learned to stay hidden, deep within Lebanon without resupply for long periods. Then, when an opportunity arose, the unit would move rapidly to the attack in close coordination with the IAF. Commanders had to be able to solve problems rapidly and think outside the box. General Erez Gerstein, killed by Hezbollah in 1999, served in the unit. By the late 1990s, even as the IDF had generally reduced its training and went on the defensive, Egoz continued to garner much success, often deep within Lebanon.

Still, despite the example Egoz set, the IDF developed sensors for detecting enemy movements instead of stationing men on the ground. That way, its advocates argued, airplanes rather than soldiers could kill Hezbollah operatives. However, some thought that Hezbollah would find ways to defeat that technology. In 1999, General Shlomo Brown said, "I'm afraid it's not the end of the story. Hezbollah will now look for tactics that will make it less vulnerable to airborne attacks, and then we'll be back to the drawing board. There is no silver bullet that will allow us to withdraw to the international border and everything will be ok."

Even Nasrallah agreed with General Brown's assessment. He said:

> I'm not underestimating the Israeli soldier's abilities: I am just saying that he hides behind his technology, his artillery, his helicopters, and his heavy gunfire, and the human element comes last in the Israeli military estimate. This is why I know it is possible to defeat the Israeli soldiers if we know how to use the elements of the battle on the ground to our advantage.

Nevertheless, despite opposition, before the 2006 Lebanon War and even in that war's wake, the IDF adopted a "limited conflict doctrine." Its goal was to target the "consciousness" of Hezbollah by using pinprick attacks to fatigue Hezbollah and wear down Lebanese society. That was little different than what Hezbollah was trying to do to the IDF. However, some strongly disagreed with that strategy. Major General Yaakov Amidror, head of the IDF's National Defense College, said regarding the limited conflict doctrine that a "mistaken assumption" is that "victory is always a matter of cognizance rather than the outcome of physical or coercive measures." In other words, Amidror thought that to win, the victor must take the fight to the enemy and defeat it on the ground it holds rather than depending on just influencing the enemy's mindset. I agree. When a nation's future is at stake, certainty is required. Concrete facts on the ground matter far more than pie-in-the-sky psychological predictions.

While debates continued on how to best approach future conflicts with Hezbollah, the IDF developed four alternative plans between 2002 to 2005. One was called "Northern Storm." It envisioned using light infantry, special forces, and the air force to attack Hezbollah from multiple directions simultaneously. Each group would operate independently and in effect swarm all opposition. The operation's initial objective would be to destroy by airstrike all of Hezbollah's long-range rockets, many of which were in the Bekaa Valley, in the first thirty minutes of the outbreak of war. Planners also intended to demolish Hezbollah's command and control center in the Dahiya region of Beirut with ground forces—even though that could take weeks to accomplish—while also using ground forces combined with airpower to eliminate the threat of Katyushas fired from southern Lebanon.

Another plan, similar in nature, was called "Defense of the Land." It called for heavy air strikes against Hezbollah and Syrian targets in Lebanon. The plan also envisioned crossing the border with ground forces in conjunction with helicopters transporting special forces to designated locations in Lebanon. However, rather than focusing on taking territory, the mission of the ground forces was to combine with airpower to hunt and destroy targets—mostly missiles. Planners thought it would take six weeks to accomplish that goal. However, when Syria pulled out of Lebanon in 2005, this plan lost its luster for unclear reasons.

After Syria pulled out of Lebanon, in 2005 the IDF developed a third plan called "Elevated Waters," which focused more on killing Hezbollah operatives.

And then there was a fourth plan, "Icebreaker." For the first seventy-two hours of a conflict, the IDF would only use airpower and artillery. Meanwhile, the IDF would mobilize ground forces, which would include activating three reserve divisions. Planners thought that the mere act of moving the army north would pressure Lebanon's government to lean on Hezbollah to resolve Israel's issues with it. If not, the mobilized ground forces would move into Lebanon.

Notice, despite the philosophical changes afoot, all four plans required incorporating significant ground forces. But then in 2005 along came Dan Halutz, a new chief of staff, who formerly had been Israel's Air Force commander and had no experience commanding ground forces. Halutz said, "Is war over territory relevant at all in the future? In my opinion, no!…Decision is the issue of consciousness. Airpower influences in a meaningful fashion the consciousness of the enemy." Not surprisingly, Halutz derided all four plans. Instead, he put all his marbles on using airpower to kill Hezbollah operatives and destroy missiles while refraining from deploying massive ground forces. In essence, he bet heavily on cognizance rather than physical coercion.

It was a bad bet.

A few months after the 2006 war ended, with criticism pouring in from all directions, Halutz resigned, and Lt. General Gabi Ashkenazi took over as chief of staff. Ashkenazi brought the IDF back to a much more traditional doctrine that included better training for regular and reserve ground forces. No longer would IDF ground units focus on the Palestinians in the West Bank and Gaza, they would learn again to fight and win a war with Hezbollah.

That's when the "Dahiya Doctrine" entered the IDF's lexicon. Its proponents recognized that political and social dynamics might well create time constraints that would prevent the IDF from achieving total victory. Therefore, its advocates believed that the goal of a future war would be to reestablish deterrence by demonstrating what the cost of that war would be to Lebanon. Fear of that, they thought, would deter Hezbollah from crossing any red lines that would initiate a war. Brigadier General Itai Brun said it well: "We used to plan for military decisions, and deterrence was the outcome. Now, we are planning for deterrence. That's the change." To do so, however, required broadcasting that the IDF would also respond against the state if Hezbollah engaged in a provocative act, rather than just against Hezbollah. Given that Hezbollah had now chosen to participate and manipulate Lebanon's government, such a view had a substantial basis. Hezbollah was no longer just a state within a state, it was now part of the state, and the state would pay the price for its perfidy.

Future Chief of Staff Gadi Eizenkot defined what the "Dahiya Doctrine" meant while he was the IDF's northern front commander. Intimating that anything related to Hezbollah would be destroyed in a future war, he said, "What happened in the Dahiya quarter of Beirut in 2006 will happen in every village from which Israel is fired on. …We will apply disproportionate force on [them] and cause great damage and destruction there. From our standpoint, they are not civilian villages, they are military bases. This isn't a suggestion. This is a plan that has already been authorized." Benny Gantz, chief of staff from 2011-2015, agreed. He said the IDF would "[hit] directly against Hezbollah and its state surroundings. Lebanon cannot claim sovereignty but not bear responsibility. If a conflagration erupts, I would rather be an Israeli citizen than a Lebanese citizen."

IDF strategist Gabriel Siboni explained the concept further:

> The closer [the] relationship between Hezbollah and the Lebanese government, the more the elements of the Lebanese state structure should be targeted. Such a response will create a lasting memory among Syrian and Lebanese decision-makers, thereby increasing Israeli deterrence and reducing the likelihood of hostilities against Israel for an extended period.

Those who feel targeting Lebanon's infrastructure as well as Hezbollah is a bridge too far should remember what Lebanese President Michel Aoun said in 2017—that Hezbollah's weapons "are essential in that they complement the actions of the Lebanese army and do not contradict them."

And so, Israel had almost come full circle. First, in 1982, using all aspects of its military might to move into Lebanon to end the Palestinian terrorist threat, then trying to carve out a security strip to defend northern Israel from terror attacks, then retreating in May 2000 in hopes of ending the conflict with Hezbollah, then fighting another war in 2006 forced on it by increasingly brazen tactics—this time with Hezbollah—without using the full measure of its power, and finally, returning to the concept of using both army and airpower to massively destroy what it had no interest in occupying.

A new concept of deterrence was born.

However, during this transformation, the Middle East also transformed. The Arab Spring had come and soon thereafter came a cataclysm across Israel's northern border with Syria that would descend into another civil war that embroiled the Syrian people. One would think that Israel would have gotten involved. It did not. One would not think that Russia would have gotten involved. It did. As for Hezbollah and Iran—while the turmoil might not have been music to their ears, it offered an opportunity. One that both would jump at.

Chapter Eleven

Hezbollah in the Syrian Civil War & After

Until 2011, Hezbollah had two parents to answer to—Syria and Iran. At first, Syria was stricter, and Iran was more ideological. Both Hafez Assad and his son, Bashar, had found Hezbollah useful for pressuring Israel and a lucrative tool for levering financial assistance from Iran. But there was a price. Syria had to let Iran funnel weapons, military trainers, and ideological leaders through Syrian territory to Hezbollah in Lebanon.

Syria needed Iran's money because it lost a huge benefactor when the Soviet Union collapsed in the late 1980s. Cagily, Hafez Assad turned ever so slightly to the west by marginally assisting the United States in the first Gulf War in return for a freer hand in Lebanon. But that warmer relationship did not translate into financial aid. For Assad to keep his people content, he needed money to lubricate Syria's economy. Thanks to its oil, Iran had plenty. However, Hafez Assad was always weary of giving Iran unfettered access to Lebanon because his long-term goal was to make Lebanon part of Greater Syria. Therefore, he made sure to keep Hezbollah under his thumb. Much like how Britain manipulated its alliances with European powers to prevent any one country from ascending in a manner that would threaten its interests, Hafez carefully controlled the spigot through which arms flowed to Hezbollah—opening it sometimes and tightening it when necessary. He also maintained his own independent power base and terrorist group in Syria. But things changed after Hafez's death in 2000, when his son, Bashar, loosened Syria's hold on Hezbollah and Iran.

Hafez had never thought Bashar would become Syria's ruler. He had bestowed that dubious honor on his oldest son, Bassel, whom he groomed for the job. But that plan ended in 1994 when Bassel died in a car accident of his making. Bashar was next up.

But was Bashar ready and able?

When his brother died, Bashar had already established a sedate ophthalmology practice. Growing up, he was introverted and a loner. Married to a Sunni woman, Bashar had the reputation of being a nice guy. Now he was next in line to rule, and after his father died, many hoped that Syria would change for the better under Bashar's guidance. However, others thought Bashar was weak and unlikely to stay in office for long after his father death.

At his father's funeral, Bashar sat next to Nasrallah while watching a parade of black-clad Hezbollah representatives march by. Hardly an indication that Syria's policies would soon moderate. Still, some hoped for fundamental change. After he was sworn in as president, Bashar gave a public speech that fanned those hopes. He promised to rid Syria of corruption, tolerate dissent, and prioritize education and the economy.

But despite the flowery rhetoric, Bashar had a ruthless side. Dreams of change dissipated as for all practical purposes Syria's police state continued. And Bashar continued his father's policy of meddling in Lebanon.

In 2004, Bashar pushed Prime Minister Hariri to amend Lebanon's constitution so that Syrian ally Lahoud could serve another three years as Lebanon's president. Meanwhile, the United States and France pushed for a UN resolution that would require Syrian forces to leave Lebanon and Hezbollah to disarm. Seeing that his hold on Lebanon might weaken if Lahoud did not retain the presidency, Bashar summoned Hariri to Damascus and asked, "Are you with us or against us?" Sure enough, a few days later the UN Security Council Resolution passed. But the Lebanese government also amended its constitution so that Lahoud could serve another term. The crisis was averted because Lahoud would not push to implement the Security Council's resolution. However, the next day, Hariri resigned—only to run for office again in 2005. But Bashar had seen enough of Hariri. In February 2005, likely at Bashar's request or order, and with assistance from Hezbollah, the equivalent of 2,200 pounds of TNT exploded as Hariri's motorcade passed by, killing Hariri instantly.

Bashar thought that would solve his problems in Lebanon. He was wrong.

No more would the international community pin its hopes for Syria on Bashar Assad's benevolence. Nor did Hariri's assassination further Syria's goals, for Syria's fingerprints were all over it. Soon, under intense international and Lebanese domestic pressure, Bashar withdrew the Syrian army from Lebanon. With the army went his power to dictate events there. And the retreating Syrians left a vacuum, which Iran eagerly filled.

After the 2006 war, Bashar Assad (whom I now will start calling Assad since we are discussing an era beginning six years after Hafez Assad had died) marveled at Hezbollah's survival. He thought Hezbollah's success against the Israelis mirrored his father's supposed success in Syria's 1973 war with Israel. Therefore, he ordered a study to determine whether the Syrian army should model Hezbollah's military organization. And, to keep his financial lifeline secure, he signed a long-term mutual defense and cooperation pact with Iran.

But against Israel, Assad refused to respond to provocations his father might well have. In 2007, Israel destroyed Syria's nuclear reactor, preventing Assad from acquiring nuclear weapons. He did not respond. Then in 2008, a likely Israeli bomb in Damascus killed Imad Mughniyah, Hezbollah's star terrorist. Once again Assad did nothing. Some Syrians saw that as weakness. For a totalitarian government, a perception of weakness, justified or not, can lead to a coup. Still, Assad maintained power.

But things began unraveling for Assad in 2010. Sunnis within Syria questioned his policy towards Hezbollah and Iran. They saw him actively supporting Syrian Shiites and Alawites (Assad's religion and a religion with links to Shiism) to the detriment of the country's Sunni majority. Meanwhile, economic equality was an issue, with Syria's failing economy only widening the gulf between the country's rich and poor. Both trends did not bode well for Assad's survival.

Then came March 2011. The Arab Spring had begun a few months earlier in other Middle Eastern countries. But until then, Syria had mostly avoided the disruptions and massive demonstrations in some Arab countries that had felled their governments. But about a month before, a group of teenagers in Daraa, a Sunni Syrian town, had spray painted a school's exterior walls, writing, "You are next doctor," and, "The people want to bring down the regime." The next day, Syrian security officials arrested the boys along with many others. Most were from important local clans. Word spread that they had been transferred to a regional headquarters in a nearby Druze-dominated province.

That did not bode well.

At a meeting with one of Assad's cousins, who was considered the most powerful person in Daraa, elders from the boys' family, fearing the boys would be tortured, pleaded for their release. He responded, "Forget your children…And if you want new children in their place, then send your wives and we will impregnate them for you."

On March 18, several thousand people protested, calling for the children to be released but also for freedom. The violence escalated, reportedly on pace with the increase in security personnel present. By the end of the day Syrian sharpshooters shot two people dead. Days later, the boys arrested weeks earlier were released alive to their parents after being beaten, burned, and having their fingernails pulled out by grown men in dingy rooms. More protests and more killings by security forces followed. A little more than a month later, security forces arrested another child during a protest, this time thirteen years old. He was returned to his family dead, his corpse showing signs of severe torture, including the amputation of his penis.

Many consider the boys' arrest the trigger which initiated Syria's civil war. Whether true or not, Assad soon found himself on the ropes. This was problematic for Assad, but also for Iran and Hezbollah. Commercial flights from Tehran routinely flew to Damascus loaded with armaments, which then were transferred by truck into Lebanon, and ultimately found their way into Hezbollah's waiting arms. If Syria's government fell, the flow of weapons coming from Iran to Hezbollah was in jeopardy of drying out.

At first, Hezbollah provided Syria with political support to buttress Assad's regime. But in 2012, things got worse for Syria. A bomb killed many Syrian high-security officers and, suffering casualties, with soldiers going AWOL or defecting, Syria's military manpower dwindled.

Next, Iran and Hezbollah tried training volunteer militias to help Assad. Iran also ignored international sanctions imposed on the Syrian regime by sending billions of dollars' worth of weapons and other assistance to Assad.

But in 2013, it was apparent that Assad would need more help. Having no choice, Iran and Hezbollah willingly provided it. Hezbollah sent its military forces into Syria and Iran assembled irregular forces from outside of Syria to come to Assad's aid. Nasrallah boasted, "We are tens of thousands of well-equipped and trained mujahedeen fighters in Lebanon ready for martyrdom. …We are a force…that will surprise every enemy."

However, Nasrallah's decision to enter the fight was not without dissent. Sheikh Subhi al-Tudayli, who led Hezbollah from 1989 to 1991, said "I know the decision [to fight in Syria] is Iranian, and the alternative would have been a confrontation with the Iranians. I know that Lebanese in Hezbollah and Sayyed Hassan Nasrallah more than anyone, are not convinced about this war." Others also opposed sending so many to die in Syria. However, no other Shiite leader in Lebanon could stand up to Nasrallah, and beyond him, Iran. Especially because Hezbollah's intervention served another useful purpose other than helping Assad and Iran—it helped protect Shiites from ISIS and other Sunni extremists then operating within Syria.

And so, despite the losses it knew it would incur, Hezbollah intervened. As a result, along with Iran's help and the aid of Russian military forces that entered Syria in 2015, Assad held on. Now, Hezbollah reaps the rewards. Syria has permitted it, along with Iran, to orchestrate a second front against Israel from Syrian territory abutting the Israel-held Golan Heights.

This intervention was valuable for Hezbollah because its combatants gained experience fighting a more traditional war when fighting in company-sized formations that maintained close contact with modern Russian and Syrian army units. From them, Hezbollah learned logistics, how to call for air strikes, and even in one instance, deploy from helicopters. In essence, it learned how professionals fight a war. Many of its fighters tasted armed combat for the first time—an experience many IDF soldiers have never had. Nevertheless, the knowledge Hezbollah gained did not produce a significant threat of invasion from Syria. Colonel (res.) Boaz Amidror, who for much of his career has dealt with protecting northern Israel from both Hezbollah and the Syrian army, told me that although the Syrian army rebuilt itself, "it is a miserable army," posing little invasion risk to Israel. And that from Hezbollah, along the Golan, the risk is more of a terror attack than an outright attempt to conquer. Especially because, unlike alongside Lebanon, Israeli settlements are for the most part not so close to the border with Syria.

Also, for a while, Israel benefited from Hezbollah's intervention. Not surprisingly, while Hezbollah focused on the fighting in Syria, Israel's borders with Lebanon and Syria were mostly quiet. Hezbollah had no desire for a two-front war, Assad was too busy surviving to bother Israel, and the various Syrian rebel groups astride Israel's border with Syria were much more concerned with events in Syria than the Israelis behind them. During this time the only deadly attack on Israelis in the north was on January 29, 2015, when several Hezbollah anti-tank missiles hit an IDF convoy on a road in Shebaa Farms. Two IDF soldiers died in the explosions and six others were injured.

That attack was in retaliation for an Israeli drone strike ten days before that killed an Iranian general and six Hezbollah operatives in a vehicle traveling on the Syrian side of the Golan Heights. Hezbollah wanted to demonstrate that it would respond to Israeli attacks that killed its members, but it did not want another war. So, Nasrallah sent messages through third parties that he would not do anything else, even if Israel responded with force. When the IDF contented itself with firing some artillery shells, Hezbollah did not fire back.

But war came close that day. The road was jointly used by the IDF and civilian vehicles. If one of those missiles had struck a civilian vehicle and killed non-combatants, war might have ensued.

Other dustups occurred over the next few years, but none killed any Israelis. Although the atmosphere on the border sometimes felt ominous, it was relatively peaceful.

The Russians Arrive

In 2015, Russia showed up in force in Syria. Russia's political connection with Syria had been longstanding, stretching back more than fifty years. And for decades, pursuant to an agreement with Syria, Russia had maintained its only naval base on the Mediterranean at the Syrian port of Tartus. Therefore, when the civil war in Syria flared, it caught Russia's attention. The Russians had enjoyed a good and profitable relationship with Assad, as they did with his father. That interest now morphed into boots on the ground and planes on the tarmac.

Russia moved dozens of aircraft and helicopters, thousands of troops, and advanced air-defense systems to Syria, deploying them at multiple locations. Then, like what is now happening in Ukraine, the Russians waged a relentless and brutal air campaign, mainly against civilians sympathetic to those opposing Assad's regime.

The Russian presence also complicated matters for Israel. Iran's escalating involvement in Syria, combined with Hezbollah's bold entrance into Syria, presented new dangers for Israel. One thing Israel could not allow was its border with Syria to become what the border with Lebanon had already turned into. Neither could Israel turn a blind eye to the rising volume and sophistication of Iranian weaponry crossing through Syria to Hezbollah's armories in Lebanon. To impede both, Israel needed freedom of action to do what it needed to do.

But newly placed Russian surface-to-air missiles were in range of where Israel's air force would have to operate. And Russian ground troops often could be found near the border region close to Iranian or Hezbollah forces deployed there. However, killing Russians, whether accidentally or on purpose, was off-limits and had to be avoided. Israel had no desire to confront a nuclear superpower. Avoiding that type of confrontation required cooperation between the Russian military and the IDF. Would that be possible? What complications would arise? We shall soon see.

By 2016, the stability Israel had enjoyed in the north began to unravel. Before that, for forty years, both Hafez and then Bashar Assad had been known quantities. Both had an interest in keeping Syria stable. Both understood the relative advantage Israel held in power. As such, both were somewhat predictable. The Syrian Civil War, coupled with the increasing involvement of Russia, Iran, and Hezbollah changed that dynamic. It created uncertainty. Now, Bashar Assad owed much to three benefactors, all very much present in Syria. Two of those benefactors, Iran and Hezbollah, were devoted to Israel's destruction and very unpredictable. The third was a nuclear power best not to rumble with. None of them likely cared much about what would happen to the Syrian people, unless, of course, it served their national purposes. And collectively, they served to minimize Assad's ability to dictate events within his own country and manage Syria's confrontation with Israel.

This would turn into a problem for Israel. A problem that might become magnified in any future war with Hezbollah because, for the first time, a war with Hezbollah might no longer be contained to Lebanon. Many in Israel recognize that fact. They warn that a new war with Hezbollah will not be the Third Lebanon War, but instead, The First Northern War.

What that war looks like now, what it may look like in the future, and what Israel has done and must do in the face of that threat, is what what much of the remainder of this book is about. But first, an instructive story about how hard Israel tried to avoid war with Hezbollah, and perhaps for the moment, how little Hezbollah wanted war.

Play Acting at Avivim

Two Russian-made anti-tank missiles raced toward an IDF ambulance on September 1, 2019. Videographers from Al-Manar TV, part of Hezbollah's propaganda arm, were in place to record the glorious explosions moments away. A week before, Israel had launched two operations: one, an airstrike in Syria that killed two Hezbollah operatives set to launch explosive drones into Israel; the second, a drone strike in Beirut that destroyed newly delivered equipment that

Hezbollah planned to use to create PGMs. Now, it was time for payback.

For days, Nasrallah had been warning that Hezbollah would respond to Israel's actions, the most egregious in his eyes being the drone strike into Lebanon. Hezbollah also issued a statement: "If we are silent about this violation, it will put Lebanon on a dangerous course in which an explosive drone will come along every two days and attack targets on our territory." Michel Aoun, Lebanon's president, got into the act too, publicly declaring that "the act of the drone attacks is a declaration of war on Lebanon…." The IDF took those threats seriously, withdrawing many of its forces from bases within eyesight of the border and changing the routes of military traffic so that they did not stray within the approximate three-mile range of Hezbollah's deadly Kornet anti-tank missiles.

But this day, the IDF messed up. An ambulance with five soldiers inside moved speedily along the road between the military base at Avivim and Kibbutz Yiron, both adjacent to the border. The ambulance was in plain view of Hezbollah operatives equipped with the anti-tank missile. The operatives must have been stationed with orders to fire on any military vehicle that came into sight. After all, Al-Manar TV was there, filming from a position on a hill overlooking the road as the ambulance moved away. The video suggests that the missiles delivered a massive explosion to the vehicle.

The reality was somewhat different.

Slowed down, the footage depicts two missiles coming in succession from a position in Lebanon, perpendicular and to the left of the vehicle. Not an easy shot against fast-moving traffic. The first clearly misses. The second possibly strikes the vehicle's rear but did little damage despite the explosion. Fortunately, all five soldiers inside scrambled out without injury. Another missile, not shown by the video, hit an empty area in the IDF's base at Avivim.

Israel responded rapidly, firing up to 100 artillery shells toward Lebanon, many of which may have landed in empty fields.

It's what happened next that makes this incident particularly interesting. A helicopter quickly arrived at Avivim, and soldiers placed a stretcher carrying an injured comrade inside the helicopter, which then took off. Shortly afterward it landed at a base in Haifa, where an Israeli television crew recorded the stretcher and soldier being taken out and moved presumably to the hospital. Meanwhile, reportedly, Nasrallah reached out to Israel by way of Lebanon's prime minister to France, Egypt, and possibly the United States. His message—Hezbollah's attack was retribution for Israel's August attacks, and it did not want any further escalation. In other words, enough is enough. Don't hit us anymore and we will not hit you.

After those few volleys of artillery shells, Israel did nothing more. And it soon became public knowledge that the injured soldier transported on the helicopter was a ruse designed to allow Hezbollah to save face. Fortunately, for all, the IDF did not suffer any injuries and Hezbollah could hold its head high having made the point that it would not tolerate further IDF strikes inside Lebanon (whereas the same does not appear to be the case for the two operatives killed in Syria and future operations). No major war broke out that day because neither side wanted it to. Nevertheless, war might have happened if several IDF soldiers would have been killed or wounded.

This is why the remainder of this book is so important. A future war may break out by accident or design. Therefore, it is crucial to analyze Hezbollah's present capabilities, Iran's role along with its proxies, and what Israel can do now, and should strive to do in the future, to overcome the threat before it. For without that knowledge, we are mere bystanders, lacking understanding of why Israel may act in certain ways, and with no role to play other than to sit helplessly by and watch.

Chapter Twelve

Hezbollah's Capability Today

Until now, we have focused on Hezbollah's growth. Now we will review the challenges Hezbollah presents today and what Israel is doing about them. Later, we'll explore what the future may hold.

Today, the proper way to view Hezbollah's military capabilities is through the lens of a sovereign nation because, unlike a terrorist or guerrilla organization, Hezbollah's military capabilities encompass multiple technologies and disciplines, including:

1. Vast numbers of increasingly accurate missiles
2. UAVs (Drones)
3. Attack tunnels
4. Amphibious capability
5. Cyber capability
6. Advanced communication assets
7. Extensive defensive emplacements
8. Significant ground forces

Collectively, these capabilities exceed those of most nations and present huge challenges to Israel. When combined with Hezbollah's activities in Syria and other Iranian proxies in Gaza, Yemen, and western Iraq, which we will examine in a coming chapter—the threat is staggering.

<u>Missiles</u>

Missiles, essentially, come in two forms: those that go up and down to attack mostly civilian or military targets from a distance; and those that travel more directly and are aimed at specific objects like a tank, ship, or plane. The missiles that go up and down carry larger payloads but are often less accurate—especially the rudimentary models. The missiles that attack a specific object tend to be much more advanced and more accurate but have a shorter range and carry smaller payloads. In general, the first category (up and down missiles) goes after civilians, infrastructure, and military targets spread apart. The second group seeks to destroy mostly nearby individual weapon platforms.

It's the first category of missiles that is the scariest and poses a significant risk to Israeli society. So, let's examine that category first.

Most experts today estimate that Hezbollah possesses 150,000 missiles. Rather than just letting our minds glaze over that number, let's analyze it. Assume Israel's air force has about 300 planes and helicopters capable of striking ground targets with missiles or bombs. That would require each of those aerial platforms to fire or drop about 500 bombs or rockets to equal Hezbollah's firepower in numbers! Viewed another way, Israel has about 8,500 square miles of land exclusive of the West Bank. Having 150,000 missiles means Hezbollah has enough to deliver eighteen of them to every square mile of the country. But it gets worse. At least half of Israel's territory is sparsely populated, thus Hezbollah has enough missiles to deliver thirty-six per square mile of populated areas. When we discuss Israel's infrastructure in a future chapter, you will see how its great concentration only increases the danger it faces. But for now, you get the idea—Hezbollah has a lot of missiles, enough to devastate Israel.

Having a lot of missiles is one thing. But the devastation equation includes other factors, too, such as payload size, accuracy, range, and firing frequency. In addition, the type of fuel they use makes a difference. Solid-fuel missiles can be fired quickly, making it difficult to destroy them before they are fired. Liquid-fueled missiles take more time to launch.

Hezbollah had 13,000 to 15,000 missiles just before the Second Lebanon War and managed to fire 4,000 of them, averaging 117 a day. The IDF destroyed many of Hezbollah's remaining missiles before they were launched, including its longer-range rockets. Nevertheless, when the war ended Hezbollah still possessed many missiles. Afterward, Iran resupplied Hezbollah, first with short-range and medium-range missiles and then, in 2009, with long-range ones. In 2012, Iran added a whole new category to Hezbollah's inventory—precision-guided missiles. Called "PGMs," they present a huge danger to Israel, which I will elaborate on later. However, let's first look at how the missiles got to Lebanon.

Iran's border is about 600 miles from Lebanon. For decades, Iran has wanted to create a land route to transport weapons of war to Hezbollah. It would be the least expensive and the most efficient way to carry large amounts of missiles, other armaments, and personnel. But it would require moving the material and people from Iran to areas in Iraq under Shiite control. Then, trucks would move the cargo into Syria, where it would be transferred to storage facilities. Eventually, the cargo would be loaded into other vehicles headed to the Bekaa Valley in Lebanon and Syria's border with Israel. In 2016, those dreams were closer to coming to fruition than ever before. Three routes showed promise: a northern route through areas of Kurdish-controlled Syria, a more central one, and a southern one.

So far, despite America withdrawing part of its contingent that supported the Kurds, the northern route remains closed to Iranian exploitation. Iran might be able to use the central one (referred to by at least one expert as the "southern route-upper branch") but it is not secure. Therefore, Iran's ability to move high-value or bulky cargo along this route is questionable. The most southern route remains blocked by American forces at the town of al-Tanf whose mission is two-fold: disrupt Islamic State (ISIS) activities and block Iran's use of that route to send supplies to Lebanon and Syria. Those soldiers have been subjected to various attacks by Iranian-supported forces and others, including a thinly veiled air attack with only a half-hour notice by Russia on a component of Syrian opposition fighters within the base. For now, there is no evidence that the United States will remove those troops manning the base at al-Tanf. Should it ever decide to do so, that road route would be open for Iran.

Unable now to create the land bridge it so covets; Iran has two alternatives it can use for moving weaponry and soldiers: sea and air. For a while, Iran tried sending war material to Syrian ports. Cargo ships, like trucks, are an economical way of shipping cargo. But they are also easy to spot and interdict. In addition, they must avoid American, Israeli, and other international surveillance. Over the years, many have been intercepted by those seeking to thwart Iranian designs, despite assorted methods of subterfuge. Has cargo gotten through? Probably. But for the process to be efficient, each ship must have a lot of weapon transshipment in its one basket; therefore, losing a shipment is expensive. And cargo ships are not an optimal way to ship personnel. That leaves flying stuff in.

Iran uses planes to send vast quantities of weapons destined for Hezbollah and many foreign militia fighters to Damascus and other Syrian airports. The amount, however, is limited for now by the few planes Iran has at its disposal for such missions. When those weapons arrive in Damascus, Syrian intelligence officers oversee Hezbollah operatives unloading the planes and then storing the weapons in special compounds before Hezbollah-operated trucks, utilizing small, less obtrusive convoys, move them to Lebanon.

You might ask why Iran doesn't send missiles by plane to Lebanon's international airport in Beirut. When I asked that question of Yossi Kuperwasser, former Director General of the Israel Ministry of Strategic Affairs and present-day Israeli security expert, his answer surprised me. "We have Rules of the Game. Everybody here plays by the Rules of the Game. There are some good rules for us. Some bad rules for us," he said. "Here's the game. Once they reach Syria, you can hit them. If they've managed to reach Lebanon [from Syria], then you cannot." Somewhat incredulous, I wanted to make sure and asked, "So the rules of the game are Israel has to get one chance to hit them?"

"Yeah," Kuperwasser answered. "If they come directly [to Beirut, the IDF can], because otherwise we won't have a chance to hit them." And then he added an explanation, "There is a logic of course behind these rules.…The main issue is that Hezbollah doesn't put Lebanon at risk."

Given that I was aware of reports that Israel has struck PGM factories inside Lebanon without any response from Hezbollah, Kuperwasser's assertion seemed corroborated by facts on the ground. Therefore, a day later, when I said to Professor Freilich that I suspected that Israel does some covert things in Lebanon that are not common knowledge and are asterisks to the rules of the game, I was not surprised when he answered, "Yeah, maybe. I mean, as long as Hezbollah doesn't respond, then it's fine."

But Kuperwasser's and Freilich's responses worried me too. The term "Rules of the Game" might sound comical, but it refers to something deadly serious—perhaps existential. They are a series of unwritten understandings, which are tested constantly. Understandings that if crossed, even unintentionally, could trigger an all-out war. Especially given the level of uncertainty that even the most capable leaders contend with daily, and with the likelihood of human error increasing with the number of confrontations, the chances of one side bending the rules of the game too far are considerable.

*   *   *   *

When assessing the lethality of missiles, we must consider their accuracy, payload, and range. And, by assessing all three variables, we get an idea of how Hezbollah will likely use each missile class as well as the danger they present to Israel.

I promise you, although the terminology used to measure accuracy might seem rather arcane, in practice, it's easy to understand. But before we discuss accuracy, I want to clear up another confusing thing. People, including myself, often use the term "rocket" and "missile" interchangeably. In addition, experts sometimes also use the term "statistical rocket" when counting Hezbollah's supply of missiles. Essentially, a statistical rocket is an inaccurate rocket. Missiles, on the other hand, are accurate. For our purposes, however, you should consider statistical rockets a subset of missiles. Nevertheless, the distinction is irrelevant to the unfortunate person standing near a warhead after it detonates. Hezbollah has 150,000 missiles—most of which are statistical rockets. Half of that total can only reach targets within ten miles of the border, but significant numbers can go as far as Haifa (thirty miles away), and some of the remainder can hit Tel Aviv and targets much farther south. This means that northern Israel is most at risk but the entire country is in the bull's eye of Hezbollah's missiles.

So, let's explain how accuracy is measured by considering the most accurate PGM missiles Hezbollah has in its arsenal, approximately one dozen SCUD-Ds. These missiles can carry a one-ton explosive warhead up to about 450 miles. This means Hezbollah can hit targets all over Israel from the Bekaa Valley with one ton of explosives with devastating effect.

How accurate is the SCUD-D?

Very!

Missile accuracy is described by looking at two numbers that together reflect the percentage chance that a missile will fall within a certain number of feet from its target. The SCUD-D's numbers are 50 percent within 150 feet. That means there is a fifty percent chance that a SCUD-D will land its warhead within 150 feet of its target. Given that one ton of explosives will eviscerate everything within 50 yards of where it hits and do significant damage well beyond that radius, the SCUD-D is an excellent weapon to use against military bases, headquarters, and particular infrastructures like nuclear reactors or industrial plants. What does this mean practically? One warhead would destroy an entire city block. Buildings would collapse, and roads and runways would be heavily cratered at the impact point. People in the open could be killed even farther away.

Next up for deadly weapons Hezbollah possesses: the Fateh-110, also called an M600. These precision-guided missiles carry warheads of more than one-half ton (1,200 pounds) and can travel about 150 miles, sufficient for hitting most of Israel's populated and industrial regions. It has a fifty percent chance of landing within a little more than one-half mile of its target, with a warhead that will devastate buildings in an area the size of "a good chunk of Times Square and maim and kill people four football fields away from the point of impact." Hezbollah would likely use these missiles against larger industrial and military targets or more populated areas where a near miss is good enough, especially if multiple missiles are fired at the same target— improving chances of destroying the target. Hezbollah likely possesses several hundred of these missiles and Iran is trying mightily to develop Hezbollah's capability to build more in factories constructed 150 feet underground in the Bekaa Valley. Even though Fateh-10s are liquid-fueled, their presence in vast numbers would be extremely problematic for Israel.

Next are the Zelzal rockets. They are inaccurate but can carry a 1,300-pound warhead up to 100 miles—perfect for hitting Tel Aviv,

Haifa, and most of the industrialized and populous areas in Israel's center with devastating effects. Hezbollah has dozens if not hundreds of these. And like the Fateh-10, a Zelzal rocket will leave most of any city block it strikes in ruins.

Hezbollah also possesses thousands of Fajr-3 and Fajr-5 rockets. Their range is only about 35 miles, and they can only carry a 120-pound warhead. But even 120 pounds of explosives will prove deadly over a broad area. Hezbollah would likely launch these types of rockets from southern Lebanon, or from slightly beyond that, and aim them toward densely populated Haifa and Hadera and their industrial centers; they wouldn't need precision targeting to cause serious destruction there. Since Fajr-3 and Fajr-5 rockets have just a fifty percent chance of falling within two miles of their targets, Hezbollah would address that by firing several of them at each target. After all, they have many thousands of them and can fire vast numbers at one time.

Then, of course, Hezbollah has more than 100,000 Katyushas of varying types. These rockets will rain terror on northern Israel, especially near the border regions. They are useful for one thing—frightening and killing civilians or soldiers unlucky enough to be where they fall. Their accuracy is abysmal, and their payload is rather small. But they're especially deadly to people caught in the open, and they'll destroy any building they strike, which makes them a terrifying weapon—especially in the massive barrages of them that Hezbollah will launch.

But it gets worse. Over the last few years, Iran has provided Hezbollah with PGM kits that can convert statistical rockets, like the Zelzal or the Fajr-3 and 5, to more accurate missiles. What does this mean? Using technology, no more sophisticated than that found in modern cellphones and in easily obtained hardware, converted rockets can maneuver to correct aiming errors and adjust to atmospheric disturbances, vastly improving their accuracy and making them more elusive making their interception more difficult and costly.

Where are all Hezbollah's missiles? Most are in southern Lebanon south of the Litani River, which Hezbollah calls its first line of defense—especially the shorter-range ones including the Katyushas, and the Grad and Fajr multiple rocket launch systems. All are stored in populated areas. But the longer-range missiles are based all over Lebanon in areas under Hezbollah's control. The longest-range ones are mostly in the Bekaa Valley, difficult for Israeli ground troops to get at. The thousands of Hezbollah's medium-range missiles also do not need to be based in southern Lebanon to hit many targets worth their large payloads. Likely, many of them are stored with shorter-range missiles in at least six regions north of the Litani River as reported by an *Alma* researcher. After confiscating land from its owners and barring civilians from entering, Hezbollah specified those areas as military zones. In September 2020, a mysterious explosion in one of those locations destroyed a building. It was one *Alma* had identified as being used to store Hezbollah missiles.

The missiles, mostly stationary, are intertwined with civilian life and tucked behind human shields. So much so that per an article written by Jonathan Schanzer, one former Israeli official said, "Every third house in Shia neighborhoods contains a military asset of [Hezbollah]." Hezbollah believes the chance of killing civilians, and bearing the brunt of the world's outrage, will deter Israel from trying to destroy the missiles. Many installations use hydraulic mechanisms that raise the missile and its launcher from the interior of a civilian building to its rooftop before launch. Others are hidden by vegetation. Some, instead, are on launchers mounted on vehicles that can be moved at will. Hezbollah has made those vehicles look like civilian trucks.

In addition to the missiles that go up and down, Hezbollah has also collected numerous rockets designed to fire directly at a specific, often moving, target. In 2006, a Hezbollah shore-to-sea missile almost sunk an Israeli naval ship. Now, Hezbollah possesses hundreds of these missiles, many with increased range and payload size as well as sophisticated guidance systems. They are harder for Israeli systems to interdict and are deployed along Lebanon's coast. From there, with their 200-mile range, they would impede Israeli naval operations in a war, could strike Israeli gas drilling facilities at sea, and present a threat to international ships seeking to unload their products in Haifa. In addition, Iran has provided advanced surface-to-air missiles that can attack aerial targets up to thirty-five miles away and at much higher altitudes than weapons systems it previously possessed. In wartime, they will challenge IAF aircraft at lower altitudes and could be a deadly adversary for IAF helicopters on strike missions or carrying troops, whether in Lebanon or near the border in Israel. And finally, Hezbollah possesses very advanced anti-tank missile systems. In the 2006 war, Hezbollah anti-tank missiles damaged more than fifty IDF tanks. Now, they are deployed in all Shiite villages in southern Lebanon. Although the IDF has greatly improved the durability of its tanks to help them endure attacks from these systems, including adding reactive armor and anti-missile systems, it's still unclear how they'll perform when multiple missiles are launched in their direction.

Unmanned Aerial Vehicles

Unmanned aerial vehicles (UAVs), also known as drones, were once used exclusively in high-tech countries like Israel and the United States but are now ubiquitous around the globe. Some are used recreationally; others in the construction and agriculture industries; but their growing use in armed conflict has become increasingly prominent. UAVs, among other things, can be used to conduct surveillance and deliver bombs and missiles with pinpoint accuracy. Some are as small as a couple of feet in all dimensions. Others are surprisingly large. Many can stay in the air for hours and a few have ranges exceeding 1,000 miles. Unlike jets and planes, UAVs don't require their pilots to be in harm's way. People on the ground and even in office-like settings can guide them into combat zones, and despite their small payloads, they are the ultimate precision-guided missile. UAVs are also cheap, which makes them a perfect terrorist weapon and a potential game changer for sovereign nations and militant groups. Hezbollah is fully aware of these features. It possesses sophisticated UAVs courtesy of Iran. Less sophisticated UAVs can be purchased from many sources.

In 2004, Hezbollah flew a primitive UAV about ten feet long, over Israel's coastal city of Nahariya. Nasrallah later bragged that Hezbollah could have loaded it with forty pounds of explosives and dropped the bomb anywhere in Israel. That one, however, crashed at sea after buzzing the city. A second flight a few months later successfully returned to Lebanon. Then, during the 2006 war, the IAF shot down several of Hezbollah's UAVs. Iran replenished Hezbollah's supply.

By 2010, Israel's counterterrorism units learned that Hezbollah possessed UAVs armed with explosives that could fly up to 200 miles. In 2012, Hezbollah again tried to penetrate Israeli air space with a UAV and again an IAF fighter shot it down. More Hezbollah UAVs followed and in 2017 the IDF shot down another one that had entered Israeli airspace by way of Syria. This time a patriot missile destroyed the UAV. Then in 2018, Iran launched a UAV from Syria, testing Israeli defenses once again. An IAF Apache helicopter shot it down.

Hezbollah launches its longer-range UAVs from airstrips in the Bekaa Valley built for that purpose. From there, not only did Hezbollah use them to conduct surveillance over Israel, but it also employed them against Syrian rebels in Syria.

Over time, Hezbollah has amassed a fleet of at least 2,000 UAVs, most of them small and provided by Iran. But small comes with an advantage. They don't need airfields to take off and many are kamikaze UAVs, designed to strike a target but not return. They can be launched from cars, boats, or even canisters—making them impossible to destroy before being launched. And Hezbollah has attempted to upgrade its capabilities. In 2020, two Lebanese brothers in an American court pled guilty to conspiring to purchase parts for upgrading Hezbollah's UAVs, violating American export law. The parts included digital compasses, engines, and other items to improve navigation and flight.

One might ask what is the danger? Besides each UAV's obvious ability to transmit critical intelligence information and attack specific targets, launched in a swarm, with preprogrammed waypoints that eliminate the need for individual controllers, they cause an incredible headache for defenses. As we have seen, Israel has done a credible job shooting down individual UAVs, but how would it fare against a swarm of them? That happened in September 2019 in Saudi Arabia when Iran (with or without the help of its proxy in Yemen, the Houthis) devised a scheme to attack a huge Saudi oil facility.

Taking an indirect route, eighteen drones raced towards the Abqaiq oil facility in the hours before dawn. The Saudis, knowing Abqaiq might be targeted, had protected it with multiple air defenses to no avail. The UAVs came in two waves, both of which struck the facility. Their GPS guidance systems ensured the UAVs struck the intended target. Several weeks passed before the site was producing oil again. As a result, the world's oil supplies temporarily dropped five percent.

Stopping similar UAV swarms from attacking targets in Israel would be difficult, but not impossible. GPS denial systems and radio jamming could do the trick. But UAVs with their own artificial intelligence or optical systems would have to be disabled by a direct strike. And, of course, Hezbollah would deploy swarms while also surging thousands of missiles through Israeli airspace. The truth is, in that environment, there are a lot of unknowns. And undeniably, UAVs traveling to preprogrammed locations or being directed by pilots from afar give Hezbollah a weapon system that, when combined with its massive missile inventory, might overwhelm Israeli defenses.

Tunnels

Attack Tunnels

For years, residents of northern Israel had warned that Hezbollah was digging tunnels under the border fence into Israel. They thought they could hear the digging. The IDF didn't acknowledge their concerns and did nothing in response.

Until December 4, 2018.

It turns out that the IDF had been aware for months that Hezbollah had been digging tunnels now extending over the border into Israel but said nothing. But by the beginning of December, the danger of inaction outweighed the need to preserve the secrecy of the IDF's detection capability. Hezbollah planned to use the tunnels to funnel motivated, well-trained fighters, called the Radwan force, into Israel, where they would divide into two groups. Group one would capture one or more border villages, likely Metula at the northern tip of Israel and Za'arit, close to where Hezbollah kidnapped the two IDF soldiers in 2006. The second group would block roads at strategic points near the tunnel exits that IDF soldiers would use to reclaim the captured towns. For example, only one road leads to Metula—which snakes up a hill and is flanked by a cliff on the left and rough terrain on the right. One of the tunnels had an exit sited to minimize the distance Radwan forces would have to travel to establish defensive positions along the road. From there, they would be difficult to dislodge and would buy time for the first group to complete its nefarious task. Combined with a barrage of rockets, Hezbollah would then have had hours or even days to do what it wanted in the captured villages—kill, kidnap, destroy, and propagandize by beaming video images throughout the world of the first Arab capture of an Israeli village since the 1948 war.

The IDF found six tunnels crossing the border and either demolished them with explosives or blocked them by pouring concrete into them. One video on the internet shows wet concrete coming from Israel and pouring into a factory in the Lebanese village of Kafr Kila—proof that Hezbollah has endangered Lebanese citizens by constructing tunnels in civilian areas. Other tunnels snake towards the border but have not crossed under it. These remain intact, and UNIFIL has not taken any steps to ensure their destruction.

I wish I could be certain that all the tunnels have been found. Most experts I spoke to think that is the case. But tunnels are hard to find, and many exist on the Lebanese border close to Israel. Could the IDF have missed one? Could Hezbollah try to surreptitiously extend under the border one of the tunnels already in Lebanon? History shows anything is possible. After the ceasefire that ended the 2006 war, the IDF found a large bunker complex in Lebanon that spread over three-quarters of a square mile and traveled as deep as 120 feet. It contained firing positions, ammo storage facilities, operating rooms, latrines, kitchens, and even hot and cold running water. Parts of it came within 100 yards of a UNIFIL post. An Israeli border post had an open view of the ground above another part. Yet its construction and operation had passed unnoticed. Sure, the IDF possesses amazing new technology for detecting tunnels. But equally sure is human ingenuity. I would not count Hezbollah out on that score.

What is startling about these tunnels—besides that UNIFL did not discover and halt their construction—was their size. Hezbollah heavily invested in their construction. Some were large enough to accommodate vehicles. Another stretched more than a half-mile. All went through hard rock. They were amazing but expensive feats of engineering that were, and perhaps will continue to be, integral to Hezbollah's war plans.

Defensive Tunnels

On August 12, 2021, *Alma* published a report by Tal Beeri entitled "Hezbollah's 'Land of Tunnels.' – the North Korean-Iranian Connection" In it, Beeri describes an enormous, triangular network of tunnels extending tens of miles that connect Hezbollah's strongholds in Beirut, the Bekaa Valley, and southern Lebanon. In addition, sub-tunnels link lines of defense in southern Lebanon. Beeri believes the tunnel network extends a total of 100 miles or more. Collectively, they allow Hezbollah to move forces safely and secretly between regions. Using North Korean know-how along with Iranian support, they permit "hundreds of combatants, fully equipped" to use them. Unlike the tunnels described in the previous section, most are infrastructure tunnels that support war efforts.

They contain sections for headquarters, weapons and supplies, and field clinics. In addition, they boast shafts that allow operatives to fire missiles at Israel and weapon systems that target IDF ground forces that come within range. Those shafts are camouflaged and open and close as needed to fire weapons. Beeri also thinks that small vehicles can maneuver inside the tunnels, which would allow Hezbollah to rapidly deploy forces small and large, surprising its enemies.

Amphibious Capability

Over the decades, Israel's northern coast, especially a few miles south of Lebanon near Nahariyah, has seen its share of Palestinian terrorists arriving by sea from bases in Lebanon. Hezbollah is seeking to copy the Palestinian seaborne playbook and improve on it. It has an amphibious unit trained in Iran to use fast-attack boats, semi-submersible vehicles, and undersea swimmer mechanisms to speed them to Israel's coastline and ports. There, they can come ashore or just affix explosive devices to ships. Israel's navy deploys patrols to stop such an attack. In fact, from the top of Rosh Hanikra, a high, rocky point along the coast of the Mediterranean that I have visited on many occasions, an Israeli patrol vessel can always be seen not too far offshore to the south. To the north, just feet away, lies Lebanon.

Cyber Capability

Here again, Iran has driven Hezbollah's development of another weapon system, this time cyber. Hezbollah now has a cyber unit capable of both defending its networks and launching offensives that can collect information or penetrate government networks to destroy or alter their functionality. Under Iran's tutelage, Hezbollah has become so capable that Major General (ret.) Yaakov Amidror says, "Hezbollah is essentially Iran's sub-contractor on this."

Now, through a special unit, Hezbollah uses social media and other media outlets to wage psychological and curated informational warfare. And its ability is so great for manipulating photographs and for creating and using fake social media accounts that avoid censorship, it now teaches courses in those subjects, for a fee, to those in the Arab world who are interested. The student has become the teacher—for profit.

Hezbollah's cyber unit, in addition to targeting Israel, provides a domestic political benefit that helps sustain its power in Lebanon. By breaking into cellular phones, intercepting Wi-Fi signals, and collecting information from a variety of social media networks and databases—private and governmental—Hezbollah keeps tabs on the private actions of Lebanese citizens and Lebanon's government. Also, the unit collects information about Arab adversaries in the Gulf Region.

In 2010, a somewhat sophomoric, but effective, Facebook false flag operation, if you can call it that, took place. It took a year to discover it. Hezbollah hackers created a fake Facebook account for a female with an image of a beautiful woman "lying on a sofa." Not surprisingly, young IDF soldiers responded favorably to her friend requests. Also not surprisingly, they readily divulged information about their bases, other IDF personnel, and even codes.

An example of targeting that Hezbollah might try at some point was Iran's attempt to infiltrate computer networks at Israeli water and waste management facilities in 2020. Despite its sophistication, the attack failed. But elsewhere, in and outside Israel, attacks on private businesses and infrastructure have met with varied success. Especially the practice of hacking into and controlling servers throughout the world, in which Hezbollah has been complicit. By doing so, Hezbollah has created virtual private networks emanating unobtrusively from those servers. Those illicit networks permit Hezbollah to communicate secretively with its minions around the world.

In addition, between 2012 and 2015, Hezbollah, through an internal group named "Lebanese Cedar," launched a cyber-attack now named "Volatile Cedar." It targeted individuals, companies, and institutions worldwide. By embedding malware on their computers, Hezbollah gained the ability to glean valuable private information. This group is now actively trying to access databases in hundreds of companies worldwide. And in 2018, the Czech Republic discovered and removed Hezbollah malware in its servers that Hezbollah had downloaded to cell phones all around the globe that had fallen prey to its phishing tactics.

Hezbollah's present control of the Ministry of Communications in Lebanon makes such activity easier to undertake without the Lebanese government interfering because now Hezbollah manages Lebanon's communication network. And, by ousting two private concerns that formerly took care of that for Lebanon, Hezbollah has created a potentially huge profit center for itself. Just another example of how Hezbollah's state-within-a-state status allows it to feed on its host.

All told, whether on its own or at the behest of Iran, Hezbollah's cyber capabilities are immense and growing. Given the uncertain nature of cyber warfare, only one thing is certain, in a general conflict with Israel, surprises are guaranteed.

Advanced Communication Assets

Initially, Hezbollah had to make do with Lebanon's institutional communication structure. But that left the organization exposed to many security concerns. Therefore, Iran funded and improved Hezbollah's cellular communications by constructing a parallel high-frequency network that featured encryption. Hezbollah also installed fiber-optic cabling that connected Shiite villages and Hezbollah's command center. Those lines made communicating safer and transferring more data, such as video, faster. And it made Hezbollah's communications more robust. Think of those links as a spider web; severing one thread does not stop communication from running through a different thread.

Lebanon's communication minister between 2005 and 2008, Marwan Hamadeh, was not a proponent of Hezbollah. However, he recognized the importance of what Iran had done when he said that Hezbollah controlling its own communication system was "a strategic victory for Iran since it creates an important Iranian outpost in Lebanon, bypassing Syria." Thanks to Iran, Hezbollah obtained an important indicium of a nation-state—control of its own communications. That, along with its army, television station (Al-Manar), and social services such as an educational system and hospitals—is all that many true sovereign nations can boast. So, too, can Hezbollah.

As we have already seen, Lebanon's government saw the danger of Hezbollah's communication network when it tried to dismantle it in May 2008. Hezbollah recognized the danger it narrowly avoided and maneuvered to make sure it would not happen again. Afterward, it forced the government to agree that communications ministers in the future be Hezbollah supporters. Since then, Lebanon's government has made no further attempt to interfere with Hezbollah's communications.

Extensive Defensive Emplacements

Now southern Lebanon is one big defensive complex backed by more of the same north of the Litani River. Hezbollah has converted southern towns and villages into fortifications complete with tunnels, bunkers, and embedded IEDs. The tunnels have ventilation, multiple exits, and electricity, and are lined with concrete. Some believe they extend north of the Litani River.

The practical impact of these tunnels is that Hezbollah fighters can pop up in front of or behind IDF soldiers, maneuver around them, set ambushes, and escape when needed. The IEDs no longer require the presence of fighters to detonate them. Instead, they can be set to explode based on the heat of passing vehicles or even the presence of active electronic jamming. In 2006, much of Hezbollah's underground effort was what the IDF began calling the "nature preserves" outside of built-up areas. Now, it is the reverse.

Why?

Because Hezbollah has no problem risking the lives of civilians if it helps kill Israelis. Inside towns, the tunnels are harder to detect and more difficult to destroy. Rather than move quickly to overwhelm the enemy, IDF units entering Lebanon will have to move slowly and methodically through the choke points built-up areas provide—and accept the casualties that will result. In the open, the reverse would be true. Hezbollah would not be able to stand up to the IDF. As a result, all southern Shiite towns from the border to the Litani River and up to the Zahrani River have been incorporated into Hezbollah's main defenses against ground attacks. And in addition to the tunnels, as discussed earlier, every village has hidden missiles. Lots of them. South of the Litani River, they are of the short and medium-range types. UNIFIL, whose operating area is south of the Litani, has done nothing to stop their proliferation. North of the Litani, medium-range missiles predominate. All told, every predominately Shiite area is a bristling fortress.

*   *   *   *

Taken together, Hezbollah's offensive and defensive capability is astonishing and exceeds that of most nations, including many in Europe. And all of it is dedicated to Israel's destruction. Long- and medium-range missiles plus UAVs will strike the industrial heartland of Israel in any future war while short-range rockets plus mortars and small UAVs will be used to cause panic in the north, resulting in long lines of refugees. Meanwhile, Hezbollah will use its entrenched forces and anti-ship, anti-tank, and anti-air missile capabilities to slow and bleed the IDF. Under cover of that, Hezbollah will try with its specialized forces to snatch a town or two for propaganda purposes and use information warfare to promote a dual message: Lebanese suffering and Hezbollah's valor and victory. In total, Hezbollah hopes that the confusion it creates, augmented by disruption from its cyber activities, will weaken Israel's military, destroy its economy, and eviscerate its people's will to endure.

As dark as this chapter has been, it is mostly an analysis of potential. Soon, we will discuss Israel's defensive and offensive capabilities—neither of which is insignificant. However, first, we will delve deep into an ongoing war Hezbollah has waged for decades against Israel abroad to mete out terror, and against the nations of the world to fund its operations. How has Hezbollah managed that? By developing and using its sprawling terrorist and criminal enterprises that have global reach and impact, from which no nation is safe. And it is to that we now turn.

Chapter Thirteen

Hezbollah in the World

Special Prosecutor Alberto Nisman planned to shake Argentina's government to its core on January 19, 2015. He was scheduled to present evidence that Argentina's president, Cristina Kirchner, had collaborated with Iran to help cover up its role in the bombing of the AMIA Jewish Community Center in Buenos Aires. But he never showed up. Instead, Nisman's mother found him dead the night before, killed by a gunshot to his head, a gun under his left shoulder. The official version was that he committed suicide. But he had no gunpowder residue on his hands even though the type of gun found would leave some. The location of the gun made no sense because Nisman was right-handed. Nor was there any hint that Nisman suffered from any psychological malady. Two years later, an Argentine federal judge reversed the suicide finding, calling it murder.

Who killed him? We can suspect but we don't know with certainty. What we do know is who was behind the bomb that killed eighty-five and wounded three hundred at the Jewish Community Center on July 18, 1994. Hezbollah.

Why in Argentina? Because Hezbollah was already there, with the human infrastructure necessary to support the operation. Hezbollah frequently takes advantage of the Shiite diaspora living throughout the world. South America has a particularly localized advantageous location, known as the tri-border area, 800 miles north of Buenos Aires, where the borders of Argentina, Paraguay, and Brazil meet.

Here, those three nations declared the region a free-trade zone. It's also a free-crime zone. Blessed with rivers, lakes, and forests many regions would envy, those same topological features make it easy to hide nefarious deeds. Therefore, it was not long before gangs and traffickers made their appearance. As did stolen goods and counterfeiting operations. The tri-border area's large Shiite population also presented an opportunity for Hezbollah, which since its beginning has always been eager to supplement the benefits Iran bestows on it with income gained from criminal activity and donations (whether knowing, coerced, or innocently given).

Seeking to escape the violence and economic disruption, the Lebanese Civil War motivated one million civilians to leave Lebanon over the following fifteen years. Many of them were Shiite. Large numbers settled in the tri-border area. With them came Hezbollah. Then, in a pattern repeated elsewhere, such as in Africa, Shiite clerics helped cultivate agents and sympathizers for Hezbollah that used mosques, businesses, and even schools as cover. Soon, organized Hezbollah cells sprouted, some of the sleeper variety that would only be activated when required. The active cells sent cash back to Hezbollah's coffers in Lebanon.

In the tri-border region, Hezbollah mastered the art of diversification. Hezbollah seed money proved instrumental in opening a travel agency that made travel arrangements for Hezbollah's terrorist and criminal endeavors while also laundering money from other illicit activities. Netflix's series "Ozark" provides a perfect example of how laundering works—injecting "dirty money" into legitimate businesses and then using transactions and bookkeeping sleight of hand to conceal its source. Other operations counterfeited money and targeted shopkeepers who had family back in Lebanon to pay protection money. Also, fake charities bilked many innocent people. All possibly run out of a four-story shopping center that Argentine police once called the "regional command post for

Hezbollah." Located in Ciudad del Este, the headquarters was (and may somewhere still be) in Paraguay's second-largest city, which is adjacent to Brazil and conveniently close to Argentina. From that safe zone, its tentacles extended to Chile, Miami, New York, and even as far as Hong Kong. Collectively, millions flowed back each year to Hezbollah's coffers in Lebanon—reportedly fifty million per year from that region alone. Still, even though Hezbollah's primary goal was to make money through mostly illegal means, it had another reason to build a base for operations in the tri-border area—to fulfill or facilitate Iran's terrorist agenda when called to do so.

That Iranian terrorist agenda came to the fore on July 18, 1994.

Planning began a year before when Iranian officials selected the AMIA building as a target and Supreme Leader Khamenei, issued a fatwa in support of the operation. The AMIA building, located in Buenos Aires, contained a community center for the largest Jewish community in South America. Iran then ordered the guy who seemed always in charge of the most heinous operations, Imad Mughniyeh, to execute the attack, which he did with his customary efficiency. Nasrallah ordered other members of Hezbollah in the tri-border area to assist. That led to the recruitment of the designated suicide bomber, Ibrahim Berro, who lived in the region. Berro was no stranger to the suicide game. In 1989, his brother launched a suicide attack against Israeli soldiers in Lebanon.

Several days before the planned event, Berro came to Buenos Aires. Two days before, Mughniyeh's henchmen parked a van loaded with explosives in a garage close to the AMIA building. Not satisfied with the van's capacity to carry enough explosives to make a gargantuan blast, mechanics had previously fitted it with new shock absorbers and larger wheels on its rear axles to increase its capability. Several hours before, Berro called family members in Lebanon, telling them he was "about to join his brother."

At 9:53 a.m., Berro raced the van down Pasteur Street before slamming the brakes hard in front of the Jewish Community Center and crashing into the building. Moments later a massive explosion emanating from the van ripped through the area. Half the building collapsed, leaving corpses mixed with wounded under the rubble. Hezbollah operatives, who had slipped into the country to assist with the attack, left two hours before the bomb went off. The local Iranian designated commander of the nefarious group, a religious leader in the area's Muslim community, did not need to slink away. Iran had named him one of its diplomats four months before.

The community center bombing, however, was not the first time Hezbollah operatives had attacked Buenos Aires' Jewish community. Two years before, on March 17, 1992, another van filled with explosives, this time a Ford F-100, also driven by a Hezbollah suicide bomber, ended its journey on the sidewalk in front of the Israeli Embassy. The ensuing explosion set off by the driver, destroyed the front facade of the embassy and a consulate building nearby, killing twenty-three and injuring 242. Most were in the buildings, but casualties included a Roman Catholic priest on the sidewalk and several children at a nearby school. After all, suicide bombing is not a precise business.

Hezbollah proudly took responsibility, claiming it was retribution for Israel's killing of Abbas al-Musawi a month before, an act that also took the life of his five-year-old son, Hussein (see Chapter Five). Hezbollah's statement, made through its Islamic Jihad alter ego, said, "With all pride…the operation of the martyr infant Hussein is one of our continuing strikes against the criminal Israeli enemy in an open-ending war, which will not cease until Israel is wiped out of existence." Hezbollah also claimed responsibility for the AMIA bombing, saying that it was a response to Israeli commandos capturing an Amal leader in Lebanon. However, the true reason for that heinous act remains cloudy. Substantial evidence exists that Iran had ordered Hezbollah to strike both targets in response to Argentina ending its nuclear cooperation with Iran. Nevertheless, Hezbollah's hands were all over that operation. And collectively, between the two terrorist acts, more than 100 died and 400 were wounded. A scorecard Hezbollah could be proud of while also sending tens of millions of dollars home to finance more mayhem.

Over the course of this chapter, we will explore some of Hezbollah's more famous international terrorist operations, the vast scope of its criminal enterprises throughout the world, its gun smuggling operations, its training of other Iranian proxy terrorists, and its extensive infiltration of the United States. Tendrils are everywhere, especially where Shiites congregate—whether in South America, Africa, Europe, or even Detroit and New York. But their presence does not answer the question posed below:

Why Does Hezbollah Engage in Foreign Operations?

Matthew Levitt, a leading scholar on Hezbollah, answers the question posed above in his fascinating eight-part podcast, *Breaking Hezbollah's Golden Rule.* He said that Hezbollah participated early on in international terrorism at Iran's behest because it shares Iran's goal of exporting the Shia Islamist revolution to the world and that by doing so, Hezbollah "demonstrate[d] it was a capable and loyal proxy force [for Iran]." The same continues to be true today.

However, Hezbollah also needs money. Lots of it. Maintaining one of the largest military forces in the world while providing services to the Shiite community in Lebanon and simultaneously dominating Lebanese domestic politics does not come cheap. In 2018, the U.S. Treasury Department reported that Iran then paid Hezbollah about 700 million annually and that it also rakes in another 300 million per year from its worldwide criminal activities, most of which now comes from the drug trade. Others estimate that Hezbollah receives a billion or more each year from its international illicit activities. Whatever the number, it is staggering and necessary for what one U.S. government official called the "A-team of terrorism."

Why is it necessary? Because things happen.

In 2009, Iran temporarily reduced its payments to Hezbollah by forty percent due to Iran's internal economic issues stemming from international sanctions. Those sanctions required Hezbollah to embark on an austerity program, something that if continued for a long time could endanger its hold on supporters and Lebanon alike. Therefore, creating supplemental sources of income was good business. Not only would that ensure a steady cash flow, but it also would provide some measure of independence from Iran. Hezbollah's independence will be necessary should Iran issue orders it disobeys, or should Iran suffer from sanctions or attacks on its nuclear infrastructure that might again disrupt subsidy payments to its kindred soul in Lebanon. And, of course, Hezbollah's intervention in the Syrian Civil War, costly in lives and armaments, was expensive. So is its ongoing attempt to establish itself along Syria's border with Israel.

However, Hezbollah does not operate willy-nilly. It follows a plan that it has twice re-shaped. The first time was in 2010 when Iran and Hezbollah agreed on a terror strategy that would prioritize targeting three groups—Israeli tourists, Israeli government targets like members of the diplomatic corps and retired government officials, and Jewish communities worldwide. Israeli tourists, an especially soft target, became Hezbollah's responsibility. Then, in 2020, an American drone strike killed Qasem Soleimani. Soleimani, revered in Iran and reviled by the civilized world, was an extremely capable leader responsible for Iran's international terror and clandestine operations. His successes and connections powered his rise to becoming, perhaps, the second most powerful personage in Iran. His demise left a huge hole. Hezbollah, with Iran's blessing, in a reformation of the plan now seeks to fill that void by taking more of a leadership role in coordinating activities by Iran's other proxies in Iraq, Syria, Gaza, and elsewhere. Once only focused on Lebanon's border with Israel, Hezbollah's gaze extends throughout the region and the world.

A Quick Survey of Hezbollah in Africa, Asia, South America, and Europe

So much terror, so much crime. So much suffering and coercion. And so few pages to cover it all. Successful operations number in the hundreds, victims in the thousands, and money in the billions. And that telling does not consider what is unknown or what has been unsuccessful. Nor does it properly account for the scale of operations or what likely is unfolding today. And then, following this part of the chapter, will come a section recounting Hezbollah's operations in the United States. Combined, the level of activity is shocking, but the detail is mind-numbing. Covering it all would fill volumes. To list them would be meaningless to the reader. Therefore, rather than bore you, I will resist my temptation to detail all, and instead satisfy myself, and hopefully you, with a few stories that will give you a taste of what Hezbollah is doing.

But before I do, I need to tell you about something well worth checking out. It is an interactive map created by Matthew Levitt that is found at www.washingtoninstitute.org/hezbollahinteractivemap/. Based on open-source materials, it documents what is publicly known, but obviously, not what remains classified. Still, the amount of information there is vast and growing (as of now, more than 1,500 Hezbollah-related events worldwide are contained in the map's database). Each event is linked by date and location. You can search by country, date, or a myriad of other filters. The information available is comprehensive. But if you have better things to do with your time, the following examples should suffice.

Africa

West Africa, like South America, has a large diaspora of Shiite Lebanese. They first came in 1903, seeking to escape their difficult lives in southern Lebanon where poverty was endemic. There, they found Christine Maronites who had previously fled Lebanon for financial reasons or to avoid the Ottoman Empire conscripting their sons into the army. Eventually, the Shiite population numbered more than the overall Lebanese Christian population in West Afria. When more radical Shiites arrived in the 1970s, the Lebanese there became much more politicized.

When Lebanon's civil war began, West African Lebanese sent money back to factions they supported in Lebanon to aid their war efforts—often money generated from illegal activities, including blackmail of legitimate businesses. Then, when Hezbollah took hold in Lebanon, so too did Hezbollah operatives arrive in increasing numbers in West Africa where, taking a page from their brethren in South America, they shook down local Shiites for more money by threatening the safety of their relatives in Lebanon. There, with corruption everywhere, a lack of legal enforcement, and large numbers of innocent Shiites to mask them; Hezbollah operatives hide in plain sight and those injured or needing a break from stress elsewhere can recuperate without fear. So, too, can they operate their criminal enterprises, which, peculiar to Africa, includes the diamond trade. It also includes a pipeline of drugs straight from the South American cartels, transited by Shiite communities through western Africa, to eagerly awaiting arms, mouths, and noses in Europe.

Arabia

In December 1983, over a period of minutes, six blasts hit buildings housing American and French embassy personnel and others doing business in Kuwait. At the American Embassy, four died, another fifty were injured. Explosions at the French Embassy, Kuwait International Airport, and oil-related installations killed and maimed others—all at the behest of Iran—and assisted by Hezbollah operatives. Kuwaiti authorities arrested seventeen individuals who became known as the Kuwait 17. For the next decade, Hezbollah would engage in terrorist operations designed to force their release, including one in which it hijacked a Kuwaiti plane, took it to Iran, and during which Hezbollah operatives killed two Americans, one of whom they tortured unmercifully, while also treating the other surviving Americans abusively.

Saudi Arabia has also seen its share of Hezbollah terrorist involvement. The deadliest was the bombing of Khobar Towers in 1996, which killed nineteen U.S. Air Force members and injured hundreds more Americans and those of other nationalities. The perpetrators were Iran and a terrorist Shiite organization in Saudi Arabia known as Saudi Hezbollah. However, important for understanding the worldwide role of the subject of this book, Lebanese Hezbollah played an important part too as documented in a criminal indictment filed in Federal Court in Virginia. That document, and other reporting, makes clear that a Lebanese Hezbollah operative had helped assemble the 5,000 pounds of explosives incorporated in the bomb and had helped load it onto the truck that penetrated the American compound before it detonated. The explosion left a crater eighty-five feet wide and thirty-five feet deep. The indictment also documents Lebanon Hezbollah's extensive involvement in training Saudi operatives in Lebanon. This chain of events—an order emanating from Lebanon, then Hezbollah training and/or oversight of foreign operatives in Lebanon, and then subsequent use of those local operatives to accomplish a terror act—was a modus operandi that would be duplicated many times over in the years to come.

<u>Asia</u>

A truck left a department store parking lot in Bangkok, Thailand on March 11, 1994, heading for the Israeli Embassy 250 yards away. Unfortunately for the driver, and fortunately for the embassy, a parked motorcycle taxi blocked the exit. Nonplussed, the truck driver crashed into the motorcycle and then headed for his target. But two other motorcycle riders, not liking what they saw, raced to stop the truck a few yards beyond. The truck driver flashed some cash in hopes of sending the do-gooders on their way. But they refused, insisting that the truck driver exit his vehicle. That gave time for the owner of the damaged motorcycle to angrily confront the driver. Not liking how things were developing, the driver indicated in sign language he had to make a call and disappeared into a nearby shopping center. Not surprisingly, he never came back.

When the police arrived, they did little other than impound the truck. Stuck with the abandoned vehicle, the police called the owner. That's when things got weird.

Upon arrival, the owner noticed that her truck had been altered. Film tinted the windows on the driver's side, making it hard to see the person driving. Also, the storage compartment had been reconfigured and an extra spring added. By doing so, the truck could now carry more cargo than normal; it could also carry a ton more of weight than its typical load. All of which was necessary, for inside the truck the owner and the police found a water tank filled with more than 2,000 pounds of fertilizer, C4 plastic explosives for use as a catalyst to initiate an inferno, and a mechanism to set it all off. Also present was a leather bag with Arabic writing on it.

The owner admitted that the person renting the truck had not supplied her with the standard documents usually required.

Therefore, she had imposed a condition that one of her employees had to drive the truck. Too bad for the employee. In addition to the fertilizer, police found his strangled body inside the water tank. Although Thai police arrested an Iranian national several weeks later and charged him with the attempted terrorist act, the configuration of the truck bore Hezbollah's signature, closely resembling methods used in the Beirut bombings in 1983 and 1984 and the AMIA bombing in Buenos Aires months later. Five years later, Philippine authorities arrested a Hezbollah operative who disclosed Hezbollah's role in the 1994 bombing attempt in Thailand as well as other Hezbollah activities throughout Southeast Asia. Unsatisfied, Hezbollah tried again in 2012, but again was stymied when explosives carried by a Hezbollah operative exploded prematurely.

Europe

Hezbollah initiated its terror operations in Europe on November 13, 1983, when bombs exploded at a train station and on a train. Two years later bombs in Copenhagen and at a synagogue injured twenty-two. Then came an onslaught in France. Hezbollah, at Iran's direction, planted bombs at fifteen locations over ten months. Germany did not escape the blitz. There, Hezbollah operatives, at Iran's direction, assassinated a leader of the Kurdish movement and three others while they ate at a restaurant. It was not a one-off. For many years Hezbollah served as Iran's specialized assassination force, going after Iranian dissidents and opponents of the Iranian regime.

In 2012, after exiting a commercial plane, a group of Israeli tourists boarded a bus in Bulgaria heading for a Black Sea resort thirty miles south. The holiday group failed to notice a white man, wearing glasses and a baseball cap, carrying a backpack. Unfortunately for him, after planting his backpack in the luggage compartment and then getting onto the bus, the bomb exploded. Whether he was a suicide bomber or an unwitting mule carrying an explosive set-off by remote control is unknown. What is known is that he was blown to smithereens and remains unidentified to this day. Five Israelis died in the blast; thirty others were injured. A similar plot, also in Bulgaria, failed a few months earlier. Hezbollah is linked to both.

Great Britain has also seen its share of Hezbollah activity. In 2015, likely tipped off by Israel, British authorities near London caught Hezbollah operatives red-handed with 6,000 pounds of stockpiled ammonium nitrate, a favored terrorist explosive ingredient. The ingredients were stored in ice packs that, to function, incorporate ammonium nitrate in small amounts. Although no imminent operations were identified, they were clearly meant for future use. Perhaps for intimidation and retribution should England refuse to support Iran's demands in the then ongoing nuclear talks between Iran and a collection of nations that included Great Britain.

The United States also tried to warn its European colleagues of other attempts by Hezbollah operatives to store ammonium nitrate for future use in their countries. In 2019, the American State Department's coordinator for counterterrorism said that Hezbollah stores those materials in Belgium, France, Spain, Greece, Italy, and Switzerland. He then elaborated, "It stores these weapons in places so it can conduct major terrorist attacks whenever its masters in Tehran deem necessary." Despite lukewarm denials from France, Spain, and Greece that they had any intelligence that would confirm the assertion, those comments were a chilling reminder of Iran's attempts to gain leverage and Hezbollah's willingness to follow through with demands issued by Iran's supreme leader.

However, the most lucrative activity for Hezbollah in Europe is the drug trade and related money laundering. The Drug Enforcement Agency (DEA) pulled back the cover on Hezbollah's European drug operations in 2016 when *Operation Cassandra*, building on operations *Cedar*, *Titan*, and *Perseus* (lots of operations there) led to numerous arrests of Hezbollah operatives linked to Lebanon and South

American drug cartels throughout Europe. French raids added to the catch. For years, tens of millions had been flowing back from Europe, by circuitous routes, to Hezbollah. There is no reason to think that is not still happening.

South America

To this day, Hezbollah engages in numerous criminal activities throughout South America, where it engages with drug cartels. The FBI said, "Hezbollah's spiritual leader has stated that narcotic trafficking is morally acceptable if the drugs are sold to Western infidels as part of the war against the enemies of Iran." Iranian religious leaders have chimed in as well with a fatwa that says, "We are making drugs for Satan—America and Jews. If we cannot kill them with guns, so we will kill them with drugs."

Admiral Fuller, commander of the U.S. Southern Command, sounded the alarm too. He testified in January 2020 before the Senate Armed Services Committee that in South America "some Hezbollah supporters cache weapons and raise funds, often via charitable donations, remittances, and sometimes through illicit means, such as drug trafficking and money laundering." Also, Hezbollah's activities in the tri-border region continue. And, due to Hezbollah's infiltration into Venezuela, where thousands of Shiites live, and where an animus for the United States is alive and well, Hezbollah's illegal activities are ongoing. So much so that investigators dubbed Iran Air Flight 744, beginning in Caracas with stops in Beirut and Damascus before ending in Tehran, as an "aeroterror" flight for which the public found it difficult to obtain tickets because its seats were usually filled by Iranian agents and terrorists. Meanwhile, the model of social engagement first created in Lebanon is now spreading in South America, where Shiites benefit from a local version of Hezbollah's social, cultural, educational, and religious largesse designed to indoctrinate present and future generations.

Unit 1800

After Israel and Yassar Arafat (on behalf of the Palestinians) signed the Oslo Accords in 1993, the region and the world entertained fleeting hopes of peace breaking out between Israel and the Arab world. Iran, however, saw those dreams as its nightmare and plotted to do anything it could to thwart that progress. Therefore, Iran decided to increase its support for Palestinian groups opposed to Israel in the West Bank, Gaza, and even inside Israel. Iran did that even though those groups were mainly Sunni Arabs. Iran also aimed to have operatives infiltrate Israel to carry out terror attacks and collect intelligence. Hezbollah was its tool for doing so. Thus, at Iran's behest, Hezbollah created Unit 1800 through which Iran funneled funds to the Palestinians for them to instigate terror operations and initiate training.

One senior leader of Unit 1800 was Qais Obeid, an Israeli Arab who also was a drug smuggler. Obeid was an ideal choice given his familiarity with Israeli life and domestic procedures. Soon, under the overall leadership of Imad Mughniyeh (he just keeps popping up), Obeid began recruiting Palestinians and infiltrating operatives into Israel, sometimes with the help of cells in Europe.

And then there was the *Karine A*.

At dawn, on January 3, 2002, Israeli commandos boarded the *Karine A*, a ship trolling through the Red Sea. It was loaded with armaments destined for the Palestinian Authority under Yasser Arafat's control, and in direct violation of Arafat's agreements with Israel. The ship had been purchased in Lebanon and then sailed to Port Sudan, where it was renamed the *Karine A*. That destination was alarming since Port Sudan already had a reputation for being a location from which Iran smuggled arms to Hamas and other Islamist organizations in Africa. There, a new crew replaced the one on board. The ship then left for an Iranian island in November 2001. That's when things got even more interesting. A ferry arrived from which eighty crates of weapons were transferred.

Next, the plan was rather straightforward before taking an ingenious turn. The *Karine A* was to sail through the Suez Canal before stopping off the coast of El Arish, a Sinai town near the Gaza Strip. There, the crew planned to drop those eighty crates into the ocean. The Iranians had designed them to float just below the surface to escape detection. Whether they would then be left to float ashore or be picked up by operatives based in the Sinai is unclear. What is clear is that the quantity of the weapons was so huge, and their quality so great, that one person in the know described them "as a force multiplier." Knowledge gained from Israel's discovery and confiscation of those weapons shocked the Bush administration and forever changed its level of trust in Yassar Arafat. In effect, the *Karine A* escapade derailed peacemaking in the Middle East, not because of Israel's act of self-defense (the mission was called Operation Noah's Ark), but because it shed light on Arafat's two-faced shenanigans.

What does all this have to do with Hezbollah? It turns out plenty, as is almost always true when Iran involves itself in the region.

It appears that Hezbollah paid 400,000 dollars to purchase the boat with the understanding that the Palestinian Authority would pay Hezbollah back. And, when asked who sent the weapons, the Palestinian captain of the *Karine A* responded, "I believe it was from Hezbollah." That came as no surprise in Israel. At least three times before, Hezbollah had successfully supplied arms to Palestinians in Gaza. A fourth attempt had failed, resulting in the capture of a Hezbollah explosive expert along with written instructions for making bombs and components necessary for making missiles and remote-control devices. That Hezbollah was found up to its neck in collaboration with Palestinian terrorists was just business as usual.

<u>Unit 3600</u>

Somewhat analogous to Unit 1800, Hezbollah created Unit 3600 to operate in Iraq and to support Iran's regional plans. Unit 3600 trained members of the Shiite insurgency in Iraq both before and after the United States toppled Saddam Hussein. According to reports, Hezbollah had 800 operatives, including trained assassins, on the ground in Iraq by 2004. Those operatives facilitated the killing of American soldiers and established charities designed to help recruit members of Iraq's Shiite community. Recruit training even included bringing some Iraqis to Lebanon. Having gained much experience fighting a modern army during its 2006 war with Israel, Hezbollah was well suited to teach those same techniques to Iraqi Shiites. One weapon of note was explosively formed penetrators, known as EFPs. Hezbollah operatives taught Iraqi Shiites to use PVC piping about eight inches long to launch soft concave metal, usually copper. The projectile fired out of that seemingly innocuous weapon could penetrate the armor on American Humvees and tanks. Collectively, from 2005 to 2011, that weapon alone killed 196 Americans and wounded more than 800, many maimed. Hiding behind Iraqi Shiites, Hezbollah was in an undeclared war with America!

One particularly heinous event in Iraq deserves telling. It started on January 20, 2007, when trucks carrying twelve men who spoke English, wore American uniforms, bore American weapons, and possessed fake American IDs, passed through checkpoints. Then they headed to where American officers were meeting with Iraqi officials to coordinate security for the upcoming Ashura holiday. When they entered the compound, the meeting was already underway, and the trucks split up. Those coming closest to the American soldiers threw grenades at them and started shooting. Others damaged nearby Humvees. One American died immediately; three more were wounded. The attackers kidnapped four others and sped off with Iraqi police vehicles in pursuit. Fearing capture, the kidnappers abandoned their vehicles and slunk away. Inside, the police found a grizzly sight. Two Americans were handcuffed. Three lay dead. Only one American was still alive. The attackers had been trained by Hezbollah in Iran. Their goal had been to kidnap the soldiers and hold them hostage. In the aftermath, the United States began to appreciate the extent of Hezbollah's involvement in Iraq.

In 2007, other Hezbollah-trained operatives undertook a similar operation, this time wearing Iraqi army uniforms and kidnapping British citizens. It took years to obtain their release.

Let there be no doubt. Much western blood is on Hezbollah's hands.

Hezbollah in America

None of us should think the United States is immune to Hezbollah's contagion. America may well be its primary target. Hezbollah has riddled America with sleeper agents, who arrived in the United States legally (two decades ago the FBI reported that Hezbollah had at least a dozen cells in the United States). Upon arrival, many obtained visas to work, some married U.S. citizens and a few have themselves become citizens. Now, unknown numbers lie in wait for activation while others engage in illegal enterprises to send money back to Hezbollah in Lebanon. A few actively plan for violent acts that target Americans on their own soil. One prior leader of the FBI's Iran-Hezbollah unit said, "Hezbollah acts like a base crime organization here in the United States," and that some "Hezbollah supporters [in the United States] are not actual members, they are just useful idiots who want to be associated with a glorious cause but don't need or want to know more."

In June 2022, George Washington University's program on extremism issued a particularly chilling report regarding two decades of Hezbollah's activities in the United States. Although the report identified 128 individuals operating out of eleven states, most incidents occurred in Michigan, California, North Carolina, and New York. And while most individuals were involved in activities such as money laundering and fraud that netted funds sent to Hezbollah, authorities identified nineteen people engaged in operational conduct such as weapons procurement, surveillance, and developing the capacity to attack Americans at home. As concerning as this report is, it likely only touches the surface of Hezbollah's involvement in the United States, for it documents what is known, not what is unknown. Iran clearly has it in for the United States. As does Hezbollah, especially after America assassinated Soleimani in 2020. Therefore, for now, although Hezbollah contents itself with using America as a "cash cow," the odds of that being their future sole active role on U.S. soil is slim. And it largely depends on Iran's dictates and the success of the FBI and other legal authorities. At least for me, that provides little comfort and much concern.

Perhaps a few true stories will serve to illustrate what Hezbollah has done in the United States.

One of Hezbollah's first American recruits was Clevin Holt. He spent three months in Vietnam but did not see any combat. Subsequently, he served his country as an Army Ranger in South Korea. However, after participating in a race riot, he was honorably discharged when the army discovered he had enlisted as a minor. Following that, Holt first planned to find a good spot in Silver Spring, MD—close to Washington, D.C.—from where he could shoot white people. However, rather than doing that, he converted to Islam and changed his name to Isa Abdullah Ali. A couple of years later he changed his religious views from Sunni to Shiite and took a job, along with a friend, in Iran's U.S. embassy. By 1980, Holt/Ali landed in Lebanon where he first fought for Amal, and where he said he used a sniper rifle to shoot at least nine Israeli soldiers during the 1982 war (he reportedly alleged killing 173 in total, but that seems farfetched).

He later became a bodyguard for Hezbollah. In 1986, he returned to the United States before leaving again to train Muslim fighters in Bosnia, where he lives today. However, Holt's story has a surprising postscript. In 2013, Matthew Levitt wrote that Holt travels back and forth to the United States without a problem, and after turning himself in to American authorities was released. This despite Secretary of Defense William Perry saying in 1996 that Holt was "a known American terrorist." I can only speculate why Holt enjoys this freedom.

Some of the financial schemes uncovered in the United States clue us into the unconventional lengths Hezbollah resorts to. In 1999, Secret Service agents learned of a credit card fraud scheme that was thought to be the largest in the country at the time. Volunteers, often single mothers living in New York, traveled the country to purchase electronics (laptops were a favored choice) with fraudulent credit cards and identification documents provided by those running the scam. These were created by embossing stolen active numbers from 130 institutions around the world on blank credit cards, also illegally obtained. At one point, up to 10,000 illegal credit cards were in use. The volunteers sent the items they fraudulently purchased to addresses in Virginia and Michigan. For their trouble, they received five percent of the purchase price. After receiving the stolen goods, some items were sent to Lebanon while others were sold, with the net proceeds sent back to Hezbollah, although the exact identity of the recipients has not been determined. Law enforcement is certain of those facts. However, the total dollar amount stolen is unknown, but known losses at just two financial institutions came to 1.7 million dollars.

The discovery of one scam led to the discovery of others. Using fake companies to obtain credit cards from unsuspecting banks, Hezbollah supporters then purchased goods with those cards and hid behind bankruptcy laws to avoid paying for them. The investigative process also uncovered ties to South American cartels, drug smuggling that even included Viagra, and methamphetamine production. Some were facilitated by an employee at O'Hare International Airport in Chicago who had access to the international terminal. For eight years he supported Hezbollah's designs by smuggling packages onto planes.

The investigation also led law enforcement to a cigarette smuggling operation out of North Carolina. Hezbollah sympathizers purchased huge numbers of cigarettes, up to 4,500 cartons at a time. Because of significant differences between cigarette taxation in North Carolina and elsewhere, the scheme involved buying them cheaply in North Carolina and then surreptitiously transporting the cigarettes for use in Michigan, where taxes were much higher. Just one minivan filled with cigarettes returned $13,000. At their peak, three to four minivan trips were made a week netting up to $50,000 every seven days. Some were purchased with fraudulent credit cards, making the net profit even more. Who was the eventual recipient of the millions earned? You guessed it—Hezbollah.

However, even though Hezbollah steals tens of millions of dollars per year in America, it also pursues a much darker purpose in the United States. By 1994, the FBI warned Americans that cell members with knowledge of explosives and firearms in New York take direction from Hezbollah and that "Hezbollah has the infrastructure present to support or carry out a terrorist act." Meanwhile, multiple investigations in the United States and Canada have tracked Hezbollah arms procurement agents. Although Iran provides Hezbollah with missiles and the like, that is not all that Hezbollah covets. Hezbollah seeks to buy all sorts of equipment including small arms, ammunition, and even hand-held rockets like stingers on the global market. Fawzi Mustapha Assi was one procurement agent furthering Hezbollah's designs. He plead guilty to providing "material support to a terrorist organization" due to his attempt to smuggle GPS modules useful for navigation and precise targeting, a thermal imaging camera, and night-vision goggles to Hezbollah. Another was arrested in a sting operation when attempting to buy stingers for Hezbollah, which could be used to shoot down Israeli fighter jets and helicopters. Others don't busy themselves with arms. Instead, they conduct surveillance, preparing for the day when they are ordered to attack Jewish or Israeli targets in the United States or Canada. In 2017, two doing that were arrested by American law enforcement.

Conclusion

For Hezbollah, North America is a golden opportunity—lots of money sloshing around, and lots of targets to attack. Hezbollah operates there much like an organized crime organization with many branches. Its activities are dictated by its need to find additional and continuous sources of income independent of support from Iran, whose wealth and largesse, subject to sanctions and the fluctuating price of oil, is not always reliable. For example, in 2019, Hezbollah had to reduce the salaries of its operatives because Iran was experiencing financial troubles; and American sanctions caused only more difficulties. In other parts of the world, as we have seen, Hezbollah has many other opportunities to make money illegally, largely facilitated by the far-flung Lebanese diaspora.

Hezbollah's need for weapons is continuous. So is its ability to strike American targets—should Iran ever give the order. In testimony before Congress in 2021, the director of the National Counter Terrorism Center said that Hezbollah has a "high threshold for conducting attacks in the homeland." And Christopher Wray, director of the FBI, emphasized that Hezbollah is not going anywhere, saying that Hezbollah is trying to create an "infrastructure in the United States." So, let's be clear, Iran, through its proxy Hezbollah, is looking to deter, and if that fails, punish the United States for acting against Iranian interests. Whether it will succeed remains to be seen.

But Hezbollah has been occupied the last few years by home-grown concerns, too, because political headwinds in Lebanon have mounted. It is to those challenges for Hezbollah to which our story now returns.

Chapter Fourteen

Hezbollah's Political Presence in Lebanon Now

"Lebanon is staring into an abyss entirely of its own making. The country's corrupt political and financial elite, coupled with Hezbollah's domination of the system, sealed Lebanon's fate." So ends the Foundation for Defense of Democracies 2020 report, *Hezbollah Finance in Lebanon*. However, does sealing Lebanon's fate mean Hezbollah's fate is sealed too?

Well, not so fast.

Over the last decade, Hezbollah's fortunes have ebbed, flowed, and ebbed again. Is Hezbollah in imminent danger of losing control? No! But Hezbollah may feel it must do more to solidify its power. To explain, we need to review the last decade in Lebanon; particularly the last three years.

In June 2011, Hezbollah hit a speed bump when its fears were realized. The international tribunal investigating Hariri's 2005 assassination charged two senior Hezbollah leaders with involvement. For a moment, a hint of political sunlight coursed through gloomy Beirut. However, storm clouds returned in 2016 when Michael Aoun became president of Lebanon. Once a force who would stand up to Syria, this former Christian commander of the Lebanese Armed Forces who had many powerful Christian enemies, to power his way to the top, forged a dependent relationship with Nasrallah. That relationship included filling many Cabinet positions with Hezbollah supporters. Aoun confirmed his dependence in 2017 when he said, "As long as the Lebanese military lacks the power to stand up to Israel, [Hezbollah's] arms are essential, in that they complement the actions of the army and do not contradict them." Which part of that he truly believed and which part he felt politically obliged to say I don't know. But Prime Minister Said Hariri, the son of the man Hezbollah had assassinated in 2005, also felt the need to kowtow to Hezbollah. He expressed a similar yet more tempered view, saying that Israel remained the primary threat to Lebanon. In Lebanon, nobody of consequence would directly confront Hezbollah.

By 2018, Hezbollah and its allies solidified their power—supporters held a majority of the seats in Parliament and dominated state institutions. Since the Cabinet oversees the military, the veto power wielded by Hezbollah and its allies seated in the Council of Ministers effectively controlled the Lebanese Army. Also important was that Hezbollah placed one of its own as Minister of Public Health so it could better provide services to Shiites by using public funding to leverage the money Iran and criminal sources provided. And so, from 2005, when it first officially entered Lebanese politics, to 2018, Hezbollah tightened its stranglehold on the Lebanese government by placing its members and allies in strategic positions to successfully increase its control over the sinews of power—despite its operatives not composing a majority of Parliament. It did so through various means. Occasionally via assassination, often through the ballot box, and always by possessing guns and a willingness to use them. A willingness unchecked by opposition parties whose memories of the last civil war left them fearful of setting off another.

But as many organizations learn—even the nefarious ones—just when things are going well, seeds of discontent often sprout. The first rumblings manifested in 2016's municipal election when a civil society group wrested forty-five percent of the vote in Baalbek, Hezbollah's stronghold in the Bekaa Valley. Six years earlier, Shiite discontent had also manifested during a vote in another Hezbollah stronghold, this time the Dahiya in Beirut. So, something was brewing—not a threat to Hezbollah's control but a concern, nonetheless. It would take another three years for trouble to bust out.

2019 Demonstrations and the Economy

"It's the economy, stupid," said James Carvel during Clinton's campaign for America's presidency. This statement is probably just as true worldwide as it is in the United States. In Lebanon—at least to some degree—it is certainly true.

On October 17, 2019, anti-government protests broke out throughout Lebanon. Shiites were among the demonstrators and 200 of the protests erupted in Shiite-dominated areas. Because Hezbollah now effectively controlled the government, the protests decried its leaders as well as others. Recognizing the threat, Hezbollah responded violently. Shiite activists faced a one-two punch of threats and physical attacks from Hezbollah's operatives. In addition, the government working in parallel with Hezbollah arrested many of the protesters. In Dahiya, Nasrallah's henchmen set up more checkpoints and used security forces the locals called "black shirts." The message was clear: love us or hate us, Shiites must support Hezbollah. The aggressive response worked. Shiite opposition declined. A few months later, when Covid-19 disrupted the social fabric, the Shiite mini-rebellion ended.

But Hezbollah still saw a need to send a stronger message. The organization was especially bothered by a Lebanese Shiite writer named Lokman Slim, who understood the power of the written word. In 2019, Slim established the "Hub" in the protester camp located in the center of Beirut, where people gathered to immerse themselves in current affairs by listening to panels, participating in discussions, and watching debates. Hezbollah knew the danger an educated mass posed, so it burned the tent housing those activities and threatened

Slim and other thought leaders. Later that night, Hezbollah activists increased the pressure, collecting outside Slim's home and painting defamatory spiel on nearby walls such as "Lokman Slim is a traitor and infiltrator," and false propaganda that "Hezbollah is the honor of the nation." Unfazed, Slim pushed on. Hezbollah doubled down. In early 2021, after Hezbollah continued to counter Slim's criticism with violent threats, Slim's corpse was found, riddled with gunshots, in his car parked in a desolate area of southern Lebanon. The message was crystal clear—criticize Hezbollah and you will die. Assassination was still in Hezbollah's playbook.

But discontent with Hezbollah persisted. What didn't was the purchasing power of Lebanon's pound (money in Lebanon is called either pound or lira). Ironically, it all has to do with the dollar bill. One hundred billion of them. That's the amount of Lebanon's debt in September 2022.

Essentially, many Lebanese banks encouraged their customers—citizens as well as organizations such as Hezbollah—to deposit their dollar holdings with them, much of which was obtained through illegitimate means. The banks, in return, provided overly generous interest rates. Many commentators viewed it as more of a Ponzi scheme than legitimate banking. Those banks, now assuming a role akin to customers, would then deposit those dollars in return for a generous interest rate in Lebanon's Central Bank, the Banque du Liban. That bank then used those dollars to finance Lebanon's government spending. But there was a problem. The Central Bank exchanged those dollars for the Lebanese pound (also called lira) at what became an unsupportable exchange rate of 15,000 to the dollar.

Confused? I'm not surprised. I'll explain.

Let's pretend the Central Bank would at one point in time exchange one dollar for 1,500 pounds of Lebanese money, which employers would use to pay salaries and people would use to buy groceries and other goods. However, what if the pound loses value?

What if the pound loses eighty percent of its value so that the exchange rate becomes 7,500 Lebanese pounds per dollar? Now, what if economic fears disrupt the flow of dollars into Lebanon? That, of course, would cause the pound to lose even more value because fewer dollars are available to exchange making each one more expensive in Lebanese currency—thereby driving the exchange rate up even further to 15,000. This inflation from 1,500 to 7,500 to 15,000 pounds per dollar is a classic example of hyperinflation. So much, that it would cause panic among customers, who would then empty their accounts before the well ran dry or the bank closed its doors—the proverbial "run on a bank."

And, of course, bank runs are never good. It just makes things worse.

That's basically what's been happening in Lebanon since 2019, where anger and frustration define the national mood. There is not enough money to cover bank IOUs. And dollars are unavailable for most—a problem since many people use dollars for daily transactions. Loans are also difficult to obtain. And as the pound's value continues to decline, ninety percent or more, goods become harder to import. This causes shortages in food, fuel, energy, medicine, and other essentials while simultaneously driving their cost in Lebanese pounds up. In one year, the cost of many basic food items increased three-and-a-half times, while electricity was only available a few hours a day. Salaries of state employees no longer covered the cost of transportation for getting to work. Now, eighty percent of Lebanon lives in poverty—up from twenty-five percent three years ago.

To make matters worse, most Lebanese banks face international sanctions—and lawsuits—for allegedly laundering money for Hezbollah. In a legal case in New York, many Lebanese banks have been sued for washing the organization's dirty money. Damages could amount to tens of millions or more. Other pending litigation involves Lebanese depositors demanding their money back. They argue that Lebanese banks engaged in a Ponzi scheme to lure deposits. And then, amid the litigation and social disruption in Lebanon, Lebanese banks closed in October 2022; many armed holdups by desperate depositors demanding their money back fueled the decision. Although back-office operations continue, front-office services for everyday banking needs were suspended.

No wonder people were protesting. Lebanon had become pretty much a non-functional, failed state. No wonder Hezbollah was concerned because now it was seen as an integral part of Lebanon's government. But then things exploded—literally.

The Explosion

On August 4, 2020, a huge stockpile of ammonium nitrate blew up inside a warehouse in the port area of Beirut, violently shaking the capital city in what experts said was one of the largest non-nuclear explosions ever. The blast had a magnitude between 3.3 and 4.5 on the Richter scale, killing more than two hundred people, injuring seven thousand, and causing fifteen billion dollars of property damage. The blast could be heard 150 miles away in Cyprus, and people felt it farther than that. The ammonium nitrate had been taken from an inoperable ship that had languished in Beirut's harbor for several months before a judge ordered its cargo removed. Taken to a warehouse, it lay dormant for six years before igniting.

Determining the responsible party was imperative. The explosion affected Lebanese citizens of all religions. Protesters took to the streets, members of Parliament resigned, and some Cabinet members, charged with dereliction of duty, also left office. The prime minister stepped down as well. Accusations of fault were widespread and naturally included the government for allowing the material to sit there for so long. Some thought Hezbollah had stored weapons in the facility. Other theories abounded, including, of course, wild accusations of Israeli involvement. The need to investigate was a foregone conclusion.

But who? Who dared to investigate a national disaster that might have been caused by Hezbollah?

The first, a no-nonsense Maronite military judge named Fadi Sawan, had a reputation for integrity. Sawan, appointed by Lebanon's Supreme Judicial Council, lasted just a few months in the position before the council fired him. The council, it turns out, was being pressured by some of the same organizations that Sawan was investigating, most notably Hezbollah and its allies.

Tarek Bitar replaced Sawan in 2021. After the appointment, Bitar said, "The Beirut explosion is sacred. From now on, I will be the guarantor of the mission. Our duty is to uncover the truth. I will go wherever the law leads me. Nothing will stop me. I do not know where the investigation will take me, but I will not let it be derailed."

Now, Nasrallah and other Hezbollah supporters are campaigning and speaking against him. And, of course, he has been threatened by Hezbollah. For now, the investigation has been slowed by political machinations. Will he survive to complete his investigation? Will a government dominated by Hezbollah allow him to continue? Will he fulfill his promises? That remains to be seen.

Will Shiites Continue to Support Hezbollah?

For the short term, at least, the answer is yes. Shiites, now forty percent of the population, have not endured as much economic suffering as other citizens because of the cash Hezbollah receives from its illicit activities and Iran. Although much of the money goes to its military, a considerable sum is used to tend to the social needs of Hezbollah's supporters. Might this model one day be extended to the rest of Lebanon, in effect buying their support? It's possible. With enough cash, Hezbollah might overcome its political hurdles by satisfying the daily needs of those who would otherwise oppose it. The path of dependency worked for Shiites. It might well work for the rest of Lebanon.

Therefore, it is worth exploring the Rabat system to understand how Hezbollah controls the lives of Shiites at an individual level. Rabat means liaison. Every Shiite village has a Hezbollah-appointed Rabat, who in effect serves as the administrator in charge and is the liaison between Hezbollah and the residents. His word is final. He determines who will receive official appointments responsible for different social functions in the town. Although Rabats are relatively autonomous, often a higher-level Rabat manages several local village Rabats. Financial aid flows through the Rabat, who then dispenses assistance to those he deems worthy. After the 2006 war, Rabats determined who got reconstruction money. Rabats also control military functions related to the village, including confiscating or leasing land and structures for Hezbollah's military use. Although the Lebanese government appoints the village's official leader, the Rabat is in charge. Still, despite the control the Rabat system offers, there is grumbling, in part because such a concentration of power can be corruptive. For example, a Rabat threatened and assaulted a woman in a village near Israel's border. Her offense? She refused to sign a temporary marriage contract with him. In other words, she refused to be his mistress.

But other problems rile the Shiite community too—money and the Syrian civil war. I'll discuss those issues one at a time.

Sanctions placed on Iran by former President Donald Trump squeezed Iran's economy. That forced Iran to significantly cut its annual funding of Hezbollah (if sanctions on Iran are lifted as part of a nuclear deal, we can expect that money to be restored, and more). Hezbollah responded by cutting its budget, mostly by reducing allocations to social services. Under its austerity program, far less money went to education, medical, and other related expenses. Soon people got laid off and even military families experienced deep pay cuts. But that was not the end of it. The shrinking pie necessitated directing benefits to those fighting in Syria, and their families, while de-emphasizing Shiites as a whole. People who once had enough dislike becoming have-nots. So, even though Shiite areas fare better with hand-outs and services than the rest of Lebanon's people, it now is less than before. That makes nobody happy.

Including some family clans.

Realizing that it was facing a cash shortage, Hezbollah looked elsewhere for funds. As mentioned in Chapter One, traditionally family leaders governed the lives of Lebanese Christians, Sunnis, Druze, and Shiites. With difficulty, the government superimposed itself on that system. So has Hezbollah—with greater success. But money woes have created hints of a divide. In the Bekaa Valley, Hezbollah aggressively sought new sources of funding due to the sanction-related cutbacks. One source of income was wresting control of some drug smuggling operations previously run by certain families, which, of course, displeased the clan leaders affected.

And then there was Syria.

For Hezbollah to come to the aid of Assad, Nasrallah needed to convince his Shiite base it was necessary. Therefore, he told them that assisting Assad's regime was required to defend Lebanon and to safeguard their "resistance." But then Hezbollah forces suffered many casualties, which impeded recruitment efforts. Standards were lowered and training and indoctrination were reduced. Hezbollah's budget was impacted, too. Costs associated with fighting the Syrian civil war limited the money being spent on improving the daily lives of Shiites—except for families linked to Hezbollah's military operations. This change in financial fortune extended to job opportunities for Shiites in the Sunni-dominated Persian Gulf, where support for Assad had evaporated. In addition, Shiites quietly questioned why their losses in Syria furthered resistance against Israel.

This antipathy for the war in Syria filtered through much of Lebanon's Shiite community. But even so, young men impacted by Hezbollah's austerity measures still agreed to fight, for it was a reliable way to earn a salary. Many of those young men died or were wounded. Then, after the civil war ended, Hezbollah continued to experience a slow drip of casualties in Syria thanks to Israel's "Campaign Between Wars" conducted in Syria, which we will address in Chapter Twenty-One. With Hezbollah failing to retaliate against Israel for those losses, its argument began wearing thin that extending the resistance front to the Syrian border on the Golan was important. A common refrain in some Shiite communities encapsulates the issue—that most major Hezbollah leaders come from the south but more "martyrs" come from the Bekaa.

And there is also the problem of returning veterans of the war in Syria. As opposed to Hezbollah's recruits in the first three decades of its existence, these fighters were not the cream of the crop. Many were more sectarian than ideological, and their discipline and conduct were problems while fighting as well as after when they returned to the Shiite communities. The fighters, having lived in a combat environment for months or years, often turned to drug use, crime, and aggressive behavior upon their return—all of which were unlikely to ingratiate a Shiite community already questioning Hezbollah's leadership.

Does all this mean that Hezbollah is losing control of its base? No. But might it be a concern for Nasrallah? Of course. Shiites provide Hezbollah with the necessary votes and, even more critically, most of its fighters. Without them, Hezbollah is nothing. With that in mind, let's examine the outcome of the elections in Lebanon that took place on May 15, 2022.

The May 2022 Elections

The results of Lebanon's May 2022 elections may be a harbinger of a rockier road ahead for Hezbollah. On the other hand, they may not. If that sounds like a cop-out, it is. Experts are all over the map on this issue. Therefore, rather than prognosticate, I will detail the facts of what happened, and then provide a sense of what may come.

All 128 seats in Parliament were up for grabs. Four years earlier, Hezbollah had wrested control of Parliament with a resounding victory that combined the twenty-seven seats held by Shiites with many won by favorably inclined Christians, Druze, and Sunni. Afterward, Hezbollah held a formidable seventy-one-seat coalition against the opposition's fifty-seven seats. The 2022 elections were not as favorable. Too many Lebanese viewed Hezbollah as more an occupier than a needed savior. Despite retaining the Shiite seats, Hezbollah's allies among the other religious sects lost handily. Now, Hezbollah can only reliably count on sixty to sixty-two members of Parliament, well short of the sixty-five needed to command a majority and approve a new president.

Also noteworthy, many Shiites in the May election stayed home rather than vote, and, overall, only forty-one percent of the eligible populace voted compared to fifty percent in 2018. This, too, indicates Hezbollah's waning support. Something new may be afoot.

Some, including Hanin Ghaddar, a native of Lebanon and expert regarding Hezbollah in Lebanon, think change is in the air. She wrote:

> On May 15, Hezbollah suffered a major defeat in Lebanon's parliamentary election, losing not only its majority control of the legislature but also all of its non-Shia-Muslim allies. Despite low turnout, threats of violence, financial difficulties, and growing national despair, the people voted for change, choosing reforms over Hezbollah and its ever-growing military arsenal.

Furthermore, Ghaddar raised questions in December 2022 regarding the loyalty of some allies to Hezbollah who are now concerned that with President Aoun out, they will not receive positions they covet in government.

On the other hand, Tal Beeri and Teddy Sapir, also experts regarding Lebanon's quagmire and researchers for the prestigious *Alma* center located in northern Israel, disagree with those atwitter over the results. They wrote, "It is a misconception and a misrepresentation to display reality as though Hezbollah allegedly suffered a defeat. Hezbollah will have the power and strength to influence….In any scenario, Hezbollah cannot and should not be ignored as a major political player in Lebanon."

Can these seemingly disparate viewpoints be reconciled? I think so. And therein lies the conundrum.

The 1989 Taif Accords, which gave fifty percent of the seats in Parliament to Christians and divided the balance among the other religious sects, does not reflect an accurate portrait of Lebanon's demographics. Today, Muslims in Lebanon outnumber Christians, so if Parliamentary seats were awarded in proportion to the size of a religion's base, Christians would not hold so many seats. Therefore, as long as the Taif Accords remain in place, something Hezbollah might consider trying to change, if Christians unite, they can maintain a political counterweight to Hezbollah. However, Hezbollah has the guns. And, demographics favors Hezbollah, too, since the Christian population now amounts to only one-third of Lebanon's citizenry. So, while Hezbollah might have suffered a political defeat in 2022 that warrants scrutiny, things on the ground remain, for the most part, the same. Hezbollah is still in control. And in government, backed by its military prowess, Hezbollah has sufficient sway to demand Cabinet positions for its supporters; influence the selection of the president, prime minister, and speaker; and delay decisions and create vacuums of power when and where it wishes to.

In 2016, it took thirty months and forty-six parliamentary sessions before concessions by Aoun led to Hezbollah agreeing to his appointment as president. This time, Hezbollah has made clear after Aoun's term of office ended in October 2022, five months after the elections, that it wanted the new president to be someone who would "protect the 'revolution.'" Arrayed against Hezbollah's choice for president is a coalition led by Samir Geagea that has been empowered by the election. Until an agreement is reached, the prime minister will temporarily assume some of the powers of the president, but he cannot promulgate any new laws. Therefore Ghaddar, Beeri, and Sapir are all correct. Change might be in the air, but Hezbollah's grip on Lebanon remains tight and won't loosen in the foreseeable future. But Hezbollah must nurture its dominance to continue it. And part of that nurturing may involve becoming more combative with Israel.

How Might Hezbollah's Internal Domestic Politics Impact Israel?

History teaches that regimes with domestic political problems often seek to gain support by finding a domestic minority or external boogeymen to blame. For Hezbollah, Israel is the boogeyman. Destroying Israel is a foundational basis for its existence. Therefore, some in the organization opposed Hezbollah's entry into Lebanon's political system, alleging it distracts the organization from one of its central purposes. On the other hand, by being a part of the political system, Hezbollah gained leverage to control other political forces that could one day pose a problem if they became stronger. Seeing Hezbollah's standing slip, Nasrallah looked for something to shore up domestic support. Attacking Israel was not an option because Nasrallah knew Hezbollah did not yet have the strength to destroy Israel. Nor would he likely have had Iran's support to attempt it because it is not now in Iran's interests to try. So, what did Nasrallah decide to do?

That's where gas came into play.

Israel contracted for a gas rig, owned by a company called Energean, to begin extracting gas below the sea bottom in an exclusive economic zone (EEZ) claimed by Israel. On June 5, 2022, the rig arrived in the Karish field, an area rich in gas about fifty miles from the coast. The Karish field was embroiled in a dispute with Lebanon over sovereignty. Seeing an opportunity to display its relevance and benefit to the Lebanese people, Nasrallah used that fact to ratchet up tensions in the region.

But before getting into that, it is important to gain a good grasp on the details of the dispute. For that, we need to go back to 1982 when the United Nations adopted rules to determine who can mine natural resources discovered under an ocean seabed. Bottom line, the rules state that a nation is entitled to exclusively mine resources found within 200 nautical miles (a nautical mile is a little more than a mile on land) of that nation's coastline. Sounds simple. But not in practice because determining the borders of that EEZ is difficult. Namely, what angle should that 200 nautical mile border take from dry land out to sea? Suffice it to say, the arguments about this are complicated. Even more so when valuable resources have been discovered whose ownership is dependent on where that line has been set.

For our purposes, there are three potential lines for delineating Israel's and Lebanon's EEZ—the northernmost is Line 1, south of that is Line 23, and even farther south is Line 29 (see the map at the beginning of this book). There is some merit to Israel's claim that its border is Line 1, but much more for the middle one, Line 23, and it is lock solid for Line 29. Lebanon once seemed to agree on Line 23 as the border, going as far as filing a document with the United Nations in 2011 that made that claim. So far, so good. Sort of.

In 2009, Israel discovered gas under the seabed off its coastline. Those discoveries were not near a disputed area, and nobody questions Israel's ownership of the gas found in 2009. But in 2011, gas was discovered in what is now called the Karish field, located well south of

Line 23, between Line 23 and Line 29. That created a problem. There was no real question that Israel owned that too, but Lebanon wanted it. The problem became more complicated when seismic tests showed the possibility that there is gas in the Qana field, located mostly north of Line 1 and between that line and Line 23 plus a little extending south of Line 23 too. All this meant that Israel held a very strong claim over the Karish field that was known to contain much gas while Lebanon had a stronger claim over most of the Qana field that might contain gas of unknown amounts.

In 2020, Lebanon—seeing dollar signs—claimed for the first time that Line 29 was the southern border for its EEZ—an obvious land grab for the Karish field.

What to do?

Negotiate some more.

But negotiation was complicated too. Technically, Lebanon still considers itself at war with Israel, so for Lebanon face-to-face negotiation was off the table. Therefore, for more than a decade, American envoys have mediated the dispute. Among the problems those envoys had to navigate was an unusual one—peculiarities of the configuration of the cliffsides leading to the sea at Rosh Hanikra where Israel and Lebanon's borders meet. Israel was determined not to accept a sea boundary that would permit Hezbollah's terrorists easy access to Israel.

In 2012, the American envoy suggested a compromise in which Israel would get all the Karish field, the sea border would be set at Line 23, and both Lebanon (55%) and Israel (45%) would share any proceeds from the Qana field. Some reports have it that Lebanon's government agreed to that in principle. Others suggest that Lebanon demanded sovereignty over the Qana field in return for giving up the Karish field. In any event, Israel accepted the proposal, but Lebanon did not. For the next ten years, negotiations simmered until 2022 when the gas rig showed up in June at Israel's Karish field. This is the point where Hezbollah chose to become heavily involved and began issuing threats.

Entry into the dispute, however, created a philosophical problem for Hezbollah. On the one hand, Nasrallah opposed any negotiations between Israel and Lebanon because that would suggest some form of recognition of the State of Israel, something Hezbollah vehemently opposes. This is the same nonsense that most Arab countries peddled for decades after Israel's creation until, for some, reason coupled with self-interest overcame hate. And, of course, Nasrallah wanted Hezbollah seen as necessary in Lebanon for "resistance" to Israel—a reprise of the reason Hezbollah manufactured the Shebaa Farms running sore. However, Nasrallah had something counterbalancing to consider—the collapsing Lebanese economy. He could not afford to be seen as contributing to or ignoring that nightmare.

Nasrallah, knowing he needed to get involved, chose a middle course.

On June 9, Nasrallah proclaimed that he considers any attempt by Israel to pump natural gas from the Karish field a theft of Lebanon's resources. That, he said, would be an aggressive act targeting the Lebanese people, to which he would respond with military action. For him, Israel's plan to extract gas was the same as Israel occupying the security zone in Lebanon more than two decades before. Both were an invasion. Of course, Nasrallah ignored two salient facts: the security zone was a part of Lebanon used to attack Israel; and the ocean boundary that Lebanon had newly asserted was mostly, if not all, an encroachment on Israeli territory, which Lebanon now desired for obvious economic reasons.

Not one just to utter empty words—at least this time—Nasrallah ordered his operatives to send four UAVs toward the gas-pumping installation between June 29 and July 3. Israeli forces intercepted all of them. But the message was clear, even though it was directed at two different groups. Regarding Israel, Nasrallah may have hoped to establish new "Rules of the Game" in which Israel could not pump gas until negotiations were completed, thus pressuring Israel to accommodate Lebanon's demands. Regarding the Lebanese people, he sent a message that Hezbollah still is "the defender of Lebanon." Nevertheless, Lebanon's government, now deep into determining who will be president and prime minister after the May 15 elections, was not pleased and insisted on continuing to work with the American mediator in hopes of finding a solution.

In a speech made on July 13, Nasrallah explained that resolving the gas issue on favorable terms was crucial for alleviating Lebanon's economic plight. He also claimed that the window of opportunity for doing so was fleeting because Israel would begin gas production in September. And he threatened war with Israel if Lebanon did not receive the share it was entitled to.

Then, seeing that his June 9 and July 13 comments had not achieved what he wanted, Nasrallah went further on July 27. In an interview on Hezbollah's television station, he threatened, "If the extraction of oil and gas from Karish begins in September before Lebanon obtains its right, we would be heading to a problem, and we'll do anything to achieve our objective." To elucidate what that "anything" is, he said, "all fields are under threat, not only Karish," and that "no Israeli target at sea or on land is out of the reach of the resistance's precision missiles." This, of course, was a clear attempt to insert Hezbollah's threats into the negotiation, giving Nasrallah the ability to argue that Hezbollah should be given credit for any deal that was made. That took care of Hezbollah's desire to be seen as an indispensable entity for improving the lot of all Lebanese. Nasrallah was also aware the Lebanese people needed to be comforted as well as defended. He said, "I tell the Lebanese people that they should be confident in the resistance's capabilities … we have not asked anyone to join a future war on our side, but it is not known if other forces might join such a war, and this is a strong probability."

In early October 2022, after continued negotiations, Israel rejected a response from Lebanon, which included their denial of an Israeli request to meet inside Lebanon for a signing ceremony (important for ending Lebanon's refusal to accept Israel and helpful for forcing a break with Hezbollah's designs). However, reports say that before this development, Israel had made significant concessions, which some believe a wily plan to give Lebanon something it needs (a way to make money in the middle of a financial crisis) and thereby something to lose, thus enhancing deterrence and the prospects for peace. Then, to the surprise of many, three weeks before elections in Israel, Israel and Lebanon reached an agreement on October 12. War with Hezbollah was averted, but at a cost to Israel.

The terms of the agreement did not include a meeting between Lebanese officials and Israelis. Nor did Israel preserve any rights north of Line 23. It also agreed to leave the determination of compensation for the 17% of the Qana field south of Line 23 for a later date to be decided between Israel and the relevant commercial company mining the area once the gas output is known. However, Israel did get one thing very important for the moment—an agreement to preserve the status quo for the buoy line extending about three miles (five kilometers) out to sea from Rosh Hanikra. This, the IDF saw as vital. In return, for the next nine miles, Israel accepted Lebanon's boundary demands before connecting the sea border to Line 23. Nevertheless, many have raised concerns that since the agreement only preserves the buoy line status quo but leaves open the possibility of further negotiation of boundary claims, Israel will face renewed claims in the future.

Who got the best deal?

Nasrallah argues Lebanon and Hezbollah did. Immediately after the agreement's announcement, Hezbollah crowed about the victory achieved and said it had the right to defend it. Nasrallah bragged that the document does not contain signatures from Lebanon or Israel and their delegations never sat under the same roof, and it does not contain any security guarantees. Therefore, there was no normalization of relations. In effect, Lebanon got the right to earn money from offshore gas deposits whose ownership was disputed but did not have to change its stance towards recognition of Israel.

As to who achieved the deal, President Aoun admitted that Hezbollah's threats—including the UAVs sent toward the Karish gas field and warnings that it would destroy the field should Israel begin operations there before an agreement, and the numerous terrorist operatives that had heightened tensions by closing close to the borders—had helped procure the result. What's more, even though Hezbollah did not sign the agreement it is widely believed that it approved every line of it. Therefore, at a minimum Hezbollah played a significant role. But more likely, Hezbollah was the driving force. For all practical purposes, Aoun outsourced the foreign policy and military arms of the state to Nasrallah.

Inside Israel, there was much controversy. Those in favor of the deal pointed to the practical aspects: Israel could now develop the Karish field and reap the financial gain. Also, war was avoided. Politically, many supporters saw two benefits. First, Lebanese media was now using the term "Israel" rather than "Zionist entity." They also pointed out that Lebanon will not be able to extract gas from the Qana gas field, of which eighty-three percent is in its territory, until an agreement is reached regarding Israel's compensation for its seventeen percent of the field. And, they say, Lebanon still has a problem figuring out how to protect the money it will earn from Hezbollah's clutches.

From my perspective, the deal hurt Israel's deterrence, a topic I will address in much greater detail in Chapter Twenty. I believe Israel's government acted in good faith but for bad reasons. With Israeli elections three weeks away, it should not have succumbed to the pressure to get it done. Sometimes nothing is better than something.

Nevertheless, for now, with Hezbollah standing down militarily while taking domestic credit for improving the gas deal, the threat of war with Israel has eased. Jonathan Schanzer believes the agreement could lead to "the continuation of the status quo for quite some time." However, there are many other known, and unknown, triggers that could initiate a conflict—not the least of which is the new threat Nasrallah uttered in February 2023, that Hezbollah would stop Israel's drilling in the Karish field should there be "procrastination" extracting gas for Lebanon in the Qana field. For all, Hezbollah must not only calculate its response based on its goals and Iran's commands, but also its need and desire to preserve its support among the Shiite population in Lebanon while maintaining and broadening its inroads within the other religious communities in Lebanon.

These are hard times. And to make matters more complicated, there is the issue of Iran and its present influence over Hezbollah. The next chapter addresses that issue.

Chapter Fifteen

Iran and Hezbollah Now

In 2017, Iran placed a large digital clock atop a column in Tehran's Palestine Square. Based on Ayatollah Khamenei's 2015 declaration that Israel would not exist in twenty-five years, the clock purported to show the number of days left before Israel's destruction. Years later, one of the many power failures that swept through Iran shut it down. However, no matter its duration, the clock was ample evidence that Iran is determined to destroy Israel.

Given the volume of diatribes regularly espoused by Iran's leaders, no objective person should doubt Iran's intentions. Both ayatollahs who have led Iran have plainly said so. One clear example of their vitriol is what Khamenei said after becoming Iran's second supreme leader, "We believe the solution to Palestine is in destroying the Israeli regime." No slip of the tongue, Khamenei and other Iranian political and military leaders have repeated that thought in several speeches—it is their badge of honor. It also is backed up by symbols of hatred that include banners in government-sponsored processions bearing the words "Death to Israel" and the firing of missiles at targets shaped like the Star of David in training exercises. So, unless you discount every message Iran has issued, Iran's strategic intent is unmistakable—the end of Israel.

How might Iran accomplish that?

Iran has no border with Israel. Therefore, marching its army into Israel is not a viable option. Nor does Iran have the capability to maintain a constant presence in Israel's skies, let alone achieve air superiority. Yes, it has missiles. And it may now, or soon, have nuclear weapons. But using them against Israel would certainly invite a devastating response from the Jewish State. Therefore, while using its present capability, or even a fledgling nuclear capability, could eventually figure into Iran's offensive strategy, using them now would likely result in the death of countless Iranians and even the end of Iran's tyrannical regime. What's more likely in the short term is Iran aiming to accomplish the following: deter Israel from launching a first strike that would eliminate its nuclear capability; provide a nuclear umbrella for Iran's proxy allies; and intimidate and influence Sunni Arab states in the region, such as Saudi Arabia, all to promote the growth of a Shiite Islamic revolution throughout the world.

But that does not mean Iran's goal of destroying Israel is limited to rhetoric. What cannot be accomplished directly and immediately, Iran believes could be accomplished through steady pressure, intimidation, and attrition. All of it designed to erode Israel's strength and its people's willingness to endure. That's what Iran's proxies are for. That, and deterring Israel from attempting to destroy Iran's nuclear weapon program. Of those proxies, Hezbollah is by far the most powerful. For four decades Iran has equipped it to confront Israel. In 2006, when Nasrallah started a war by kidnapping two Israeli soldiers, Tehran was not pleased. Why? Because the time was not right. From Iran's perspective, all Nasrallah did was diminish the forces Hezbollah had been strengthening with Iran's help for the last twenty-four years, leaving Iran without a key deterrent against an Israeli attack on its nuclear industry.

So how did Iran respond to Hezbollah's misstep? By providing funds to help rebuild and replace that which Israel destroyed, and to improve Hezbollah's military capabilities—including over the next decade and a half replenishing the stock of missiles Hezbollah lost in the 2006 war and then increasing it more than ten-fold. Iran did not do that out of the goodness of its heart. Nor did it pour so much military capability into Hezbollah's hands just for show. At some point, Nasrallah knows there will be a quid-pro-quo. Iran will expect Hezbollah to use them, likely not when Nasrallah decides to do so unilaterally, but when Iran orders it to. Or conversely, should Hezbollah want to use its weapons to launch a war—Iran's permission will likely be desired if not necessary.

Whether Hezbollah's fealty to Iran is all-embracing is an important question for Israel's policymakers. For them, it is one set of calculations for deciding under what circumstances Hezbollah might strike Israel, of its own volition, or in some limited manner. Something it might do for a variety of reasons, such as a dispute over offshore boundaries. But it's another set of calculations for determining whether Hezbollah would obey an Iranian order to attack Israel. This is a hugely important question for Israel should it ever decide to launch an air attack against Iran's nuclear program or confront Iran in some way that would provoke a devastating response from Tehran. Even without an Israeli provocation, that question requires consideration. The Iranians may at some point determine that the moment has come for its proxies to launch a devastating blow. An attack that might shake the nation to such a degree that Iran's declared policy to destroy Israel would have taken a giant step forward without risk to the Iranian home front.

I posed the question of Hezbollah's obedience to several experts. One I met at a boisterous coffee shop in Northern Israel. There, over successive cups of coffee, Yoram Schweitzer and I discussed the issue. Yoram leads the program on terrorism and low-intensity conflict at Israel's Institute for National Security Studies (INSS). He also is a joy to spend time with. Using the INSS's platform as a base, he is a well-regarded and frequent lecturer, researcher, and author in his area of expertise, which includes Hezbollah. Previously, he held positions in Israel's intelligence community and served as a consultant to the office of Israel's prime minister and the Ministry of Defense. Therefore, one might think he would give me a definitive response to the question of Hezbollah's subservience to its Iranian masters. Don't think that. Yoram told me:

> Believe me. It's almost like a Shakespearean dilemma. We are debating from day and night, ten years ago and now among every [circle], including in [and out of] the intelligence [community], whether Nasrallah is more Lebanese or more Iranian, whether he will listen to the dictates of Khamenei.

> First of all, there is no answer, no clear-cut simple answer. Of course, he has Lebanese [allegiance]. Faithful specifically to the interest of the Shiite community and [of] course by his soul, guts, and his religious loyalty, he is inclined to listen to the Supreme leader, personally the Supreme leader, not all the other people around them.

But listening is not automatically complying. Yoram explained that Nasrallah understands a war with Israel would bring death and destruction to Lebanon and Hezbollah. He knows that it's only Hezbollah's military prowess that keeps its many enemies in Lebanon at bay. A war with Israel would surely substantially weaken it—or worse. And a depleted Hezbollah is a vulnerable Hezbollah. On the other hand, Yarom said that Iran built Hezbollah "for this situation to deter Israel," and Nasrallah well knows that should he refuse an order to attack, Iran would likely cut his financial lifeline. That, especially given Lebanon's precarious present economic situation, would end any chance the nation has to recover and Hezbollah to thrive.

In the end, Yoram was careful not to hazard a definitive prediction. Partly because Iran considers Nasrallah experienced in Middle East affairs, Yoram told me Nasrallah is just as much consulted as ordered to execute Iran's wishes. But if directly ordered to attack Israel, he would comply though he would try to maneuver the situation not to reach that stage because of the likelihood that an all-out war would devastate Lebanon. An opinion he supported by referencing what has happened in recent years, during which Israel, as we will see in Chapter Twenty-One, has done so much to interfere with Hezbollah in Syria without suffering retaliation. On the other hand, Yoram pointed out to me, the confrontation over offshore drilling, discussed in depth in Chapter Fourteen, proved that Nasrallah was willing to "take [the] risk of military escalation and execute a brinkmanship policy towards Israel when the topic at hand was fundamental and even critical to the needs of Lebanese economic survival."

Still, after saying, "They don't want war," Yoram concluded, "I'm not sure."

Others, however, are more certain. When I met with Dr. Eitan Azani, whom I introduced in Chapter Six, we discussed whether Nasrallah would always obey Iran. He said:

> Hassan Nasrallah…is now controlled by Iran. Initially, the relationship between Nasrallah and Iran was more of a mentor-mentee dynamic. However, after the 2006 war where Hezbollah's strength was depleted, the relationship transformed into one of command and control. Nasrallah's autonomy is now limited, and the organization controlled by [its benefactor].

Not a surprise since Iran now funds Hezbollah to the tune of $700 million a year.

Nasrallah, however, is very sensitive to perceptions that he is Iran's stooge. In February 2022, during an interview with Iranian state television, he said that Hezbollah might not get involved if Israel and Iran end up in a war. However, many feel he said that to satisfy domestic political concerns rather than highlight the daylight between Iran's needs and Hezbollah. I also note that Nasrallah did not say what he would do if Iran asked, but only generically indicated that he might not get involved. A slim reed indeed with which to hold hopes of Hezbollah's independence from Iranian demands.

Days before I spoke with Yoram at the coffee shop, I met with Brigadier General (res) Erez Maisel. For many years Erez held leadership roles at northern command that included a stint as commander of the IDF's International Cooperation Unit tasked with coordinating its efforts with the many other national militaries operating in the region. On his LinkedIn page, Erez self-describes part of his background as "Over 20 years of creating and delivering actionable intelligence." After spending an hour and a half with him, I realized that was an understatement and that I was in the presence of a man with prescient insights based on a lifetime's experience, study, and leadership. Regarding Hezbollah's obedience to Iran, I asked Erez what the impact would be if Nasrallah was no longer in charge due to his death or otherwise. Erez responded:

> As long as Nasrallah is there, I believe it's going to be Lebanese. [But] Nasrallah, like all of us, will one day go somewhere else and then you'll get, probably, some young idiot running the show. And who knows because younger idiots tend to make more mistakes. Nasrallah already had a war. You know, he knows what it means to make mistakes here….

Maisel was right to point out that what drives Nasrallah may not drive the institution of Hezbollah under a new leader.

I could succinctly argue both sides of the question posed in this chapter with equal persuasiveness. Perhaps Nasrallah's response to an Iranian demand for war would be based on his perception of how willing and capable Iran will be to rebuild Lebanon afterward. Perhaps it also will be based on Nasrallah's domestic calculations, including the possibility that he is losing power in Lebanon, so why not shake things up? The truth is, we won't know what Hezbollah will do if Iran asks it to initiate a war with Israel—until, that is, Iran asks. There are just too many variables—known and unknown. But if the answer is yes, will it then be too late for Israel to mount an effective response? What can Israel do to lessen the danger it faces? The next section of this book explores answers to those very questions and more. But before we get there, we need to consider the other threats Israel would face in a war with Hezbollah—namely, Iran's proxies in Syria, Gaza, Western Iraq, and Yemen.

For now, though, I leave you with one sobering thought, a definitive truth quoted from a fact sheet on the American Jewish Committee's website: "Hezbollah is the long arm of Iran."

Chapter Sixteen

Iran's Other Proxies

Hezbollah's fealty to Iran has been established, yet as discussed in the last chapter, one facet of their relationship remains uncertain—how might Hezbollah respond if Iran orders the organization to wage war with Israel? Only time will tell.

But Hezbollah is not the only game in town. Iran has other, weaker proxies with which it has much influence. They include Shiite militias now assembling in Syria along its border with Israel; Hamas and Islamic Jihad in Gaza—two Sunni groups that share Iran's agenda to destroy Israel but likely have more independence than other proxies; Hezbollah in Western Iraq; the Houthis in Yemen; and a developing situation in the West Bank possibly pushed in part by Hezbollah's agents. Today, Hamas and Islamic Jihad present the greatest danger to Israel after Hezbollah. The mounting situation in Syria, if ignored, will be a much greater threat in the future. Cumulatively, these additional proxies present a grave concern.

Why?

If Israel and Hezbollah clash in the future, Iran will likely order all its proxies to join in the fray. That's especially likely if Israel and Iran go to war. Israel would then be attacked from multiple directions by swarms of missiles and UAVs. In addition, terrorists spilling out of Lebanon, Gaza, and Syria would seek to cross multiple borders to kidnap and kill Israelis living nearby. To defend against that, the IDF would have to scatter its missile defenses throughout the country and disperse its offensive capabilities to deal with all the threats enveloping Israel—never a good thing in a war, which usually requires concentration of effort to win. In addition, incoming fire from Iran's other proxies would hasten the depletion of Israel's stock of Iron Dome missiles and other interceptors already stretched thin by the fight with Hezbollah. And, with the involvement of all the proxies, few locations in Israel would provide an out-of-range haven. If all this were to happen, even a military as powerful as the IDF would be challenged. Let's examine each of the proxies to see why.

Syria

During the civil war and after, three outside entities—Iran, Hezbollah, and Russia—have played a significant role in influencing and managing Syria. Because of their interventions, Syria's ruler, Bashar Assad, survived the war.

Now, Iran and Hezbollah, are busy creating a second front from which they can strike Israel. In addition, they want to open and maintain a land corridor extending from Iran through Iraq and then by one of three routes, through Syria to Lebanon. Success would ease Iran's supply of modern weapon technology and PGM manufacturing capability to Hezbollah. At present, the Kurds are tenuously blocking the northern route. And despite former President Trump having removed most American soldiers from Al-Tanf, remaining forces still block the southern route. A more central route, where Iranian bases are still being constructed, shows more promise for Iran. Opening any of the three paths would aid Iran economically by allowing it to sneak goods to Europe, bypassing sanctions now in place. It would also benefit Hezbollah militarily. No longer would Hezbollah need to primarily rely on Iran flying weapons and manufacturing components to Damascus and then trucking them to Lebanon (we will explore this in more detail in Chapter Twenty-one). However, keep in mind, both the aerial path and the land corridors require support, tacit or overt, from Syria.

Despite helping Syria for decades, Russia's reasons for involvement are more difficult to discern if viewed as a balance between interests and costs. Clearly, however, Russia sees a geopolitical advantage in maintaining its air and naval bases in Syria, which allows it to project Russian power into the Mediterranean and play a role in Middle Eastern affairs. Whether that is worth the cost of doing so in today's environment is debatable. But whether worthwhile or not, Russia's presence requires Syria's acquiescence.

Assad's primary goal is to remain in power and regain control of his country. His secondary goal is to recover the Golan Heights from Israel. Syria's historical dream of incorporating Lebanon into a greater Syria is now a distant one. For now, at least, his efforts are more focused on remaining in power which requires significant military support and money from Iran. It also requires material and military support from Russia. The price for such help has been Syria's losing its sovereignty. Iran and Hezbollah with the assistance of their proxy militias now control large swathes of Syrian land, especially on the Syrian Golan where the IDF strives, with much success, to prevent military forces from planting themselves. Iran also holds territory in eastern Syria, which supports the creation of the central land corridor mentioned above. Russian forces, primarily based along Syria's northwestern coast, hold much smaller sections.

All this creates problems for Israel.

Reports suggest that Hezbollah has moved some missiles to hardened sites in Syria, of which some incorporate civilian shields like in Lebanon. In addition, despite having transferred some to Hezbollah, Syria likely still commands an inventory of missiles with varying ranges, many of which can carry chemical weapon payloads. This is worrying since Syria probably still possesses some chemical weapons.

On the ground, Iran and Hezbollah's plans and actions are frightening. Across the border from the Israeli-held Golan Heights, they seek to create a situation like what exists in southern Lebanon—a warren of defensive and offensive positions manned by well-trained militia. All of this, they work towards, supported by a sympathetic population that provides a civilian shield to protect military assets placed in its communities. Already there are twenty thousand militiamen, trained and bolstered by experienced Hezbollah and Iranian operatives, active in the border region.

Insidious, also, are the demographic and cultural changes the region's population is undergoing.

Now, Iran funds and fosters there the creation of health, religious, educational, and other welfare services closely aligned with its views. By unilaterally increasing economic well-being in the region, it is attempting to shift loyalty from Syria's government. This is an old, well-worn playbook used successfully in Lebanon. However, the Iranians dealt exclusively with a Shiite community in Lebanon predisposed to viewing them favorably. That is not true in Syrian communities close to Israel, which are a mix of Sunnis, Druze, and others. In fact, prior to the civil war, Shiites only composed about one percent of the citizens of Syria. But Iran has an answer to that—population transfer and conversion.

Iran has initiated a transfer program in which Shiites from other areas of Syria and many from Iran and Iraq, are moved to the region at Iran's behest. In conjunction with that inflow, Iran has blocked members of other religions who had fled the area during the Syrian civil war from returning. Alone, however, this religious cleansing and repopulation project is too modest to supply the border area with enough people who owe their allegiance to Iran. It's also necessary to inspire those from various religious backgrounds still living there to support Iran. To accomplish that, the Iranian toolbox includes programs designed to foster allegiance and, in some cases, outright conversion to Shiism. Foundations and Hussainiyas (places for Shiite religious gatherings) are the funnels for pushing Iranian culture and religious ideology on the locals. Iran uses them to offer money, charity, employment, food, etc. Also, those organizations seek to establish ties with large, influential families in the region. The goal is to cultivate and then enhance local sympathy for Iran. Since the region is impoverished, and there is little to offset Iran's local designs, this plan has a good chance of succeeding.

The process of indoctrination began in 2018 after high-level representatives of Ayatollah Khamenei visited the area. Soon after, welfare foundations funded by Iran to the tune of tens of millions of dollars established themselves in the region. One of those foundations appears to have its roots in Hezbollah. Another glorifies Hezbollah to local youths. Iranian money has been augmented by donations from the Red Crescent and the UN meant for civilians in the region which were redirected to support Shiite militias. In addition, some local mosques have found themselves with new management. They, along with the Hussainiyas, will provide the infrastructure for growing new or already established Shiite communities. It is the Lebanon playbook all over again, but in Syria.

So far, however, money has been the driving force behind the growth of local militias that support Iran and Hezbollah—not ideology. One reason Iran promotes these militias is to increase its presence and control over the local population. That is why their duties include suppressing local opposition, recruiting more activists sympathetic to Iran, and providing security for visiting officials. In addition, the militias have a military function. They help Hezbollah smuggle weapons and drugs, support Hezbollah or Iranian military operations, and collect intelligence regarding Israel. Some have been involved in the limited number of terrorist operations launched against Israel from Syria in the last few years.

Many militia members had fought the Syrian regime, Hezbollah, and other irregular Iranian militia units during the civil war as part of the Free Syrian Army or other groups including even ISIS. Now, those same people, in return for monthly payments to their families ranging from $50 to $100, have joined the new Iranian-supported militias supported targeting Israel. Many do so despite having previously benefited from Israel's "good neighbor project" which provided medical treatment to them and their families. Such is the power of money and the frailty of past kindness.

Some of the militias operate under a "Syrian Hezbollah" nomenclature. Others are affiliated with local so-called civic associations. But all are part of the radical Shiite axis that receives orders from Iran and, at times, Lebanon Hezbollah. Often the militiamen are based in civilian homes. Homes, like those in southern Lebanon, that now contain weapons, observation posts, and missiles. Thus, the process of intertwining women, children, and other non-combatants in Syria with implements of war has begun.

If the past is prologue, Iran and Hezbollah may soon attempt to restrict UNDORF, the United Nations Disengagement Observer Force which has policed the Golan Heights region since 1974. The UN created UNDORF to enforce limitations near the boundary, known as the purple line, that Syria and Israel agreed to as part of their disengagement after the 1973 October War. As such, UNDORF plays a role analogous to UNIFIL in Lebanon where Hezbollah restricts UNIFIL from patrolling certain roads or entering designated villages and areas. Those restrictions, which Chapter Seventeen will explore, facilitate Hezbollah's assembly of weaponry in southern Lebanon and helped create a massive redoubt there. If the militias place similar restrictions on UNDORF along the Golan Height, the same will undoubtedly happen there. It may only be a matter of time before we see that.

Israel's declared goal is to prevent Iran and Hezbollah from establishing bases in Syria near the border with Israel. So far, it has largely succeeded. In addition, Israel has striven for years to prevent Iranian weapons from crossing Syria's border into Lebanon. To do so, as you will learn in Chapter Twenty-One, Israel uses its airpower to destroy missiles in Syria on their way to Lebanon and to demolish other targets that pose a threat. But Russia's presence and assistance to Syria complicates Israel's mission planning.

Russia's presence requires that Israel must liaison with its forces in the region. This is because much of Syria, as well as Lebanon and northern Israel, is within range of Russia's advanced S-400 surface-to-air defense missile systems located at Russia's Khmeimim air base in Syria and at the Syrian port of Tartus, where Russian forces are also established. In addition, Russia employs other anti-air systems at its bases and on its naval forces in the Mediterranean and has provided Syria with less advanced surface-air missiles. Until now, Russian and Israeli military representatives have maintained coordination agreements designed to avoid an inadvertent incident that would result in the loss of Russian or Israeli lives and military assets. Even so, to avoid conflict with Russian forces Israel's ability to conduct missions is hampered to some extent. However, an unfriendly Russia willing to employ those defensive missiles would endanger IDF forces operating in Syria's skies and impede Israel's ability to stop Iranian arms from reaching Hezbollah. This explains the constraints Israel faces regarding Russia's war with Ukraine. Some have criticized Israel's stance, but others recognize that Israel needs to be able to operate in Syria. Doing so requires not poking the Russian bear too forcefully. With that in mind, Israel has supplied Ukraine with humanitarian aid and offered early warning technology but has refrained from supplying weapons systems. It's simply a manner of survival—for Israel as well as for Ukraine.

Hamas, Islamic Jihad, Houthis, And Hezbollah Iraq

None of these groups present an existential danger to Israel on the ground. But all of them, especially the Hamas and Islamic Jihad Palestinian terrorist groups located in Gaza, present significant dangers through the air with their growing stockpile of missiles. Although most are short-range and inaccurate, these missiles are still dangerous, especially when launched in bunches. In 2021, Hamas and Islamic Jihad launched several hundred a day toward Israel. This stressed Israel's defense so much that after that confrontation ended it asked the United States to resupply it with a billion dollars' worth of Iron Dome missiles. Reportedly, Shiite forces in Western Iraq and the Houthis possess missiles capable of reaching Israel, too. They also have UAVs that likely can do the same. Their threat stems from their location. Although fewer in number, their missiles would fly toward Israel from a different direction than those coming from Gaza, Syria, or Lebanon.

The West Bank

In recent months, some experts have raised alarm regarding the increasing flow of money and arms into the West Bank sent by Hezbollah and Iran. In the short run, this assistance is designed to destabilize the West Bank by weakening the Palestinian Authority while also providing means to strike Israeli interests with terror attacks. However, the long-term goals are likely no different than elsewhere—create another base from which missiles can be fired at Israel and to divert Israel's resources in a war.

Combined Impact of Proxies in a War with Hezbollah

Will these other proxies help Hezbollah or Iran in a fight with Israel? Given that their survival depends, to varying degrees, on Iran's munificence, one must assume they will obey Iran's orders, rather than hope they will not. In Syria, there is little doubt, given Hezbollah's and Iran's control, that missiles based there would be fired at Israel. For Hamas and Islamic Jihad, the infrastructure to align with Hezbollah is already in place. In 2019, Iran established a nerve center in Lebanon to coordinate all Iranian proxy activity. It was used during Hamas' and Islamic Jihad's fight with Israel in 2021 to provide them with information gleaned from reconnaissance drones launched from Lebanon and Syria. It may also now be engaged in coordinating Hezbollah activity in the West Bank to create another front, this one internal, from which Israel is threatened. Therefore, it appears that Iran has prepared for those two Palestinian groups to join the fight. And, whether Iran orders them to act or not, an all-out war with Hezbollah that distracts the IDF may seem to Hamas and Islamic Jihad a golden opportunity to further weaken Israel, moving them closer to achieving their own malevolent goals of destroying Israel. After all, over the past decade, they've intermittently fired missiles at Israel; and they've also initiated several missile wars with Israel in the past. As for the Houthis and Hezbollah in Iraq, although they are not proximate to the fight, they are beholden to Iran. Thus, given their loyalty to Iran, and since many of them desire to destroy Israel, it would be foolish to think that Iran's proxies will not act in concert with Hezbollah should Iran demand it, or if they perceive a benefit from doing so.

When coupled with Hezbollah's massive inventories of missiles, an attack by the other proxies will only further stress the IDF's ability to protect Israel from missile strikes. Combined, these forces will add significant pressure on Israel's Iron Dome defenses and require Israel to conserve its supply of Iron Dome missiles. I will discuss Iron Dome in greater detail in Chapter Eighteen, but for now, know that reports indicate that Israel presently has around ten Iron Dome installations. Although they're mobile, if the other proxies attack, using Iron Dome to defend against their incoming missiles from multiple directions would prevent Israel from focusing its entire inventory on the huge mass of missiles that will fly south from Lebanon. Adding Iran's other proxies to Hezbollah's involvement in a war would place many more demands on Israel's air force, which would already be pushed to destroy thousands of targets in Lebanon. Powerful as it is, the IAF will not be able to eliminate threats everywhere at once, especially those located in the more distant proxies. That delay will mean that more missiles will fly toward Israel. Meaning more will get through.

Chapter Seventeen

UNIFIL and Lebanon's Armed Forces

UNIFIL is an acronym for the United Nations Interim Force in Lebanon. The UN established UNIFIL in 1978 as part of a ceasefire agreement. Then, as discussed in Chapter Three, after a terrorist attack in Israel killed or wounded more than 100 civilians, the IDF moved into Southern Lebanon to clean out PLO terrorists based there. Essentially, in return for Israel's withdrawal, the international community created UNIFIL and charged it with confirming that withdrawal and assisting the Lebanese government with regaining control of southern Lebanon. For the previous eight years, the region had been dominated by Palestinian terrorists who repeatedly traveled from Lebanon to kill civilians inside Israel. Supposedly, with UNIFIL's help, things would change. UNIFIL received a mandate to patrol an area stretching approximately sixteen miles north of Lebanon's border with Israel. The plan also called for the Lebanese Armed Forces (LAF) to return in sufficient force to ensure peace in the area UNIFIL would patrol.

Except things did not work out as planned.

Soon after UNIFIL's forces, composed of soldiers from a variety of nations, arrived in Lebanon, they found themselves in a hostile environment filled with PLO terrorists unwilling to cooperate. In short, despite the high-minded UN scheme, the PLO had no interest in seeing UNIFIL's mission fulfilled. Near Tyre, a coastal city in southern Lebanon, PLO operatives killed three UNIFIL soldiers and wounded ten others. Rather than respond forcefully, to avoid future clashes UNIFIL worked a deal with the PLO in direct opposite of its mission—UNIFIL soldiers would no longer approach within 500 yards of PLO posts and UNIFIL would not hinder PLO terrorists seeking to cross the border into Israel. Furthermore, the agreement included an understanding that if PLO terrorists found themselves in danger of capture or death from IDF forces pursuing them, they could surrender to UNIFIL forces, thereby receiving UNIFIL's protection. And so, from the very beginning, UNIFIL proved to be a toothless entity that shielded terrorists and impeded the IDF.

Over the next four years, the PLO built up a force of approximately 15,000 soldiers, prepositioned tanks in dugout positions, and initiated more and more terrorist operations and rocket and mortar fire targeting Israel from Lebanese soil. It was UNIFIL's first failure, and not its last. The continued PLO terrorist operations coupled with the threat of more, prompted Israel to again enter Lebanon in 1982, this time with massive forces, to eliminate the risk the PLO posed to Israeli citizens in northern Israel. That invasion, as discussed in Chapter Three, jump-started the rise of Hezbollah. Thus, UNIFIL's early failures to perform its mission directly led to the situation Israel faces today. Hezbollah should thank UNIFIL for its existence.

But it gets worse.

UNIFIL's failure to intervene with the PLO has continued with Hezbollah.

After 1982, Hezbollah and Amal replaced the PLO's presence in southern Lebanon with their own armed Shiite fighting forces, which grew over time. UNIFIL did nothing to stop them. Rather than aggressively rooting out weapons held by the Shiite militias, UNIFIL contented itself with manning checkpoints and initiating desultory patrols, usually in conjunction with the LAF. During those patrols, UNIFIL rarely entered towns or villages without Hezbollah's permission. It also allowed Hezbollah to dictate when and where it could go. Perhaps that would be understandable if UNIFIL's primary goal was its preservation. But it was not. Three times Israel withdrew from Lebanon—in 1978, 2000, and 2006—each time with the clear understanding that UNIFIL would follow the UN's mandate and disarm militia groups in southern Lebanon, meaning Hezbollah in 2000 and 2006 and the PLO in 1978. All three times Israel would be disappointed by empty promises encapsulated in UN Resolutions.

UNIFIL did not disarm the PLO. It did not disarm Hezbollah. Not once. Not even close. Regarding Hezbollah (same with the PLO), it didn't even try. Instead, a year after the IDF pulled back to the security zone in 1985, Hezbollah initiated attacks on UNIFIL soldiers, mainly French ones. One roadside bomb killed three. Eventually, France pulled its troops out. The Dutch had already done so in 1985. An Irish UNIFIL battalion suffered casualties, too. It left in 2001. With UNIFIL not willing to carry out its mandate and patrol southern Lebanon aggressively, Hezbollah ran wild—and UNIFIL felt deterred.

Then things got even worse.

In October 2000, when Hezbollah kidnapped three IDF soldiers in the Shebaa Farms, a UNIFIL soldier filmed the event. Filmed it rather than stopping it from happening! And there are some reports that Hezbollah used UN vehicles with UNIFIL markings on them. When Israeli authorities asked to see the videotape, the UN first denied possessing it before admitting it had two copies. Shockingly, it took ten months for the UN to accede to Israel's request to view the unedited videotape—important for ascertaining the condition of those kidnapped and how it happened.

As part of negotiations that ended the 2006 war and led to Resolution 1701, the UN agreed to increase UNIFIL's numbers to 15,000 and mandated that it assist the LAF per the Lebanese Cabinet decision of July 27, 2006, and the relevant portions of the Taif

Accords that called for "Disbanding of all Lebanese and non-Lebanese militias." As such, the resolution stated that "there will be no weapons or authority in Lebanon other than that of the Lebanese State." It also authorized UNIFIL to take all necessary action in areas of deployment of its forces and as it deems within its capabilities, to ensure that its area of operations is not utilized for hostile activities of any kind, to resist attempts by forceful means to prevent it from discharging its duties under the mandate of the Security Council." All parties understood that Resolution 1701 referred to Hezbollah. Since Hezbollah had instigated the 2006 war, which led to the resolution, and was the only organized, non-state actor in Lebanon at the time that had what amounted to an army, this was the only understanding that married the words of the resolution with facts on the ground. Israel agreed, perhaps naively, to stop fighting in 2006 based on that understanding.

To accomplish UNIFIL's established goals, the UN secured agreement from France, Italy, and Spain to add their soldiers to the UNIFIL contingent. The UN hoped that adding those well-trained Western European forces would prevent Hezbollah from filtering more weaponry into southern Lebanon. As we will see, that didn't happen. Even the UN's aspirations for a 15,000-man UNIFIL force fell short; it never again comprised more than 13,000 soldiers.

At first, adding the European soldiers, some of whom were elite, seemed to make a difference. But Hezbollah did not like the interference. Near Kfar Shuba, Spanish troops found an unwelcome gift— IEDs planted by Hezbollah. Whether at the initiative of a local commander whom Hezbollah subsequently replaced, or ordered by Hezbollah's central command, the message was clear. So were the other threats that UNIFIL's forces received daily.

And, making matters worse, UNIFIL feared that Al-Qaeda operatives who had filtered into relatively ungoverned southern Lebanon would try to kill UNIFIL soldiers. Recognizing that Al-

Qaeda followers are Sunni and that Hezbollah is a Shiite organization, UNIFIL knew the two would not cooperate. That led UNIFIL to coordinate with Hezbollah. Soon, plain-clothes Hezbollah personnel accompanied Spanish soldiers on their UNIFIL patrols.

Some peacekeeping operation—the very people that UNIFIL was supposed to be monitoring and preventing from engaging in wrongful activity were now part of the patrols sent out to do so. As a result, Hezbollah always knew the time and route of each patrol. When the patrol would seek to enter sensitive areas, Hezbollah officials would prevent them—declaring it was private property. Really? Resolution 1701 does not contain a private property exception. UNIFIL had been neutered—now no more than a show pony.

Then things got worse yet.

In June 2007, a roadside bomb killed six Spanish UNIFIL soldiers. Who placed the bombs has never been conclusively determined. But before the explosion, there is mention that Spanish officials had observed Hezbollah construction activity north of the Litani River. UNIFIL got the message. It stopped observing Hezbollah's construction activity and increased its coordination with Hezbollah. A French UNIFIL official said, "UNIFIL relies heavily on cooperation with Hezbollah, there is no way it could perform its mission without this form of tacit coexistence." Perform its mission? UNIFIL was, and still is, fully aware that Hezbollah has continued to increase its military presence and strength in southern Lebanon. But rather than do something about it, UNIFIL ignored it. That's not performing a mission. That is avoiding it.

As the years rolled by, Hezbollah continued to assert its will on UNIFIL. In late 2011, Hezbollah blocked patrols in areas where they had not been an issue before. Three years later, when the European Union declared that Hezbollah's military wing was a terrorist organization, Italian officers then commanding UNIFIL became concerned that there would be violent repercussions for UNIFIL in

Lebanon. This came at a time when LAF soldiers joined only ten percent of UNIFIL's patrols. But what was the UN's response to the increasing threat posed by Hezbollah, its rapid armament, and the LAF's minimal involvement? Nothing. The UN did not shore up UNIFIL's eroding strength. Instead, these years saw UNIFIL's manpower decrease from 13,000 (already 2,000 less than what had been envisioned when Resolution 1701 passed) to 11,000. Also, the Europeans began withdrawing their forces from UNIFIL, reducing the overall capability of UNIFIL's contingent. Its forces weakened; so did UNIFIL's credibility. Meanwhile, the UN did nothing to ensure that UNIFIL would fulfill its mandate by patrolling where it needed to.

In 2017, Hezbollah took international and Lebanese media on a tour of the southern Lebanon front. During the tour, Hezbollah operatives wore uniforms, carried weapons, and flew Hezbollah's flags. It was an ostentatious display of Hezbollah's armed presence. When confronted about Hezbollah's violation, a UN representative said, "UNIFIL personnel did not observe unauthorized armed personnel when they encountered the media group." In truth, UNIFIL soldiers did not see, or at least report, what they did not want to see. The phrase "Go along to get along" certainly applies.

Then, in a July 2017 report to the Security Council, UN Secretary-General Antonio Guterres said, "In accordance with its mandate, UNIFIL does not pro-actively search private property for weapons in the south unless there is credible evidence of a violation of 1701, including an imminent threat of hostile activity from that location." That was a declaration of impotency. UNIFIL was supposedly there to help ensure peace. But Guterres made clear that UNIFIL would not do anything unless it was certain a gun or rocket would be fired imminently. His statement embodied what had been happening since the force's inception— UNIFIL would do nothing about anything.

Have things improved since 2017? Has UNIFIL taken a more proactive approach? The short answer is no. As a result, Hezbollah has been on the move—enabled by the lame "private-property defense" that it and the LAF raise.

To gain a deeper understanding of how UNIFIL's failure to fulfill its mandate plays out, let's look at three examples of Hezbollah's misconduct that UNIFIL has not stopped or even documented in detail.

The first example involves unauthorized firing ranges. Remember, only the LAF and UNIFIL are authorized to have weapons in southern Lebanon. Many times, however, UNIFIL soldiers in helicopters have observed Hezbollah using land in southern Lebanon for training, including weapons training—a clear violation of Resolution 1701. Uniformed operatives fire their weapons and make no attempt to disguise their activities. Whenever UNIFIL has attempted to inspect these locations, LAF and occasionally Hezbollah operatives invoke the private land exception, preventing UNIFIL's access.

The second example is the attack tunnels, which were discussed in Chapter Twelve. Hezbollah dug them to allow its Radwan force to infiltrate Israel and overrun settlements there. It was bad enough that UNIFIL was unaware they existed. Perhaps worse is that when the Israelis brought the tunnels leading into Israel to UNIFIL's attention, it failed to do anything about the tunnels remaining on the Lebanese side of the border. Nor did it castigate Hezbollah for constructing them. When writing about the tunnels in a March 2019 report to the Security Council, the UN's secretary general could only bring himself to say that Israel "expose[d] and neutralize[d] tunnels *allegedly* [italics added by the author] built across the Blue Line by Hezbollah." "Allegedly?" Who does the secretary general think built those sophisticated tunnels if not Hezbollah? UNIFIL is a UN force entrusted with ensuring that Resolution 1701 is implemented and the best thing the secretary general, the highest-ranking officer at the UN, can say is "allegedly?" Come on. If the leader of the UN cannot bring himself to state the truth, what does that say about the prospects of UNIFIL performing its purported mission?

Let's review again what really happened at one tunnel location. On December 24, 2019, the IDF neutralized a tunnel by pouring concrete into its shaft, which extended into Israel near Metula. Two days later, UNIFIL officials saw that same concrete oozing out of a building in Lebanon about 100 yards from the border. The IDF released a humorous video of that which can be viewed at several locations, including: *https://www.timesofisrael.com/idf-releases-film-of-liquid-flowing-from-attack-tunnel-into-lebanese-village*. Soon after the liquid began oozing out of the structure, people in civilian clothes blocked the roads, preventing UNIFIL representatives from inspecting the location closely. Later, LAF members denied UNIFIL access because—of course—it was private property.

No wonder UNIFIL frustrates Israel. Hezbollah built attack tunnels that crossed the border which had only one purpose—to send terrorists into Israel for the express purpose of conquering a village and killing its citizens. Then, when exposed, UNIFIL does nothing. It doesn't squarely finger Hezbollah and it does not inspect the tunnel. It just writes milk toast reports that have no impact.

When I met with former IDF spokesperson Lt. Col. Jonathan Conricus, who retired in 2021, we discussed UNIFIL's stance on the tunnels. Visibly frustrated, he told me:

> We exposed six cross-border tunnels, every place where Hezbollah dug a tunnel, we brought UNIFIL and we showed them on a map and gave them specific coordinates of each and every location where Hezbollah had dug the tunnels from the Lebanese side, and the exact house where they dug the tunnel from. We told them, 'This is a violation of 1701. It is within your

mandate. Go inspect and document your findings so that you can report on it.' But they didn't go to even one of those places.

The third example has to do with Green Without Borders (GWB). On June 30, 2013, GWB formally declared itself a Lebanese nonprofit. On its blog, GWB states that its mission includes planting trees and caring for forests, fighting forest fires mostly in Shiite areas of Lebanon, and establishing public parks and nurseries. Sounds benign, doesn't it? It's not.

In 2017, the Daily Star quoted GWB's president as saying, "We do not hide this [affiliation with Hezbollah]." In the nonprofit's written materials he admits, "The trees are the shade of the resistance," and that planting of trees serves as "a veil on the eyes of the enemy in addition to a wall behind which the resistance fighters protect themselves." Closely aligned to GWB is Hezbollah's construction unit. This leads us to today's problem.

During the 2006 war, the IDF destroyed Hezbollah's military positions along Lebanon's border with Israel. For the next decade, Hezbollah contented itself with establishing new military positions in and around villages in southern Lebanon. That changed in 2017 when Hezbollah resumed establishing positions along the Blue Line—a practice that continues today. Among them are sixteen small, custom-made containers scattered along the Lebanese side of the border that can house several personnel. Hezbollah operatives guard them around the clock. The structures sport GWB flags; but that doesn't fool anyone because the prefabricated containers have nothing to do with any forestry project. Manned by Hezbollah operatives, including some from its Radwan strike force, they have one purpose—gather intelligence. Well, maybe they have two purposes because a UN report in 2020 documented UNIFIL's opinion that Hezbollah launched missiles from two GWB sites. One published picture goes so far as to show a Hezbollah operative standing next to a GWB structure and flag while holding binoculars for observing events in Israel. Even so,

UNIFIL has neither stopped construction of the GBW structures nor inspected them. When UNIFIL has asked to do so, Hezbollah operatives and LAF soldiers refuse the request, often accompanied by threats and the tired private lands excuse or by statements that they are closed military zones (that a closed military zone is a valid excuse tells you all you need to know about UNIFIL fulfilling its mission). As a result, the GWB sites remain in place as part of Hezbollah's military infrastructure and the situation along the border today looks much like it did just before the 2006 war broke out.

By now, I suspect you have got the idea. UNIFIL has not even acted as a speed bump to slow down, let alone stop, Hezbollah's machinations and armed occupation of southern Lebanon.

Does UNIFIL Do Any Good and Should it Leave Lebanon?

My answer to the questions posed above begins with what the secretary general has written in recent years to the Security Council:

1) The number of incidents affecting UNIFIL's freedom of movement is unacceptable. The mission's access throughout its entire area of operations…along the full length of the Blue Line is critical to the implementation of its mandate.

2) I remain concerned about the presence of unauthorized weapons in the area between the Litani River and the Blue Line, including the rockets launched on 25 April and weapons observed at firing ranges in the UNIFIL area of operations. All constitute violations of Resolution 1701 (2006).

3) The continued self-acknowledged maintenance of unauthorized weapons outside of State control by Hezbollah and other non-State armed groups represents a persistent, grave violation of resolution 1701 (2006).

So, what is UNIFIL good for? By the secretary-general's admission, UNIFIL has failed to achieve the most important reason for its continued existence—blocking Hezbollah's placement of a well-armed force on, or near, Israel's borders. As a result, war has become more, not less, likely. That war will be more deadly and destructive—not less—than previous wars. And a new war will be more difficult for Israel to end quickly. This is not what Israel agreed to, and these are not the conditions the UN promised in return for Israel agreeing to stop fighting in 2006. So, should UNIFIL remain in place?

To formulate my opinion, I read several studies and spoke with several experts in Israel, many with high-level decision-making or operational experience dealing with UNIFIL and Hezbollah. Combined, they presented a mosaic of frustration, anger, and necessity.

Brigadier General (Res.) Erez Maisel laid out the present problem best, writing:

> Unfortunately, the past few years have seen the force turn into a growing 'white elephant:' It cannot prevent Blue Line violations (UNIFIL access is denied), it is unable to deter clear Hezbollah infractions (such as Radwan light infantry activity) and is unable to rollback what is clearly a major Hezbollah intelligence collection effort.

However, there is a view that UNIFL, along with the LAF, provides some limited benefits. Jonathan Conricus told me, "The primary contribution that UNIFIL has made, I think, is the liaison mechanism that exists and is facilitated by UNIFIL between Lebanon in general, indirectly to Hezbollah, and Israel." Theoretically, by providing that mechanism, UNIFIL reduces the chance of conflict and provides a forum where Israel, the LAF, and even Hezbollah indirectly can address their concerns. But while likely true to some small extent, the process is hardly one that inspires comfort.

Periodically, representatives of the IDF, the LAF, and UNIFIL sit in a small room, adjacent to Rosh Hanikra at the only border crossing between Israel and Lebanon, and there, under UNIFIL's auspices, supposedly hash out their differences.

> Conricus, who "participated in dozens of them" as secretary of the Israeli delegation during his two-and-a-half-year stint along the northern border as head of the liaison unit with UNIFIL gave me a sense of what those meetings are like.
>
> The Lebanese officer doesn't even look into our eyes. He doesn't speak to us. He looks at UNIFIL and says, 'Tell the Israelis that they did 1, 2, 3.' You're sitting right across from him. You're looking at him and thinking, how juvenile are you, really? We are right in front of you.
>
> Even so, Conricus said they are important meetings "that help dismantle hostility and tense situations along the border."

So, does UNIFIL make a difference in that setting? After all, it's illegal in Lebanon for citizens to communicate with Israelis. Therefore, does UNIFIL's presence as an intermediary provide the LAF with a needed excuse allowing it to deny its personnel are having direct conversations with Israelis? Perhaps. But perhaps it also makes it easier for the LAF to avoid dealing with the IDF. Expedient in the short run, I'm not sure that is good in the long run because it continues a ridiculous practice that more perpetuates conflict than promotes conciliation.

When I asked experts at *Alma* whether UNIFIL is beneficial or detrimental, I encountered a mix of responses ranging from "they get in the way" to conceding that UNFIL has "certain limited benefits." After more discussion, I came away with the impression that those benefits include minimizing the chance of an accidental war but do not include preventing a war that Hezbollah or Iran might want.

A good example of this is when Israel moved to destroy Hezbollah's tunnels snaking across the border into Israel. To ensure operational security, the IDF gave UNIFIL only thirty minutes notice. Then, at each location where the IDF dug to uncover the tunnels, it placed a liaison team with flags that included UN personnel to verify Israelis were not crossing the Blue Line into Lebanon. This was important to avoid providing Hezbollah with a pretext to fire at Israelis engaged in the operation. It worked because Hezbollah was not ready to go to war over the discovery and destruction of its attack tunnels.

Professor Freilich is not only a former member of Israel's National Security Agency. He is also a prolific author, having penned two award-winning books on Israel's national security policy, a forthcoming book about the cyber threat to Israel, as well as numerous articles and podcasts related to Israel's security. When I met with him outside a coffee shop in Tel Aviv, he was short and to the point about UNIFIL. It is "better than nothing," he said. However, he indicated his dissatisfaction with the status quo and criticized the United States for not pressuring the United Nations to make UNIFIL more effective. He told me, "UNIFIL does not require more forces. It requires them doing something and having the backing to do it."

But Yossi Kuperwasser, whom I introduced in Chapter Twelve, has a much dimmer view of UNIFIL's continued involvement. He said, "UNIFIL, I never liked this. I never liked the entire idea of [a] peacekeeping [force]." Then, when I prodded in a questioning tone, "It creates an illusion of safety," Kuperwasser responded, "More operational problems. Once something starts, you have to make sure that you don't hit them…. Had they performed some positive role, I wouldn't mind, but they don't. And they can't, and it just gives [Hezbollah] cover."

However, when we continued to discuss UNIFIL, it became apparent that although Kuperwasser appreciated the value of having a liaison, he was more focused on whether UNIFIL should have an operational component rather than just a political purpose. He told me:

> I don't want anybody to fight for me. I can fight myself....We need, maybe, somebody [that] can hold a meeting between us and the Lebanese army if something goes wrong and some coordination is needed. But forces on the ground, they really are unnecessary. It's a waste of money and a waste of time. And I won't say it's a risk, but they are humiliated in Lebanon. Why [would anybody] send his soldiers to be in this position? I mean, they do that because they get a lot of money from the UN, but it's really unjustified.

In August 2022, the United Nations had an opportunity, and some had the will, to address UNIFIL's role and make changes deemed necessary. Every year, the Security Council must renew the mandate for UNIFIL's existence. This time, some members, including the United Arab Emirates and the United Kingdom, pushed for stronger language in a resolution for renewing UNIFIL. Both wanted to explicitly condemn the presence of any weapons outside Lebanon's government's control and the UK wanted to explicitly pinpoint Hezbollah as the offending party. France eventually submitted a draft with stronger language condemning "armed groups" that continue to possess weapons outside State control. France also wanted the resolution to contain language indirectly calling to remove restrictions on UNIFIL patrolling in southern Lebanon without the LAF.

On August 31, 2022, after further discussions, a new resolution authorizing UNIFIL for another year passed. It included the following:

> The Council reiterates that UNIFIL does not require prior authorization or permission from anyone to undertake its mandated tasks, and that it is allowed to conduct its operations

independently. It calls on the parties to guarantee UNIFIL's freedom of movement, including by allowing announced and unannounced patrols. The Council condemns the harassment and intimidation of UNIFIL personnel, as well as the use of disinformation campaigns against peacekeepers.

The proof will be in the pudding. To my mind, the resolution includes many empty words that will not be backed by any change, as indicated by the document's use of the word "parties" rather than identifying Hezbollah and the LAF, which are the only parties impacting UNIFIL's freedom of movement. If the Security Council will not name the offending parties, why should Hezbollah and the LAF change their conduct? Over the years, Hezbollah has succeeded in cowing both UNIFIL and the LAF. As a result, UNIFIL never fulfilled its mandate. Now, since the Security Council cannot take forceful action to back up its resolutions because of Russia's and China's veto power, nothing will change. Therefore, it is unlikely that any member nation providing troops to UNIFIL will be inclined to risk their soldiers' lives which Hezbollah, as history has shown, will not hesitate to take if confronted.

Nor did it take long for Hezbollah to respond to the August 31 renewal of Resolution 1701. A senior Hezbollah official said that the statement from the UN "turns the [UNIFIL] forces into occupation forces whose role would be to protect the Israeli enemy through pursuing the people and the resistance." It's clear where Hezbollah stands. The same is true for the LAF, which complained about the August 31 UN resolution. After much ado, UNIFIL buckled. It tweeted on September 26 that it would not operate independently of the LAF. So much for "announced and unannounced patrols."

Then, just three months after the UN's latest attempt to add textual teeth to UNIFIL's mandate, facts on the ground extracted them. A two-vehicle UNIFIL convoy got lost in an area of southern Lebanon filled with Hezbollah supporters. A mob reportedly fired twenty-seven shots at the vehicles, killing an Irish UNIFIL soldier. Another was critically wounded. Why? Because UNIFIL's vehicles had deviated from their usual route. In response, a Hezbollah official said it was an "unintentional incident" and requested that Hezbollah not be "inserted" into what occurred. According to the newspaper *Nidaa al-Waran*, a UNIFIL commander told a Hezbollah representative, "If you are not directly responsible for the incident, then you bear the responsibility of mobilizing the popular environment in the south against us."

Ireland sent investigators and Hezbollah has turned over an alleged culprit to Lebanese authorities but has denied that the suspect is a member of the organization. Nevertheless, I doubt that any final determination and denunciation will be made, if ever, regarding Hezbollah's role. Not because of ambiguity, but because of politics. There is no ambiguity because nothing of that magnitude happens in south Lebanon without Hezbollah's approval. Politics, however, will play a large role. Remember, UNIFIL goes along to get along. Meanwhile, the incident will likely have its intended effect. UNIFIL will be less motivated to deviate from its normal routes and less inclined to embark on the "unannounced" patrols the UN is supposedly now calling for. Jonathan Schanzer's remark, "Hezbollah has effectively boxed in UNIFIL. They can't even get lost," rings all too true.

So, should the UN continue to pay a half billion dollars to field a now 11,000-soldier force that failed to prevent Hezbollah's armed deployment along Lebanon's border with Israel and that does nothing to impede it now? The question is presently even more pertinent because Hezbollah has placed much of its long-range missile capability north of the Litani River—outside of UNIFIL's purview. That long-range capability enhances and magnifies UNIFIL's abdication of responsibility within its operational area which includes permitting Hezbollah to place tens of thousands of shorter-range rockets in civilian structures to shield them from attack. Don't these synergistic missile deployments coupled with armed operatives training to invade Israel and defend a glut of Hezbollah military infrastructure in the south render the present form of UNIFIL obsolete? Isn't a UNIFIL that has botched its mission now standing in the way of corrective action Israel might need to take soon to ensure its security? And doesn't UNFIL's mere presence create a false worldwide misconception that things are under control?

I conclude that the answer to the three questions posed above is yes. Therefore, UNIFIL, as presently constituted, should be abolished. It does nothing to diminish Hezbollah's ability to create mayhem inside Israel. On UNIFIL's watch, Hezbollah bored sophisticated attack tunnels into Israel, added tens of thousands of missile-launch sites in southern Lebanon and untold numbers of defensive positions, openly conducts armed training of its soldiers, creates border posts for intelligence and attack purposes, and generally has created an intolerable situation that leaves the initiative with Hezbollah. All of that has been materially aided by UNIFIL's presence, which engages in an illusion of watchfulness while in some ways shielding Hezbollah from the IDF. Nor does UNIFIL accurately report the truth—that Hezbollah and the LAF systematically and purposefully thwart UNIFIL from accomplishing its goals. A daily occurrence given its inept failure to report and inspect where Hezbollah's illegal weapons caches that violate Resolution 1701 are being kept in villages, even when they explode for lack of proper storage. This isn't an issue of lack of knowledge—UNIFIL knows full well what is going on. Nor is it a lack of a mandate—UNIFIL has the full right to go wherever it wants. Instead, the issue is UNIFIL's lack of will and the UN's passivity—or worse.

On the other hand, preventing the outbreak of an accidental war is an important objective. But doing that does not require a sizable military force. It just necessitates a diplomatic corps of resourceful individuals who feel secure where they are based and when they're on the move. At most, that requires a few hundred soldiers and maybe a few dozen civilians, all based in a couple of strategic locations in southern Lebanon and tucked out of the way should war break out. So, although Conricus says UNIFIL may be "better than nothing," a better option would be a downsized, reconstituted UN force focused on negotiation and prevention of accidental conflict since UNIFIL has failed to fulfill the mandate given to it by the Security Council. That would eliminate a sham peacekeeping force that is not honoring its mission and replace it with something useful.

However, if UNIFIL is disbanded, the Security Council will still have much to do if it wants to play a constructive role. Should Hezbollah, or the LAF, impede remaining UN forces or liaison individuals, the Security Council should call them out by name, rather than avoiding a specific reference. Also, whether UNIFIL is disbanded or not, all violations of Resolution 1701's prohibition against arms held by non-state actors should be reported by name in monthly reports. Not because outing them will stop Hezbollah, but because it will lean into Hezbollah's ability to change international focus from its conduct to Israel's defensive responses. And it will make it easier to impose more international sanctions against Hezbollah and offending individuals and countries that support it.

The Lebanese Armed Forces

And then there is the question of the LAF. Kuperwasser clearly expressed his views to me:

> [As for] the Lebanese army, I think [it is] totally penetrated by Hezbollah [which] is a much bigger and stronger armed force than the Lebanese army. So, what is the point here? We just waste money on a fake belief that there is a Lebanese state. There is a

Lebanese State, but its ability to perform is totally dependent on the goodwill of Hezbollah.

Nevertheless, in February 2022, the Biden administration repurposed $67 million of aid to the LAF and another $16.5 million to Lebanon's Internal Security Forces. Why? To provide both organizations with "livelihood and support." However, the administration did not institute controls to protect these funds from leaking to or being manipulated by Hezbollah—a likely result given Hezbollah's pervasive presence, financial shenanigans, and willingness to use force to achieve its means.

Why would the United States send this latest batch of aid? Since 2006, the United States has provided more than four billion dollars' worth of security and other assistance to Lebanon. To what end? A senior State Department official testified before Congress that the money was meant to help the LAF continue to "serve as an institutional counterweight to Hezbollah." And the State Department said security assistance is for "[strengthening] Lebanon's sovereignty, secure[ing] its borders, [to] counter internal threats and [to] disrupt terrorist facilitation." But during those years, Hezbollah has prospered, ensnared the LAF, and taken Lebanon's political process captive. Meanwhile, the LAF has done little or nothing to stop Hezbollah, and in many cases has facilitated it.

It is, of course, important to recognize the ongoing, devastating financial crisis in Lebanon. This crisis has caused the LAF to stop feeding its soldiers meat and reduced monthly salaries for the lowest ranks to $100, one-eighth of the buying power they enjoyed before the financial crisis. That motivated the United States and other nations to provide the recent wave of funding, as well as weapons and training, thought to be required to keep the LAF from collapse. But what did the money really buy?

The UN assigned the LAF a mission as a predicate for UNIFIL to help keep southern Lebanon, between the Litani River and the Blue

Line, "free of any armed personnel, assets, and weapons other than those of the Government of Lebanon and UNIFIL." But that has not happened. Despite the LAF's presence and mandate to patrol the region alongside UNIFIL, and its job to establish checkpoints and other measures to prevent Hezbollah from infiltrating fighters and armaments, the opposite has happened. Hezbollah has grown exponentially stronger in southern Lebanon while the LAF, at best, has looked the other way and, at worst, has been complicit. Furthermore, it has been complicit by using the "private property" argument to prevent UNIFIL from inspecting suspicious locations—thereby preventing UNIFIL from accomplishing its mission. Recently, the LAF has even prevented UNIFIL from placing cameras at strategic spots, "citing local concerns."

So maybe a smaller LAF presence would be better—especially because the LAF has become quite cozy with Hezbollah. One study used cellphone location data to demonstrate that LAF members "shop in the same markets, visit the same cafés, and swim at the same beaches as Hezbollah fighters." The study also used the same cellphone data to prove that the "LAF allows Hezbollah fighters to move freely throughout its territory while itself being constrained to specific movement corridors through Hezbollah-controlled areas."

When I asked experts that I spoke with concerning UNIFIL whether the international community should support the LAF, their answers reflected disdain for the LAF and their conviction that Hezbollah controls it. Tal Beeri from *Alma* explained that not only is the LAF forty-five percent Shiite but many of them are related to Hezbollah members. And if they're not related, they're likely friends with Hezbollah members who grew up in the same villages and attended the same schools. So, favors are done.

Professor Nagel, who has held many high-level positions including head of Israel's National Security Council and acting national security advisor to the prime minister, was emphatic regarding the LAF. "I think it is crazy," Nagel told me, "to give…money to [the LAF] because [the money and equipment]…will find itself in the hands of Hezbollah… . And [the LAF is] not stopping Hezbollah from doing whatever it wants in south Lebanon."

Even Professor Freilich, who was open to a future role for UNIFIL, was much less accepting of the LAF in its present form. He told me:

> [The] LAF has become counterproductive in the sense that Hezbollah controls what they do today, and as a matter of fact, a lot of the arms, or I don't know some of the arms that they get goes from LAF to Hezbollah. So…I would target it….You have to know which units the stuff goes to, and if it doesn't go to them, it stops, and the stuff has to be accounted for on some sort of regular basis.

And yet, Freilich conceded the LAF provided a benefit, however minimal. Without the LAF around, Hezbollah would assume full control. Now, the LAF's presence forces Hezbollah "to take into account that there are some other players in Lebanon." Pretty thin gruel, I think, for the United States to continue funding the LAF without significant overhaul and accountability.

The bottom line is that something is very rotten with the LAF. The money the international community pours into the LAF does not translate into shrinking Hezbollah's influence and danger. If funding does continue due to the argument that Lebanon must have a government independent of Hezbollah (however farfetched that reality may be), comprehensive controls must be placed on the funds provided. Financial support must be made contingent on the LAF facilitating UNIFIL's mission, not impeding it. And controls and continual audits are needed to make sure weapons and money stay in the LAF's hands rather than filter to Hezbollah. But even with all that, I have doubts. Because LAF representatives refuse to engage directly with the IDF on matters of mutual concern, because the LAF is riven with turncoats more supportive of Hezbollah than the government, and because Hezbollah retains a large say in LAF operations; further international funding is bad policy and counterproductive. It would be far better for conditions on the ground to reveal the truth rather than have that truth masked by a thin veneer of uniformed LAF soldiers who have no desire to do what is necessary to stop Hezbollah.

Conclusions

Let's begin with the good things, meager as they are. In concert, UNIFIL and the LAF (grudgingly), supply an indirect communications conduit between Israel and Hezbollah. But there are other ways to do that. And while UNIFIL does hold the ground where its units are based, that's a mere few hundred square yards at best at multiple locations. Perhaps also, UNIFIL's presence tempers Hezbollah's public display of its activities, although that impetus is lessening by the day.

Now for the bad. UNIFIL's presence is a farce that gives the false impression—as well as an excuse for the world to think or disingenuously argue—that Hezbollah has been restrained. It has not. Furthermore, it does nothing to help the Lebanese government control southern Lebanon, a purpose that is farcical given Hezbollah's political and practical control of the government. And UNIFIL just gets in the way. If war breaks out, the IDF will already have its hands full trying to avoid killing civilians. Adding thousands of international soldiers to the mix only makes targeting more difficult and regrettable accidents more likely.

As for the LAF, it is an empty bag of tepid air. Although it spouts off upon occasion, the LAF only marches with Hezbollah's permission. And when it does, it's only to stop conflicts between Sunnis and Shiites or to fight against enemies that Lebanon shares with Hezbollah like ISIS and related groups in Syria. In southern

Lebanon, the LAF helps shield Hezbollah from scrutiny and has done nothing to prevent southern Lebanon from becoming Hezbollah's heavily armed canton. And, in the event of a war, like UNIFIL, it will be in the IDF's way. Their only purpose, then, would be to publicize fatal accidents that will create international sympathy and domestic support for Hezbollah's war with Israel.

Therefore, in short, UNIFIL's mandate should end, and its soldiers be removed by the UN from Lebanon—leaving the important mission of preventing an accidental war to others equally well or better suited to mediate disputes. As for the LAF, it does more harm than good. More money—even if it's monitored—is not the answer. The cash will only fan Hezbollah's flame because money is fungible. Instead, the LAF should be subjected to the "school of hard knocks." If it wants international funding, it must earn it by first showing that it can be trusted to make a difference. As a prerequisite for further funding, it must create a demonstrable track record of reining in Hezbollah in southern Lebanon—which includes supporting UNIFIL should it continue to exist in some form, intercepting and imprisoning armed or uniformed Hezbollah fighters, and demolishing Hezbollah's outposts anywhere throughout the country. Only then should money flow. And then only commensurate with the LAF's benefit and effort.

Chapter Eighteen

Israel's Defenses

Israel's defensive capability is comprehensive—but porous if attacked in mass. Yes, the IDF's ground forces are much bigger and far more proficient than those of Hezbollah and the other Iranian proxies combined. And yes, its air force is an immensely capable organization that would, in the event of war, wreak havoc on Hezbollah. But for the IDF's defenses to claim without any reservation "mission accomplished," they must stop all incoming missiles targeting civilians, infrastructure, property, and military sites, which the IDF cannot do. Not even close. Also, to succeed, the IDF must thwart any Hezbollah attempts to cross the border into Israel. The IDF, even with the help of citizens in border villages, probably cannot stop them all— especially if Hezbollah launches a surprise attack. In a war, Israel will also have to block cyberattacks—especially those targeting its economy, the IDF, or government secrets. If the past is any indicator, Israel cannot hermetically seal the nation from that, either. And to fully succeed, the IDF must stop unmanned aerial vehicles (UAVs) from sneaking into the country and causing havoc. That will prove impossible.

But even if the bar is lowered, Israel faces significant problems. To win an all-out war with Hezbollah, the IDF must prevent Hezbollah from crippling Israel's economy, and it must limit Israeli casualties while also minimizing Lebanese civilian casualties. In addition, Israel must avoid conditions that might create the perception that it has lost.

Otherwise, even if Hezbollah is decimated and the IDF is left controlling large swathes of Lebanon and Syria—Israel will have suffered some measure of defeat that could leave the Jewish nation struggling to maintain the level of deterrence and domestic support it needs to survive. Israel can accomplish what is necessary to prevent that, but it will not be easy and there will likely be setbacks and surprises. However, to "win," Israel will need the freedom to do what is needed—even if circumstances require striking first—without significant political ramifications, foreign or domestic. And, because nothing is certain in war, Israel must do more now to ensure its success. Today, the margin of error for achieving victory is too small.

Winning a war against Hezbollah and Iranian proxies will require Israel to further implement a multi-layered defensive approach and to make bold offensive moves. This chapter shines a light on the IDF's present defensive arm. That requires examining IDF defensive systems and measures taken to protect the civilian population. While it is not my intention to explore in detail all of Israel's defensive measures— some of which the public is not privy to—by the end of this chapter you will be well acquainted with the issues the IDF faces and how it will meet them. Unfortunately, everything is not perfect. More needs to be done.

Israel's Infrastructure and Population

Before we examine Israel's defenses, I need to present what needs defending. Today, about 9.5 million people live in Israel, excluding Arab residents in the West Bank but including almost a half million Jewish citizens who live there. All told, ninety percent of those people live in urban areas squeezed into a nation about the same size as the state of New Jersey. Let's dwell on that for a minute. From north to south, it takes no more than a few hours to drive from one end of the country to the other. In the north, it's a ninety-minute drive from the easternmost boundary with Syria to the coastline in the west. From many locations in the country's center, it is only a few minutes' drive from the West Bank to the Mediterranean Sea. Those wishing to walk could complete the journey in less than a day. As such, except for the desert region in the south, the country is tiny.

Most Israelis live in the center of the country, in cities and suburbs located south of Tel Aviv and extending north to Haifa. There, people and industry compete for space. Factories, chemical plants, and other indicia of a modern, thriving economy dot the landscape. Tall buildings are everywhere, 344 of which are at least twelve-stories high and twenty-nine soaring 500 feet or more. That is more than Boston, Dallas, or Seattle. Between Netanya and Haifa, only forty miles, 100 of those buildings crowd the skyline. Some are offices, others are residential. Many have hundreds or more people living or working in them. One hit from a SCUD-D, Fateh-10, or a Zelzal missile could cause any of those buildings to collapse, killing many people. Likely, Hezbollah would target at least some of them with precision-guided missiles (PGMs), coupled with hordes of less accurate ones. And even if the missiles with huge payloads missed their target, they would strike populated areas in the surrounding region, causing massive numbers of deaths and injuries. If many missiles struck at once, or even over the succeeding hours or days, the result would be unspeakably tragic. Israel's economy and society would be shaken to their core.

Unfortunately, given how densely populated the nation's center is, some areas as much as any city in the world, Hezbollah's medium and long-range missiles will not miss that tens of square miles core if they are not intercepted—even those that are not precision-guided.

Then there is infrastructure.

In 2018, Israel's Home Front Command, tasked with hardening Israel's ability to withstand blows from Hezbollah and/or other attackers, identified fifty critical infrastructure systems throughout Israel. Extensive damage to any of them would severely impact Israel's economy. Damage to many of them would cause the economy to shut down. Let's look at a few scenarios.

Missiles striking Ben Gurion Airport or Israel's main ports in Haifa and Ashdod would stop Israel's economy cold. Damage to runways or docks would prevent planes from landing and cargo from unloading. Even after repairing them, the fear of more missiles would prevent tourists and goods from flying into or out of Ben Gurion Airport. Those same fears would stop ships from docking. Ships laden with the goods Israel's economy needs and ships required to transport Israeli goods for export would disappear from Israel's coasts. Why? Insurance. Even those intrepid souls willing to pilot their cargo ships to Israel would be stymied by the prohibitive cost of obtaining insurance that would be in force while Hezbollah's rockets fly.

Another vulnerable point is Israel's heavy industrial facilities, which include chemical plants near Haifa. Even from a hotel window on Mount Carmel, their concentration is apparent. Missile strikes among those storage and production facilities could easily set off secondary explosions that would cause massive fires wrapped by plumes of smoke loaded with caustic substances. The fires would be incredibly difficult to extinguish, and the fumes would cause a choking nightmare for those living nearby. Meanwhile, the resultant loss of productivity would be a huge blow to Israel's economy. And like the cities and suburbs, because of the huge area encompassed by the industrial plants and chemical storage facilities, Hezbollah need not only use PGMs to attack those targets because they are widespread. If one missile hits an industrial zone, it would be problematic and, depending on where it fell, dangerous. If multiple missiles strike the area, it would likely be catastrophic. And, as shown when Iran attacked Saudi Arabia's oil refineries, swarms of UAVs striking sensitive industrial targets can wreak havoc as well.

Then there is Israel's transportation network. The coastal plain is about twenty miles long and ten miles wide. Two major highways link

Tel Aviv and Haifa. Interchanges connect north-south routes with east-west routes. A couple of well-placed rockets, likely PGMs, would halt traffic. That would interfere with civilians fleeing south and wreak havoc with trucks carrying food, medicine, and other goods to the north. But even worse in the short term, it would diminish the IDF's ability to rapidly move military units north, where they would be needed to defend the borders and move into Lebanon to stop Hezbollah's missile launches. Missile strikes blowing up vehicles and damaging roadways, tunnels, and interchanges would cause massive traffic jams everywhere. Bodies would lay strewn in the streets. Panic and mayhem would only exacerbate the congestion, and traffic jams would become enticing soft targets for UAVs and more missile barrages.

The electrical grid and power generation infrastructure are also exposed. Modern life requires electricity to function. Without it the banking system would grind to a halt, communications systems would not work, and the lights would go out. Thunderstorms, ice storms, and wind events often damage isolated machinery that temporarily stops the transmission of electricity to thousands. We all have experienced it. Within hours or days, it is repaired. The outages are annoying but during the short time it takes to repair the damage, we deal with it. However, in a war, when PGMs or UAVs strike machinery, the machinery is not just damaged; it is likely destroyed, which will likely impact a wide-spread area. And you can be sure, Hezbollah will target the most critical infrastructure. We have seen Russia do the same in Ukraine, with far fewer rockets than Hezbollah and Iran's other proxies possess. So, should the missiles and UAVs strike successfully, it would take weeks, if not months, to restore power to countless homes, businesses, and factories. Israel's economy would grind to a halt. It could take years to restore the country's former economic vitality.

This is what is at stake. I have only named a few critical systems. There are many more including water, communications, offshore gas structures, and other heavy industry. This is what must be defended. And this is what cannot sustain many missile strikes, if any, without severely impacting Israel's strength and confidence.

But the danger is greater than what I've yet described.

Northern Israel will be hit hard in any future war. Towns and villages at, or near, the border will face salvos of Katyushas. Even though those missiles are inaccurate, collectively they can deliver tons of explosives laced with shrapnel to a small area. Their payloads contain steel designed to fragment and spray 6 mm spheres, submunitions, or thousands of irregular fragments over a killing zone with a thirty-yard radius. In the 2006 war with Hezbollah, one struck and caved in a roof in Haifa, killing eight people and wounding twenty. Another struck just outside of Kibbutz Kfar Giladi, killing twelve soldiers.

In the north, Katyushas will also set forests and agricultural fields aflame, as they did in 2006. Massive blackouts will hamper social services. Hospitals will be overwhelmed with traumatic injuries and suffer from shortages of medical supplies like insulin and blood products, especially if Hezbollah targets transportation bottlenecks.

In the early hours after a war begins, isolated kibbutzim and villages on the ridges bordering Lebanon will likely have to deal with casualties on their own. Meanwhile, overwhelmed public services will desperately triage where they can help the most with the assets they can bring to bear. And, in the confusion, amid fire and smoke and explosions, Hezbollah will try to occupy one or more of those exposed communities.

If 2006 is a guide, many in the north will stay put, but hundreds of thousands will try to flee, and Israeli authorities may attempt to evacuate those most exposed who are willing to leave. But most of the roads are two-lanes and often winding and hilly, and with rockets falling, people panicking, and with the army heading north it may take days to get civilians out. And, I must mention, anyone coming or going—be it civilians leaving or troops and supplies arriving—face another potential danger; many Arab towns have a chokehold on the transportation network. If the flare-up in Gaza in 2021 is a guide, Arabs living near those bottlenecks, perhaps instigated by Hezbollah operatives, may riot and actively attempt to impede traffic flow.

Who's to know what effect all of this will have on people's desire to return to northern Israel after the war is over. What changes in society will all this physical and psychological trauma cause? If Hezbollah is left unchecked, will the spirit of Israel survive, and after a war will it retain or recover its vitality? The remainder of this chapter considers Israel's defenses. The next chapter discusses Israel's civil defense preparations.

Israel's Missile Defenses

Effective missile defense is essential for Israel to emerge victorious in a war with Hezbollah. Let's examine why. In 2021, during a war they instigated, Hamas and Islamic Jihad fired 470 rockets at Israel from Gaza during the first twenty-four hours of fighting. And a total of more than 4,300 during the eleven days of war—an average of 400 per day. Although a third of the missiles fired malfunctioned and fell short in Gaza, sixty penetrated Israel's defenses. Hezbollah is now able to fire up to 4,000 missiles into Israel on the first day of fighting after which, by one estimate, 2,000 more per day. That is ten times the daily average fired from Gaza on the first day in 2021 and five times more on succeeding days. In addition, Iran's other proxies, including Hamas and Islamic Jihad, will fire their missiles—several hundred per day. Even if the percentage of missiles that penetrate Israel's defenses is the same as it was in 2021 (though it likely will be higher because of the number being fired from multiple directions), that translates to 250 missiles or more hitting targets in Israel on the first day of a war with Hezbollah, and at least 125 on each succeeding day. Based on my calculations, a two-week war would mean that 2,000 missiles might hit targets in Israel.

To increase its chances of creating mayhem in Israel, Hamas tried using swarm tactics, firing up to 140 rockets over a few minutes—fortunately, with little success. However, Hezbollah, who can fire far more missiles simultaneously and for a longer duration, will likely test Israel's ability again to prevail against swarm tactics. Until they've been challenged, we will not know how well Israel's defenses will perform in that environment.

Then there is the matter of delivering large payloads to their targets. Fortunately, in 2021 most of Hamas's missiles were short-range, poorly guided, and had relatively little explosive power. Few, if any, had much precision-guided capability. The same goes for Islamic Jihad's missiles. That's likely still true today. Hezbollah, on the other hand, has many missiles with powerful warheads and precision guidance, which, if not intercepted, will strike their intended targets.

To meet the challenge, Israel possesses a multi-layered missile defense system that attacks incoming targets at different stages of their trajectory. Those incoming targets will include missiles of various types, mortar shells, and UAVs. This leads us to the concept of trajectory. Most missiles and all mortar shells have three flight phases: ascending after their initial launch, reaching the top of their path, and descending. Others, like cruise missiles, fly pretty much straight to their targets. Most travel on a predetermined path but some are maneuverable. All, except UAVs, fly fast.

Each of those characteristics presents challenges. So, let's see how Israel's missile defenses stack up against what it will face.

The most famous Israeli anti-missile system is the Iron Dome. It kills Katyushas, other shorter-range missiles, mortar shells, and even UAVs. But as good as it is, it does not always succeed. That is why reportedly two missiles were fired at projectiles targeting Tel Aviv, perhaps to the chagrin of other communities for which only one Iron Dome missile was allocated against threats. When employed against Hamas in 2021, Iron Dome intercepted about ninety percent of what it targeted, leaving alone those that it calculated would land where they would not cause harm. Then, in 2022, when used to defend against the 1,175 rockets and mortar shells that Islamic Jihad fired at Israel, Iron Dome achieved a 96% success rate—likely because of improvements in both hardware and software.

Until recently, Iron Dome consisted of a battery of three or four launchers, each containing twenty preloaded missiles. Therefore, every battery had at least sixty or eighty missiles ready to go. Launcher reloads do not take long and time can be saved by swapping out empty launchers with preloaded ones. Still, time constraints make it doubtful that reloads or swaps can be accomplished fast enough to stop a swarm attack. Now, I learned in one of my interviews, each battery can control more than four launchers.

The missiles can be employed against targets from two-and-a-half miles to forty-three miles away from the battery (although Israel is reportedly working on extending that range). However, despite its maximum range, at least one article in the public domain suggests that Iron Dome is most effective in defending about 100 square miles, which equates to a ten-by-ten-mile square. This makes sense to me since at its speed of Mach 2.2, it would take about 24 seconds to travel 10 miles, but a whopping minute-and-a-half to go forty-three miles. That's probably way too long to intercept most incoming missiles and mortar shells that do not have far to travel to their target. Fortunately, however, each launcher system can probably be separated by some distance from its accompanying radar. So that would allow each battery to defend a wider frontage.

At present, Israel has ten batteries for the entire country but plans to build up to five more. Therefore, my back-of-the-envelope estimate is that Israel presently has two batteries placed to defend northern

Israel, plus two more for defending the offshore gas rigs and Haifa. Israel might move one more Iron Dome installation north, if necessary, but doing so could leave defenses in central Israel too weak to contemplate. This means that only four hundred Iron Dome missiles might be available to be fired at any one moment to defend an area ranging from Haifa to the Golan Heights and that includes the entire Galilee and the northern border region, some 1,700 square miles. It is not nearly enough but putting more there would leave the rest of the country—including Tel Aviv, Jerusalem, Beersheba, the Dimona nuclear reactor, and Eilat—more exposed to massive devastation.

But remember that I wrote "until recently" regarding launchers being attached to Iron Dome. On my last day in Israel, I interviewed Uzi Rubin at a Tel Aviv coffee shop near the Kirya, a major urban IDF base and civilian center devoted to Israel's defense. Uzi spent eight years overseeing the development of the Arrow anti-missile program, won the Israel Defense Prize in 1996, and today is a highly respected analyst of missile defense systems. So respected, one peer I interviewed spoke of him with awe and reverence. At first sight, he appears like any other aging man who might care more about grandchildren than his former work. I dispelled that thought within moments of meeting him. He is concise, intense, and knowledgeable, but also warm, and engaging. Our short hour together left me wanting more.

Uzi told me that Iron Dome now is an array. Meaning, the IDF can place radar in multiple locations separate from launchers but still leave everything interconnected. The number of launchers per site is no longer limited. In effect, you can have "as many as you want—dozens of radars, hundreds of launchers." I did not bother asking to what extent that had been accomplished; I knew that the answer to the question would be secret. However, since I have not yet seen anything written about that capability, I suspect it is a work in progress. Therefore, my estimate of four hundred Iron Dome interceptors in the north ready to be launched may be low. I hope so.

Iron Dome's genius is that its battle management system collects information gleaned from the battery's radar to determine whether an incoming missile or projectile will strike a sensitive target. If not, they are left alone. If yes, the battle management system directs a missile launch to intercept it. Generally, and with great success, Iron Dome missiles hit the incoming projectile at the top of its trajectory although they now can also hit UAVs flying on a flat trajectory. However, if the incoming missiles or UAVs maneuver, Iron Dome isn't as efficient. Similarly, if incoming missiles or UAVs appear to be on a harmless flight path, but then maneuver to a more threatening path, it might be too late for Iron Dome to react.

Aware that defensive systems must be affordable, Iron Dome's designers did their best to reduce its cost. That is why the system ignores those incoming projectiles that will land in empty regions. Uzi told me, "Iron Dome was a huge step forward because they used cheaper technologies to make this. Did a lot of value engineering. Broke accepted practices and went to other practices, all kinds of things. It amazed me." Still, each missile costs about $50,000. When compared to what it intercepts, which cost anywhere from several hundred to several thousand dollars to make, it's not an enviable tradeoff.

For defense planners concerned with comparative costs, PGMs also present a special problem. Since PGMs can maneuver, it makes it difficult to discern early in their flight where they'll land, assuming Iron Dome can distinguish between PGMs and unguided munitions, which is unlikely. Battery radar systems can't discern where a PGM will land until late in its third stage of flight—a more difficult time to shoot down missiles—so Israel must fire more missiles to shoot down suspected PGMs.

How does the threat of PGMs affect Iron Dome's usage and viability? I discussed this with Professor Nagel. More than a decade ago, Nagel headed the committee which was responsible for Israel's decision to develop the Iron Dome. He told me, "If [there are] too many PGMs we have to assume that all [missiles] will hit [an] occupied area. So, we have to launch much more [Iron Dome anti-missiles]." To make matters worse, if Iron Dome can't determine the accuracy of a PGM until late in its flight, the approximate 100-square-mile cone of protection each Iron Dome installation provides is reduced. As Nagel put it,

> The more accurate, the more it maneuvers, the smaller area Iron Dome can defend because we have to wait for the missile to come to me. Because…I have to wait until the point I know…it is not going to maneuver. [Therefore, it protects] a smaller area. So, I need more batteries and I need more missiles.

History provides an example of why this need for more missiles is concerning. In 2014, before any Iranian proxies had PGMs, the United States replenished Israel's stock of Iron Dome interceptor missiles during its seven-week-long fight with Hamas that erupted after Hamas kidnapped and murdered three Israeli teenagers. Then, it was facing an opponent with far less capability than Hezbollah now, but some argue that Israel agreed to less favorable ceasefire terms because of its shortage of Iron Dome missiles. Bibi Netanyahu says otherwise in his 2022 autobiography *Bibi, My Story*, but does admit Israel ran short during the fighting two years before. Seven years later, after presumably firing thousands of interceptors at the projectiles launched by Hamas and Islamic Jihad from Gaza toward the Jewish State, Israel recognized the mounting challenge of having many Iron Dome missiles in stock. Therefore, it asked the United States to re-supply it with an emergency replenishment grant of one billion dollars' worth of Iron Dome interceptors. That sum likely paid for roughly 20,000 interceptors. However, that number isn't as impressive as it might sound. Remember, Hezbollah has 150,000 rockets. Twenty thousand rockets might only be enough to shoot down less than fourteen percent of them! Unless, of course, the air force succeeds in destroying large numbers of Hezbollah's missiles before they are launched.

Now I hope you understand. As effective as Iron Dome is, it is not foolproof. Especially, when facing 150,000 rockets or more. In a war with Hezbollah, Israel, when using Iron Dome, will have to prioritize for the first time between people, industry, and the IDF. Israel's twelve military airfields will probably be its top priority; its planes need to keep flying to diminish Hezbollah's ability to fire missiles. Troop concentrations, weapons depots, and command and control centers will likely receive equal priority. Second, Israel will have to protect its infrastructure. As discussed above, Israel's ability to prosecute a war with Hezbollah and recover in its aftermath depends on electricity production, heavy industry, transportation capability, and the like—all required to tend to the needs of the population and the economy—remaining relatively unscathed. Israel's several major population centers will likely be a lower priority for Iron Dome's protection—not out of indifference but out of necessity. Still, they all will require some protection because just one unguided missile falling anywhere within hundreds of yards of its target can kill tens or hundreds of people and wreak havoc in densely populated areas. Smaller towns, villages, and kibbutzim will draw the short straw. As war with Hezbollah begins, and maybe for some time after, little of Iron Dome's supply will be devoted to protecting them as it did in wars with Hamas. Simply put, Israel doesn't have enough interceptors to defend against the rain of incoming missiles that will darken its skies.

Fortunately, in addition to Iron Dome, Israel possesses two other technologies capable of shooting down missiles. David's Sling is Israel's highly maneuverable middle-range missile defense system. It can destroy threats 30-200 miles away. Therefore, fixed installations of David's Sling in the center of Israel offer protection for the entire country. Even though it can be used to intercept mortar shells, David's Sling has a different primary purpose. It will be used to take down incoming aircraft, cruise missiles, and ballistic missiles. Unlike Iron Dome, David's Sling's *Stunner* missile is designed to strike its target directly rather than explode near it. Most likely, it will be used against Fateh-110 and M-600 rockets as well as other medium- and long-range missiles. However, since they cost about one million dollars each, they must be used sparingly.

The last of Israel's well-known triad is the Arrow-3. At $2.2 million each, it has a unique purpose not relevant to a conflict that involves just Hezbollah. The Arrow defends against ballistic missiles fired from Iran and other distant locations. Because it intercepts rockets outside of the earth's atmosphere, it will be used to destroy missiles that may carry nuclear warheads.

In addition to the triad, I should not omit the Barrak-8, which is designed to protect against cruise-type missiles with flat trajectories. Relatively immune to jamming, it is useful for intercepting short-range, highly maneuverable missiles. As such, Israel's navy uses them, and they're likely deployed near crucial land targets such as the nuclear reactor at Dimona and perhaps heavy industrial targets near Haifa.

All these defensive systems are great to have, but their effectiveness has also created a bit of a public relations problem. Many mistake Iron Dome for a virtual dome that makes Israel impervious to missile attack. And while it has performed exceedingly well in fights with Hamas, that may not be the case against Hezbollah. Israel's defenses are insufficient to fully protect all targets from Hezbollah's stock of missiles. And Hezbollah possesses countermeasures. Hamas employed jammers to interfere with Iron Dome's operational capability. Certainly, Hezbollah, with Iran's help, has learned from Hamas's experience and improved upon it. Also, Hezbollah's continued acquisition of PGM missiles will further stress Israel's missile defense systems. One report revealed that an experienced technician needs only a few hours to install improved guidance systems on many of Hezbollah's rocket types. Finally, there is the fog of war. In an all-out war with Hezbollah, surprises, miscalculations, and confusion are inevitable. Under pressure from a growing legion of missiles, it is unlikely that facing five to ten times more incoming warheads on any given day, Israel's weapons systems will work as they have before.

What to do? Make cheaper missiles. Because, as Uzi wrote in a September 2022 article for the Jerusalem Institute for Strategy and Security (JISS):

> With everything else being equal, producing and firing rockets is cheaper than shooting them down. Contrary to Clausewitz's dictum that defense is easier than offense, in the case of missile warfare, and at the current state of military technology, the opposite is true: rocket and missile offense is easier than rocket and missile defense.

Uzi thinks it is necessary to develop anti-missile systems that utilize missiles costing less than half of Iron Dome's missiles—maybe even one-tenth of the cost. Make them "cheap as a cannon shell," he said. Until then, the offense has a huge advantage.

However, it is not enough to have cheap interceptor missiles. Defensive systems must locate what's incoming. Present radar systems are capable enough to detect most missiles. But Hezbollah's current stock of UAVs, and the cruise missiles that it may one day possess, present a more difficult challenge. They fly low and straight, contrary to the three phases of missile flight I described above. To do a better job of locating them, Israel's defense gurus may have found at least a partial answer—an old-fashioned balloon, which is also called an aerostat, that became operational in March 2022.

I discussed aerostats with Seth Frantzman, a senior correspondent for the *Jerusalem Post* who writes about military affairs and is the author of a recent book, *Drone Wars,* which contains everything you ever wanted to know about drones (I call them UAVs). He told me:

> The cool thing about an aerostat I think is that you can put a lot of sensors on it, so you can be doing video. You can be putting [on it] half radars. You can listen for things...and it just sits there....If you have to monitor 24 hours a day, one huge, large area, it probably saves man hours and, and saves you from having to fly drones around that. Drones are very noisy. You can hear them. Usually, they sound like flying lawnmowers.

Seth then said, "They can also see people and maybe over the horizon monitor tunnels, buildings, etc. So, I assume from a standpoint of monitoring that, having a big balloon with lots of sensors on it is good."

Will missile defense alone provide an answer to Hezbollah's missile arsenal, especially if used in concert with other Iranian proxies' missile stocks? Definitely not! In the end, Uzi told me it is likely the IDF will:

> Need to prioritize [missile] launcher destruction over other offensive countermeasures. This is a far from simple requirement since the enemy is doing its best to ensure the survival of his launchers by camouflage, deception, and deployment within densely populated areas to achieve the effect of human shielding. The keys to success in launcher destruction are very accurate and timely intelligence, cutting-edge remote surveillance technologies, and sophisticated low-lethality weapons to minimize collateral casualties.

So far, Israel has been unable to prevent Hamas from launching numerous missiles—Hamas either possesses too many launchers or utilizes too many fake ones. Presumably, Hezbollah possesses far more launchers than Hamas. Perhaps recognizing the difficulty of the mission, one source Uzi referred to said that the IDF prioritizes launchers third after storage centers for the missiles and missile manufacturing centers. Further complicating matters, to get the launchers the IDF will proactively need to go after them by air. As a result of Hezbollah's basing strategy, Lebanese civilians will die during these attacks. And it's wishful thinking to believe that ground forces will not be required as well. During those ground attacks, many Israeli soldiers will also die.

Lasers

I was not planning to address the issue of lasers—I was going to leave that to Star Wars fans—but then, in February 2022, Prime Minister Bennett said he thought Israel might deploy laser systems, now called Iron Beam, that could become operational within a year (other reports have said it will take a few years). Perhaps Bennett was being aspirational when he said, "This will enable us, as the years advance, to surround Israel with a wall of lasers that will protect us from missiles, rockets, UAVs, and other threats." But Bennett's comment, like Reagan's Star Wars dream, does lay out a future path of hope if only Israel can find the way.

Whenever lasers become operational, developers say they'll be used to hit targets at high altitudes in all types of weather and to defend large areas. Brigadier General (res) Dr. Danny Gold said, "From the moment a laser is on the target(s) it takes a few seconds before they are downed." Likely, they would be used in conjunction with Iron Dome. But to be viable, a laser anti-missile beam must be so intense that each pulse of energy can destroy its target while its projector must be cheap to build and power, and also must reenergize rapidly for another shot.

Unfortunately, Uzi doubts that a useful laser weapon can be developed in the near term. One problem, he told me, is that just because laser beams move at the speed of light, they don't "kill at the speed of light." And, echoing Danny Gold, the beam must remain focused on the target for two to three seconds. Forgetting about the issue of the weather reducing effectiveness, if a laser beam must be focused on a target for two seconds to destroy it, and a hundred or more rockets are coming at the same time, an effective defense requires a lot of lasers, so they better be cheap. Right now, they are not. Each projector costs millions of dollars. That is far too much to be viable.

There is also a range issue. The farther the laser beam must travel to hit its target, the less killing power it will have. And, of course, countermeasures exist. The simplest might be thickening the shell of the incoming missile. That could require a laser beam to remain focused on the missile for more than two seconds.

Power is a problem too. For lasers to become viable as a weapon, the mechanism must have access to sufficient energy to produce the laser beam. That requires powerful generators nearby to create even a low-power beam. Perhaps a recently announced collaboration between Lockheed Martin, an American firm, and Rafael, an Israeli firm, will address this problem. "We don't have a technology problem or a scientific problem anymore," said the CEO of Rafael USA, "It's now an engineering problem... . It's a question of when, how long it will take…. I think realistically this is an effort that…will take two to three years before we have an operational system working." Perhaps that is because the present plan for Iron Beam is to use the existing Iron Dome infrastructure to aid targeting, making it stationary rather than mobile, and accepting that it will only have a range of a few miles. Still, the CEO's projection of two to three years for an operational system seems wildly optimistic. Uzi is in the same camp as me. He told me, "Unfortunately, Naftali Bennett's 'Laser Wall' seems at this time to be a very distant prospect, if feasible at all."

UAV Threat

UAVs or drones—call them what you wish. But for our purposes, I will consider drones to be of the smaller quadcopter type purchased in toy shops. Pretty much anything else I consider a UAV. Collectively, UAVs present a growing problem for which airtight solutions do not yet exist. Cheap to build, slow and small, and able to fly low on pre-programmed routes—they present a potentially huge challenge for Israel.

Uzi and I spent considerable time talking about the subject and he has written extensively about drone use. As has Seth Frantzman. Neither left me encouraged.

In a January 2022 report published by the Jerusalem Institute for Strategic Studies, Uzi explained that there are two basic classes of UAVs. The first are rather large and expensive. They can carry PGMs or dumb bombs but also are used by Hezbollah for surveillance. These UAVs require a runway to take off and return to. Israel has shot down at least three of them over Israeli airspace by using aircraft, and in one instance, a helicopter. The second UAV type is much smaller and designed for Kamikaze missions that end with them crashing into their target. Fortunately, most Kamikaze UAVs carry no more than a forty-four-pound payload. Unfortunately, especially in a swarm attack that might come in low from multiple directions, that is enough for these highly accurate aerial vehicles to punch devastating holes in critical infrastructure or to destroy military vehicles and aircraft on the ground.

Uzi told me he believes Hezbollah and others will use Kamikaze UAVs to destroy infrastructure and military targets because their payloads are too small to cause large numbers of human casualties. I am not so sure. Nothing would be more unsettling for civilians to hear than buzzing in the skies that herald attacks they have already experienced or heard of.

Cumulatively, UAVs will strain Israel's defenses. To defeat them, they must first be detected, which is difficult to achieve because they fly low and slow (technically difficult for radar to deal with) and on unpredictable flight paths. Some specially constructed UAVs will be more difficult to find because the materials used to make them provide some protection from radar detection. Also, Uzi told me, Israel's defenses must cover all 360 degrees of their potential approach because, unlike missiles, UAVs can be maneuvered to come from any direction by ground-based controllers or through preset GPS coordinates—they're only limited by fuel capacity which limits their range.

And then there is another problem. Once they're detected, defenses must be sufficiently robust to overcome swarm attacks designed to overwhelm them. A problem made more difficult when factoring in the cost of interception. Many UAVs cost 2,000 dollars or less to make. Using an F-15 to fire a million-dollar missile at a $2,000 UAV is not an enviable trade-off—and financially unsustainable in a war.

What is the answer? There are multiple candidates, but none inspires confidence in an all-out war. It's relatively easy to shoot down individual drones. Ground-based fire can do it cheaply. Planes and helicopters can do it expensively. Iron Dome's radar has been reconfigured to identify UAVs for its missiles to destroy—albeit at a present cost of $50,000 per UAV. Lasers might one day provide a more cost-effective answer. Jamming GPS systems could have an impact. And Uzi told me that microwave beam generators could even play a role, although, if not used carefully, they might fry critical Israeli military and civilian electric circuitry. Combined, all these defensive systems will have an immediate impact, which will only grow as technology develops. But I doubt that, in the fog of war, they will provide an airtight answer amid competing needs.

What will? The same approach Israel can use to defeat missile attacks. By taking the battle to the enemy, of course—from the air and by ground forces.

Tunnel Detection

In the spring of 2022, I entered a kilometer-long attack tunnel built by Hezbollah that extended from Lebanon into Israel near the town of Zar'it. An IDF officer led us underground down endless well-formed wet stairs into the dank tunnel. Around me were well-built walls and sophisticated infrastructure that included dedicated wiring, lighting, communication equipment, and other mechanisms. From where we stopped the tunnel went farther down; twenty-two stories in all. When the tunnel was discovered, its exit into Israel was disguised by trees and natural ground cover. Now it has a door with a Mezuzah affixed to it! Despite the exit being closed and camouflaged, the IDF found it, along with five others. Are there more? How did the IDF do it? Will the IDF detect future similar construction efforts?

In the north, the IDF found tunnels with modified technology that it already used along the border with Gaza. That technology has also been used by the United States to find drug tunnels along the southern border and to locate ISIS tunnels used to infiltrate American bases in Syria, Iraq, and elsewhere.

Jonathan Conricus told me that the IDF had been working on tunnel detection for twenty years and that the technology was first successfully used to find tunnels in October 2017. Developed in conjunction with the United States, the IDF has used it to locate approximately twenty border attack tunnels extending from Gaza into Israel that it subsequently destroyed.

But the composition of the ground matters. Along the border with Gaza, Conricus explained, the ground is mostly composed of sandstone. In the north, however, solid rock is under the border between Israel and Lebanon. This made detection more difficult and required tweaking the technology. Testing took place at a military training ground in northern Israel situated atop similar underground geology. When engineers were positive they had solved the technical challenges solid rock presented, the technology was used in December 2018 along the Lebanese border. As a result, six tunnels stretching into Israel were located and then demolished.

Have all the tunnels snaking under Israel's border from Lebanon been found? I asked five different Israeli experts and gathered that the answer to that question is yes, but that many others that stop short of the border remain. One day, Hezbollah could attempt to extend them. Most of the experts also expressed a degree of uncertainty, such as Professor Nagel, who said, "I'll never tell you that I am 100% confident that there are no more."

What do I think? In war, there are always surprises. And it's unclear how long it would take to extend or branch off the many tunnels that come near but don't cross the fence line. Historical experience in Gaza demonstrates that tunnels continue to be built and found, but I have no way of discerning the average lag time from creation to discovery. Given that tunnel discovery is more difficult in the north and given that I have driven along those border roads on multiple occasions without seeing obvious signs of an ongoing detection process on the ground and considering the wide separation between IDF bases—I am not so sanguine that other tunnels crossing into Israel do not exist. Or that existing tunnels cannot be rapidly extended, which, before they're detected, would provide Hezbollah with dangerous opportunities to attack. Therefore, in a war, the only sure way to prevent Hezbollah from infiltrating Israel through tunnels is to overrun their entrances in Lebanon. That, like so much else, would require ground forces.

Naval Defenses

Looking south from the cliffs of Rosh Hanikra, one always sees an Israeli naval vessel. I have visited this spot a dozen times; a naval vessel was always present. It's common knowledge that Hezbollah possesses a naval arm trained to infiltrate Israel by surreptitious means using small boats and underwater technology. It's a historical fact that Palestinian terrorists have snuck into Israel via the Mediterranean Sea to kill helpless civilians. And it's certain, with gas soon to be extracted from the Karish field in the Mediterranean, that Hezbollah now has juicy targets at sea to strike. Ripe for picking, too, are the industrial and port areas of Haifa that lie adjacent to the ocean. That's why an Israeli naval vessel is always present to defend the sea border.

Arrayed to defend against Hezbollah's seaborne threats, Israel's navy maintains a large base at Haifa, thirty miles from the border with Lebanon. It is home to multiple missile boats, submarines, and small warships—the most modern equipped with both the Barak air-defense system and capable of using the newly operational naval version of C-Dome (the ship-based version of Iron Dome). Israel's elite naval commando unit, Shayetet 13, is based farther south.

Hezbollah's fledgling naval operation poses little existential risk to Israel. But that does not mean it isn't dangerous. In a confrontation, Hezbollah will attack fragile targets, which will complicate any defensive tasks Israel's navy must carry-out. Defensive tasks will also be hampered by the many square miles of ocean that Hezbollah's naval arm can use to mask an underwater approach and its ability to target gas rigs at sea with swarms of missiles and UAVs. That is why C-Dome is a welcome addition. Now, Israel's naval vessels can multi-task—providing on-site protection against attacks by air and sea. As such, they play a crucial role.

Summary and Conclusions

Hezbollah has based much of its weaponry in a myriad of civilian structures. In a war, missiles and UAVs will fly from them toward

Israel. And Israel will respond. Where possible, Israel will seek to use airpower. But there is no escaping that ground forces will need to play a significant, and bloody, role. Simply put, Israel does not possess a defense capable of sealing its citizens, infrastructure, and military assets from Hezbollah's reach. Israel's defenses can soften the blow but not eliminate it, and large swathes of devastation and dismay will be left in its wake. If Hezbollah's gut punches are ignored, they'll grind Israel down to a whisper of its former self. That leaves only one solution. A solution Israel is fully capable of imposing on its enemies—an overwhelming and comprehensive offensive operation by air and ground that will eviscerate Hezbollah's military capability and reset realities on the ground for years or decades to come. In short, Hezbollah's shadow over Lebanon would disappear, and for any remaining segments, there would be new Rules of the Game.

But that will take time.

For an IDF offensive operation to achieve the necessary results, it will take days or weeks—not seconds or minutes. Although the air force would launch immediate attacks, not all targets can be hit in the opening hours of a full-fledged war. As capable as Israel's air arm is, there are many more targets than there are platforms from which to launch munitions to destroy them. And for some locations, multiple sorties will be required to ensure success. But not all the important targets can be destroyed by air. And airpower cannot hold the ground. Therefore, ground forces must dig out deeply held weapons and those too entwined with civilians to risk airstrikes. Ground forces will also have to chase Hezbollah from strategic locations and prevent terrorists from crossing the border. However, once the war begins, it will take days before ground forces will be present and ready to enter Lebanon in large numbers. Until then, Israel will count on its standing air and ground defenses to minimize damage to its home front.

And Israel will count on Home Front Command. So, it is to that we now turn.

Chapter Nineteen

Home Front Command

Seeking to split Arab nations from the coalition the United States had built to liberate Kuwait in 1991, Iraq's Saddam Hussein launched forty-two missiles at Israel hoping to draw it into the Gulf War. Collectively, the missiles only directly killed one Israeli. Others died due to indirect causes like heart attacks and ill-fitting gas masks. But Israel's government realized the nation had dodged a bullet. It could have been much worse.

Understanding that Israel's response to Iraq's missile attack had been scattered and disorganized, the IDF established Home Front Command (HFC) a year later. Until then, the IDF had three territorial commands that corresponded with Israel's three regions (south, central, and north). HFC became the fourth command. Charged with civil defense, HFC was not given any authority or ability to take offensive operations. Rather, it was created to relieve the other three commands from worrying about Israeli civilians behind the front lines. As part of its duties, HFC now had the responsibility and authority in a crisis to manage civilian first responders such as firefighters, emergency medical responders, and the police.

Unfortunately, fiscal reality got in the way. Post-Gulf War legislation mandated that new residential homes must contain a room in which residents could shelter in place from missiles equipped with explosive or chemical warheads. This mandate strained HFC's ability to perform all its missions because the government did not sufficiently fund it. As a result, constructing shelters in new homes was the only mission HFC managed well. Complicating matters, HFC found itself with little clout. In effect, HFC was the weak sister to the three combat commands. And, it appears, HFC's failures in its first fifteen years stemmed from it not grasping the depth and complexity of its responsibility. This became apparent when the Second Lebanon War broke out in the summer of 2006 after Hezbollah kidnapped two IDF soldiers.

During the thirty-four days of war in 2006, a daily average of 117 rockets rained down on Israel's northern communities—close to 4,000 in all. As a result, thirty-nine civilians died, more than 2,000 were injured, and 12,000 buildings were damaged. Israel's economy sustained a fifteen-billion-dollar loss (in 2022 dollars). Meanwhile, hundreds of thousands of people fled northern Israel. In the aftermath, few believed HFC had done a credible job.

HFC faces a far more difficult task today than it did in 2006. The IDF estimates that 7,000 missiles may hit residential areas during a Third Lebanon War. Worse, many of those missiles will carry larger payloads and strike regions farther away than in 2006. And some of them, due to better guidance, will home in on areas where they will inflict the most damage. Crucial for Israel, HFC must not repeat its dismal 2006 performance. It must accomplish its mission. Why? Professor Freilich provides the answer in his seminal book *Israeli National Security*, in which he wrote:

> Israel's home front and military rear are now the primary battlefield. Iran, Hezbollah, and Hamas know they cannot defeat Israel militarily today, but view its home front and military rear as an Achilles heel, a strategic vulnerability that provides them with the basis for an effective, decades-long strategy of 'attrition until destruction,' designed to neutralize Israel's superiority, undermine its society, and ultimately lead to its collapse.

Is Israel's home front better protected now than in 2006? Yes. But not enough. HFC is bigger and it has created six regional headquarters that will work closely with the national police's parallel administrative divisions in a crisis. HFC also conducts numerous comprehensive drills, including a recent one that simulated its response to Hezbollah missile attacks that destroy eighty buildings over several days and cause 300 casualties—a mere fraction of what would happen in an all-out war with Hezbollah.

And in 2007, Israel established the National Emergency Management Agency (NEMA). Now under the Ministry of Defense's jurisdiction, NEMA was designed to be a civilian entity charged with coordinating all organizations working on behalf of civilians in a crisis, including HFC, which is a military command. Arguably, NEMA would supplement HFC's work by forcing other ministries of government beyond HFC's control to respond accordingly. However, it's unclear if NEMA and HFC would work well together. Frankly, it's unclear what NEMA would do. And, because NEMA in many ways duplicates HFC's role, NEMA might muddy HFC's primary responsibility to coordinate military resources and civilian services under the command of the IDF. This is bound to cause delays and problems. Invariably the two organizations will differ regarding control, division of resources, and mission vision. Having said that, NEMA and HFC recently agreed on a division of responsibilities based loosely on whom they report to. Essentially, HFC is to deal with defensive measures such as early warning, shelters, and civil defense. NEMA's job is to make sure that food, medicine, and other supplies remain available for civilian consumption. In November 2021, the two organizations conducted a joint exercise to work out the kinks. Whether the exercise succeeded in doing so and whether their division of labor can withstand the stressors of war remains to be seen. I'm pessimistic.

So, having slogged through some organizational goop, what is HFC's primary mission today? Simple—cultivating and sustaining a national resilience that permits the continued function of civilian society and "preservation of a reasonable emergency routine." This requires HFC to prepare the public in routine times, devise solutions for anticipated problems, inspire confidence before and during a war, and perpetuate a perception of success in the aftermath of a war that in many ways was lacking after the 2006 war.

Is that happening? Yes and no. Although HFC has come a long way, based on the interviews I conducted and articles I reviewed, much remains to be done and there is much confusion.

First some good stuff. About 40 percent of Israel's housing now has safe rooms that provide at least some protection against missile attacks. Also, Israel now has a robust missile attack warning system that pinpoints where missiles launched will strike so that just people in the target zone need to seek shelter. That system is supplemented by phone apps available for download on iTunes and Android that provide timely incoming missile information. All of that is helpful, even though Israel's housing base is loaded with unplanned and unrecognized housing in the Arab communities that complicate pinpoint phone and siren-warning technology. After all, why will you be warned if nobody knows you are there?

However, the more I dug into the issue, the more I became concerned regarding how ready northern Israel is, let alone the rest of the country, for a future war with Hezbollah.

Seth Frantzman, in his folksy way, said it best, "If there's a conflict [with Hezbollah], people need to understand this is not like Gaza. They can't sit on their porch and sip coffee and watch Iron Dome go to work."

When it comes to the maintenance of bomb shelters, complacency born of fifteen years of relative peace has created a false sense of safety. Because missiles have not come, especially for those not living astride the border, some don't consider shelters that important. As Seth put it regarding 2006, "People said, wait, I don't understand. I thought we all have bomb shelters, and everything works. And you're like, well, no, the bomb shelter in your building,…Yossi is using it as his storage space." Or, shelters may not be suitable for human use, damp and dank from years of water leakage and ignored maintenance; filled with rodents, insects, and other denizens of dark, unused spaces. Although I observed and entered shelters that seemed suitable, I also stood outside one public shelter at a border community that had been left in disrepair for many years before being brought up to speed. Numerous others I've seen from the outside do not inspire confidence. I'm sure there are many suffering from neglect. The same with shelters in individual residences. How cluttered are they? Are they ready to host people at a moment's notice? How long people will have to remain in the shelters is also a problem. Do they have sufficient supplies? Acknowledging human nature and frequently laggard governance suggests that the condition and inventory of supplies in each shelter will vary greatly, all impacting people's willingness and ability to stay in them for extended periods.

Much more likely than sheltering in place, people will likely want to evacuate instead. But how will that be accomplished without costing lives? And should people leave? Picture hundreds of thousands of people threading their way south on twisty, two-lane roads while military convoys chug north, with rockets exploding all around them. And where will these people go? In 2006, Israel's central and southern regions were out of Hezbollah's rocket range. That is no longer the case, especially because Iran's proxies would likely join the battle. For answers to these and other questions, I met with several experts, some with HFC command experience.

Teddy Sapir lives on a kibbutz in northern Israel. During the 2006 war, he was happy that his wife and children evacuated south to Jerusalem and Tel Aviv. Teddy, however, remained at the kibbutz where a small, armed emergency unit stayed put to defend their homes. The same would likely be true today. Meanwhile, he told me, HFC would take command of all civilian emergency services.

Retired Gen. Erez Maisel is also a proponent of evacuation. He said that Israel wants "all our settlements on the border [to] evacuate because [if] Hezbollah's [Radwan unit] comes through the border, we won't have to deal with hostage situations." But, Erez told me, those that stay, including quick reaction units that live in the settlements, will be protected—those closest to the border by Northern Command alone. For those farther away, HFC will work to protect them while also ensuring the continuity of municipality services.

I was confused about where this hand-off would occur, so I pushed Erez to explain it further. But he only revealed that where HFC's responsibilities begin is based on the local road network. When I asked who runs the evacuations, Erez told me that "the whole evacuation is run by Northern Command because they are the pushers" but, in the villages, HFC personnel will be positioned to ensure that the roads are clear of any interference. Erez did not seem too troubled about the problem of army units coming north while civilians headed south. Still, he admitted, those first "twenty-four hours will be very long hours."

However, not everyone thinks evacuating civilians is a good idea.

High in the Golan Heights, on the southern slopes of Mount Hermon, sits a small enclave called Nimrod. Once a paramilitary IDF base, it is now home to a few seemingly intrepid souls. There, an isolated collection of eclectic homes overlooks the Golan and the Shebaa Farm ridgeline. To reach it, I had to drive up a narrow road that connects the enclave to a much busier two-lane road below. Finding it was a bit of a challenge. Upon arrival, I stopped my car to look around and get my bearings, and that's when Lilach Ashtar, who oversees village security, walked up to my window toting a gun. I saw the gun first, and then I saw Lilach. She was whom I had come to see.

We met in her home where she served me the inevitable cups of coffee that most meetings with Israelis include. It did not take long for me to form a lasting, positive impression of her. She was tough and nice—and captivating. Also, certain, and clearly capable.

In the 1980s, Lilach was the IDF's first female company commander of men, or as she called them, "boys." She also served in many intelligence roles in Lebanon. including interfacing with female terrorists captured there before the IDF withdrew in May 2000. Later, Lilach served as commanding officer for a 400-person territorial defense unit charged with responding to emergencies along a portion of the border with Lebanon. Now, she is responsible for leading Nimrod's quick reaction force in emergencies and is still involved with the IDF.

After exchanging pleasantries, we discussed the issue of civilian evacuation. Lilach told me that she studied the problem for the army and concluded, "We can't move people. We have to do the opposite. Why? Because we need the roads. Think about [it]. [We] need to move thousands [of soldiers]." So rather than write evacuation plans, Lilach wrote the opposite.

What she told me confirmed my concerns. Although there are several modern highways in northern Israel, most roads leading from them to the borders with Lebanon and Syria feature just one lane in each direction and wind through rocky hills. Lilach wouldn't tell me how many troops would be streaming north at the outset of a war, but she was clear "it can't happen if people are on the roads and [that] it is not only the little roads, [but] the main roads will be blocked [too]." Therefore, she created a "staying plan" in which communities must prepare to stay in place for a week.

Lilach also confirmed that police and fire would work under the territorial commander's direction in an emergency.

Feeling less than certain about HFC's mission and capabilities, I also spoke to Shay Shemesh. It was one of my most enlightening conversations while conducting research for this book. Shay is forty-five but looks thirty and is in great physical condition. When I asked about his background in the IDF, his understated response told me more, in a few moments, about him as a person than conversations with others that took hours. Shay served in the Golani brigade as well as other elite units. He said that matter-of-factly, but I knew that the Golani brigade is one of the IDF's most revered and demanding combat units. I was in the presence of an unassuming but special person. Shay's service included leadership positions ranging from platoon commander to brigade executive officer. After retiring, he accepted a reserve position as chief of staff for an HFC unit responsible for the Western Galilee (part of northern Israel). His sector includes seventeen Arab or Druze communities plus three larger mixed Jewish ones. In his spare time, Shay studies archeology. Here was the person I was looking for to explain Home Front Command.

Knowing our time together was limited, I grudgingly concluded our chit-chat and dove into the topic.

Home Front Command's origin, Shay told me, was tied to Israel's early days in 1948, except then it was called Civil Defense. Its purpose was to rescue civilians endangered by aerial bombardment and shelling from ships at sea. People manning anti-aircraft defense units also belonged to the organization. Most members were older reservists who could no longer serve in combat units. Trained to perform emergency services, they would cooperate with police, fire departments, and health services to save people trapped or hurt in buildings struck by bombs. This organizational structure was acceptable for the first four decades of Israel's existence because, for the most part, the IDF prevented Israel's enemies from striking Israeli cities and civilians. But that changed during the Gulf War in 1991. Not just because Iraq's missiles laden with explosives struck Israeli soil, but because of the realization that one day those missiles might carry chemical weapons. Israel could no longer just depend on older reservists. A new, invigorated organization to deal with threats to the home front was now required in the modern era, in which missiles would surely penetrate Israel's defenses. Shelters would be required on a large scale. So would protection from chemical attack. Out of those needs, HFC was born.

Soon after, Israel mandated that every new residence must have a bomb shelter. In a multi-unit structure, that meant every apartment—not just the building. Every new public building also had to have a shelter. All this required the HFC, under command of the IDF but legitimized by the Knesset, to coordinate with private concerns and local entities. And that coordination required digging deep into aspects of Israeli society—especially construction. As is typical in most societies, new buildings require permits from the fire department and other agencies. In Israel, new buildings also require HFC permits certifying that appropriate shelters are present. HFC also works with local authorities to ensure that factories, fuel depots, and other critical infrastructure have built-in protection.

However, I wondered where the money comes from to fulfill HFC's requirements. Does HFC dole out funding?

"No," Shay said. "Home Front Command does not actually give funds, but it can…designate funds… . Each local authority has its annual budget. Some of the budget is money…it gets from the government and some of it is collected…from taxes." Then, HFC declares, "this percentage should be designated for that. And [HFC] at the end of the year … [checks] to see how it was actually used," because as is true worldwide, sometimes governments try to use allocated money for things different than their intended purpose. In essence, HFC is a watchdog making sure the appropriate amount of money is devoted to passive security measures. Meanwhile, in peacetime, the local governments and their emergency personnel, like the police, remain in charge of internal security.

However, things change when the national government declares an emergency.

During peacetime, including floods, fire, and the like, local police departments under the command of the Ministry of Internal Security are responsible for internal security. This is true even though some members of civilian emergency services are reservists for HFC. The police then call upon fire and rescue services as required. But when the national government declares an emergency, control of the police and all other emergency services shifts to HFC. Then, people like Shay, who soon will command HFC operations in a portion of western Galilee, take charge of all emergency services and resources.

Simple? Not so. During COVID, which was not declared a national emergency, HFC and local authorities butted heads when they tried combining their resources. The same thing happened during the Second Lebanon War in 2006, when decisions, such as whether to close schools, caused friction between HFC and local authorities, even though it was a declared national emergency. Other examples also exist, whether a national emergency was declared or not, in which local authorities and HFC found themselves at loggerheads because politics is local, and city mayors and their ilk, I surmise, dislike ceding control. Nevertheless, Shay told me, "There is no other organization like the IDF that can deal" with the range of issues encountered in a national emergency such as a war with Hezbollah.

Yet, even in a national emergency, local police are better prepared to deal with local security issues than HFC reservists. So are firefighters and ambulance personnel. Therefore, HFC must be judicious in using its command authority. And HFC must think carefully about whom it recruits as reservists. For example, if called to duty as a reservist, will a person whose profession is a firefighter, police officer, or doctor honor their obligation to HFC, or will they use their specific skills to continue serving their community?

This, and other factors, makes selecting individual reservists for HFC complicated. Shay explained that after their mandatory military service, most soldiers must serve as reservists in the IDF. From that pool, the IDF designates where they will serve, including with HFC. Shay interviews those who show an interest in HFC, but he, like others, is picky. It does him no good to have a roster of reservists who will not or cannot report when needed. Therefore, those who plan to move abroad, for whatever reason, are unlikely to pique his interest. Same for those with other issues that would prevent their rapid deployment in an emergency. Having a great unit on paper is not enough. Paper will not save lives—only well-trained and motivated people able to serve on a moment's notice will.

Now that I understood HFC's structure and coordination problems, I asked, "How prepared is HFC for a real war with Hezbollah?"

Shay responded candidly. In a four-front war dealing with incoming fire from Lebanon, Syria, Gaza, and internal issues; Israel does not have enough Iron Dome protection to sufficiently reduce the number of missiles that will strike within its borders and does not have enough shelters in individual homes. The Arab community's residences, Shay told me, are even further behind than the Jewish ones. He explained what I had heard elsewhere, residences of Jews and Arabs alike built before 1991 do not have shelters. Multi-family buildings do have shelters within them or in the neighborhoods surrounding them, but that is not sufficient if you have no more than a ten to sixty-second warning.

Shay mentioning the Arab communities caught me off guard. Not because I discounted them, but because I was unaware their housing presented more issues for HFC than the Jewish communities did. It turns out that within those communities there are significant governance issues. Frequently, inhabitants build houses without permission or permits. Those homes may be fire traps, may not be able to withstand earthquakes, might be in flood plains, and all too often lack shelters. Until now, their lack of shelters has not been a huge problem because Hezbollah and Hamas usually target Jewish cities. But cities are increasingly mixed, and during an all-out war, the lack of shelters in Arab homes is sure to translate into unnecessary casualties in those communities.

Unfortunately, Arab communities in northern Israel also pose another potential problem in times of war—rioting and terror attacks. Until 2021, Israel's Arab population stayed neutral during wars and caused few problems. But that might be changing. During the May 2021 multi-day battle with Hamas in Gaza, some Israeli Arabs left their homes to block roads, infiltrate Jewish villages to kill citizens there, and burned police stations and attacked police and fire personnel as well as members of their communities. One day there were ninety distinct riots nationwide. In short, there was madness. This shocked and saddened many Jewish Israelis, especially those who had tried to improve their relationships with local Arab communities. And it surprised HFC.

"It's a very serious problem," Shay told me; because chaos often attracts criminals, who loot and kill. Adding this social phenomenon to the ongoing conflict between Jews and Arabs only exacerbates problems. Magnifying the issue further, in any future conflict, Hezbollah's agents and sympathizers are sure to incite riots that may be larger than in 2021. As a result, for example, firefighters seeking to extinguish a fire in an Arab town will face two dangers—the fire and anyone creeping up on them from behind.

Furthermore, in a future war, Shay predicted that troops and equipment flowing through Arab villages on roads leading to the borders will face, where bottlenecks exist, attacks from domestic Arab terrorists that will slow convoys and cause them to bunch up. This channelization of forces would create juicy targets for Hezbollah's missiles. Even though the IDF has established a reservist brigade to deal with those channels, they will do nothing for Jews in their homes. Jews in nearby villages and mixed Arab and Jewish towns, many of which lack a police station, will find their homes and residents facing both random and calculated attacks. In his sector, Shay said, "I don't have enough personnel and don't even have enough weapons [just twenty weapons for each of three rescue battalions] to provide security." Local police departments won't have enough, either. In 2021, many calls to the police went unanswered. This, of course, will create a dilemma for reservists called to duty. Should they go to the army or stay home to defend their families?

This lack of resources is not unknown. HFC is talking about its inability to protect citizens because many of its personnel are not combat soldiers. But talking is not doing. And while there is much of the former today, it's unclear how much there is of the latter.

I then asked Shay about the Druze because the Western Galilee has several Druze villages. Shay told me that civil disturbances will not be a problem there because, since 1948, Druze living in Israel have aligned themselves with the Jewish state. As such, they are drafted and serve in the army, which, Shay said, is "one of the best means of bonding …Israeli society." Shay feels the same about Arab Bedouin voluntarily serving in the IDF. "I trust them," he says, "As I trust myself." Same thing for Arab Christians who live in some northern Israel towns that have low crime rates compared to Arab Muslim towns. It is the hardcore Arab Muslims, Shay explained, who are the problem. The ones who don't serve in the military and who have complicated nationalistic aspirations that don't include living in a Jewish state. Nor do they desire to live in other Arab states. Instead, they hope one day to remain where they are—but without the presence of any Jews. Meaning, the end of Israel.

Our conversation then moved to the issue of evacuation. I expressed my concerns about the practicality of mass evacuation given the road network and told Shay about Lilach's plan to remain in place. To my surprise, Shay mirrored many of her thoughts:

> When you have an all-out war, you have attacks everywhere. So, it's not realistic to evacuate people because you can't evacuate them. If you have missiles fired from everywhere, you can't evacuate people. If you evacuate them from southern cities, if there are attacks from Gaza, we evacuate them to Tel Aviv, but Tel Aviv takes [fire] from both directions. You don't have anywhere to go….But if you have only a regional one-front conflict, like only for Lebanon, or only from, from Gaza, you can temporarily evacuate people. And we did that [before]. Evacuate[d] people and put them…in a different region that is not being attacked.
>
> [B]ut we have two problems with it. First, we anticipate that if you have a local issue, a local conflict, eventually it will become an all-out conflict because a war with Lebanon will be with Syria too, and eventually with Gaza and the West Bank too, and Israeli Arab(s). And so, you can't start evacuating people from the north to the south and then back and forth. You can't do that. Second thing is if you have refugee camps, you have [a] really serious problem. You need to feed them. You need to protect them. [I]t's an issue because if you [build] a refugee camp, people come from the north [to] near Tel-Aviv and then rockets would start being fired at Tel-Aviv and it will happen eventually.

"Then they are all concentrated," I said.

"Concentrated under tents."

What a perfect target for Hezbollah missiles.

Furthermore, Shay said, "We need to clear the roads for our troops….And because we have a small army, sometimes we need to move them between sectors, and we need the roads clear." They can't be clogged by frightened civilians fleeing missiles and UAVs, targeted strikes that may damage interchanges, and marauding domestic terrorists bent on mayhem.

Therefore, because of all the problems that accompany a mass evacuation, Shay said it is important to separate the populace into categories based on the danger they will face. Today, Israel's vigorous shelter program, which is still a work in progress, protects many Jewish communities and will protect even more in the future. Thus, those people can stay home. However, because Hezbollah is targeting them for capture, HFC may need to evacuate up to 10,000 people living in border communities. Even though Hezbollah's success, at most, would be fleeting, the consequences for those people taken and the propaganda surge that would result is something that Israel cannot afford. That's why HFC is not planning for a mass evacuation—only a much smaller, targeted one. And then there are the Arab communities. Lax residential licensing enforcement has caused a problem that politicians, who prefer to kick the can down the road, especially when faced with cultural barriers, have yet to fix.

The problem is time. Hezbollah might start a war without notice—perhaps a massive missile attack or just an attack on a border village designed to capture it. "And those villages," Shay said, "don't have the means to protect themselves. And not only that, we disarmed most of the settlements. We ourselves as a government."

I was incredulous.

Three years earlier, I visited Kibbutz Hanita, located directly on the border, where I met the commander of that kibbutz's civilian reaction force. The kibbutz had guns at the time. What about now? What changed? Shay answered my question based on his knowledge as a commander, coupled with his experience living on a kibbutz where he wears yet another hat—commander of its local reaction force. "Until a year ago, we had…ten or fifteen guns [including M-16s] the police department gave us.…If something occur[s], I open the armory. I call my squad, I give them the weapons, and we can protect ourselves." But since local Arab terrorists and criminals had stolen many weapons from kibbutz armories, and even though many more guns have been stolen from IDF bases, authorities decided to collect weapons from individuals and store them at central locations. Of course, that defeats the purpose of the weapons. By the time authorities identify an emergency and distribute those weapons to communities in danger, it will be too late. But it gets worse. The authorities refused to provide residents with permits to purchase their own weapons. All to reduce the number of weapons illegally circulating on the street. Especially the Arab street. A noble cause with a frightening impact.

This refusal to allow settlements to maintain their own weapons arsenals will create another problem in addition to the problem of defending against border incursions. Shay explained that arms legally possessed by civilians (people living in Judea/Samaria, those who have attained a specific army rank, school bus drivers, and the like) have dropped from 300,000 to 150,000. That drop combined with a population increase has left only 1.5% of the civilian Jewish population possessing legal firearms, as opposed to the previous figure of 4.5%. While that might still sound like a lot, approximately 400,000 illegally possessed weapons are circulating in Arab communities, mostly in the hands of criminals and would-be terrorists. In the chaos of a general war, 400,000 versus 150,000 weapons make for bad odds. So bad that Shay admitted that, although he volunteers with the police, has a senior HFC command, and leads his local community's quick reaction force: "I don't have any solution…to protect my own family."

This left me disconcerted. Hoping to quiet my concerns, I asked whether the border communities have any hope of defending themselves from a determined attack by Hezbollah's Radwan unit. Shay responded that some in those communities do possess personal pistols and that they can lock their doors at night. Combined, he said, that will reduce Radwan's ability to slaughter civilians before the IDF arrives in force. His response did not alleviate my concern. I've walked through many of those communities. I know how close they are to the border and how easy it would be for a determined group to force its way in. To my mind, those shorn of guns have been stripped of the ability to defend themselves. When Hezbollah kidnapped IDF soldiers in 2000, and again in 2006, they used massive missile and mortar barrages to distract and slow an IDF response. Simultaneous with any surreptitious attack on a border community, Hezbollah will almost certainly do the same. Without more than a few scattered pistols and hastily locked doors, I fear residents and communities will fall to Hezbollah's sword.

Nearing the end of our time together, I asked Shay whether there is any program that ensures the border communities have sufficient food, medical supplies, etc. to hold out several days without resupply. He said no. But his "no" was not one of despair. Shay was certain the IDF would never permit one of the settlements to remain isolated for several days, no matter how challenging the road network is, and no matter how trying the obstacles are.

During our last few moments, I inquired about the more populated Israeli towns, like Nahariya or Kiryat Shmona, near, but not on the border. I inferred from his response that there would be no planned evacuation for people living in those cities. Instead, they would have to rely on shelters now in place and missile defense systems such as Iron Dome.

At the end of the interview, I asked what I thought would be my final question. What, I inquired, would you do today if you were made commander of HFC, and the prime minister said to you there will be a war with Hezbollah in two years? Shay responded that Israel has lots of good, well-trained manpower in their twenties and thirties doing little to further Israel's defense. Therefore, he would build more light infantry brigades under HFC's command. Each would be assigned an area to protect. Each would learn all the idiosyncrasies of its sector—including priorities of the politicians, local police department concerns, etc. In a national emergency, the members of those brigades would be drafted. They would then have the weapons, training, and local knowledge to protect the citizenry. In November 2022, Dr. Yagil Henkin mirrored this suggestion in an article he wrote that is posted on the Jerusalem Institute for Strategic Studies' website.

Shay's hope for more manpower in tune with local needs is not in place today. HFC knows it only has enough resources to defend its installations and convoys, not the entire population.

Unable to resist, I snuck in a follow-up question, asking if there was anything else on his wish list—no limits. Shay's final words to me were:

> I think we should wake up and smell the coffee. Like you say, we have a very serious problem. We should stop avoiding it. I really have to say, it's not like professional, but you should grow a pair of balls to deal with things. And not only think about the present, we should think long-term and we should combine all the parts of each of Israeli society. On the one hand to hug everyone, to give them the opportunity to be equal all parts of Israeli society, but on the other hand [we] will have to force them to follow the rules, to force them to work together to firstly not to act against their own country.

> We have to do that.

Most Israelis I spoke with had little knowledge of Home Front Command's origin, purpose, and capabilities. You now know far more than they do. I see that as a significant domestic problem because what I learned alarmed me. Israel has the framework in place to provide a vibrant civil defense. It has done so regarding threats emanating from Gaza, but it cannot do so in a full-fledged war with Hezbollah. If the 2006 Second Lebanon War is any guide, given the present threat, the institutional framework today is not nearly sufficient to protect Israeli citizens and society in northern Israel, and likely to a lesser degree elsewhere in Israel. That leaves a gap Hezbollah will exploit and one that restricts Israel's freedom of action. Much more needs to be done.

Time is running out.

Chapter Twenty

Deterrence

Before discussing Israel's deterrence strategy regarding Hezbollah, it is important to define the word deterrence. In Chapter Ten I provided a working definition of deterrence. But now it is time to be more precise. I searched for a simple, but relevant, definition that covers the nuances of this complex term and found two. Oddly enough, one came from David Petraeus, a retired American general and former CIA director. He said, "Deterrence is founded on an adversary's perception of your capabilities and your will." Gabi Eisenkot, a former IDF chief of staff, wrote something similar in 2019, saying: "Deterrence…involves discouraging the nation's enemies from acting against it based on military and security force buildup and the preparedness and willingness to counter the enemy's intention to violate the sovereignty, daily life, and security of the nation's citizens."

Therefore, deterring Hezbollah requires considering three things: how much harm Israel can do to Hezbollah; Hezbollah's and Iran's perception of the same; and whether they believe Israel has the will to accept the consequences of doing so. Can Israel significantly harm Hezbollah? What might Israel need to acquire to do so? How has, and should, Israel shape Hezbollah's perception of Israel's capability and willingness to strike it? And is Israel's ability to establish deterrence impacted by Hezbollah's relationship with Iran? The rest of this chapter is devoted to these questions. Chapter Twenty-Three addresses Israel's will to fight.

Soon after the end of the Second Lebanon war, Nasrallah told an interviewer, "We did not think, even one percent, that the capture [of the IDF soldiers] would lead to a war at this time and of this magnitude….If I had known on July 11…that the operations would lead to such a war, would I do it? I say no, absolutely not." Proof positive, I think, that Israel's deterrence had failed before the 2006 war. But now, many Israeli experts, including some I spoke with, point to that statement as proof that, since 2006, Hezbollah has been deterred by its knowledge of what Israel would do to it, and Lebanon, in the event of another war. Surely, they say or write, after experiencing those catastrophic blows and equipped with the knowledge that the IDF's capabilities have vastly improved since then, Nasrallah is deterred from launching a full-fledged attack on Israel. But is he? Also important is whether Iran is deterred from slinging Hezbollah at Israel. I'm not so sure about either. Just as plausible is that the can has been kicked down the road, whether due to Israel's deterrence or Hezbollah's and Iran's design, but that one day soon that road will come to an end. We shall explore that concept.

But before we do, let's eliminate any doubt about Israel's offensive capabilities. As long ago as 2017, IAF Commander Maj. Gen. Amir Eshel said, "What we could do in thirty-four days during the Second Lebanon War, we can now do in 48 hours," and while doing so employ "four to five times" the total firepower of air operations compared to the Second Lebanon War." In 2019, Petraeus expressed his confidence regarding Israel's deterrence of Hezbollah. Summarizing the IDF's force structure, he said that Israel had dramatically improved its anti-missile defense systems while also establishing a robust offensive structure that would employ rockets, artillery, other indirect fires, and especially its air force, which flies "the most sophisticated aircraft in the world, the F-35." Since then, the IDF's defensive and offensive systems have surely improved. As has the IDF's ability to acquire targets. Yaakov Lappin wrote in

December 2022 that the IDF now uses advanced artificial intelligence systems to identify many more targets with information gleaned and collated from sensor systems already in use. Those targets can then be hit by weapons designed to do the job, but not destroy anything else. Therefore, he writes, if ammunition is stored on one floor of a seven-story building in a crowded town, the IDF can accurately deliver an explosive projectile tailored to the job that will destroy the target but not knock down the building or injure non-combatants scattered elsewhere in the structure.

Similarly, new techniques offer the prospect of doing what Uzi Rubin said was crucial—destroying rocket launchers. Eran Ortal wrote that it's possible to detect rocket launchers by saturating suspected regions with air and ground sensors. Then, if that information is integrated with appropriate offensive systems, those launchers could be destroyed before they shoot and then scoot. While that might not prevent the first rocket launch, it would stop the second.

Combined, these new techniques make war more palatable for Israel if it can destroy Hezbollah's offensive weaponry before it can be used. As a result of these advances and increased force structure, now in the event of war, thousands of targets inside Lebanon will be attacked daily with greater accuracy than ever before. That, combined with the IDF's well-configured and rapidly moving ground forces, which now train constantly to carry the fight into Lebanon—something that was not the case in 2006—means Israel can obliterate Hezbollah and destroy Lebanon if it so chooses. But to establish deterrence, Israel's rhetoric must make it crystal clear what Israel will do if there is a war. Then, Hezbollah must be convinced that the IDF has the capability, and Israel's government has the willpower, to execute Israel's war plan.

In 2008, Gabi Eizenkot initiated that process. While serving as commander of Israel's northern front, he said, "What happened in the

Dahiya quarter [the built-up area where Hezbollah's headquarters was located that the IDF destroyed in the Second Lebanon War] of Beirut in 2006 will happen in every village from which Israel is fired on. We will apply disproportionate force on it and cause great damage and destruction there. From our standpoint, these are not civilian villages, they are military bases." Harsh, but reasonable given that Hezbollah hides its missiles, command posts, tunnels, and other military infrastructure in some 200 Shiite villages in southern Lebanon and that in many circumstances there is no other way to prevent the weapons hidden there from being used to kill many Israelis in a future war. Two years later, Eizenkot reiterated that while casting blame, saying, "Hezbollah is the one that is turning these areas into battlegrounds." And then Eizenkot spoke of deterrence without expressly saying so: "I hope this will restrain them…but if not, we need to explain ourselves and to others that this is something that Hezbollah has brought upon itself since it is building its combat zones inside these villages."

In 2012, then Prime Minister Netanyahu buttressed Israel's deterrence posture when he explained that if Hezbollah provoked a war, "As far as we're concerned, the Lebanese government is responsible for whatever happens in its jurisdiction," and therefore Israel would not differentiate between Hezbollah and the Lebanese state. Again, harsh but fair—especially since Hezbollah now participates in, and by many measures, controls Lebanon's government. Former Prime Minister Naftali Bennett further illuminated Israel's intent in a 2017 interview with *Haaretz*, while he was serving as a legislator:

> The Lebanese institutions, its infrastructure, airport, power stations, traffic junctions, Lebanese Army bases—they should all be legitimate targets if a war breaks out. That's what we should already be saying to them and the world now. If Hezbollah fires

missiles at the Israeli home front, this will mean sending Lebanon back to the Middle Ages.

Professor Nagel expounded similar harsh rhetoric when he said to me regarding Nasrallah, "He knows he'll be dead. He knows that [Hezbollah's] next confrontation against Israel…will bring back Lebanon to the stone ages." And then there was Gabi Ashkenazi, another former IDF chief of staff, who expressed the sentiment best, "In the next war, it will be forbidden to ask who won."

Has the message gotten through to Hezbollah? Jonathan Conricus, who recently retired as the IDF's international spokesperson, thinks so. He told me that Israel's biggest "media or perceptional success over the years has been getting our enemy to understand that the destruction they dealt with in 2006, and have been dealing with since, will be a fraction of what will happen again if they attack us." I don't think that Conricus is wrong. Israel's messaging has been consistent, on point, and clear. Nasrallah would have to be tone-deaf not to have heard it. But does it matter?

Jonathan Spyer thinks it does. I met with Spyer in a restaurant at First Station, a converted Turkish train station now home to funky restaurants and walkways. Spyer is the author of *Days of the Fall*, based on his undercover journalist trips to Syria and Iraq. He also wrote *The Transforming Fire*, anchored in part, on his undercover journalistic trip to Lebanon that included spying the route he took during the 2006 war from the vantage point where Hezbollah's operatives shot at his tank. Spyer's books fascinated me. Every page left me marveling at his courage. Even if he had nothing relevant to tell me, I was determined to meet him. Our hour-and-a-half conversation did not disappoint. Regarding Hezbollah, he told me:

> I think it is deterred.…Hezbollah is a complex organization.…They are Lebanese after all, and they do understand that if they want to continue ruling Lebanon as well, [and] if that war happens…one way or another, with the smoke

and ruin, it would be hard for them to reassert again. I mean the big war, the great Northern War.

Amos Yadlin thinks so, too. Yadlin, a former general in the IAF and former head of the IDF's Military Intelligence Directorate, told the Jewish News Syndicate, "Deterrence is that your enemy, who has the capability to pull the trigger, after doing the calculation the cost-benefit analysis of what will happen, is not doing it." Therefore, he, as is true of many experts I met with, believes Hezbollah has been deterred from attacking Israel.

Maybe.

Or maybe it is waiting for the balance of power to shift in its favor. Or when Lebanon's domestic politics dictate that Hezbollah must take a swing—as it almost did with the off-shore gas issue coupled with its relatively poor showing in recent elections. Or very likely when Iran orders an attack. Call these intervening semi-peaceful years that now amount to almost two decades a product of deterrence if you want. Or just call it what it might be—a simple calculation that the time has not yet been right.

But one thing is certain. Israel's ability to take Lebanon apart does not deter Iran. To modify a well-worn phrase, Iran is happy to use Hezbollah to fight Israel to the last structure in Lebanese villages and the last Hezbollah operative if it suits Iran's purpose. Until then, the Iranians want Hezbollah to remain intact and be ready to respond should Israel attack Iran. That is why Iran was unhappy when Nasrallah started the Second Lebanon War. But Iran's control is also why all of Israel's deterrence strategy may mean little because it is focused on just one party—Hezbollah—rather than Iran, too.

Knesset legislator Nir Barkat sees a need to deter Iran to deter Hezbollah. In a September 2022 interview with Fox New Digital, he said, "We have to make sure that Iran understands that if…and when they use their proxies to attack Israel, it's not going to be the Third

Lebanese War, it will be the First Iran War, and we will attack Tehran." Whether that is politically and militarily feasible or even believable is beyond the scope of this book. However, Barkat's thought highlights my concern. Does Israel's present deterrence strategy fail to deter the most necessary party?

Eizenkot, meanwhile, may have alluded to the problem—intentionally or not—in 2015, while working as IDF's chief of staff, when he wrote, "Deterrence must be specific and adapted to each enemy; it must be based on an ongoing analysis of the enemy's characteristics, considerations, capabilities, identity, and decision-making processes." Based on Iran's significant influence on Hezbollah, a deterrence strategy that does not account for Tehran is flawed at best and nonexistent at worst. Spyer thinks Iran is deterred from permitting Hezbollah to attack Israel for now because it wants Hezbollah intact to deter Israel from attacking Iranian nuclear facilities. So, "right now [they] have to be very, very careful because otherwise the instrument for the future apocalyptic war gets destroyed so actually [Iran] is deterred." Of course, as discussed in Chapter Seventeen, it is unclear whether Hezbollah would honor an Iranian order to go to war.

Fortunately, I have found little evidence of Israeli complacency, which is a danger of misplaced reliance on deterrence. The IDF now constantly drills for war with Hezbollah, while steadily improving its offensive and defensive capabilities. But Israeli leaders haven't taken the next step—linking Hezbollah's behavior to its deterrence policy with Iran. For now, Iran knows that if it attacks Israel, the IDF will respond. Better, I think, would be to warn Iran that if Hezbollah starts a war, Iran won't go unpunished.

Unfortunately, Hezbollah is also practicing deterrence. The Rules of the Game are undoubtedly supported by Hezbollah's deterrence of Israel. As such, Israel's perception that it would suffer a heavy price if war broke out with Hezbollah ensures that Nasrallah's threats are heeded. That has impacted Israel's behavior. For ample evidence of Hezbollah's deterrence in real-time, one need only look to the IDF's unwillingness to strike provocative targets in Lebanon. But has that deterrence impacted Israeli policy in other ways? To answer that, we need to look no further than the offshore gas field crises that simmered for ten years before almost boiling over in 2022.

Let's review again what happened. During the summer of 2022, before a deal was reached, Nasrallah jumped full bore into the dispute—launching four UAVs at Israel's working gas-pumping installation and then threatened that if Israel extracted oil from the Karish field without a deal in place, Hezbollah would strike Israeli targets on land and sea. To attack the gas rig, Hezbollah might have aimed anti-ship missiles at the Karish oil rig, as it did in 2006 to strike an Israeli naval vessel. Alternatively, Nasrallah could have ordered a swarm UAV attack, as Iran had in Saudi Arabia, or he could have used his naval unit. For that, Hezbollah has divers trained to use boats, mini-subs, and other craft to surreptitiously attach explosives to targets in the ocean. In addition, in preparation for some form of confrontation, Hezbollah's operatives had positioned themselves close to the border in many places. The threat was clear.

Israel reacted strongly to the threats, prepositioning naval craft, an Iron Dome battery, and soldiers. But since Hezbollah may have targeted more than just the Karish oil rig, if fighting would have started, in the fog of war Hezbollah might have attained some success somewhere.

Could Hezbollah have executed a pinprick attack short of war? Sure. But Hezbollah's mere attempt, let alone any level of success, would have instigated a massive response from the IDF—something U.S. Secretary of State Anthony Blinken acknowledged in September 2022. That attack most certainly would have led Hezbollah to respond, bringing matters to a fever pitch and leading to the First

Northern War, involving Hezbollah, Lebanon, Syria, Gaza, Western Iraq, possibly Iran, all of Israel, and possibly elsewhere.

A gas deal was reached, though, and war did not break out. But did Israel strike the deal because it served its interests or because Hezbollah's threats deterred Israel from starting gas production in the Karish field? Experts differ. Some focus on the agreement successfully preventing a war. Others point to Israel maintaining the buoy line status quo and gaining an unfettered ability to start gas production in the Karish field, as well as the potential for earning royalties from the Qana field. But those opposed speak of the price Israel paid. As a result, Hezbollah solidified its political position after an election that produced equivocal results. Nasrallah began a messaging campaign to Lebanon's populace that its recent involvement, after many years of fruitless negotiation without it, had caused Israel to fold in fear of Hezbollah. Second, the crucial sea border within twelve miles of Rosh Hanikra has not been finalized—it's just frozen for now—which leaves the possibility that that issue, and other areas being disputed, will become part of a future borderline crisis instigated by Nasrallah. Third, it is unclear where Lebanon's share of the money will go. Remember, Hezbollah controls Lebanon's government. Will the money go to the people desperate for economic relief, Shiites only, Hezbollah, or even Iran? Today, we do not know.

If the doubters are correct, and I think they are, then Hezbollah's ability to deter Israel played a role. Months before, Israel's position in the negotiations was much more hardline—and, given the facts, fair. What changed? Perhaps politics related to upcoming Israeli elections was one element, but Hezbollah's threats were certainly the driving force. Israel did not want war. Was Hezbollah conducting a high-stakes bluff? We will never know. But its messaging was exquisite. The Qana field, from which Lebanon won most of the benefits, was once called the Sidon field. Lebanon renamed it Qana to remind the world of a mistaken IDF strike in 1996 that killed many Lebanese citizens, which Hezbollah then capitalized on for propaganda purposes, even though Hezbollah operatives were the underlying cause of the attack. No doubt the renaming was instigated by Hezbollah for propaganda purposes and to emphasize its determination. Since deterrence involves perception, it was the perfect prop.

Unfortunately, the gas negotiations are not the only instance where Hezbollah has pushed the envelope to expand its deterrence umbrella. When, despite sanctions on Iran, Hezbollah arranged for Iranian oil to be shipped to Lebanon, it threatened to retaliate against Israel if it tried to block the shipments. And, of course, there is the issue of overflights. Knowing where Hezbollah stores its missiles and locates defensive positions is critical to the IDF. Hezbollah threatened to shoot down Israeli aircraft flying over Lebanon. Israel changed its operations as a result. Therefore, deterrence between Israel and Hezbollah goes both ways.

Determining where Israel's and Hezbollah's deterrence intersect requires knowing what each side perceives and calculates based on different goals, as well as recognizing each side's capabilities and thresholds for pain. It's a determination grounded in some facts but susceptible to subjective, faulty assessments. Let's hope that balance favors Israel, but there is no guarantee it does.

And then there is the problem of accidental war. Deterrence only marginally impacts the likelihood of that. But the outbreak of an accidental war is a real risk. Yadlin said, "Looking at all the Arab and Persian leaders, they know how to make mistakes. So, this is one concern." In addition, Yadlin worries about what he called "under-the-threshold" activities that either Hezbollah or Israel do not think will trigger an all-out war but about which they could be wrong. What is rationally perceived as a threshold by one side may not meet the rational or emotional red lines of the other side. Therefore, deterrence only goes so far, and the desire to enhance it adds its own risks of accidental war.

One of those under-the-threshold activities is the war between wars that Israel is presently conducting in Syria. It is to that we now turn.

Chapter Twenty-One

Israel Mows the Lawn

Lacking the will to pay the awful price in blood, treasure, and international condemnation required for rooting Hezbollah out of Lebanon, Israel sought an alternative. Beginning in 2013, Israel has cleverly focused on interdicting weaponry and PGM manufacturing machinery on its way to Lebanon from Iran. In addition, on an ongoing basis, Israel has acted to prevent Hezbollah and Iran from establishing military bases along Syria's border with Israel. To prevent this attempt to create another Shiite front, Israel has used its air force to destroy targets and killed some particularly capable Iranian military officers operating in Syria—the most recent, as of this writing, by a roadside bomb outside Damascus in November 2022 and possibly by missile strike in February 2023. Collectively, this process constitutes Israel's Campaign Between Wars (CBW) or *Mabam* in Hebrew. Sometimes it is referred to as "mowing the lawn," the lawn being Syria and sometimes Western Iraq. But most pointedly, it doesn't include Lebanese territory.

Why not?

Because the Rules of the Game dictate that if Israel attacks targets in Lebanon, Hezbollah will retaliate by striking targets in Israel. And, to further complicate things, those byzantine rules extend to Hezbollah personnel in Syria. However, weapons in transit are fair game. So is destroying Syrian and Iranian bases in Syria and Iraq as long as Hezbollah operatives are not killed. Killing them exposes the

IDF to Hezbollah's retribution. Due to the nature of these intricate understandings, this chapter is required reading for sorting out Israel's efforts to slow Hezbollah's march while still abiding by the Rules of the Game.

Generally, the last leg of the journey for weapons being delivered to Hezbollah involves trucking them from Syria to the Bekaa Valley. There, they are usually first stored in bunkers located in Shiite villages. But getting them there is a cat-and-mouse game, in which the trucks are the mice and Israel's air force the cat. While those caravans are en route, Hezbollah stops electrical and phone service in pertinent regions of Lebanon hoping to prevent Israeli agents on the ground from alerting the IDF that the caravans are coming. However, to avoid tipping off the Israelis, Hezbollah intermittently turns off those services even when nothing is being transported.

Since the 1990s, the methods Iran has used to deliver weapons and the lethality of those weapons have transitioned. While he ruled Syria, Hafez Assad was cautious; so only light weapons and some anti-tank missiles, mortars, mines, and ammunition made the trip, none of which posed a strategic threat to Israel. Just pinpricks that cost lives. Some made the journey because of Syrian policy, and others arrived because corrupt Syrian officers had smuggled them to their destinations.

After Assad died, Syria and Iran grew closer; as did Syria and Hezbollah. When Assad's son Bashar assumed control of Syria, he allowed Iran to send longer-range missiles to Hezbollah, including M-600 missiles. Whether Bashar did so, at least in part, because in 2007 the Israelis had destroyed Syria's secret nuclear reactor that was under construction, is conjecture. The deliveries were coordinated by Muhammad Suleiman, a Syrian general, until 2008 when he met an untimely death. While dining with friends on the balcony of his home overlooking the ocean, a sniper's bullet felled him. The gunshot came from a boat anchored near the beach. Likely, it was an Israeli operation.

Still, the weapons kept coming.

Then came the Syrian Civil War, and in 2011, as rebels took more and more Syrian territory, Bashar Assad transferred some Syrian weapons to Hezbollah for safekeeping—including surface-to-surface and surface-to-sea missiles. In exchange, Hezbollah agreed to return those weapons upon request and, reportedly, not to use them against Israel without Syria's permission. In addition, because there was no land corridor, Iran relied more on flying weapons to Damascus International Airport as the first step in their journey to Hezbollah. Reportedly, after the civil war started, Iran had no other choice; Turkey was no longer turning a blind eye toward ignoring trans-shipments passing through its territory. Hezbollah personnel would then unload those weapons under the watchful eye of Syrian security, a practice that continues today. The weapons are then stored in Syrian warehouses until Hezbollah transports them to Lebanon in convoys of no more than a few trucks. This became the primary method for sneaking advanced weaponry to Hezbollah, although Iran also used cargo ships to transport weapons to Latakia, a seaport in northern Syria.

Two years later, in 2013, Iran introduced new technology to Hezbollah—precision-guided missiles (PGMs). At first, Iran's Quds Force was responsible for moving PGMs out of Iran. Israel's air force was successful in thwarting this effort. Then, in 2015, Iran switched tactics. Rather than transfer the missiles from where they were built in the homeland, it tried to enable Syrian factories to manufacture PGMs. Israel successfully interfered with that effort as well through targeted air strikes. But Iran refused to be denied and took a different approach in 2018. Assuming that, per the Rules of the Game, Israel would not strike PGM factories in Lebanon, Iran began surreptitiously moving—by land, sea, and air—materials required to manufacture PGMs to Lebanese soil. In 2019, seeking to put an end to this new endeavor, Israel arguably violated the Rules of the Game. An Israeli drone struck a target in the Bekaa Valley that purportedly contained equipment for making PGMs. Although tensions in the region escalated after the attack, Hezbollah did not respond meaningfully.

Some researchers believe that Israel has largely succeeded in halting Iran's and Hezbollah's PGM programs. They think that Hezbollah only possesses a few dozen PGMs. Others put the number in the hundreds. But whatever the number may be, it's growing. Total prevention is impossible. Relying on detection and interdiction to prevent such destabilizing weapons from being constructed in the future are thin reeds indeed. There isn't a perfect solution for preventing domestic production in limited amounts or transshipment of PGM kits on Iranian flights to Syria or Beirut (to this day Iranian planes land at Beirut's international airport, some under the guise of bringing medical supplies). Especially when a well-trained team given the proper tools and materials can convert a "dumb" missile to a PGM in three hours at a cost of about $10,000. Therefore, I am not optimistic.

This brings us to the CBW, which many also refer to as the war between wars.

Lieutenant Colonel. (res.) Sarit Zehavi, founder and president of *Alma,* while speaking to a group of foreign military personnel on top of Mount Bental overlooking the Syrian landscape, discussed the guiding psychological philosophy of the CBW. She said, "You know your enemy, his nature, you know that [if] you humiliate your enemy he will be obliged to respond. So don't humiliate your enemy. You never admit you carried out the attack unless you have a specific interest in doing that." And until recently, Israel was quite circumspect about its hundreds of air strikes designed to prevent Iran from arming Hezbollah and creating bases along Syria's border with Israel.

The operational goal of the CBW is to decrease the threat level while simultaneously improving conditions on the ground should war come. In addition, by repeatedly demonstrating its willingness to act, Israel hopes to deter Hezbollah, maintain the IDF's freedom of action by narrowing the scope of what the Rules of the Game proscribes, complicate Hezbollah's planning, and limit the organization's freedom of action. By April 2022, according to one writer, Israel had conducted more than 400 airstrikes to further the goals of the CBW. Others, quoting Israeli sources, put the number at hundreds in 2020 alone. In 2019, outgoing Chief of Staff Gadi Eizenkot said the number of targets hit since the CBW began several years before, was in the thousands. During the fall of 2022 and heading into the winter of 2023, Israel appears to be increasing the frequency and brazenness of its attacks. What's the exact number of air strikes? How frequent will they be now? Jonathan Schanzer, the author of *Gaza Conflict 2021* and a prominent expert regarding the Middle East, obtained this quote from a senior Israeli official, who joked, "Who's counting?"

Although the number of air strikes remains debatable, their targets are well established. In the past, most CBW strikes have targeted air defense systems, UAV bases run by Iranians, and PGM missile systems headed for Hezbollah. The strikes have killed more than 300 people on the ground, including Iranian commanders, Syrian military personnel, Iranian-backed militants, and, perhaps, three civilians (possibly due to Syrian munitions falling back to earth). Now, Israel has widened its scope of targeting. In the summer of 2022, Israeli planes dropped ordinance that damaged runways at the international airport near Damascus and weeks later did the same to an airport near Aleppo. The clear intent behind those attacks was to interdict Iran's increasing attempts to use civilian air traffic to carry munitions of war. On September 17, 2022, another Israeli air strike hit storage facilities near the northernmost runway of Damascus' supposedly civilian airport. Those facilities, which store incoming weapons and PGM production equipment destined for Hezbollah, are managed by a Lebanese unit inserted within Iran's Islamic Revolutionary Guards Corp (IRGC). The fall saw more strikes at airbases and military posts that killed Syrian and Iranian soldiers. Tal Beeri, head of the research department at *Alma,* assessed:

> The message is clear. So long as Iran's air corridor for smuggling weapons from Iran to Syria and Lebanon continues, the Syrian state will be as responsible.…So long as Syria won't act, the airport will continue to be a target.…The messaging is not aimed at Iran—that is a lost cause. It is determined to continue trafficking arms to Hezbollah. It is aimed at Syria.

Notably, most Israeli strikes have not elicited a response from Hezbollah—one remarkable exception being an attack on February 24, 2014, when Israeli jets destroyed a building storing weaponry bound for Lebanon. For that Hezbollah promised to retaliate and did. But, except for a roadside bomb in Shebaa Farms that wounded four IDF soldiers, the retaliation came mostly from Syrian soil. Otherwise, the IDF did not incur any casualties.

Iran has tried, unsuccessfully, to physically intimidate Israel into taking a step backward; its messaging efforts have attempted to do the same. On February 10, 2018, an Iranian UAV flew into Israeli airspace. Israel's air force (IAF) shot it down. Israel then destroyed the command-and-control center in Syria responsible for operating that UAV. During that operation, a Russian-supplied surface-to-air missile (SAM) shot down an Israeli jet. That led to the IAF destroying multiple SAM sites in Syria. The next three months saw more IAF strikes hitting Iranian bases and missile storage sites in Syria, all designed to prevent Iran and its proxy Hezbollah from establishing bases in Syria and transporting weapons to Hezbollah's waiting hands.

When, on May 9, the IRGC fired twenty rockets at IDF positions on the Golan Heights, (four on track to strike civilian or military locations were intercepted by Iron Dome and the rest fell harmlessly), the IDF struck back hard, hitting all known Iranian sites in Syria (numbering in the dozens) and Syrian SAM sites.

However, in September 2018, Israel's ability to mow the lawn in Syria became more complicated. When Israeli aircraft struck multiple targets in Syria, Syria's missile defenses tried and failed to shoot them down. But one Syrian anti-air missile struck an unintended target. When the missile whistled past the IAF plane it was targeting, rather than immediately fall to the ground, it kept flying. Twenty-five miles off Syria's coast, the missile inadvertently struck a Russian reconnaissance plane tracking developments. Its Russian crew died.

Rather than blame Syria for the debacle, the Russians blamed Israel, charging that the IDF had only provided them with a one-minute warning of the impending strike and, even worse, that the Israeli planes used the Russian plane to cover their strike. Israel presented proof that refuted those nonsensical charges. Nevertheless, the Russians continued to blame Israel, perhaps as a false pretext for what followed. Later that month Russia gave the Syrians a much more advanced missile defense system. As a result, Israel's aerial missions have become more complicated due to the need for new operational procedures that placate the Russians and that take extra measures to avoid the more advanced missile defense systems Syria now possesses.

In the past, Iran tried to send its contraband by air, land, and sea. Airplanes and ships can store more cargo than individual trucks can. But they're also easier to track and disrupt. The air route usually incorporates Damascus International Airport, but that has been the subject of much Israeli activity in recent years. The sea route has used the Port of Latakia in northern Syria as its terminus before trucking the landed goods to Hezbollah. However, in 2021, two IAF air strikes destroyed Iranian shipping containers there, causing Russia to put its military forces in Latakia to stop the shipments. Even so, it is likely some Iranian goods for Hezbollah still make their way there.

And now there is the matter of civilians smuggling Iranian PGM kits, and others being transported on civilian airlines. *Alma* published a startling photo taken in 2021 in which members of Iran's soccer team are shown arriving at Beirut's international airport for a two-day stay. This didn't seem, on the surface, too unusual; however, each person in the picture was wheeling multiple large suitcases on a cart. *Alma* wondered what they contained. It was a lot of luggage for ostensibly a forty-eight-hour sojourn.

Even more concerning is what Mahan Air, an Iranian airline that began operations in 1992, is up to. Mahan Air is based at Imam Khomeini International Airport near Tehran, operates passenger and cargo flights and is Iran's largest private airline. It used to fly to Europe, but that was largely stopped by sanctions placed on Iran. In 2022, according to Tal Beeri, it flew at least 110 times to Damascus International Airport, thirty-nine times to Beirut, and another twelve to Syria's Aleppo airport. Its CEO, according to Beeri, has been involved with the IRGC. Is Mahan Air smuggling arms and PGM equipment destined for Hezbollah? I can't answer for sure. But perhaps that is why Israel has bombed Syria's civilian airports near Damascus and Aleppo. And perhaps that is why a December 2022 article in the *Times of Israel* reported that Israel has warned Lebanon it may strike the airport in Beirut if smuggling is ongoing. Not an empty threat since Israel has released pictures of purported PGM factories built underground about 300 yards from Beirut's airport.

But opening a direct land route to Lebanon remains of high priority for Iran and Hezbollah. Although Iran will continue to move illicit goods from time to time by sea and air depending on the level of risk it perceives at that moment, it will always need a road route that provides continuity for its supply of Hezbollah. Today, a shaky land corridor extends 1,100 miles from Tehran, running from where many of Iran's military industries are, to Damascus. It snakes across the border of Iraq, into Syria, and around remaining concentrations of ISIS fighters still entrenched in deserted areas of Syria. It is a corridor by which Iran sends military goods to Hezbollah and avoids export sanctions to send banned goods to Europe. Periodically, reports emerge of Israel's interdiction of that route, both in Syria and in western Iraq.

The route used is one of three potential paths. The other two routes, as mentioned previously, remain blocked for now—to the north by the Kurds and to the south by American forces at al-Tanf.

Is there any realistic hope that Israel will succeed in choking off future Iranian attempts to further arm Hezbollah? I think not. In 2006, before the Second Lebanon War began, Hezbollah had up to 15,000 missiles. It used nearly 4,000 in the war, and Israel destroyed many others before they could be launched. Still, Hezbollah ended the war with an inventory of several thousand missiles. Now, sixteen years later, Hezbollah's missile inventory has increased by an average of 9,000 missiles per year—many of which carry a much larger payload and are far more accurate than what Hezbollah had in 2006. As a result, today Hezbollah boasts an inventory of 150,000 missiles that threaten Israel's existence as a modern, vibrant state. Thus, mowing the lawn is an improper metaphor. Israel's CBW has not cut the grass to a manageable length. At best, it has only slowed Hezbollah's missile count, not prevented its monumental growth to a frightening level. Tal Beeri wrote that the CBW has had seventy percent success in preventing weapons from being transferred and about ninety percent success in preventing Iran and Hezbollah from building military infrastructure on Syrian soil. However, despite the CBW's significant success, he calls the CBW a "Sisyphean campaign." The more it succeeds, the more Iran and Hezbollah find new alternatives—one of which may be hiding arms shipments among supplies ostensibly sent to help victims of the 2023 massive earthquakes in Turkey and Syria.

So, is the CBW working or is it just delaying the inevitable? To determine that, let's compare its goals with its achievements.

A February 2022 article in the Israeli newspaper *Haaretz* addressed the question I posed. The author wrote that, in 2018, the IDF articulated five goals for the campaign, which were:

> Reducing the existing and developing threats to Israel; deflecting the prospect of war and creating better conditions for winning one; maintaining and strengthening deterrence; increasing Israel's 'equity' as an asset in the eyes of its partners; and maintaining the IDF's freedom of action while reducing that of the enemy.

In response to the questions posed, "security sources" candidly told the article's author that, although the campaign has stopped much of Iran's attempt to establish itself on Syria's border with Israel, it has not been so successful regarding Hezbollah because Hezbollah has "put a price" on attacking its members and assets, especially in Lebanon. Another official was quoted as saying, "In Lebanon, we're deterred. We're walking on eggshells there."

I agree.

The lack of CBW activity in Lebanon makes clear Hezbollah has deterred the IDF from destroying weapon systems and production capabilities that leak into Lebanon. Israel is so hesitant to provoke a military response that when a Hezbollah UAV infiltrated Israel, Israel's weak reaction was to just task its warplanes with circling menacingly over Beirut. And when Hezbollah fired an anti-tank missile at an IDF vehicle inside Israel, the IDF replied with smoke shells—not explosives. Unfortunately, the IDF's messages appear to have been designed as face-saving gestures rather than to have a real, measurable impact. Hezbollah now brags with impunity about its UAV incursions into Israel. Meanwhile, since Hezbollah now has the means to shoot down Israeli UAVs, the IDF has restricted its use of UAVs for reconnaissance. The contrast in approaches is evident.

Therefore, I am concerned. But is my concern that the CBW is not working justified? The experts I spoke to were all over the map.

Seth Frantzman told me there was little evidence that the CBW has slowed down overall Iranian entrenchment in Syria. And, Seth said, that regarding Iranian air defense systems and Russian ones: "There's a bit of a black hole of information." Although without a CBW, Seth admitted that it is unknown how much more Iran would have accomplished.

As for PGMs reaching Lebanon, Seth said to me in early 2022:

> According to the foreign press and you can read it also in our book, we think that there are [a] few hundred. They want [a] few thousand. We want zero. Now, the leakage is not because of a lack of intelligence. We have that. But sometimes you have that intelligence and you're not doing things because of other reasons. Because you don't want to kill too many innocents.

> Yet pinning down the exact number of PGMs Hezbollah possesses is an art rather than an exact science. In September 2022, Jonathan Schanzer highlighted a few estimates, some in agreement with Seth and some suggesting less. But one thing is certain. The number is growing.

While Yossi Kuperwasser agreed that there is leakage (Seth's term), he said, "Every rocket that we stop on the way is one less rocket. Because of that, I think it doesn't mean that the effort is irrelevant. The effort is relevant. It has to go on." When I asked if there were any negatives to continuing the CBW, Yossi answered, "Nope. So far, we do that without paying a price"—meaning Israeli lives have not been lost. But then Yossi made another comment, which might seem a bit whimsical, but which others have also expressed, just differently: "At the same time, there is another, not actually a goal, but a prayer, that something's going to happen in Lebanon and the Lebanese save the country and regain control of the country. This can happen."

Professor Freilich said something similar. In a hopeful but somewhat dubious tone, he said, "Maybe we can gain enough time here. Maybe eventually Syria will no longer be around. Maybe something good will happen in Iran. And maybe in the meantime, we'll save maybe hundreds or thousands of lives." Freilich then alluded to November 1977 when President Sadat of Egypt surprisingly announced that he would travel to Israel the following week to seek peace. That shocked everybody. So did the secret 2020 meeting in Saudi Arabia between Israeli Prime Minister Netanyahu and Saudi Crown Prince Mohammed bin Salman. As did the groundbreaking meeting held in Israel in 2022 between Israel's foreign minister and the foreign ministers of four other Arab nations, three of whom had signed diplomatic agreements with Israel only two years earlier. Freilich told me that if someone would have predicted all that, he would have responded, "What are you smoking?" The same shock, he said, could come one day from Damascus. "Does Assad really want to be beholden to the Iranians forever?" Freilich asked. And look where Israel is now compared to 1948. "Aren't more Arab states [at] peace with us today?"

Freilich and Kuperwasser are certainly correct that change could come—but maybe not in time to avert a war with Hezbollah. So, should Israel continue with its CBW?

General Maisel told me that the CBW "is past its prime. It's not effective anymore. It's costing too much…and that's interfering with the IDF preparing for the real war." Maisel compared the issue to running a business. "It's always about how much you invest [and] what you get out of it… . Sometimes you say to that investment, I need to do something else." Maisel thinks the CBW is "not about striking Hezbollah." Nor is it the main effort. "The big effort is to make sure they understand that they can't go to war with us." Maisel is most concerned about Hezbollah in Lebanon.

Jonathan Spyer's thoughts about the CBW focused on the growing threat in Syria. Although sympathetic with the concept of degrading the strength of Israel's enemies, his concern was:

> We tend to ignore the actual nature of large parts of the Iranian project in Syria specifically because we can't really deal with them by air warfare [which is] what we do well. So, we ignore it, but the fact is that Iran is moving [Shiite] population into [south Syria], Iran is creating long-term Hezbollah-style organizations that don't go away. Staffed by Syrians themselves, the [CBW] doesn't address [this]. And it seems to me that when war comes all these things would be very important. So, I think the campaign is good in my opinion. But it allows us not to think about certain things because we're doing well with the campaign. The generals can get up to 80% of the capacity that would otherwise have been there, that's all cool, but it doesn't take into account other capacities that are being built.

I had heard much the same about Iranian activity in Syria from Sarit Zehavi and read much about it in articles on the *Alma* website. But the intensity with which Spyer spoke struck me, especially because of his personal experiences in war zones in Syria and mingling with Shiites in Lebanon. So, I asked him if there is a way to address the issue of Iran winning the hearts and minds of people living in Syria near its border with Israel. He said:

> We need to understand the absolute centrality of what's taking place here is the Iranian method for asserting what I call, it's not my term,…for inserting a kind of deep state of their own into the territory of another state. Usually, when you say deep state it emerges from the particular state itself, but this is something different, it's a foreign country inserting its own deep state

complete with armed forces and political structures and social structures into another state and in so doing hollowing out the neighboring state….You can do that in a state, which has a functioning electoral structure, like Lebanon or Iraq. Or you can do it in a state with one which does not have electoral structures, like Syria. The methods will differ because of the nature of the state, but the essential goal and the essential project is the same.

This project is already advanced in Syria, arguably in Lebanon, …it's completed….In Iraq and in Syria, the method is in process, considerable progress has been made. And if you look at the project process that way, then yes, you realize the limitations of air warfare. Airpower is great, but you know, history is full of examples where air warfare for all its awesome capacity, it's not able to deliver every outcome you want. It's not the answer to everything. Right? And one of the things that it's not an answer to in my view is this.

So, I asked, how should Israel address the problem?

Israel can't do it alone. Israel can do it in cooperation with other allied forces because what you have to do [is] develop local allies and you have to sponsor and support strong local allies. [However], I think in Lebanon it's pretty much a done deal and they can have it. The counter to Hezbollah is so weak, so demoralized…,[but in Syria] and Iraq it's not done.

And there are many forces on the ground [that] can work with a sponsor. And I think there needs to be greater attention to that. Go to systemization of that, and cooperation with allies. Allies including [the] United States of America, United Arab Emirates—different countries bring different capacities as an ally….So…we need to develop other friends, I mean, we and the

Emiratis and others need to be working the way the Iranians work in a certain way.

Not exactly like [the Iranians] We don't have to create a revolutionary guards corp. We [need] a systematic approach to understanding that space, that battlefield, between the Mediterranean Sea and the Iraqi/Iran border to Lebanon or Syria. That's where the future of the region in many ways is being fought out and we have fallen behind in spite of our many capacities because…in this area, the Iranians reign supreme. And they've been allowed to export [their doctrine] when it comes to the cultivation of local allies and utilization of them, and the hollowing out of states and the building of power on the ground.

We've been, uh, deficient in that area. And I think that's somewhere where we have to up our game. Again, doesn't mean we're completely not there. We are there, but more attention and more seriousness have to be paid to them.

Enthralled, I asked if Iran and Hezbollah are providing social services, as they are in Lebanon, to Syrians in the border region while preventing the Syrian state from doing the same. Spyer responded affirmatively. Then I asked, "Is there a way to counter this?" Spyer said yes but that it requires both financial and military support. Expounding on that, he said:

[Syria] isn't really a state. The state is kind of fiction, but there is this arena of competition in which a variety of different communities and forces [are] moving. [S]o what you have to do is you have to develop your own clients, your own strong clients. If they're not strong, then make them strong, help them to be strong, financially, militarily, whatever it takes.

So that in that arena, you have players and you have people working with you who are stable and capable who can stand up.…All the things that they do, we can also do. And these are the currency of what they've understood early on to be the currency of power in that space. So, we can play that also.

We can do this. 'We' I define very broadly. I say that what I think we can now begin to talk about is the regional alliance of which Israel is a part, which consists of US-aligned Arab countries, Kurds, and Israel. This is now an emerging thing. Since the creation of the I2U2 structure [Author Note—I2U2 is a new national grouping composed of Israel, India, the UAE, and the U.S formed in 2021], and since the Negev summit that was a good signpost on that road, it is great to embrace the crystallization of that counter-alliance.

This alliance has been successful. It does know how to do this stuff. We're not hopeless at it and we need to do more of it and get into the game, you know? Cause that's where the future will be decided.

Spyer's thoughts are an important contribution to divining a solution to what's occurring in Syria. After surreptitiously slipping into Syria from Turkey, he is among the few Western reporters, and probably the only Israeli one, who witnessed firsthand the failures of forces opposed to Assad during Syria's civil war. After having eaten with them, spoken with them, and suffered with them—Spyer's views on developments and solutions in Syria should be heeded. He saw how the lack of external support wreaked havoc on opposition groups' ability to sustain themselves against Syrian forces supported by Iran and Russia. On a previous surreptitious trip to Lebanon, he saw the methods Hezbollah uses to solidify its social control there. Spyer sees the danger and argues persuasively for his solution.

And then there is the issue of Iran and the region. Jonathan Conricus said in a Podcast in late 2022 that Iran has "invested tremendous efforts to bridge the 600-mile gap" between the Iranian nation and where it wants to be forward deployed along Israel's border in order to threaten Israel. And that its strategy for doing so involved taking advantage of Syria's destabilization due to its civil war. Conricus considers the Israeli Air Force's efforts in stopping these Iranian designs "quite remarkable." He then added that the CBW is signaling to other nations in the region—such as Bahrain, the UAE, Morocco, and Saudi Arabia—that Israel can be counted on to oppose Iran. During the same Podcast, Jonathan Schanzer added another important point. He thinks that the CBW is serving a purpose in addition to keeping Iran at bay. Schanzer said that it might be the platform from which Israel will seek to destroy Iran's nuclear program as part of a process that includes many methods rather than just an airstrike.

So where does that leave me regarding the Campaign Between Wars, which, as of this writing, seems to be intensifying? I have a few thoughts. First, without the CBW, Hezbollah would be stronger and both Hezbollah and Iran would have better established themselves on Israel's Syrian border. For now, although Iran is making progress with its social goals, its ambition to establish many bases in Syria near Israel has been thwarted. In that sense, the CBW has achieved one of its goals.

Second, the CBW has slowed but not stopped Hezbollah's acquisition of statistical missiles, PGMs, and UAVs. In essence, the CBW has left a leaky faucet that now has filled Hezbollah's tub with weapons that pose an existential threat to Israel. Furthermore, because of the Rules of the Game, Hezbollah moves about Lebanon with impunity—building defensive positions, tunnels, and missile launching sites in civilian homes—not a good thing should a future war break out.

Third, it is likely time for something more and maybe something less. If Israel has the resources to keep doing what it is doing while embarking on a new mission to win hearts and minds across the border in Syria, then fine. Especially, in conjunction with its Sunni Arab allies who want to rein Iran in and are willing to join with Israel to do it. If not, it might be time to find an affordable balance between Israel's military activity in Syria and an increased focus on the growing societal changes that could pose the greatest threat in the long run.

Fourth, Schanzer's CBW platform concept makes sense to me. In late January, Israel used its own UAVs (reportedly quadcopters) to strike Iranian missile and UAV production facilities inside Iran. Since Russia attacked Ukraine in 2022, Israel has been criticized by some for not doing more to help Ukraine despite Russia's presence in Syria which a provoked Russia could use to much complicate Israel's prosecution of the CBW. But by attacking Iranian facilities engaged in producing weapons for export to Russia, Israel may have found the perfect path for helping Ukraine. Reducing Iranian armament production has a dual benefit—it both lessens the number of weapons available to send to Hezbollah and it reduces the flow of weapons to Russia. By accomplishing that within the framework of the CBW it may avoid antagonizing the Russians too much.

Fifth, the time has come for Israel to take on more risk by confronting the growing threat in Lebanon. Preferably, Israel should do this quietly, so Hezbollah is not publicly humiliated and forced to respond, but if that is not possible, then overtly. The tub, now filled in Lebanon, needs draining before it overflows.

Chapter Twenty-Two

Israel's Media Outreach

"Every time we win the war, we lose the word war," said Professor Nagel about Israel's failed communication strategy. Changing that dynamic is necessary.

Jonathan Conricus agrees.

Lt. Col. Conricus led the IDF's International Media Branch for four years before retiring in 2021. He was the public face of the IDF and oversaw its public diplomacy and social media operations. Previously, Jonathan held numerous liaison positions with the IDF in northern Israel, including interfacing with UN forces in Lebanon and on the Golan. He also spent time in New York, working as an IDF representative at the UN. Earlier, he was a warrior, having served as an infantry platoon and company combat commander. Jonathan first came to my attention during the IDF's tunnel operations along the Lebanese border in late 2018, and again during Israel's fight with Hamas in 2021. Then he appeared daily before the international press corps, eloquently responding to tough questions and maintaining his composure during trying times. Given his background, I knew he could provide me with contemporaneous insights into the proficiency, or lack thereof, of Israel's public diplomacy and the challenges it faces. We agreed to meet in Tel Aviv in the lobby of my hotel.

Early on a sunny morning, an extremely tall man wearing a leather motorcycle jacket and carrying a helmet strode purposely through the entranceway. Immediately, I knew it was Jonathan, even though his no longer regulation locks and facial hair threw me off a bit. Civilian life had certainly given him a different, more relaxed appearance but hadn't, I soon learned, affected his fierce dedication to Israel. After a few pleasantries, we found a quiet area to speak.

Straightaway, Jonathan emphasized that Israel's communication strategy must change and that his opinion was based on personal experience.

> I think that the way the state of Israel handles or mishandles communications specifically, international communications, is a strategic shortcoming, which is a critical liability for the state of Israel. We are neglecting international communications on a national level. We're neglecting it!

His passion and forthrightness surprised and pleased me. Just that statement alone proved his willingness to speak frankly during my interview of him. But then he hit the nail on the head (I'm sorry for the colloquialisms in the last two paragraphs, but their use informs my impression of Conricus—who is earnest but relaxed, experienced but inquisitive—and a nice guy).

"We don't have a strategy in place," Jonathan said. "We're not allocating resources, energy, time, personnel, and access. And too many senior Israelis fail to understand the importance of information preparation of the battlefield on an operational level and on the strategic national level." Then, seeking to make a distinction between domestic and international concerns, he continued:

> We spend a lot of time convincing the convinced as in communicating to Israelis, posturing, deterrence, shows of strength, et cetera, et cetera, for the purposes of keeping the Israeli public feeling safe, which is super important. But what we almost always overlook, and under plan, underfund, and under support is how we position ourselves in terms of international

public opinion and how we communicate our challenges and our activities to the world.

His comments reflected a truth I had felt for a long time. But to get to the root of the problem, I thought it important to understand the process presently in place. Conricus told me that after the 2006 war, the government founded a new office, under the prime minister's direction, responsible for disseminating information. In theory, it is supposed to coordinate all governmental media activities—including the foreign ministry, IDF, police, other ministries, and the social footprint of 190 Israeli embassies around the world. In practice, not so much. For the last six years of Netanyahu's previous tenure, petty politics prevented anyone from being appointed to oversee the office. Instead, a caretaker had limited authority to harmonize messaging from various branches of government. And Jonathan told me, based on his experiences, the office has never adequately performed its assigned mission. This left, in essence, two independent components—one tied to the IDF's Spokesperson's Unit for Public Affairs, in which Jonathan was responsible for communicating to the international community, and the other comprised the Foreign Ministry and the various embassies.

The Information Office changed in 2021 when Prime Minister Bennett took office and continued that process when Lapid took over. They appointed seasoned professionals who started to turn the ship around and implement a better culture. With Netanyahu's return as prime minister in 2023, time, and Israeli politics, will tell whether those changes will be supported, reversed, or altered.

What is Jonathan's main critique of the messaging done to date?

> They're not dealing enough with humanizing Israel, especially in times of conflict, and especially when there's a battle of narratives between the Palestinian narrative and an Israeli narrative. And even though I think they've done a lot of progress in terms of social media, it's still far from where I think it should be.

In essence, Israel's media strategy focuses on facts but often fails to include stories that people can relate to and that touch hearts and move minds. Hezbollah does not make that mistake. An example Jonathan gave me—even though it involved a terrorist organization in Gaza rather than Hezbollah in Lebanon—is illustrative.

In 2018, on multiple days Hamas sent tens of thousands of people to the fence separating Gaza from Israel to break through it. Hamas probably didn't care if they succeeded. Instead, Hamas' purpose was to generate incidents that would create horrible pictures it could capitalize on. If they could infiltrate into Israeli villages or kill or injure Israeli civilians, so much the better. IDF soldiers, after first trying verbal warnings, water cannons, rubber bullets, and tear gas that proved ineffective, stopped rioters that continued to press forward by shooting at their legs below the knee. Lethal force was used only after the local commander felt the rioters presented a clear and imminent danger. Still, Hamas achieved its goal. Even better for its purposes, were deaths and injuries among the rioters. On the day Israelis, U.S. government representatives, and supporters celebrated the American embassy being moved to Jerusalem, dozens of Palestinian rioters in Gaza died near the fence line (many were members of Palestinian terrorist organizations) and many more were injured. Jonathan said:

> Who do you think was tasked with explaining that to the world? Me. Why was I alone doing it? Because it was a very uncomfortable situation. Hugely unpopular, and very difficult to explain to the world why we are shooting so-called quote-unquote unarmed, peaceful protesters, which they were not. Instead, they were sometimes armed, sometimes with Molotov cocktails, sometimes with firearms. And were cutting open the fence to try to use violence to get into Israel with the aim of killing, lynching, or abducting Israeli civilians.

Since Israel had failed to highlight the potential for mayhem to the world before the storm of protestors materialized or while they were gathering, Jonathan's task:

> was very hard. Because when you see horrible images on the Palestinian side; civilians wounded, or killed, smoke and mayhem, and all that you see in response is just the green silhouette of an Israeli military spokesperson in combat gear, of course, the humanizing story and any human feeling would be toward the stories of suffering and the hardship on the Gaza side.

Instead, Jonathan said:

> In a situation like that, what should have happened was the State of Israel should have said there's military activity, but let's talk about the Israeli civilians who live just a few hundred meters from the fence, whom the IDF is defending. Because, if the IDF won't block these tens of thousands of Palestinians here, then we'll find them in a village, and they'll butcher Israeli civilians or, if they managed to get through, the IDF might be forced to kill anybody who went in because we wouldn't be able to take the risk of having our civilians butchered by Palestinians.

But that did not happen. There had been many social media threats against Israel's citizens emanating from Gaza before the riot. Israel did not publicize them. There was no attempt to elucidate the dangers Israel's citizens faced during the months leading up to the arrival of the protestors at the fence. Nor was there any discussion of the IDF's commitment to respond in a manner that posed the least danger to Gaza's citizenry beguiled by Hamas' callous disregard for their lives. Instead of a unified, coordinated response using all of Israel's communication capabilities and potential, the IDF alone was left to respond after the event. Alone, Lt. Col. Conricus was a "big guy in uniform" before a suspicious international media thirsting for sensationalism at Israel's expense. He was "trying to win hearts and minds while representing the military—facing powerful visuals, bad visuals of wounded, civilian looking people on the other side. You must understand that it's a situation that cannot be won from a media point of view."

Jonathan then pointed me to a related *New York Times* story, and an accompanying professional and compelling seventeen-minute video about the terrible accidental death of a Palestinian medic on June 1, 2018, during later protests along the Gaza border. It was a journalistic endeavor that could not have been accomplished without access to witnesses and videos taken in Gaza—access that could not have been gained without Hamas' acquiescence if not collaboration. Millions must have been spent by the *New York Times* to produce the video, untold hours spent putting it together, but of the seventeen minutes, less than a minute was devoted to an edited interview of Jonathan presenting Israel's response. And only seconds were devoted to the danger the rioters presented to Israel and the difficult choices and risks that necessitated. I watched the video twice. If I had known nothing of the history of the region—Israel's constant, unflagging, but not always successful attempt to avoid civilian casualties when confronted, and the perfidy of Hamas that harvests the blood of dead Palestinians they incite to achieve its media operational goals—then I, too, might have been influenced to view Israel's actions that day poorly.

Where was Israel's response? It was left to spokespersons like Jonathan who were not provided with the tools to succeed. There were no slick videos or in-depth stories about the suffering of Israelis along the border and the daily risks they face living there. There was no exposé on the hate-filled pronouncements by Hamas' representatives who are very open about the organization's goals and views—the destruction of Israel and contempt for Jews. And there has been little or no attempt to prepare the information battle space before bullets are fired and rockets fly. As a result, Israel time and time again loses the word war, as Jonathan did in the wake of the *New York Times* article.

In addition to telling its story more compellingly, Israel should use its world-class intelligence capability to gather information for the express purpose of divulging it to the media. "Many times," Jonathan told me, he was "sent empty-handed to fight the media battle." An example of that is what Israel should have done leading up to Israel's May 15, 2021, bombing of the *al-Jalaa* building during the 2021 war—a war in which Hamas fired 470 rockets at Israel on the first day, followed by 3,000 more over the next ten days of fighting. Only Iron Dome protected many Israelis from violent deaths and prevented financial losses that would've been in the billions. Knowing that, Hamas ran a jamming operation designed to blunt Iron Dome's effectiveness. It was in the *al-Jalaa* building in Gaza City. The building also housed the offices of Al Jazeera, the Associated Press, and other news organizations.

The building was a legal, approved and vetted, military target. Striking the building stopped the jamming and crimped a related research and development operation; it also destroyed assets owned by another terrorist operation, Islamic Jihad. But when Jonathan learned of the plan to bomb the building, he advised against it. Jonathan told me that, while the building was a legitimate military target, the presence of news organizations inside made it a magnet for bad publicity. "It was a stunningly poor target to attack from a PR perspective," he said. "I mean, I could think of maybe just a few worse targets to attack in Gaza—a hospital or an orphanage."

In hindsight, Jonathan said:

> What we should have done was for the IDF Chief of Staff to summon a presser. We invite the agencies, CNN, AP, all the big ones, and say, listen, this is what's going on. And we'd invite them an hour before the strike and say, 'Listen, this is what's going to happen in this building. Here is our intelligence on what

we know Hamas is doing. They are trying to jam the Iron Dome from that building. And inside are Hamas militants. That's what was the intelligence we had, which is the justification for the strike. Then we should have said that we're going to make sure that no civilians are hit, and we will warn the tenants in advance, but that ultimately, we need to strike that target to save Israeli lives.

For a target of this magnitude, we should have had a professional dossier to give to everybody and we should have live-streamed the presser on our platform while saying 'See, this. It is Hamas trying to use international journalists as their human shields. And they're trying to jam the Iron Dome from here, and we're not going to have it.' That would have given us the initiative and might even have turned the situation in our favor—despite striking a location also used by the international media.

When I responded that he was advocating for using information about the impending strike as an offensive weapon, Jonathan said, "Exactly." Instead, "We just did it, you know, in a stupid kinetic-focused thoughtless way of oh, that's a target. I have a hammer. Let's smash it." To which I added, "Let Jonathan clean it up."

After we both agreed that Israel's attack on the *al-Jalaa* building diminished international sympathy for Israel's plight and hurt its image, I asked Jonathan a question. Could he translate his experience into a plan for preparing the information battle space for a preemptive attack that Israel might need to launch against Hezbollah?

His answer then, based on personal experience and conjecture, was more a further expression of the problem than a solution.

We've been trying over the years; diplomatically government to government, minister of foreign affairs, Prime Minister Netanyahu was involved in it personally, military level, public diplomacy level, visitors, AIPAC, and European legislators. So, there's really been an effort. However, I personally think it's very difficult to establish how effective it has been. My pessimistic assessment is that we are not getting the message across about how dangerous the situation is in Lebanon and Israel, despite the fact that we've said the numbers and people come to the north and we've shown it. I think people aren't listening because there's nothing really happening.

Then, speaking of the threat that Hezbollah's 150,000 rockets, many hidden in or below civilian homes, pose to people living near the border or even in Haifa, Conricus said, "We are not where we want to be. In terms of how the issue is framed in international media." Nor is Israel where it needs to be with political leaders in Europe. If you ask them what is going on in Lebanon, they are conversant with its economic issues and things like the explosion at Lebanon's port in 2020. But regarding regional issues involving Hezbollah and the threat it poses, "It is very down low. We are not succeeding in that. And when will, of course, people listen? When rockets start firing. And we pummel Hezbollah."

By that time, it will be late to state Israel's case.

But months after I interviewed Jonathan, I had the opportunity to hear him speak on a Podcast conducted by the Foundation for Defense of Democracies. During that program, he concisely explained a related problem and provided a solution. International reporting shapes the opinion of both government and the public. Jonathan said that the problem with international reporting is often context and the order of events. All too often, it is not clear what happened first that led to Israel's response. He proposed that early in the planning process for military operations or governmental activity, consideration must be given as to how the world will interpret what Israel will do, and how Israel can best show, rather than tell, what it wants the world to understand. Jonathan contended that by judiciously using information gathered by its intelligence services and visuals, not just rhetoric, press coverage will be more balanced.

I agree with Jonathan's assessments. Using my adult children as a barometer, they generally support Israel, but their busy daily life prevents them from digging deep to discern the truth when they are exposed to emotional images and sound bites calculated to garner sympathy for the causes of those who would see Israel's destruction. The same is true for many others who favor Israel, as well as for the many who would sympathize with Israel's plight if they only knew the truth. Reciting dry facts in response does not cut it. Neither does running an inconsistent information campaign that's poorly tailored to how people consume news today. How, I have often wondered, should these people be reached? How can the truth be humanized and disseminated in a manner that defeats the effective efforts mounted by Israel's enemies?

However, Jonathan does think that one informational message has been sent and received successfully. One that stands against a war breaking out, which Jonathan acknowledges could still easily happen. And that message is:

> How well Hezbollah understands that we will be very, very fierce with Hezbollah and with anything around Hezbollah. That message maybe could be our biggest media or perceptional success getting our enemy to understand that the destruction that they dealt with in 2006, and have been dealing with since, will be a fraction of what will happen again if they attack us. I think this message is maybe the only one that has successfully been understood by the intended recipient, Hezbollah. Does the U.S. government know? Do the French know? Do the Russians or Chinese? Naa. Not enough. Not enough. But I think Hezbollah understands, that's maybe most important.

Routinely, all the other experts I spoke with echoed Jonathan's concerns. Some amplified them. Seth Frantzman told me Israel should articulate to the international community:

> [T]he degree to which Hezbollah is an illegal terrorist militia that is occupying illegally southern Lebanon, that is using extra-judicial means in terms…of killings and extra-legal means in terms of stockpiling of weapons. I think [it] would be a good thing for Israel to always keep hammering on about and pave the way, for the feeling that…Israel is not in the wrong…*because I think, unfortunately, Israel does sometimes wait too late to even explain what the point of the conflict is* (italics added). And then…there is a ready-made anti-Israel course in the west…that will always run out and immediately…protest Israel's actions. [Given] the fact…that if there is a conflict,…Israel is seen as the more powerful country and you will see people fleeing southern Lebanon, and then [it] will be, oh, look what Israel is doing. You know, Israel is as bad as what the Russians did to Ukraine.
>
> So, I think Israel needs to hammer home the point that Hezbollah is not a political party. It's an illegal militia of the type that Americans, for instance, have heard about. Like with January 6th,…this is a militia involved in the attempted coup attempt in…Lebanon. You can't have an illegal militia with weapons everywhere occupying a third of your country. And I think western countries understand that. But you have to remind them and not allow Hezbollah to claim that it's a non-government organization that provides welfare services in southern Lebanon and just happens to have an armed wing, which is not what it is. [So] I think that countering that argument…is probably worthwhile. And I think Israel sometimes isn't good at preparing the messaging or even deciding what the message is if there's a conflict.

Seth then turned, as Jonathan Conricus did, to the May 2021 war with Hamas and the bombing of the building:

> I think we saw that in the May 2021 war, there was no messaging. It was like, well, Hamas is bad. It's firing rockets at cities. You're like, yeah, but people have heard this before. That was not great. Optics. Let's blow up a building that's full of media. [Of] course, Hamas is not stupid. They look at a building full of media and they're like, well, let's put a headquarters next to it. They're not stupid, but you have to be smarter than that. And always be ahead of that. Ahead of that lie, if you want to explain what exactly you're doing.

Professor Nagel also alluded to the 2021 war with Hamas to explain the problem:

> One hundred-fifty Palestinians were killed and injured from missiles Hamas fired [that fell short in Gaza]. No one wrote about it….But if two children have been [killed by] a missile that we sent against a Hamas post inside a school, everyone is writing that. So, we have to enlarge [the conversation]. We have to make sure that the world hear[s] us, we have to spend much more effort in PR and communication and in media and social.

Nevertheless, Nagel candidly said, "In the end, I think we will lose the communication war, the public or the publicity war." Still, he believes it's a necessary fight, even to just convince Israel's citizens that the government does all it can to protect them.

Yossi Kuperwasser, whom you may remember held leading roles in Israel's intelligence and strategic affairs communities and is an editor of an in-depth book on this subject, *The Cognitive Campaign: Strategic and Intelligence Perspectives*, thinks that Israel does much to reach foreign decision-makers but still not enough. And, he emphasized, it is important that the public at large also understands the danger Hezbollah poses to Israel.

When I pointed out that I thought the Biden administration's release of classified material had had a salutary impact on world opinion leading up to Russia's invasion of Ukraine, Kuperwasser said:

> We do…the same. First of all, we exposed those tunnels. We allowed everybody to visit and get a big impression as to what happened. Secondly, we do share information about the location of rockets inside the houses in south Lebanon, how almost every house in the south is a military target. And we do share from time to time some information about the behavior of Hezbollah towards UNIFIL and how they prevent them from performing [their] task. But it's…not consistent enough. It's not frequent enough. It's not getting the results we need. We need more. We need everybody to know how terrible Hezbollah is. It's about how dangerous they are.

Do you have any thoughts, I asked, how that should happen?

> Yes. I think we should be more open and using information that we have, and more vocal and have better access to…people whom we need to reach for this effort. We don't have enough because unfortunately we are too much identified with the international right. We should be non-partisan. Should be in the middle definitely on that issue. [Still], [w]e are moving forward in convincing more people to [identify] Hezbollah as a whole as a terror organization. It's not that this battle is not being fought or it's neglected. No, not at all, but not enough is being done.

Kuperwasser then told me a story to drive home his point about using intelligence.

> I have a group of people that [I] work with. I brought them over for a tour to study the threat from the north. [W]e were speaking and sitting with the deputy chief of staff. He shows all the stuff

about [Hezbollah]. And some of the stuff, I didn't know, I mean, [he] showed it to foreigners and how come I don't know about it? And definitely, they don't know about it. If you want to impress them with information that nobody saw. Okay. That's fine. But I didn't feel that this was the case. It's just information that they held. They didn't [bother] to make everybody know about all kinds of clips of Hezbollah people [violating UN mandates] dressed in civilian uniform…harassing UNIFIL people in the south.…[T]his tells you what we are dealing with.

His story resonated with me. Why doesn't Israel move heaven and earth to prove Hezbollah is the one increasing the risk of war? Kuperwasser agreed that Hezbollah spits in the face of the UN, saying: "We can show evidence, right? Of course, not on everything, but enough to help us. [But] we don't capitalize on these opportunities enough." Nevertheless, I learned through multiple interviews, there is a growing awareness in Israel of this problem. That makes me hopeful, sort of.

But much work needs to be done. And Kuperwasser, like Jonathan Conricus, remains concerned. "We don't have somebody," Kuperwasser told me, "who is in charge of all the efforts and see[s] how one effort will help with the other effort, how they build each other. We [are] too much divided."

Well, maybe the situation is not that hopeful, after all.

Another stop on my quest to understand Israel's information issues was with Dr. Azani, whom I introduced in Chapter Six. He told me that Israel needs to work on this problem "all the time." And that "one of the problematic issues that people don't understand within this field is how the images influence people that are not part of [this] area because, at the end of the day, the narrative of the weak is stronger than the narrative of the strong." So true—even if the narrative of the weak is false.

Azani further explained, "Because you are fighting [an] international outlaw…you face huge problems because they [use]…society as a human shield and they use it in every place." That, in my opinion, necessitates finding ways to attack Hezbollah that limit collateral damage while explaining in clear, simple, and compelling terms why methods that will likely cause civilian casualties might be necessary. This must be done before and after any attacks and people are harmed. In essence, Israel needs to set itself up for success by preparing the informational battleground.

I then questioned Azani about word choices because I strongly believe the descriptive words we choose to use sometimes undercut our arguments. Often, Hezbollah is called a terrorist organization that operates as a state-within-a-state. I told him, however, that I hesitate to use that vernacular because it does not amply describe Hezbollah's chokehold on Lebanese politics and its unchallenged military strength, which in my mind means that the State of Lebanon and Hezbollah are, for all practical purposes, one and the same. However, Azani pushed back on my thought ever so slightly by introducing me to the term "hybrid terrorist organization" that I discussed in Chapter Six. As you may recall, a hybrid terrorist organization is one that has three legs: a terror or military leg, a social leg, and a political leg.

Azani was correct that Hezbollah matches that definition precisely and has emphasized one leg or the other, as it sees fit, to maximize support for it and to avoid international opprobrium. But for me, when explaining what Israel faces simply, it is better to emphasize how little daylight there is between Lebanon and Hezbollah. And that, if war does break out, Israel will find it nearly impossible to differentiate between the two because, for all practical purposes, Hezbollah is now Lebanon.

I also discussed this issue with Jonathan Spyer. Considering that, as a writer, he has seen with his own eyes what failed states look like in Lebanon and Syria, and that he is an expert analyst, what Spyer thinks matters. Spyer told me he agreed with my thoughts regarding Hezbollah's status, even though some oppose linking Hezbollah too closely to statehood because they are glad that the United States and France support the "organs of the Lebanese state." He said:

> [We] should have clarity....I think we should define Hezbollah as the state. It's not like some out-of-the-box weird thought. They control the majority in the cabinet, they control the majority in the parliament, they control at least one of the main intelligence organizations. They control large numbers of officers within the regular army who get their positions because of their connections to Hezbollah. So how much more, what do you actually need [to do] without actually proclaiming we're changing the name of the country to Hezbollahstan tomorrow? I agree, state it clearly. And part of that statement is to precisely say…in future conflict[s] this will be the working assumption that we take. There won't be a conflict between us and Hezbollah. There'll be a conflict between us and…the governor of Lebanon…the colonial governor-general of Lebanon, [who] on behalf of Tehran is Hassan Nasrallah.

But Spyer was uncertain if Israel would take such sweeping steps to redefine the relationship between Hezbollah and Lebanon. He told me, "The problem is that for better or for worse, the people who control policy here, are people who come from the combat echelon. Fighters become information-warfare generals and fighters become prime ministers. And that's all good. And there's a reason for it and it's not necessarily bad." But, Spyer said:

> Every aspect of warfare isn't about fighting. The general view…has been [that information warfare], that's a kind of luxury that some other idiot has to deal with. The real positive people deal with capturing the hill and some other dufus comes on, and…has to explain it.

It's very hard to change this perspective that values kinetic activities (meaning the application of force) over cognitive activities (the battle for minds). But, Spyer says, "Your ability to conquer the hill, how anybody even lets you anywhere near that attempt is to a great extent…determined by the political and even to some degree media landscape, we are able, or not able to create."

How true.

Before I end this chapter, I think it's important to highlight how Israel's information system operated during the 2006 war on a local level—where the fighting was happening. To do that, I had a fruitful conversation with Jonathan Davis. Now Vice President for External Relations at Reichman University, Davis (yes, he is the third Jonathan I interviewed for this chapter) has a storied past. He made Aliyah as a very young man from the United States and then served in a paratrooper reconnaissance unit that performed many behind-the-lines missions in Syria and Iraq during the 1973 war. As a reservist, he fought in the 1982 Lebanon war, and then he was an IDF spokesperson during the intifada and the 2006 Lebanon War. These experiences made me eager to meet him, whether he had much to say about Israel's information warfare or not. But, to my fortune and yours, he added much to my knowledge base.

As part of my preparation for the interview, I read an article Davis wrote about an event in Lebanon. It revealed much about the man. In 1982, he and two other sharpshooters occupied a rooftop position in the southern Lebanon city of Tyre; their job was to protect IDF soldiers below. They had been ordered to refrain from shooting civilians—unless, of course, they were enemy operatives—but navigating the gray area between suspicion and confirmation was easier said than done.

Davis told me:

> When you're walking in some orchard [in Lebanon], you know that within one second you may need to open fire, for your life

and the life of your comrades. So…your weapon is cocked and ready for action. And your finger is two-thirds of the way on the trigger already….You're very tense. The same was true that day on the rooftop.

Suddenly, they saw movement behind a curtain covering a doorway below. They held their fire for ten seconds, even though that offered enough time for a grenade to be thrown at the troops in the street. Then a man stepped out from behind the curtain. He was old, half-blind and deaf, and carrying a white flag. That day, Davis' forbearance saved a life. What had stopped them from firing? The IDF had instilled in them the value that you never shoot civilians unless you are certain they are the enemy. And Davis explained to me, even though bad unintended things happen, like "there could be a missed shell that lands in the wrong place and does kill innocent civilians. That's part of the price of war. But I have found over the years that the honor code of the IDF with regards to saving lives of civilians in combat areas goes the extra mile."

After the war, the foreign ministry sent Davis to speak on college campuses in the United States. To the students he spoke about those tense moments on the rooftop. Israel needs to do more of that to push back against the tide of hateful propaganda assailing college kids today.

What motivated Davis to write the 2018 article about his experience on the rooftop in Tyre? "It was the idea that we're endangering our brothers and at the same time, obeying humanistic orders of the IDF and having to find the balance between the need for life versus human rights and being in that gray area and not being overly impulsive."

Davis first began his spokesperson duties as a reservist, for a few days a year in the 1990s. Then came the 2006 war. His job was to assist the foreign press corps prowling near the fighting to write articles about the battle and to appear on television and radio. Doing so required Davis to speak up. Otherwise, since foreign correspondents were (and still are) barred from attaching themselves to IDF units, his silence would leave a vacuum of reliable reportage that Hezbollah could fill with lies.

In addition, because the IDF didn't permit journalists to embed within its units, that deprived the public access to sound, accurate reporting that could shed light on Israel's plight—and perhaps even improve Israel's image. When I asked Davis if he thought embedding produces a more favorable environment for sympathetic reporting, he told me:

> When you're living and breathing with them for weeks on end, and you're getting to know who these people are and who their families are, and you're witnessing losses and you're seeing different things, it's quite possible that an embedded member of the foreign press might be a little more objective.

Our conversation then shifted to how he did his job. Davis said they would generally hold one or two meetings a day: an early meeting to determine that day's agenda and itinerary for each spokesperson, and then a second meeting later to summarize the day's events and progress. Sometimes his agenda included escorting members of the press to Israeli units within Israel, including artillery units firing into Lebanon. Other times, he would arrange interviews with IDF soldiers whom Davis knew spoke the reporter's language fluently and had just left the fighting in Lebanon for a rest break.

Unfortunately, although there was some coordination between the foreign ministry and his office, Davis said representatives from the foreign ministry "weren't usually in great numbers in the field," and gently suggested that perhaps more should have been on the scene. After the war, Davis told me, suggestions were made that more needed to be done in this arena to coordinate efforts. And that, he thinks, "[A]ll kinds of organizations have to work closer…with each other and on the same page in order to be able to…best present what needs to be presented."

However, Davis said, the press invariably changes its attitude toward Israel. Then, like piranhas, there comes a feeding frenzy (my words) when innocent civilians are accidently wounded or killed:

> That makes for a great headline which many of the foreign press like to latch onto because it's a human interest story. …That despite [their knowledge] that we will do everything we can for the purpose of human rights and for the purpose of being humanistic Zionists. [However], we would rather be a live over-dog than a dead underdog.…And so, you realize that you still have to defend the country…and you realize that Hezbollah [is] firing rockets into Israel in order to deliberately kill as many people as they can, including innocent Arab civilians.

Davis said that a good spokesperson is objective and leaves politics out of it. But the truth is irrefutable. Hezbollah was firing missiles at Israel to kill people. Israel was trying to stop them and protect the people of Israel. That was the message. It's not for nothing, he said, that "we're called the Israeli defense force" rather than the "Israeli offensive force."

The problem is time. A war with Hezbollah has a very different time issue than a war with Hamas. And that time problem needs to be communicated to the world now, not later. In a war with Hamas in Gaza, Hamas is incapable of killing thousands on the ground in Israel's major cities. Therefore, the IDF can risk operational effectiveness by warning civilians in areas it intends to strike, even if that results in hidden missiles being fired before the IDF can destroy them. Iron Dome can likely deal with them because Hamas can only fire so many missiles at one time and does not possess an overwhelming stockpile. That, however, is not the case regarding Hezbollah. Davis said:

> [We're] going to have to react. Very, very quickly and do something in a short amount of time. So [to prevent] a humanitarian wipe-out

on the Israeli side…your priority now is going to be to disconnect all air activities for Hezbollah, to disconnect all harbor activities for Hezbollah, to disconnect all electricity for Hezbollah, to disconnect all [military asset] housing abilities of Hezbollah. And what you're left with here is something that may happen within seconds or minutes of the other side unleashing.…There may be less time to play chess here. And so, therefore, there could be a lot of rubble on the other side.

So, Israel must explain that story in advance. What works in Gaza will not work in Lebanon because the stakes are higher, the area is larger, and Hezbollah's capability is much greater. And even though Israel might not win the information battle, Davis told me in one of the sports analogies he used in our discussions, "When it comes to the way people objectively see Israel…my gut reaction would be that even if we…lose the basketball game,…I think we should try and lose…by six or seven points, put up a good fight, and not lose in a blowout of 40 points."

*   *   *   *

Winning the information war with Hezbollah will be hard. Preparing the information battle space properly will also be difficult. Israel must do both to succeed. Should Israel have to launch a preemptive strike, its motivation and necessity must be understood worldwide in advance. And when calamity invariably occurs, and Lebanese civilians die in a war—either started by Hezbollah or initiated by Israel as a defensive measure—that tactical tragedy cannot be allowed to morph into a strategic nightmare. Hezbollah wins by not losing. The death of Lebanese civilians strengthens its hand by driving the international community to press Israel to stop fighting before it achieves its objectives. Therefore, the stakes are high for Israel to launch a successful information strategy now.

What is truly unfortunate is not that Israel is held to a high standard. It should be. It is that Hezbollah is not held to any standard at all. And in an ironic twist, Iron Dome has proved to be a boon to Hamas' and Islamic Jihad's propaganda, as it will for Hezbollah. Since Iron Dome has intercepted most of the deadly rockets fired from Gaza over the last decade, that success has perversely led to those terrorist organizations being viewed as underdogs deserving of a whitewash whenever Israel defends itself. A whitewash even though those organizations are indiscriminately trying to kill innocent Israeli citizens while Israel does its best to protect them. A whitewash even though Israel does its utmost to preserve the lives of those civilians who live where the terrorists callously store their weapons.

This problem will manifest to a far greater degree in a war with Hezbollah. Israel's critics will ask why it must respond so destructively when it has Iron Dome. This book answers that question and much more—Hezbollah can overwhelm Iron Dome. But most will not read this book. Nevertheless, their hearts and minds must be touched by the truth. How can that be accomplished?

It can be done by telling numerous, simple, fact-based, relatable stories to generate empathy, repeating those stories to ensure they're heard, and by being creative. As managing partner of a law firm, I presided over many conversations about how best to market and brand ourselves. I quickly learned there is no "one" way. Trying to find "the" answer was a recipe for finding no answer. For Israel, as it was for my law firm, it is vital to embark on multiple, simultaneous, creative, and synergistic paths. Many would fail, some would succeed, but all would likely have at least some incremental benefits. The same is true in politics. Choosing one way to the exclusion of all else is unlikely to achieve a victory. To win an information war, victory must travel on a plethora of interconnected paths all leading to the same place.

In Chapter Twenty-Six, we will explore this concept further. But for now, I will leave you with this thought from Jonathan Davis that echoes Professor Boaz Ganor, "The definition of a terrorist is a person who deliberately murders innocent civilians in order to achieve their political aims." That is precisely Hezbollah's aim today. It's simple. Hezbollah wants to kill Jews and destroy Israel. So does Iran. Hezbollah is willing to let innocent Lebanese citizens die if that will help it achieve its goals. When I heard Davis enunciate his definition of a terrorist, I realized Israel needs to reiterate that concept to people worldwide day after day, week after week, through every means possible. Since those running Iran are willing to publicly hang people for being gay; since Iranian proxies supported by Hezbollah in Iraq happily bomb Sunni mosques; and since Hezbollah indiscriminately launches missiles at Israeli cities, kidnaps its soldiers, and builds terror tunnels to capture towns inside Israel—one can only imagine what Iran's proxy, Hezbollah, has in mind for Israel's citizens given the opportunity. This is the story that Israel and its supporters must tell—every day, every week, every month, every year. Through every communication means imaginable. And where possible through the experiences of people suffering under Hezbollah's thumb or exposed to Hezbollah's attack. It will take money and ingenuity and manpower—certainly more than the paltry sixty-person unit that I was shocked to learn was all that Jonathan Conricus had under his command. But it is a message that must be shouted from the rooftops, reverberating wherever people of reason reside.

Chapter Twenty-Three

Israel's Will to Fight

In May 2000, days after the IDF withdrew from Lebanon, Nasrallah taunted, "Israel is weaker than a spider's web." It was a memorable way of saying that, despite Israel's material and technical superiority, it is vulnerable to non-stop war and bloodshed. In Nasrallah's eyes, caring about the lives of its soldiers and citizens and having an allegedly self-indulgent society that embraces Western values makes Israel fragile. Nasrallah has repeated the phrase over the years. But is it true? *Is Israel weaker than a spider's web?* The answer to that question will, in large part, determine Israel's future.

This chapter is based on several interviews I conducted in April 2022, comments made in multiple articles, proclamations by a slew of political and military leaders, and my study and analysis of recent events—including the agreement Israel and Lebanon made with the United States regarding the undersea gas deposits discussed in Chapters Fourteen and Twenty. Combined, they inform my answer to the question posed. But, before we get there, I need to discuss Israel's psyche regarding IDF soldiers.

* * * *

Eight days into my April 2022 trip to Israel, I stood with Sarit Zehavi and her husband, Yaron, in a gravel parking lot a couple of miles south of the Lebanese border, adjacent to the remains of an airfield Britain's

Royal Air Force used in the 1940s. Then, it was vibrant. Now, it is a vast field of overgrown grass hiding remnants of concrete hangars.

A few days earlier, I had met with General Gershon Hacohen at his home chiseled into a mountainside that offers an expansive view of the Golan and Shebaa Farms. "Hezbollah," Gershon told me, "created a complicated threat. And if there would be a Nobel Prize for military invention, I would give them a Nobel Prize because they [constructed] a strategic threat to Israel without the conventional equipment like submarines, air force, and armor. They succeeded to build a military force fitting to their own limitations." Hacohen confirmed what I already knew; Hezbollah is a growing danger. But is Israel willing to do something about it or is it the paper tiger Nasrallah suggests? On that score, I quizzed Sarit and Yaron.

Sarit and Yaron are the parents of three boys and two girls. During Sarit's military career, she held many positions in the IDF that informed her of the threat Hezbollah poses. By any measure, she is both tender and tough, realistic, and resolute. Her husband, Yoran, also served in the IDF, retiring as an officer in a distinguished infantry unit. Sarit told me:

> Nobody can understand…Israeli mothers, [who know] since the child is born, know at the age of eighteen, he will go to the army. We all know that. And we all know that we defend him until the age of eighteen, and from the age of eighteen, he defends us. So, the [lives] of the soldiers; they are our brothers, our sons, our husbands [also daughters].

Sarit spoke resolutely here, but, when she continued, her serious expression made what followed especially profound.

> That's why for us there is very little tolerance for waste of life. For us, it's very important that if a prime minister decides to go to war, there is a very high justification for this. If you cannot justify going to war, you can't go to war. Yet, if there is a good reason

and Hezbollah kills Israelis or puts the state of Israel under an existential threat—we will all stand behind our prime minister no matter what.

Sarit had come close to answering whether Israel had the willingness to fight, but her explanation fell just short of what I was looking for. However, she did make me realize that my question was too simple. My question should have included how imminent, how definite, and how existential the threat must be for Israel's population to willingly risk a war with Hezbollah or back the government's decision to start one.

Nobody, especially Sarit, doubts that Hezbollah is a complicated, dangerous, and growing threat. But where does acknowledging this lead? Are Israelis willing to fight now or at least risk a fight to avert a nightmare later?

And what role does anger play?

In 2006, Hamas terrorists moved through a tunnel leading from Gaza into Israel. They exited the tunnel; kidnapped Gilad Shalit, an IDF soldier manning a tank; and dragged him back to Gaza, where they held him captive for years. Three weeks after Shalit was taken, Hezbollah operatives crossed the border fence in northern Israel to ambush an Israeli patrol, killing three soldiers and kidnapping two. "We [were] pissed off by that," said Colonel Boaz Amidror, and two days later the IDF struck back and the 2006 war with Hezbollah ensued. But soon, domestic support for the government waned.

Why?

Professor Nagel supplied part of the answer, "Leaders see the wide picture, but most of the public are willing to suffer in order to finish the war fast." Professor Chuck Freilich echoed that thought, telling me, "The public is always fully behind the leadership at the beginning." But he somberly added, "They stay fully supportive as long as they think that something's being achieved." Illuminating the issue further, Jonathan Spyer said, "The country was all up in arms because of the kidnapping…so [the prime minister]…could order aggressive action because the country was angry. And so, he had that window."

The observations of Freilich, Nagel, Spyer, and Amidror summarize past events fairly. Israel's incursions into Lebanon before 2006 did not free the country from terrorists based in Lebanon—even though the players changed after the First Lebanon War, the threat persisted and grew. After Hezbollah's kidnapping of the two IDF soldiers in 2006, the Second Lebanon War dragged on for thirty-four long days. Israel did not destroy Hezbollah. Nor did it take new territory that would protect the country. Hezbollah's leadership remained intact while its focus on destroying Israel did not waver. Israel's various confrontations with Hamas in Gaza yielded similar outcomes. Essentially, Israel justifiably gets pissed off by terrorist attacks, kidnappings, or missile strikes, decides to retaliate, but then is prevented from responding with full force by politicians succumbing to domestic concerns or international pressure, or IDF leadership looking to limit casualties, and so the dynamic on the ground goes unchanged.

In effect, Israel mows terrorist grass while its civilian population perseveres. Then they watch as the terrorist weeds grow back. That's infuriating. When wars, like those in Lebanon, drag on too long without furnishing significant benefits—especially in 2006, when the war disrupted the home front, killed many civilians and soldiers, and damaged property to the tune of billions of dollars—the public loses faith in the government and military and begins to question their tactics, strategies, and targets. This is especially true when Israeli soldiers have died in combat or targeting errors have killed Arab civilians. That's what happens when anger drives decisions; and instead of using a comprehensive strategic plan to end a threat for an extended period, soldiers engage in tit-for-tat exchanges that accomplish little except putting people at risk.

So, what have we learned from the 2006 Lebanon War as well as Israel's wars over the last forty years? We know that if an enemy provokes or attacks Israel, Israel will fight. But how hard and for how long? And does Israel have an undue concern for the lives of its soldiers that affects its ability to make sound military decisions? Nasrallah believes that it does—and he relies on that belief.

Jonathan Spyer told me, "Because politicians…never stop being politicians…[they] have to take into account that Israeli society is immensely…sensitive to casualties where anybody can make a plausible argument that actually there was no reason for this war." Of course, he said, "If the "fight's on, we all get it. Then the Israeli psyche is very resilient. But if there's the slightest sense about my son who just got killed or hurt, there is no need for it," even based on a newspaper editorial, then there is a problem. That is why it's difficult for the government to take aggressive action.

But what are the origins of Israel's deep concern for its soldiers, a concern so profound their lives are sometimes placed before the nation's needs? I think it derives from the bond between soldiers and society and from valuing a civilized viewpoint more than pioneer instinct. Those realities then drive calculations about the necessity of war and the value of peace.

Soldiers and Citizens

Colonel Boaz Amidror is a tough guy who has served in dangerous places. Although many people had told me similar things, the way Boaz explained the different attitudes in Israel toward soldiers and citizens was instructive. Speaking in powerful, clipped sentences in English, which is not his native language, he told me, "You don't risk the life of soldier if it's not an important thing to do." That Israelis say, "Every soldier is our son." And that, "Soldiers don't choose where they go." Civilians, on the other hand, have freedom of choice. They can go where they want when they want.

Therefore, if a soldier is killed or wounded, it is in part because the IDF placed them in harm's way. Whereas, if a civilian suffers the same fate, it is because their personal decision led him to the spot where he suffered his misfortune. That is why Israeli sensitivity for the lives of soldiers is bigger than for civilians. However, Boaz admitted, "If there's children involved or many civilian casualties, that changes everything.

In the end, Boaz explained to me, it boils down to luck versus duty. A soldier's job is to defend the country. If he is killed doing that, he has been killed in furtherance of that service. On the other hand, if a civilian is killed, it is bad luck that his choice of where to go led to his demise. Still tragic, but not as impactful as the soldier whose orders sent him to his death. Boaz admitted, "It's a different approach. But, he said, "This the way the Israeli people think."

Shay Shemesh, who taught me so much about Home Front Command, agrees. He told me, "I can tell you that sometimes when there are civilian casualties (that's) OK. But if a soldier is dead, they say, wow. He went there to fight for all of us. … Sometimes they are younger, like our children." Then he expounded further, "The people in Israel are so sensitive to soldier casualties because they are heroes. It's not like someone going to work and was stabbed…OK. Sorry. Poor thing, poor guy. But then a soldier dies, he's a hero. [He] went there to protect us." Of course, there are exceptions to this matter-of-fact acceptance of civilian casualties. Sarit Zehavi pointed to an important one: "I think [it is different when] rockets fall on a kindergarten."

Still, avoiding soldier casualties, especially meaningless ones, is important to Israeli society. Sarit was very clear but fatalistic on that point. Soon, her oldest son will enter the military. She accepts that one day Israel's soldiers might have to enter Lebanon again and that soldiers will die. But, if politicians decide to do that, she doesn't want a "fake war....If you fight, fight!" she said. Half-measures are unacceptable and useless.

Unfortunately, Israel's government has not always abided by Sarit's dictum. Whether it was good policy or not, despite a bunch of geopolitical musings, the prime minister's decision to pull out of Lebanon in 2000 was much driven by the desire to protect soldiers, even though the decision left the civilian population exposed. Seeing that no civilians were dying in northern Israel at the hand of Hezbollah, mothers did not want to see their children soldiers die for what they thought had become needless reasons. The same fear of soldiers dying affected tactics and strategy in the 2006 war. Over thirty-four days, Hezbollah fired thousands of rockets at citizen targets in northern Israel while, for the most part, the IDF sat, relying mainly on airpower and artillery fire to quell the threat. Then, when airpower alone did not work, the IDF launched pinprick attacks with little upside, during which numerous soldiers died. Not good. The same fear of soldiers dying has guided Israel's hand during its many flareups with Hamas in Gaza—with Israel electing to use mostly stand-off measures rather than ground incursions in force to root out the terrorist infrastructure there.

Lilach Ashtar, whom I first introduced in Chapter Nineteen, is not a fan of that type of thinking. Sitting inside her unique home that was centered on a large living room area with high ceilings, after discussing Home Front Command, we turned to her disdain for the undue focus on soldiers' lives. Of course, she feels that their lives are important and must not be wasted. But, she said, "In my time, when we joined the army as a soldier, we know we might die. It wasn't a joke. It's like roulette." Then she posed an interesting question, using a term that General HaCohen had also used: essence. "What is my essence?" she asked. What am I made of? I will never forget her serious visage when she expressed that word, and how she used it. What is my essence? I've thought about that much since then.

Lilach criticized the concept that soldiers are everyone's kids, even though she, too, is a mother. But, she emphasized, "No, he's not a kid. He's a soldier,…and when he's a soldier, [he] can die." I asked her when that essence changed. "I think Lebanon was the first time, 1982." Then, because of concern for the soldiers, Lilach said, "We moved out of Lebanon because we didn't think about the kibbutz near the fence, we thought about the soldier."

"That was when Israel started to be normal," Lilach said sarcastically, "but we're not normal. We're not in a normal situation."

This sensitivity to soldiers' lives is even greater today and significantly influences policy decisions. It also affects decisions made in battle, which Boaz Amidror told me is a good thing because "it forces commanders to be responsible, professional, to think before they act, [and] to only do things that are important." Spyer even said that "one of the reasons why the Campaign Between Wars is so great and so popular is because hardly anybody's actually involved. … Hardly anybody's been killed, thank goodness, maybe no one." However, because the fear of soldier casualties—and the potential of war—might cause political decision-makers to hesitate or even refrain from doing what's necessary, that fear and passivity could harm Israel as a whole and reward Hezbollah's more aggressive actions. In the long run that would only increase the risk of war and more soldiers dying.

Necessary Wars

We should internalize Sarit's accurate and succinct summary of the present geopolitical situation in the north:

> This is the situation.…You have a terrorist organization on the other side of the border, or [an entity] who doesn't recognize our existence. And I think this is something that people outside of Israel don't understand. It's not about land. It's not about

religion. It's not about ego. It's about our very existence over here. Are we entitled to live here or not?

Yaron, Sarit's husband, added a practical appraisal of reality. He said there are times when Israelis need to fight back or "learn…to [swim] a lot." And by that, he meant fleeing by swimming across the Mediterranean. Together, their thoughts lead me to conclude that not only is a future war likely, but it also might be necessary.

So, what is a necessary war?

Shay Shemesh and I delved into that question. His answer exposed two issues, "One is quality of life and the other is life itself." Shay explained:

> When … Israel was established, and after the Holocaust, we talked about our existence. So, if Arab countries attacked us, they wanted to eliminate us completely, so we fought for our existence, so 1,000, 2,000, 5,000 casualties,…it's a price we have to…pay for our mere existence.

> But now we don't talk about life itself. We talk about quality of life because no one, we believe,…can really risk and jeopardize our existence as a country because we are the strongest, we can deal with them [even though] they can really hurt us. So, we don't talk about life itself. We talk about as a nation, a quality of life. And when you talk about a quality of life…you say, okay, it's like a give-and-take game and it's all a different perspective."

> And then when people say, okay, should we go to war on this issue? It's not an existence/existential issue, it's only a quality of life issue.…We don't fight for our existence. And now Hezbollah is arming itself. Okay,…if you attack them, they will retaliate, and we'll have war. So [some people say] let them arm themselves. They can't really risk our existence.

> And there is another issue.…Sometimes, the Israelis are more sensitive to army casualties than to civilian casualties.

Shay, like others, had alluded to the nub of the issue—soldier casualties versus civilian casualties influencing policy.

Given that a war to decimate Hezbollah's military strength could cost the lives of hundreds or even thousands of IDF soldiers, would an Israeli prime minister willingly risk that loss if everything is quiet, new houses are going up, and tourism is booming? The decision might come down to this: If Israel starts a war, will the populace perceive it as a necessity or as a choice? If Hezbollah were close to having a nuclear weapon, people might support a vigorous response. So far, though, Hezbollah's possession of 150,000 missiles that could devastate Israel, has not motivated the public to press for an immediate campaign to destroy the threat. And, I think, Israel's strategic goals will dictate how strongly the public supports a war. If war only buys a couple of years of peace, Professor Freilich said that most Israelis would balk at risking their son's life for such a short-lived reward.

So, what then is the value of peace? And does preferring a shaky peace that risks hell in the long term indicate that Israel's society has softened?

Peace Versus the Pioneer Spirit

Sarit and Yaron live near Israel's border with Lebanon. For them, the risk of war is not theoretical—it's their reality. A reality that can take their lives, the lives of their children, demolish their homes, and end their way of life. As the wind whistled past us at that abandoned British airfield, we discussed their concerns. But when our conversation bled into Yaron's suggestion that Israel should act unilaterally inside Lebanon to diminish Hezbollah's threat, Sarit asked him if he wanted to "take the risk of war…while everything is quiet, and no rockets are coming?"

Unfazed, Yaron answered, "But you know it's not quiet. You know it's a matter of time….It's a fake quiet." And although he admitted, "I don't want to take the risk of [war]," Yaron also insisted, "I think when it's quiet, you give them time to prepare for war."

"That's right," Sarit answered. "So, postpone the date….That's the whole idea of the Campaign Between Wars. Postpone the war and be prepared for it."

"I don't think it wise. In the end, it will blow up in your face."

"You see, we disagree. [The difference between] mothers and fathers," Sarit said with a smile. Yaron, of course, rebelled at the notion that there was a difference, but I wasn't about to step into that squabble!

A couple of days before the three of us spoke, Sarit and I visited the spot where many decades ago her father, as a child, had crossed from Syria into Palestine (then under the British Mandate). It is a spot that Sarit holds with great veneration and that stimulates great emotion within her. I could see it in her eyes and hear it in her voice. Her father's courage on that journey and during what followed (which I detailed in my book *Living in Heaven, Coping with Hell*) is part of her heritage and a foundation for her love of Israel. After that, we had lunch at a coffee shop. There, I tried to ask Sarit a direct question about whether residents in the north are aware of the acute threat Hezbollah poses. But to preface my inquiry, I stated that she and her family were pioneers. Sarit was quick to correct me, "We don't feel like pioneers."

Although Sarit's response did not answer my intended question because I had introduced another thought—that change in perspective from pioneer to resident offers a clue into Israeli attitudes. At least Lilach and General Gershon HaCohen think so.

Lilach told me that when she was growing up, all the kibbutzim considered themselves the frontier. "So, you really have meaning, you know, people need a goal, need meaning, something." But then cities came, and people lost their "essence." And, she said, "When you lose the essence, you lose everything." There's that word "essence" again. Sorry—the concept of "essence" captivates me.

My conversation with Gershon about pioneers started with a bit of his personal history when he showed me a hundred-year-old picture of his ancestors, pioneering Jews that were plowing fields. "Do you wish you lived in those days?" I asked.

"Yes."

Then I asked him what he would do about Hezbollah if he were prime minister. His answer began with his reflections on the past. In short, he praised Ben Gurion, Israel's first prime minister, for recognizing that to entice Jews to come to Israel he needed to create conditions for two different walks of life: the bourgeois and the pioneers. This was the "tension," he said. And in cities like Tel Aviv, the two could mix, synchronize, and build the nation's identity, with the town dwellers living their lives among cafés and theaters, and the pioneers coming to the city periodically to enjoy the same. Heady stuff from this philosopher general.

But then we got down to the nitty gritty regarding Hezbollah and the danger it presents:

> I must find a way for preemptive attack. On the other side, I have no conditions to do it. Not regarding the international support legitimation, et cetera. Also, regarding the internal support, no one can…go to a war without creating consensus and acceptance of the people about a kind of conviction about what we are going to fight for.

> There are more than 1,000 Hezbollah elite troops that can cross this night…to take Metula, Misgav Am, Shlomi, what would we do? And so, I will prepare the people and [help] them to understand that I cannot promise them to be secure in the same way that I'm committed to secure Tel Aviv because they are [on] the border. It is a frontier. It is like…it's a buffer zone. And like the shock absorber of the car.

And what's the duty of [a] shock absorber in the car? That you will drive in the field and get the feeling that you are not feeling differently than [on] the excellent road. Who will be getting the shock? The shock absorber. If [they] claim to you they are sitting comfortably and [they are] getting the whole shocks, this is your duty. But it means not just to prepare them [for] that. It is to give them an identity of pioneers. A liberal society cannot do that because liberal society, the basic story of it, is everyone in a way paying his duty in the same way that he's paying taxes. After that, he is free to live his private life.

If we're speaking about pioneers [on] the frontiers, that's how [they] partner [with] the security forces to the [benefit] of the country.

Powerful stuff. Gershon and Lilach are calling for residents of northern Israel to take risks, willingly, for the common good. To be the nation's "shock absorbers." To be pioneers.

Others are willing to pocket present peace in hopes of a better future. They point to the situation after the 1973 war when Egypt and Syria launched a surprise attack on Israel that almost overwhelmed the nation. Who would've ever thought, they say, that four years later Egypt's president would break through three decades of hatred by visiting Israel and eighteen months later signing a peace treaty? Things can happen quickly in the Middle East. Massive demonstrations now course through Iran daily. If Iran's government falls, so might Hezbollah. Therefore, enjoying a guarded respite from violence is not necessarily a bad idea. But also, those who appeal for a return to a pioneer mentality have a point. Being willing to fight is an effective way to prevent a fight. Fearing a fight often guarantees one. Therefore, the tension between Israel's pioneer mentality and its hunger for sustained peace is the key factor in determining if Israel has the will to fight. If war is thrust upon them, all Israelis will fight hard without respite. But not all Israelis are willing to risk a war that would jeopardize the peace they now enjoy—especially if leadership has done a poor job explaining why going to war is necessary. Unfortunately, with Hezbollah's mindset so murky, it's difficult to find a middle path that incorporates the best of both perspectives.

Are the Israeli People Ready for War?

Let's be honest. Lilach is a hardliner. But that doesn't make her wrong. Consider this statement of hers:

> I think we're not prepared, and we are not doing a great effort to be prepared. I think we lost so many thing[s] in…Israel, but the first thing that we lost is the meaning, the vision.
>
> Look at the quality of life, see how many good cars [are] on the road. See, everything is so nice. You have…the coffee and everything. Just be around Kiryat Shmona, [that's] a very nice place. And they have the students, you know, the parties and everything is so nice. So…it's like…everyone will say…it will be war with Hezbollah, but nobody really [understands] what does it mean? They take the responsibility out of the people. They really take the responsibility out of the people and say now we'll do it for you. [Everything will be OK.] And You feel OK. And in the meantime, the generals are playing a strategic game. What will Khameini do, what will Nasrallah do? I don't care what Nasrallah would do. I care what is my essence? What [is] the thing that we should [do]?

Lilach continued, "The army wants to make you sure that…everything is okay. So, they [don't] let us be prepared. [But] we can be prepared….It's not like Hezbollah is a huge enemy." A worthy enemy? "Yes, but it's manageable." Then Lilach said that Israel should explain that Iron Dome will not save the day. Israel's leadership must tell people the truth, she says, and challenge them. And it must teach history in a manner that illuminates the challenges its founders faced and overcame. Instead, Lilach is concerned that this period of safety and security has made people feel comfortable, eliminating the need for them to accept personal responsibility. In her vision for an enviable essence, she hopes people return to pioneer ways. Lilach already has.

Gershon, of course, agrees with Lilach. He told me leadership must explain the reality to the people because "the best way to prevent a war is to be really ready to [go to] war." However, he said, "If you want to escape to your small private life by just ignoring all threats you will be very happy today and tomorrow. But the day after I cannot really promise." Thus, he said, "To lead, we must bring an awareness of the crisis situation." But he candidly admitted that leadership must also be aware of what might come after a war starts—rockets hitting Tel Aviv from many directions, and then pressure for a ceasefire, which might press Israel into relinquishing the Golan Heights, Shebaa Farms, and other disputed areas. Therefore, any consideration of war must also consider how it might end.

Is Israel Weaker Than a Spider's Web?

Yaron Schweitzer once headed the International Terrorism Section of the IDF's military intelligence directorate, was a private consultant to the prime minister's office and is now a senior research fellow at the Institute for National Security Studies. He also is a likable fellow and was a joy to spend a few hours with. But he was gruff and clear about Israel's willingness to fight: "I believe in spite of everything…that Israel is strong enough, is determined enough."

Nevertheless, Nasrallah's spider web speech struck a raw nerve because, as propaganda does, it conflated truth with falsehoods. Yes, Israel desires peace and will go the extra yard to attain it. No democratic society, given the choice, embraces war. But that principle is nothing to be ashamed of; it is a strength. It ensures that Israel won't go to war without giving the decision its proper weight. And it highlights the salient difference between Israel and those Lebanese citizens whom Nasrallah holds in a vise—hope versus darkness.

However, it's only virtuous to avoid war when the decision is based on reason rather than emotion. It is here that Israel's political process, which has held five elections in the last four years, undercuts Israel's citizens. For two decades, too many times Israel's leaders have feared the consequences of lost lives more than the deleterious effects of poor policy decisions. This is not the fault of the people. It is the fault of those who lust to lead. It results in politics trumping policy and shaky governments that lack enough continuity for a prime minister to rule versus react.

When convinced of the necessity of war, or provoked by its enemies, Israelis band together to join in the fight. However, for more than two decades the government, no matter who the prime minister, has not done an admirable job of defining and readying the population for a necessary war with Hezbollah that Israel might have to initiate. Nor has the government made any attempt to reverse the psychology that makes soldiers' deaths more tragic than civilians' deaths. I know that sounds harsh, but not only is it the duty of soldiers to protect civilians, but it is also the highest calling of government, too.

As a result, future Israeli governments may act too cautiously to curb Hezbollah's growing strength out of fear of that casualties will cause them political peril. This caution limits the IDF's freedom to do what is necessary and increases the likelihood of the very results the government is trying to avoid. Part of the reason for political timidity stems from pessimism caused by Israel's failure to end threats from Lebanon, despite having tried four times to do so over the last forty years. But those failures illuminate the path that Israel must travel in any future war with Hezbollah. Israel must see it through until it ends with a discernible victory that eliminates the Hezbollah threat for at least a decade if not forever—nothing less. Otherwise, if Israel starts the war, the public will see it as a failed war of choice. And if Hezbollah starts it, absent its clear defeat, the war will be seen as an ostensible success that empowers Israel's enemies.

Therefore, until Israel's government convincingly reverses the old mindset, Nasrallah's reference to the spider web will continue to sting—whether true or not. Also, if he continues to believe Israel is a vulnerable target, or if domestic needs push him hard enough, Nasrallah might once again fail to recognize the danger of Israeli anger or the risk of crossing Israeli red lines and try to tweak what he sees as a weakening opponent.

Then, there could be an accidental war.

Chapter Twenty-Four

If War Comes

"Operations we do when we can; wars only when we must," said Benny Gantz, former IDF chief of staff, defense minister, and deputy prime minister of Israel. His comment, with or without his intention, highlights the difference between the Campaign Between Wars and a future war. When Israel mows the lawn, it is an operation. It could be preventing Hezbollah, or Iran in Syria, from encroaching; it could be interdicting weapons transfers; or it could be slowing down Hezbollah's procurement of an existential threat to Israel—such as too many PGM missiles. Unless there is an emergency, CBW planning requires Israel to weigh the risks versus the benefits of every action.

Wars are something different. Their objectives are much broader than an operation's. And the risks are greater. Although some wars are planned, others are a byproduct of miscalculation—such as Hezbollah's failure in 2006 to appreciate how Israel would respond to the kidnapping and killing of IDF soldiers. Wars can also be triggered by accident—like a small-scale Hezbollah attack on an IDF military target that accidentally causes civilian casualties. Israel would likely respond violently, and then Hezbollah might feel obligated to respond even more violently, launching an all-out war.

An accidental war nearly broke out in 2015 when Hezbollah missiles killed two IDF soldiers in a military vehicle and came close to striking a civilian transport. Fortunately, only the driver was in the vehicle, and he jumped out to safety. That day, an abundance of luck likely prevented a war. If a missile had struck the car while passengers were inside, a war might have ensued.

Wars can also break out without warning. A surprise attack by Hezbollah poses a great risk to Israel. Thousands of missiles would fly without notice, possibly from multiple directions, toward an unprepared Israel, while Hezbollah's Radwan units would attempt to invade unsuspecting Israeli towns.

Wars can also be preemptive or preventative. A preemptive or preventative Hezbollah attack would unfold similarly to a surprise attack, except for the degree of preparation. If Israel launched such an attack, the course of events would differ from what I will describe in this chapter; they would be so different that the subsequent chapter is devoted to discussing an Israeli preemptive or preventative attack.

But what if Israel doesn't initiate the war? What if it breaks out for a reason other than Israel responding to Hezbollah's egregious actions? What might that look like and how would it play out?

Hezbollah

Likely, Hezbollah would have four wartime goals: surviving, preventing Israel from achieving its goals, retaining its ability to rearm and influence Lebanon's government, and creating a public perception that Israel lost. To accomplish that, Hezbollah will focus on destroying Israel's economy and demoralizing its people. It's estimated that Hezbollah can fire anywhere from 1,500 to as many as 4,000 rockets into Israeli territory daily. Hezbollah operatives will also try to infiltrate Israel to terrorize and temporarily occupy one or more Israeli towns. Once the operatives are across the border—whether in Metula, Manara, Misgav Am, Hanita, Za'arit, or any other place adjacent to the border—they'll kill and/or kidnap Israeli civilians and plant Hezbollah's flag for propaganda effect. Meanwhile, terror groups coming from Syria into the Golan Heights will try to do the same, likely with less success. Hezbollah will try to infiltrate Israel from every angle—moving over, around, under, and even through border defenses. To mask those intrusions, Hezbollah will fire a massive barrage of rockets, mortars, and other munitions along the entire border.

In addition, Hezbollah will employ fast attack craft, semi-submersibles, and other means to attack up and down the coastline near Nahariyah, Acre, and even Haifa as surface-to-sea missiles strike Israeli natural gas extraction facilities in the Mediterranean.

No matter what happens, Hezbollah's media arm will surely produce and spread propaganda on a global scale. Much of it will be manufactured videos and images. Then, in the face of Israel's furious response, Hezbollah will continue fighting, at any cost, until the international community already predisposed to criticize Israel at the drop of a hat, and now prompted by the media's biased depiction of destruction and civilian death in Lebanon, forces the fighting to stop—surely at a time not of Israel's choosing.

For Hezbollah, a strategic victory means achieving its four wartime goals. To do so, Nasrallah knows he must endure many tactical defeats, which will include losing much of his armament and trained manpower. Lebanese civilian casualties will not concern him. Instead, the more civilians who die, the more likely he is to achieve his goals. It is an absurd but well-considered formulation. Their deaths will inflame Shiites and many others in Lebanon to hate Israel while simultaneously galvanizing the international community to demonize Israel and thwart its war strategy. On the other hand, Nasrallah believes that the more Israelis he kills—soldiers and civilians—the more Israeli society will fracture from despair. Thus, Hezbollah's concept of victory does not hinge on military success but rather on the perception of Israel's defeat.

A few years ago, to prove Hezbollah's targeting capabilities and further deter Israel, Nasrallah released a video with satellite images of targets in Israel that included their location coordinates. They comprised part of Hezbollah's comprehensive database that contains targeting information necessary for hitting infrastructure, population concentrations, military bases, and other targets. Included are Haifa's petrochemical plants and numerous locations in Gush Dan, the densely populated region in central Israel that includes metropolitan Tel Aviv. The database also has targeting information on locations in the Negev, including Beersheba and the nuclear reactor in Dimona. It even lists *Alma's* location, Sarit Zehavi's northern Israel research and education non-profit that regularly reveals Hezbollah's activities.

Israel

In a future war, Israel's primary goal is to defeat Hezbollah definitively and clearly. Anything less will allow Hezbollah to claim victory and grow even stronger—as it did after the 2006 war. Retired Major General Yaakov Amidror opined that in any future war, Israel must not only destroy Hezbollah's capabilities but also leave it unable to rearm when the war ends. To accomplish that, Amidror envisions a two or three-week intensive phase during which IDF ground forces take control of most of southern Lebanon while the air force ranges throughout the country to destroy missiles and other targets on the ground. A second phase lasting several months would follow, with the IDF combing through the region it holds to destroy all Hezbollah infrastructure and weapons. Then, after withdrawing, Amidror says the IDF must respond aggressively to any attempt to filter new weapons back into the region. In short, a total reset of the Rules of the Game, in which there are no sanctuaries.

I agree with Amidror. It is fine to implement a policy of mowing the grass if doing so returns the mowed area to a pristine state. However, mowing the grass is not a sustainable policy when, following each mowing, weeds regrow higher and thicker. To return the region to a pristine state, the next all-out war must be just that—all-out. The

IDF must destroy the regional Shiite threat not only in Lebanon but also in Syria, too, if attacks emanate from there during the conflagration. Additionally, it would be nice if, as a byproduct, the war helped reduce Iran's influence in Syria and Lebanon and freed Lebanon's government from Hezbollah's control. However, because both of those aims would be hard to achieve, Israel should limit its purpose to ending the military threat and must steel itself to do so. Then, as a former northern commander said, if successful, "It won't be another second Lebanon war, but the final northern war."

But what if Israel tries instead to limit the scope of a future war?

A more limited response to some Hezbollah provocation might see the IDF restrict itself in the opening stages to an attempt to destroy the PGM missiles and other large statistical missiles that are most dangerous to Israel's infrastructure. That would require thousands of air strikes using planes, missiles, and UAVs but would not include much involvement of IDF ground forces other than some localized special forces operations.

However, since Hezbollah hides its missile assets in or near civilian structures, it is doubtful that a limited war would stay limited because even an Israeli limited plan of attack would entail an enormous number of air strikes and a significant impact on Lebanese civilians. Nasrallah would face immense pressure to respond immediately—and aggressively—or else Hezbollah would risk losing credibility with its supporters, and Israel will have established overwhelming deterrence by eliminating Hezbollah's biggest threat. If Nasrallah pulls his punches and only fires a few missiles, the result would be similar. Israel's missile defenses would deal with them, issuing a massive blow to Hezbollah's credibility. And if Hezbollah held back, it would face another problem stemming from uncertainty. The IDF would surely not repeat its mistake of 2006 when it failed to mobilize large numbers of ground forces immediately. Then, seeing large IDF troop concentrations near the border, Nasrallah would be left guessing whether Israel planned to supplement its air strikes with an invasion into southern Lebanon to root out missiles. Therefore, Nasrallah would likely feel he had no choice but to fire Hezbollah's missiles before losing them. This, of course, would lead to the same robust Israeli ground incursion into Lebanon that Israelis advocating for a more limited response had sought to avoid. Furthermore, to garner Israeli domestic support, a ground incursion would have to echo what Amidror suggests rather than be a pinprick, which would still draw blood from IDF soldiers with little benefit.

Another scenario that might at first limit the scope of battle would be if Hezbollah decided to strike a target in Israel in response to an Israeli CBW operation that kills Hezbollah operatives. Since killing Hezbollah operatives crosses a red line for Nasrallah, failing to retaliate would diminish Hezbollah's deterrence and basis for existence. But that impetus almost led to war in 2019 when, as part of the CBW, an Israeli air strike on the outskirts of Damascus killed two Hezbollah members who had been trained by Iran to fly UAVs. It was part of a series of attacks designed to foil Iran's plans to send explosive-laden UAVs to attack military targets and infrastructure in northern Israel. Afterward, the IDF knew Hezbollah would respond. Soon, as described in Chapter Eleven, Hezbollah struck. Fortunately, no Israelis were injured but the IDF engaged in a publicized helicopter evacuation of a soldier bandaged to feign injuries. This permitted Hezbollah to save face since it had destroyed a vehicle and ostensibly injured IDF soldiers. But since no soldiers were injured or killed, Israel felt no need to respond. However, if Hezbollah's retaliation had caused casualties, military or civilian, things might well have gone much differently. Israel might have launched a massive response and very quickly Hezbollah would have faced the same choice that it will face should Israel try to destroy its PGM missiles—should it respond with everything it has or not?

Therefore, since even a limited war might well lead to an all-out war, let's examine what that would look like.

Israel's Ground Attack

Alone, Israel's standing army is too small to win a war with Hezbollah. Winning requires mobilizing the reserves. But if war starts with little or no warning, it will take up to four days for troops to reach the northern borders in sufficient numbers to initiate a powerful ground offensive. And those days will be harrowing. The first stage of mobilization will see reservists report to mobilization centers throughout the country. There, they'll face the threat of Hezbollah's PGMs and UAVs sent to kill and disrupt those concentrations. Then their movement north will be complicated by Israeli civilians streaming south to escape the fighting, Israeli Arabs blocking roadways, and damage to Israel's transportation network caused by Hezbollah's rocket fire. When those soldiers reach the border region and mass for an attack into Lebanon, they will face Katyushas fired in such massive numbers that Iron Dome will not be able to stop them all. Meanwhile, those few soldiers in place from the beginning of the war will have their hands full preventing Hezbollah's operatives from invading towns and villages along the border and raiding the northern coastline.

Since Israel will want to achieve its objectives quickly and its troops will be endangered by remaining stationary, four or five days after mobilization begins the IDF would probably initiate an aggressive ground campaign into Lebanon. It might initiate the campaign even sooner using specialized regular army units and reservists who arrive in the early hours of fighting. But the battle will be challenging. Lebanon's road network in the south channel's movement. Only three routes allow rapid advances northward: along the coast, in the center through the Salouqi/Hojeir Valley, and to the east through the Hasbani and Shebaa Valleys that lead to the Bekaa

Valley. All three routes are susceptible to anti-tank ambushes. Tanks that reach the Bekaa Valley will then encounter another problem—a natural tank trap composed of a valley floor about six miles wide flanked by steep mountains. The Syrians used the topography in the Bekaa Valley to good effect during the 1982 War. In the 2006 war with Hezbollah, the IDF incurred significant casualties and tank losses in the Salouqi Valley. Today, a better-prepared IDF will move aggressively north on all three courses, even though fleeing civilians and Hezbollah operatives in well-prepared defensive positions will impede its progress.

And then there is the matter of international forces. UNIFIL has thousands of troops housed in many bases throughout the region. Because the IDF will not want to harm them, their mere presence will complicate efforts to move quickly.

The current war plan is called *Momentum.* Rather than fight in large division formations, the IDF's organizational structure will revert to past days, fighting in smaller, brigade-sized units spread throughout the countryside, which, due to their more localized and responsive command structures can better deal with Hezbollah's village defenses. To improve the readiness of both the regular army and reservists, the IDF has increased the number of military exercises simulating a northern war. Training now includes the use of simulators and emphasizes rapid maneuvers. To simulate battle conditions as much as possible, the IDF employs multiple urban warfare training centers built to look like Lebanese villages, towns, and refugee camps. The largest contains 600 structures that include mosque-like edifices, multiple-level buildings, and even tunnels.

To succeed, while the air force ranges throughout Lebanon looking for PGMs and other targets susceptible to air strikes, IDF ground forces will need to swiftly stop Hezbollah from launching missiles based in southern Lebanon. Otherwise, Israel's home front will face devastation. To do so, ground forces will move past the Litani

River and into the Bekaa Valley. Since speed is of the essence, troops will first focus on rapidly reaching their end point, cutting off Hezbollah's entrapped forces from resupply and reinforcement. Then they'll mop up. Complementing the movements of the regular army, special operation units will land from the air and possibly sea to attack from unexpected directions. All will receive massive support from the air, ground artillery, and the navy. Soldiers and firepower will attack Hezbollah from every direction. All IDF ground forces will likely coordinate with a plethora of aerial platforms, including large numbers of UAVs equipped with sensors that reveal Hezbollah positions and equipment. Once the enemy is detected, IDF units rapidly inserted into the region, together with a myriad of weapon platforms, will quickly attempt to destroy the enemy before it can inflict unacceptable losses on the IDF and the home front.

Still, the battle will be fierce and ground units will probably face determined opposition as soon as they enter Lebanon, where they'll encounter tunnels, mines, and other defensive positions deeply enmeshed in villages dotting the region. Between those villages, southern Lebanon's lush foliage will mask other defensive positions. House-to-house fighting is inevitable. It is unavoidable that civilian structures will be destroyed. Would it be easier to flatten those villages from the air and use tunnel-busting explosives to destroy Hezbollah's underground bunkers and tunnels wherever they're found? Sure. But doing that might violate international rules of war. It certainly would invite international condemnation. So Israeli soldiers, fighting on the ground, will pay with their blood for Hezbollah's cynical perfidy that values killing Israeli soldiers more than the lives of Lebanon's civilians.

Depending on how events unfold, IDF ground forces might also enter areas besides Lebanon, such as Syria. The objective of moving into Syria would be to push Hezbollah and other Iranian proxy forces back from the Golan Heights border while destroying missiles located there. Since opposing numbers are comparatively few, the terrain is relatively open, and the Syrian army is now a shadow of its former self, the IDF should be able to accomplish this without too much trouble. And since Israel already has a security presence in the West Bank and might receive tacit cooperation from a Palestinian Authority opposed to Hamas, the IDF's activities there will likely involve more policing than attacking; and the problems of the area, no matter how the media might portray them, will likely be more of a nuisance than an existential threat.

However, Gaza presents a much more complicated problem. If Hamas and Islamic Jihad support Hezbollah by launching their rockets while attempting to send terrorists across the border, the IDF may have no choice but to move ground forces into Gaza to stop the rocket launches, especially if Israel's supply of Iron Dome missiles runs low. That would result in a bloody house-to-house fight in crowded streets. The IDF would suffer many casualties and would need to employ large numbers of troops that could distract from the main effort in Lebanon and Syria. Civilian casualties and damage to property in Gaza would be significant. Especially because the IDF would have to move hastily to shut down threats emanating from Gaza so that it could better concentrate on Hezbollah.

And then there is the problem of Arab communities in the northern regions of Israel. While most would remain peaceful, some will not, especially if Hezbollah's provocateurs stir things up. It would not take many of them to inflame the region. As discussed in Chapter Nineteen, Home Front Command lacks the resources to keep the road network in northern Israel open if the region's Israeli Arabs riot on a large scale. The same could be true in more central areas of the country, such as Lod which saw riots in 2021. Since that road network is crucial for moving troops to Lebanon and supplying them, the IDF will have to siphon soldiers from the main battle to deal with the threat. In preparation, it has already established one reserve brigade to accomplish this task. But more might be required.

All told, in a major conflict with Hezbollah, IDF ground forces will need to move rapidly into Lebanon and possibly Syria and Gaza, while defending Israeli towns along the northern border and keeping peace in Arab towns astride northern Israel's road network. It's a daunting task that will stretch the IDF's capabilities to its limits.

Israel's Air Attack

In February 2021, the IDF conducted a large-scale military exercise designed to simulate a sudden outbreak of war with Hezbollah, both Iranian proxies and Syrian forces in Syria, and with Hamas and Islamic Jihad in Gaza. Israel's air force (IAF) simulated launching 3,500 aerial strikes each day—the same number of targets attacked in all thirty-four days of the 2006 war! That same month, Israel conducted an air defense drill to practice defending against missile attacks and UAVs.

In the days before the bulk of the IDF's ground forces reach the border and move into Lebanon, the IAF's primary goal will be to destroy missiles and launchers belonging to Hezbollah and other combatants. To meet the aerial onslaught, Hezbollah will use its growing surface-to-air hand-held missile inventory and Syria will use its advanced ground-based surface-air missiles to blunt the IAF's efforts. Nevertheless, the IAF must succeed. In 2006, of the 4,000 missiles launched by Hezbollah, many hundreds struck urban areas in Israel. They damaged or destroyed thousands of homes along with schools and hospitals. Now, Hezbollah and its allies may be able to fire more than that amount in the first day of fighting and collectively possess more than forty times the number of missiles fired at Israel in 2006. Therefore, Israel's economic well-being depends on what the IAF can achieve during the first few days of the war before ground forces finish the job.

Fortunately, today's air force can accomplish much. In the first two days of the 2006 war, the IAF destroyed many of Hezbollah's middle- and long-range rockets. Over the next thirty-two days, IAF planes flew thousands more missions over Lebanon. Eleven years later, IAF commander Amir Eshel said, "What we could do in thirty-four days in the Second Lebanon War, we can now do in forty-eight hours." Since then, the IAF's capability has increased.

However, it will prove impossible for the IAF to fully prevent terror from the sky striking the home front. Israel's enemies possess far too many missiles. Therefore, like Iron Dome, Israel's offensive operations must prioritize going after the most dangerous missiles with longer ranges, payload capacity, and accuracy. Hezbollah has scattered these missiles throughout much of Lebanon; some are likely also based in Syria, Gaza, and Western Iraq. Thus, operations will need to continue at a rapid pace throughout the region surrounding Israel—twenty-four hours a day—for many days or weeks. It will not be easy. And it will be made more difficult if enemy missiles get through Israel's defensive missile screen to strike one or more of Israel's airbases. To prevent that from happening, Israel's missile defenses will prioritize protecting those airfields over Israeli civilians, who will suffer greatly as a result.

In addition to its other tasks, the IAF may also target Lebanon's infrastructure. The reason for this must be conveyed to the international community now, not just then. Bridges, power-generating stations, and communication facilities will likely be destroyed for two reasons. One is for military purposes—much of that infrastructure supports Hezbollah's war efforts. The second is political. Lebanon's people must understand that if they do not rein in Hezbollah by government action or otherwise, then they cannot avoid responsibility for its failure. This is especially true now that Hezbollah is so integrated with Lebanon's government that it controls Lebanon for all practical purposes. A nation that causes a war bears the price for that war. There is no free lunch.

<u>How International Laws of War Impact the IDF</u>

Hezbollah does not hesitate to put civilian populations at risk by embedding and hiding weapons in civilian areas. And since those weapons are purposed for causing injury and death to Israeli civilians and soldiers, the IDF must destroy them if war breaks out. However, international law for armed conflict requires participants to do everything feasible to mitigate the risk of civilian casualties. Since Hezbollah ignores it, honoring that dictum puts much pressure on the IDF.

So how will that international law restrict IDF operations in a war with Hezbollah?

First, let's make sure we understand what the law is. While the Law of Armed Conflict does demand that combatants only target military objectives, it does not preclude using force in civilian areas if military targets are present. Article 51 explicitly states that the defending force may not use civilians to garner immunity from attack. And Article 57 contemplates attacks that will cause civilian casualties. However, the attacker must do what is feasible to reduce harm to civilians and not attack when the military value of the target does not outweigh the risk of civilian harm. Hmm. That is a very subjective standard. The IDF, being sensitive to the bias with which many nations view it and, to further honor the traditions and morals of a democratic society, does everything it reasonably can to hold up its end of the bargain. But I must emphasize that it does so unilaterally. Hezbollah does not demonstrate a scintilla of those same scruples.

To fulfill its responsibility, the IDF has integrated assessment procedures in its decision processes, at both high and low levels of command, that ensure that the Law of Armed Conflict is honored. Examples of IDF techniques to minimize civilian casualties, even at the risk of losing tactical advantage by sacrificing the element of surprise, include:

- Providing warnings to civilians near the target by dropping leaflets and sending texts and telephone messages to those in danger of being injured if they remain. Consider that for a minute—much effort is put into identifying the contact information of civilians living in target areas so they can be warned but these warnings could also result in combatants evacuating themselves and their missile from the target, too!

- Rooftop knock warnings, which is shorthand for striking the roof of targeted buildings with munitions that cause little damage but that make a loud noise heralding more powerful explosives to come. By doing so, civilians within the building get an audible message to immediately evacuate.

- Firing precision-guided missiles that use the least explosive power necessary to fulfill the mission. This minimizes collateral damage to surrounding areas.

- Utilizing specially calibrated tank shells with reduced explosive power so that only the room targeted will be destroyed. I will never forget the lesson in tank-gun accuracy I received. A former unit commander on the Golan Heights pointed out a distant building to me. He said that the tank I was leaning against could easily fire a round through any of the windows in view.

- Unfortunately, as I previously mentioned, Hezbollah does not feel constrained by the Law of Armed Conflict. Instead, it ignores them, as it did when it fired thousands of rockets at Israel in 2006. And as it will fire Katyushas again in a future war, which Hezbollah knows are far too inaccurate for striking specific targets but extremely useful for terrorizing population centers because they kill indiscriminately. It's not as if Hezbollah does not understand the Law of Armed Conflict. Hezbollah's frequent attempts to convince others to accuse

Israel of doing what it itself routinely does is ample proof of that. It just uses the laws when it wants to for its advantage.

<u>How A War Ends, Matters</u>

Israel will not want to stop fighting until the cost of continuing the fight is greater than the value of what it can still reasonably achieve. However, the choice to end a war is not just for Israel to make. Hezbollah, Iran, and perhaps even Hamas and Syria will also have a vote. Their choice will be based on the same calculation but with a different perspective. Therefore, there are three basic scenarios for ending the war:

A. Israel has caused so much damage to Hezbollah and any others participating in the fighting that Israel can unilaterally stop the war when it wants because the cost to its opponents of continuing the fight is too steep for them to bear. This is the best scenario for Israel because it would be free to fight until Hezbollah would no longer have the power to threaten Israel, Iranian forces and proxies would likely have been removed from areas in Syria abutting Israel, and the Lebanese government might then be able to restrict Hezbollah's ability to regenerate.

B. Israel is forced to stop its attacks because of failures on the battlefield, heavy soldier or civilian casualties, or because the international community mobilizes more pressure for a ceasefire than Israel can withstand. It will happen if Israel loses the support of the United States, but it could also happen even with its support. This would be a terrible result for Israel, and one that would constitute a win for Hezbollah, which may only agree to stop fighting at a price that's difficult for Israel to swallow.

C. A coordinated end to the fighting with or without external pressure on both sides. Absent third-party mediation, this would be unlikely. However, unless Israel has concrete demands that it sticks to, which include actual disarmament of Hezbollah and that Iran is removed from the region, Hezbollah and many others would view words unaccompanied by real enforcement measures as a victory for Hezbollah.

Achieving a definitive victory, as outlined in the first option above, is critical to Israel's future. Since the next war will undoubtedly leave Israel with significant economic damage and cause many military and civilian casualties, Israel cannot afford to end the war with the possibility of having to fight another round soon. Anything less will seriously impair the nation's morale, endangering Israel's future. That is why a partial victory would be a defeat. That is also why it's so important for Israel to increase its chances of winning its next war with Hezbollah. The next chapter explores one way of doing that.

Chapter Twenty-Five

Preemptive or Preventative War

"I think we need to seriously consider a preemptive strike in Lebanon," former major general and Israeli national security advisor Yaakov Amidror told a reporter at Al-Monitor. "We made two fatal strategic errors in the past in our dealings with Hezbollah. One more mistake will leave us regretting it for generations to come. We must not let Hezbollah cross that red line." When asked to identify those errors, Amidror responded:

> The first mistake was that we let the organization grow dangerously powerful when we withdrew from Lebanon after the First Lebanon War. The second mistake was that we didn't insist that Security Council Resolution 1701 be enforced after the Second Lebanon War. Now Hezbollah has grown to almost monstrous proportions. We will pay a very steep price if we allow it to have such a large number of rockets and precision missiles. Israel is a tiny country. We have very few advantages, so we cannot make that mistake. We are now facing a watershed moment. We must be prepared to bear the cost of a preemptive attack if it turns out that Hezbollah has, in fact, accumulated capacities that it did not have in the past that would bring about a drastic shift in the balance of power. As soon as the Hezbollah monster acquires exceptional capacities, we would be facing a tiebreaker. Under no circumstances may we allow that to happen.

*   *   *   *

This has been a difficult chapter to write because it is about Israel attacking Hezbollah without warning. Some people might think that doing so is immoral. Others may applaud that choice. But wherever you land on that moral spectrum, one thing is certain—lots of people will die if Israel makes that choice. Therefore, because of the seriousness of the issue, let's make sure we are on the same wavelength regarding the terminology. I will try not to be obtuse.

Preemptive war, sometimes called "anticipatory self-defense or anticipatory attack," is an offensive operation undertaken in the face of an *imminent threat* that will cause *unacceptable harm*. An imminent threat means there is high confidence that the enemy will attack very soon. If we are referring to individuals, killing one person is unacceptable harm—especially if it is you, a loved one, or a child. But the conflicts this book discusses do not lend themselves to such a granular view. Instead, the issue is determining what constitutes unacceptable harm for a nation. To my surprise, however, there is no universally accepted definition for that. Therefore, I will soon supply you with a way to think about unacceptable harm, guided by the words of Uzi Rubin. But for now, remember that a modern nation depends on power, water, transportation, communication, and even banking to function. If an enemy destroys that nation's ability to generate those services and/or kills hundreds or thousands of civilians, that enemy has caused unacceptable harm.

The terms *preventative war* and *preemptive war* describe two types of similar yet distinct wars, both of which aim to prevent the enemy from inflicting unacceptable harm. But the terms differ regarding how soon the enemy will likely strike. And like unacceptable harm, both terms have many definitions. I present for your consideration one definition most applicable to Israel's concerns with Hezbollah. As such, preventative war is a war initiated when a nation strongly expects that an enemy already is, or soon will be, able to inflict unacceptable harm and intends to do so in the foreseeable future. This is especially true if delaying an attack will make it impossible for a nation to eliminate the threat when it becomes imminent.

The decision to launch a preemptive or preventative war is a serious matter. Such a war would invariably cause much damage and loss of life in both Israel and Lebanon. Given that, should Israel consider launching such an attack? To answer that question, we need to analyze and answer the following questions in detail:

1. What benefit would Israel reap by striking first?
2. What conditions might cause Israel to strike first?
3. Would a preemptive or preventive attack on Hezbollah be legal under international law and does that matter?
4. How might Israeli politics obstruct the decision to attack, and would Israeli citizens support it?

However, before answering those questions, I will lay out the factual foundation upon which such a weighty decision may one day be made.

The Factual Foundation

Hezbollah, backed by Iran, intends to destroy Israel. Nasrallah's words, as well as the words of Iran's past and present leadership, are consistent on that score. And words do matter, especially when they're consistently expressed for decades in various forums by people in leadership. Especially when those words have been backed up by terrorists sent by those leaders to kill and kidnap Israelis. These words fit hand-in-hand with Hezbollah's procurement and development of weapon systems capable of fulfilling the leadership's goal. For decades Hezbollah, lacking the means to fully execute its objective, settled for annoying and terrorizing Israel. Now, that has changed. Its growing arsenal of weapons poses a growing existential threat to Israel that left unchecked jeopardizes its future.

Also relevant to this discussion is that Hezbollah is a terrorist organization—called a hybrid terrorist organization by some—that has ensnared Lebanon. Now the Lebanese government has limited free will if any. Simply put, Hezbollah has devoured Lebanon. Placing a placard embossed with a country's name on a United Nations table does not make a nation. Especially if that government refuses to meaningfully confront the monster it facilitates and cannot, or refuses to act, without consent from the terrorist entity that dominates it. We could debate for hours whether Lebanon still exists in anything other than name only and whether Hezbollah is now Lebanon. The phrase "form over substance" comes to mind. But for our purposes, we can pare the issue down to one inescapable fact from which all else stems— in Lebanon, Hezbollah calls the shots.

Furthermore, as Hezbollah's threat to Israel grows, so does the threat of the other Iranian proxies—Hamas and Islamic Jihad in Gaza, Iranian-inspired militias in Syria, Hezbollah of Iraq, and even the Houthis in Yemen. All those proxies now have menacing weapons and growing ground forces. And further, a nascent Hezbollah effort in the West Bank presents the potential for future problems for Israel. Alone, Hezbollah's capabilities are fearsome—able to inflict unacceptable harm. When combined with the other proxies—those capabilities are nearing or may have already reached the level of existential threat. And that is without Iran joining the fight.

For now, Israel has primarily responded by strengthening its already powerful military; attempting to deter Hezbollah by word and by deed, the success of which is uncertain; and by continuing the Campaign Between Wars. Fortunately, by all counts, the CBW has been remarkably effective for reducing the immediate military threat. Iran has found it difficult to establish its forces and those of its proxies along Israel's border with Syria, Iran's attempts to send more destructive missiles and PGM technology to Hezbollah have been largely frustrated, and Israel has reportedly even hit targets in western Iraq and now Iran itself. But the CBW alone will not stop Hezbollah's threat from growing. It will only slow and disrupt it. Sarit Zehavi told me, "This is the Eisenkot doctrine,…saying let's postpone the war. That's the whole idea of the Campaign Between Wars. Postpone the war." Postpone it until when? Meanwhile, closer to Israel's beating heart, the many flareups with terrorists in Gaza coupled with Israeli and Egyptian quarantine measures have reduced the number of rockets now in the hands of Hamas and Islamic Jihad.

Still, the enemies haunting Israel's borders continue to obtain even more weapons of an increasingly lethal nature, just as the number of terrorists in Syria targeting Israel continues to grow. Hezbollah didn't always have 150,000 missiles. A decade ago, it had neither PGMs nor UAVs. And for years, Syria was embroiled in a civil war that foreclosed stationing operatives there who threatened Israel. Now, things have changed. What was a growing danger has become a malignant nightmare.

Therefore, the CBW has not proved itself capable of eliminating the threat Israel is currently facing; it has just kicked the can down the road. But that road is becoming far more dangerous with each passing day, and the road's end is near. Yesterday, if Hezbollah and Iran's other proxies had started a war with Israel, the impact on Israeli society would have been destructive. Today, it could be devastating. Tomorrow might be worse. For Israeli men, women, and children—for infants breathing their first breaths and elderly struggling to enjoy the fruits of their labors in their remaining years—death and despair lurk and leer just around the corner. Would you accept living your life subject to that increasing threat? A real threat that Hezbollah ostentatiously proclaims with its flags and banners along the border. Or, other than fleeing, would you try to do something about it?

The borders are peaceful today. But in this volatile region, that can change tomorrow. And every tomorrow after that will be no different except for one thing—the threat will increase unless Israel does something about it.

<u>What Benefit Would Israel Reap by Striking First?</u>

Hezbollah's ability to cause unacceptable harm stems from its collective use of its missiles, UAVs, and Radwan forces. The missiles and UAVs will soar through the skies while Radwan operatives snake their way into Israel's homes. But what if Israel strikes first? Would that mitigate the damage?

Israel's primary defense against Hezbollah's missiles is Iron Dome and, to a lesser extent, David's Sling and Arrow for ballistic and cruise missiles. Bases for the latter two are in the center of the country because of their long range, which amply covers all of Israel. But Iron Dome installations, due to their comparatively short range, are scattered throughout the country. Thus, many Iron Dome installations are not positioned to interdict a concentrated attack from the north. Nor should they be given potential threats emanating from Iran's other proxies. While that might be fine for a small dust-up with Hezbollah, Israel lacks sufficient Iron Dome installations and missiles to intercept everything Hezbollah will send its way in an all-out war— and that doesn't include the rockets the other proxies will be firing at Israel which will make matters worse.

Two variables are relevant when analyzing how dire the situation is—Iron Dome's collective successful interception rate and how many missiles Hezbollah can launch per day. Let's assume Hezbollah could launch 3,000 missiles on the first day of a first strike (estimates are 1,500-4,000). If we assume that only two-thirds of the missiles fired will hit sensitive areas if not intercepted (others might still start forest fires), that leaves 2000 missiles that must be stopped. If we further assume that Israel's missile defense systems will perform against Hezbollah as they did in 2021 and 2022 against rockets coming from Gaza alone, then Israeli defenses might shoot down 95 percent of

Hezbollah's missiles. (an optimistic projection for a war with Hezbollah given the complex, confusing airspace that defense systems will operate in and that missiles will arrive from multiple directions.) Unfortunately, that still leaves 100 missiles that will penetrate Israel's defenses and strike sensitive locations on the first day alone.

In addition, UAVs will also strike targets. Hezbollah has hundreds, possibly thousands, of them. In the past, Israel has used planes and helicopters to shoot them down. But that was when no more than three were in the air simultaneously. If Hezbollah strikes first, lethal swarm attacks will descend from the sky. Individual UAVs within those swarms will be hard to detect and interdict because they're small and fly low and slow—which makes them difficult for radar to differentiate from ground clutter. While some will be shot down, with smoke in the air and ground detonations everywhere, many will get through. Especially because Israeli air assets will be tasked with striking targets in Lebanon and elsewhere. And the number of penetrating UAVs will increase if Hezbollah's first wave of missiles significantly damages IAF bases.

Why is the prospect of 100 missiles penetrating Israel's defenses and innumerable UAVs hitting their targets during day one so concerning? Because Hezbollah only needs to damage or destroy a limited number of targets to inflict unacceptable harm.

To illustrate the point, in 2021, Uzi Rubin conducted a fascinating, unique study of Greece. After only two days of noodling on the Internet, he determined that Greece's twelve thermal power stations and four hydroelectric dams supply 63 percent of the nation's power supply. And that people living in Athens depend on one water treatment plant that has five critical locations. Furthermore, he found that 90 percent of the cargo ships bringing food, fuel, and other items to Greece, and that carry exports out, depend on one seaport with three cargo terminals. Similarly, 97 percent of international travelers visiting Greece pass through two airports. For fuel, the nation has only three refineries. Internet communications funnel through one space link and one undersea cable terminal station. Combined, these key locations total thirty-one pressure points, which, if damaged or destroyed, would paralyze the nation. But Uzi was charitable. He hypothesized that maybe there are sixty more pressure points that he failed to discern or mention, such as military bases, banking centers, dense population regions, and even tall buildings (think 9/11). That totals to approximately ninety pressure points, each of which is susceptible to devastation if they're hit with a half-ton warhead or many smaller ones.

Uzi's presentation of this analysis is preserved on a YouTube video. Based on my impression of Uzi after meeting him, along with his credentials and the respect his peers afford him, I'm confident his analysis is accurate and have little doubt about why he used Greece to make his point. A large-scale missile attack on Greece could potentially devastate its society and its ability to function; the same is true in Israel. Even if the particulars between the two nations vary, they're close enough to make Uzi's point noteworthy. Speculating how such an attack would affect Greece allows us to hypothesize how one might affect Israel. Israel has one airport through which most international travel flows and a handful of seaports, the main one of which is in Haifa. Israel has two refineries, perhaps nine power plants, and one nuclear reactor. And its industrial production, chemical plants, and population centers are concentrated on a land mass one-sixth the size of Greece.

Thus, if enough well-placed missiles survive Israel's missile defenses, they could shut down Israel for an extended period and kill thousands. And if Hezbollah damages IAF runways and radars, the IAF will be unable to quickly destroy Hezbollah's missiles before they're launched, and even more UAVs will fly into Israeli airspace. Those UAVs will inflict damage that could prevent evacuations, impede IDF mobilization, and destroy industrial sites—just as the twenty-seven UAVs Iran launched from Houthi territory did to a Saudi refinery. That's unacceptable harm.

How many critical pressure points does Israel have? Is it thirty-one or ninety? More? Less? I don't know. But a 2018 report produced by the Washington-based think tank JINSA chilled me. In it, the authors wrote that Home Front Command and Israel's National Emergency Authority had classified fifty infrastructure systems in Israel as critical, requiring a "broad defense." That's chilling because, by my calculations, at least 100 of Hezbollah's missiles will penetrate Israel's defenses and strike targets on day one of an attack. If other Iranian proxies join the fight, that number will be higher. This will create a situation that UAVs will only exacerbate. If some of the missiles have large payloads and are accurate, not many of them will have to strike their targets in Israel to cause unacceptable harm. Even if the missiles that escape interdiction are inaccurate, Hezbollah could still potentially inflict unacceptable harm on the first day—And if not the first day, what about the second, or the third, or the tenth day? Unless Israel's defensive efforts blunt its capability, Hezbollah can do this repeatedly, every day of a war lasting weeks not days—especially if Israel's stock of defensive missiles dwindles and Hezbollah has weakened Israel's ability to swiftly launch a comprehensive response that takes out its missiles.

How could this happen? By design or accident. Hezbollah could launch a surprise attack on Israel for a myriad of reasons, or an accidental war could break out—one in which Hezbollah strikes the first blow.

One way to alleviate the danger Israel faces—perhaps the only way—is for Israel to strike first, to reduce the number of missiles in Hezbollah's inventory which can destroy Israel's economic, civilian, and military pressure points. Specifically, that means destroying on the ground as many of Hezbollah's PGMs as possible, as well as any rockets capable of carrying large payloads and, if possible, UAVs too. If Israel can reduce the daily number of missiles it must intercept in a future war with Hezbollah to somewhere between 500 and 1,000— especially if those missiles are inaccurate and carry smaller payloads, like Katyushas—then Israel can significantly limit the damage it will sustain. But if Israel does not strike first, it will leave Israel dependent on Hezbollah's forbearance for starting a war. But that forbearance will not last because of Hezbollah's desire for peace. It will only last until Iran says otherwise or until Hezbollah believes that it will benefit from striking first. That's a calculation Nasrallah could make as Hezbollah obtains more PGMs or if he perceives that Hezbollah's domestic opposition is gaining so much strength that it would be to Hezbollah's domestic political advantage to initiate a limited confrontation with Israel even though it might spiral out of control.

An Israeli first strike could work if Israel knows where Hezbollah's more capable missiles are being stored and if the IAF can hit thousands of targets inside Lebanon within a very short time frame without mobilizing first. Following that, after destroying all known targets, waves of IAF planes and UAVs would have to maintain an air presence in the skies of Lebanon for a sustained period to eviscerate any missile launchers being raised or loaded. The first wave of attacks would be to reduce the number of launchers and missiles still in storage. The follow-up strikes would likely be a race between launcher identification and missile launch.

But what about the Radwan forces?

The Radwan are highly trained individuals whom Hezbollah tasks with conquering Israeli border villages. Trained troops number in the thousands. I have walked and driven along Israel's borders with Lebanon many times and in many places. Israeli military bases and villages are spread wide apart, often by several miles. Between them is rough, hilly country loaded with underbrush and undulations and sometimes agricultural fields. Along the entire border is wire and metal fencing containing detection measures. In many places, the fences are supplemented by tall concrete barriers and even bulldozed changes in the topography. Israeli patrols pass by periodically. All these defensive measures are important. None are airtight. They will not stop a determined force from penetrating the border. If it concentrates close to the border in sufficient strength, a Radwan force can penetrate Israel whenever it wants. It won't survive for long inside Israel, but that wouldn't be its mission anyway. Hezbollah would deem it a success if a Radwan force temporarily takes an Israeli town or village, plants a Hezbollah flag there for a few hours, and likely kills and kidnaps its citizens.

But it is highly doubtful that Radwan soldiers are crouching twenty-four hours a day at their jumping-off points. They have families, too. They take days off. They train in locations removed from the border. Can they be mobilized for an attack without Israel knowing? Maybe—especially if the scope of their mission does not require large numbers. Therefore, the IDF cannot count on detecting their movements. Given that, the best defense against what may be an inevitable attempt to conquer an Israeli village might require Israel to attack when Radwan forces are not ready. By destroying transportation nodes and making road movement difficult, the IDF could slow Radwan's mobilization. Furthermore, Israel could create confusion by using targeted strikes to kill Radwan leaders. That would buy time for step two—deploying active-duty IDF soldiers on the borders and mobilizing IDF reserves. Then, step three—a major move into Lebanon after reserve divisions have reached the scene. Before that, specialized IDF units might conduct limited attacks, by air and sea, that focus on Hezbollah's pressure points and those missile sites easy to eliminate, if any.

I fully realize that what I just wrote is a civilian's suggestion of a battle plan, which, in real life, would be infinitely more complicated and dangerous than what I have detailed. And even the best-laid plans go wrong once a war starts—the enemy will not act entirely as expected, intelligence will not be perfect, and friction gumming up the works will mount as more and more things that must go right inevitably go wrong. And, as Mike Tyson said, "Everyone has a plan until they get punched in the mouth"—there is that too.

Even if it works as planned, an Israeli preemptive or preventative attack would undeniably precipitate a response from Hezbollah that would cause Israel grievous harm. However, a surprise attack from Hezbollah would be even worse—a potential knockout blow. It's a difficult choice for Israel. Now let's look at a few scenarios that might cause Israeli leaders to select that option.

What Might Cause Israel to Strike First?

Below, I list four plausible scenarios that could lead Israel to launch a preemptive or preventative war. Each has numerous offshoots, too many to describe. And, of course, many other hypothetical fact patterns would pose the same issues. But considering these four alone will give you an idea of what might force Israel to start a war.

1) Hezbollah obtains a critical mass of PGMs

A critical mass of PGMs is the quantity of PGMs, especially those with large warheads, Hezbollah needs to inflict unacceptable harm on Israel. On the first day of the war, Hezbollah will launch thousands of rockets toward Israel—the hypothetical I presented earlier in this chapter had Hezbollah firing 3,000. If the other Iranian proxies fire another thousand rockets, we get to 4,000. Based on my earlier calculations, perhaps 135 will hit targets rather than 100 if only Hezbollah fires its missiles. But if we assume that a proportional number of that 135 will be PGMs, and due to their maneuverability, PGMs will be harder to shoot down (which is likely), and accept that the stressed environment with so many rockets in the air will complicate matters, the success rate for interdicting PGMs will probably go down to 90 percent or less—meaning 10 percent of the PGMs fired will puncture Israel's defenses. Then, because of their accuracy, 50 percent or more of the PGMs that evade interdiction will hit their designated military, infrastructure, or high-population targets rather than a general area.

This reduces the calculation of a critical mass of PGMs in Hezbollah's hands to a simple question and formula, which is expressed as follows:

> If Israel has fifty pressure points that must be defended at all costs, and one PGM strike with a large warhead will cripple its target, how many PGMs does Hezbollah need to launch to inflict unacceptable harm on Israel?

The answer is 1,000 PGMs (1,000 x .90 (percentage shot down) x .50 (accuracy) = 50 targets destroyed or significantly damaged).

How accurate is my calculation? Those connected with Israel's government and in a position to influence policy are reluctant to answer that question. Understandably, they do not want to declare a red line that either will be crossed without response—decreasing Israel's deterrence credibility—or that would pressure decision-makers to launch a reflexive attack without sufficient contemplation. However, there is no shortage of other reputable experts, employed by think tanks or elsewhere, who study this issue. Their estimates of the tipping point range from 500-1,000 PGMs in Hezbollah's hands. Collectively, they add credence to my back-of-the-envelope estimate that 1,000 PGMs in Hezbollah's hands could cause Israel unacceptable harm if Hezbollah can fire them in conjunction with thousands of other missiles that would mask the more dangerous PGMs and inflict significant harm by themselves.

It's unclear how many PGMs Hezbollah has now. Estimates range from tens to hundreds. However, they are cheap to make because, as Uzi Rubin told me, cell phone technology, used in conjunction with low-cost commercial technology, can be used to create inexpensive guidance systems. And that those systems can incorporate easily obtainable targeting data from sources ranging from companies operating commercial satellites to Google Earth. And equally worrisome, Iran and Hezbollah are constantly scheming to get more PGMs into Lebanon—either by building them there or finding better ways to get them there. Has the CBW stopped them cold? It's doubtful. Can Israel count on its prodigious intelligence capability to know with certainty how many PGMs Hezbollah currently possesses and will obtain soon? Also, doubtful.

That leaves Israeli policymakers with a stark choice. As they become more certain that Hezbollah will soon obtain the critical mass of PGMs needed to inflict unacceptable harm, are they willing to depend on Hezbollah not using them? And is Israel prepared to see its deterrence dissipate because of the growing PGM threat that might invariably diminish Israel's willingness to respond to provocations? Or will Israel determine it has no choice but to act?

2) <u>Israel or the United States decides to attack Iran's nuclear facilities</u>

For decades, Israel has successfully delayed Iran's nuclear weapons program by using a variety of measures—including cyber-attacks and targeted assassinations. Also, some would argue that the JCPOA, which Iran agreed to in 2015 and from which the Trump administration withdrew in 2018, significantly delayed Iran's nuclear program by setting constraints on it. Others differ as to degree. And they argue that by unfreezing 100 billion dollars of Iranian assets, the JCPOA helped finance many other malign Iranian activities, which included arming Hezbollah with PGMs and other weaponry plus financing Iran's and Hezbollah's involvement in Syria. However, though I'm sorely tempted to, I will not dive further into that dispute.

But it is important to recognize that, despite what Iran says, its actions betray its eagerness to acquire nuclear weapons. As of the end of 2022, most experts think that if Iran proceeds full speed ahead, it will have nuclear weapons within months or sooner, assuming it does not already secretly possess them. Coupled with that, Iran presently has missiles that can reach Israel. Nevertheless, most experts opine that it might take a year or more for Iran to be able to marry a nuclear warhead with the missiles already in its larder that can reach Israel. Given the difficulty of having a 100 percent reliable intelligence network and the subjectivity of analysis, that is, to me, a slim reed on which to rely. Meanwhile, its centrifuges continue to spin and consequently the amount and purity of enriched uranium in Iran's hands, a necessary component of nuclear weapons, grows. Therefore, as Iran's capabilities increase and its rhetoric remains vitriolic, Israel may decide that, despite the risks and complexity involved, it must try to destroy Iran's nuclear assets by air—something it did in Iraq and Syria when those countries pursued nuclear weapons. For one thing is certain, Israel's current policy is clear—it will act to prevent Iran from obtaining nuclear weapons.

However, if Israel attacked Iran, Iran would surely respond by ordering Hezbollah and its other proxies to attack Israel—a war that Hezbollah would initiate in the middle of what probably would be a multi-day effort by the IAF to destroy nuclear infrastructure in Iran. At that moment, Israel would have trouble dealing with an attack by Hezbollah and others. Powerful as it is, Israel likely does not have sufficient resources to destroy Iran's nuclear capability quickly while also stopping Hezbollah and other Iranian proxies from devastating the homeland.

Therefore, before attacking Iran, Israel might well attack Hezbollah to eliminate its capability to disrupt a future IDF attack on Iran's nuclear facilities. That might also be necessary if Israel learns that the United States plans to attack Iran's nuclear facilities, as unlikely as that may be. Unable to effectively respond against the United States, such an attack could easily prompt Iran to order Hezbollah and its proxies to strike back at Israel—an attack that it might join.

3) <u>Israel learns that Hezbollah will soon launch an all-out attack on Israel or undertake a more limited operation that Israel will have to respond to—likely leading to an all-out war with Hezbollah</u>

In this scenario, Israel receives intelligence of a Hezbollah plan to launch an all-out war. In that case, even if Israeli intelligence does not think Hezbollah possesses sufficient weapons to inflict unacceptable harm on Israel, would Israel risk waiting for Hezbollah to strike first? And even if what Israel suffers does not amount to unacceptable harm, that would mean little to the many who will lose their lives. Nor will it assuage the feelings of those who will have to live with and repair the destruction, made much worse because Israel chose not to launch a preemptive attack.

Similarly, if Israel becomes aware that Hezbollah will soon do something short of an all-out war yet still unacceptable, policymakers may decide to strike first. Why? Because if Hezbollah's plan is so reprehensible that Israel must respond violently, then Hezbollah might have little choice but to counter with an all-out war—leading close to where Israel would be if Hezbollah conducted a full-fledged attack out of the blue. We almost saw this scenario play out in 2022 when Hezbollah threatened to attack Israeli offshore gas extraction installations. If that had happened, Israel's response would have been devastating for Hezbollah and Lebanon. Possibly, only Israel's agreement with Lebanon on ocean boundaries forestalled that outcome. But likely, Hezbollah will make new demands in the future backed by similar threats. Then, Israel will again have to decide whether to launch a preventative war—a choice some would say Israel averted by caving on its negotiating position after Hezbollah threatened to attack the offshore gas installations.

4) <u>Iran will soon possess nuclear weapons because neither Israel nor the United States is willing to use force to prevent that from happening</u>

If Iran is left free to develop nuclear weapons, it will diminish Israel's ability to deter Hezbollah. That means if Israel or the United States do not attack Iran's nuclear facilities, their forbearance may lead to Israel having to launch a preventive strike on Hezbollah.

Why?

Because Iran may threaten to employ its nuclear weapons against Israel if the IDF uses force to constrain Hezbollah, or should Israel want to attack Hezbollah for any future reason, such as to reduce the number of PGMs it possesses. Israeli policymakers would have to take Iran's nuclear threats seriously, making them less likely to vigorously respond to Hezbollah's future provocations and therefore reducing Israel's deterrence. That, and the presence of Iran's nuclear umbrella, would embolden Hezbollah to act more aggressively, making life in northern Israel a chilling prospect and increasing the likelihood of an accidental war. One that might only be forestalled by an Israeli first strike before Iran builds deliverable nuclear weapons.

Is it Legal for Israel to Strike First Against Hezbollah—And Does that Matter?

I promise to keep this section concise. In return for doing so, please excuse me for not digging deep into the nuances of international law. But at the outset, I'll say this. I am not sure that it matters. Complying with international law is one thing if a nation is dealing with something less than its very existence. If the issues are existential, compliance is something else. In that case, complying with international norms and law might be based more on recognizing what the other side would do in response to an action rather than what an international court would demand or what other nations might think. Still, a nation that prides itself on its morality must comply with international law to the degree that's possible and that's consistent with what it believes necessary to survive.

To make myself clear, I provide the following individualized example of the dilemma Israel faces: *What if a person that has attacked you before approaches your home, in which your children are sleeping, with a flamethrower in his hands or a suicide vest strapped to him? Do you have to wait until the first sheets of flame burst forth or an explosion takes down your house before you fire your gun to stop him?* The law might say yes in some circumstances. Eliminating the danger to your children might require you to say no. The risk is too great to gamble with their lives.

Don't like the individual example? What about how the West dealt with Hitler? There is little doubt that history would have been quite different if the West had stood up to Hitler in the 1930s. In 1936, his still-weak army marched into the Rhineland. In 1938, the growing German army grabbed Austria. Then, also in 1938, Neville Chamberlain met with Hitler and agreed he could occupy the Sudetenland in Czechoslovakia, after which Chamberlain proudly announced that he had returned home from Germany bringing "Peace for our time." If the West had instead initiated a preemptive or preventative war rather than follow a policy of appeasement, that war would have been won at a lower cost than what ensued. And the lives of millions of civilians would have been spared—including six million Jews.

Having digressed, let's get back to the legality of preemptive and preventative war. As discussed at the beginning of this chapter, preemptive war requires the certainty of an imminent attack. Preventative war is based on a strong expectation of an attack in the foreseeable future. Both should only be contemplated to prevent unacceptable harm, which could equate to the survival of a society— or even something much less.

Legal scholars debate back and forth regarding when and whether a nation may launch a preemptive attack. They search through history and make tortured analyses of the UN charter. They note Article 2(4) of the UN charter, which forbids nations from using or threatening force against each other. And they highlight Article 51, which says the charter does not preclude the "inherent right of individual or collective self-defense if an armed attack occurs against a member of the United Nations, until the Security Council has taken measures necessary to maintain international peace and security."

Do those words mean that a nation must wait until it's attacked or is the intent to permit a nation to act first if waiting will risk incurring unacceptable harm? If the United States detects that Russia is about to launch thousands of nuclear-tipped missiles at American soil, is the United States required to first absorb a blow that would destroy the country before doing anything militarily to mitigate the attack? What would you do if you were president?

Regarding preventative attacks, there is more unanimity in professorial circles that a nation cannot attack first. But there is also disagreement. In 2002, shortly after 9/11, President George W. Bush's administration crafted a document detailing its national security strategy. It said in part, "As a matter of common sense and self-defense, America will act against [such] emerging threats before they are fully formed." That administration argued in support of its approach that because deterrence doesn't have the same impact against terrorist groups or rogue nations as it does against most countries of the world, different considerations are required for them than for normal nation-states. Soon, in keeping with that policy, American forces invaded Iraq and interceded in Afghanistan.

Since then, American presidents' policy has been in line with the principal Bush enunciated. President Obama approved the targeted killing of terrorists, surged troops into Afghanistan, and authorized special operations in foreign countries without their permission—including the killing of Osama Bin Laden. President Trump ordered Iranian General Suleiman killed, ordered the bombing of targets in Syria on one occasion, and permitted many special operations to continue. Although President Biden withdrew American forces from Afghanistan, he authorized a drone strike in Kabul that killed al-Qaida leader, Ayman al-Zawahri, and has supported military operations by special forces in other countries, too. So, Bush's principle that approves preventative attacks remains alive and well. And at least the Western world, for the most part, is okay with that.

Where does Hezbollah fit into this legal mosaic? It is certainly not a traditional nation recognized by the UN. Nor is it a signatory to any treaties or international understandings. Instead, many nations around the globe consider Hezbollah a terrorist organization. None of them consider it a nation. And I agree with those who call it a hybrid terrorist organization. Or is it a rogue state as referred to by Bush in his national security directive? That might be true since an accepted definition of a rogue state is one that threatens world peace. Per that definition, Hezbollah is certainly a rogue state. After all, it acts as a state within a state that exists more in name than practice due to Hezbollah's control of it. And it threatens world peace because Hezbollah espouses Israel's destruction, is gathering the means to do it, and conducts criminal acts abroad that have, in the past, included mass killings. If America faced such issues with an entity like Hezbollah, it would not hesitate to launch a preventative strike. Wait a minute! The United States did and does act that way towards Al-Qaeda and other similar entities. Why should Israel's right to defend itself be any different?

How Might Israeli politics get in the Way of Making the Decision to Attack and Would Israeli Citizens Support Such a Decision?

It's been many months since I met with General Gershon HaCohen at his home in Nimrod. But our time together is indelibly stamped in my memory. He is a warrior, a philosopher, a historian, and most of all a deep thinker. While we spoke much of war, family, and children; we also spoke of politics and preemption. He told me:

I'm aware of the impossibility of the Israeli state to just go out of the blue to preemptive attack. Especially after the Russian adventure [in Ukraine]. Because everyone will say here is another Putin come just out of the blue to destroy everything. Nobody will listen that [Hezbollah has] more than 150,000 rockets [targeting Israel], but also it is very necessary to be aware that it [might be] necessary to [launch an attack on Hezbollah]. So, there is a tension. And here is the beginning of strategical leadership to make a synchronization in a complicated situation in which the main tension is absolutely beyond solution.

Wow, I thought, HaCohen hit the nail directly on its head. It's about leadership. In April 2022, when we spoke, yet another Israeli prime minister's political support was in free fall. Since then, a caretaker prime minister took over, new elections occurred, and Benjamin Netanyahu won again. He became prime minister in January 2023. Will he remain in power for long? Will he have free reign to do what is needed to be done on behalf of Israel or will he focus more on his political longevity? We will see.

But one thing is certain. There must be transparency. For Israel to embark on a preemptive or preventative attack, the seeds for doing so must be sown with Israeli citizens and the international community well before such an attack occurs. Israel must conduct a sustained campaign to explain the danger it faces, unvarnished by reassuring tones. That is a prerequisite for launching a preventative war—although maybe not a preemptive one. Will Israel's present or future prime ministers have the time and the will to do so before a scenario develops that demands a decision? I hope so, but given the topsy-turvy nature of Israeli politics, I am not optimistic.

And there is one other constituency that must be influenced—the president of the United States and Congress. For Israel to launch an attack without at least the acquiescence of the United States would be exceedingly dangerous. Unexpected things happen in wars. Israel will need America's political and material support. Resolutions will be raised in the Security Council that require a veto because they are one-sided and very much against Israel's interests. Missiles and ammunition will run out. Therefore, an Israeli preventative attack would be very risky without at least tacit American political approval and resupply. And while Israel might have to launch a preemptive attack without American support because there is no choice, it would be far better to know that the United States will have its back. Because there is no escaping that need, it must be established, loudly and consistently, in public and private, that Israel faces an existential challenge so that American leaders will never mistake a sober Israeli decision to strike first a war of choice rather than a war of necessity.

<u>My Thoughts</u>

I am an American citizen writing this from the comfort of my home. I do not live in the region. I have not witnessed the terrible nature of war, nor do I have my skin in the game, only my heart. It will not be my home destroyed in a Third Lebanon War or, as some label it, the Northern War. It will not be my family and livelihood endangered. It will not be my eyes witnessing the suffering. It will not be me shouldering the devastation. Therefore, no matter how much I care for the safety and security of Israel, my opinion should always be questioned.

But perhaps that separation adds credibility to my thoughts because I care but am not subject to group thinking. Nor do I look at the problems Hezbollah poses from the inside out. My gaze is from the outside in. Visceral memories of Israel's wars already fought do not encumber me. Rather, it is my appraisal of what is coming that drives me. Although I am hopeful, hope doesn't guide me because hope is a beacon that dispels despair but not a foundation for thoughtful policy.

Where does that lead me? To the conundrum of preemptive and preventative war. Either requires much of Israel beforehand. Neither should be undertaken likely. Both must be in Israel's playbook.

Why?

Because I do not think Israel can put all its eggs on its defensive capability while Hezbollah picks and chooses which offensive plays to use. Uzi Rubin, speaking of Israel's missile defense, said the defense system is robust, "but not robust enough." Is building up Israel's defenses the answer? It is certainly part of it. But while Israel is doing that, Hezbollah will build up its offensive capability. So will Iran's proxies. Nothing Israel is doing today will reduce Hezbollah's present strength in Lebanon or prevent it from growing. At best, the CBW will only slow that increase. Therefore, even though the CBW might degrade the strength of Iranian proxies in Syria, on balance Israel's enemies will grow stronger. Only a preemptive or preventive first strike by Israel will reverse that inevitability. Therefore, even though it presents many risks, launching one now might be a reasonable alternative, and in the future, a necessary one if, and only if, it would likely prevent Hezbollah from inflicting unacceptable harm in Israel in the foreseeable future and can avoid unacceptable harm consequently, or at least mitigate it to some degree.

And, of course, Israel might have to initiate a preemptive strike if it learns that Hezbollah will soon possess weapons of mass destruction. A November 2022 Saudi media outlet raised that concern when it reported that Hezbollah will soon move chemical weapons, now stored in Syria, into southern Lebanon. While that outlet's reliability is unclear and the type of chemical is not disclosed (was it mustard gas versus or something like chlorine gas readily available from civilian sources), the report raises a question. If Hezbollah obtains chemical weapons, does that provoke the same need for an urgent response as Hezbollah procuring biological or nuclear weapons? The scope of this book does not permit a detailed answer, but I would assume Israel's decision on when and how to respond would depend on quantity, potency, and delivery capability.

But I am certain of this—any war that Israel starts must begin with the purpose of preventing Hezbollah from inflicting unacceptable harm and end with having succeeded in doing so for a long time to come. Such an attack must be a bolt from the blue to maximize its chances of success. When it ends, Israel must speedily withdraw from all territory taken in the fighting. Anything less will be derided by Israelis, serve as a rallying cry for the Lebanese, sap the IDF of its strength, and be castigated by the international community ready to feast on any weakness or ambiguity.

There are several prerequisites for such a war. First, Israel's government must embark on a coordinated communication program that relentlessly educates Israelis about the growing danger of, and the potential need for, waging a preemptive or preventative war. Second, Home Front Command must be strengthened, invigorated, and empowered. And Israel must increase the number of homes that are equipped with shelters. I will write more about this in the next chapter. Third, Israel's intelligence services must determine with confidence where Hezbollah's PGMs are located as well as those statistical missiles that carry larger payloads. Fourth, Israel must gain knowledge of the lives and locations of Radwan's commanders at the unit level so that, if necessary, they can be killed. Fifth, Israel's air force, naval-based missiles, and ground-ground missiles must collectively be able to destroy, from a standing start, without mobilization, Hezbollah's most dangerous missiles and kill many of Radwan's leaders in the opening hours of a war. Sixth, the IDF must plan and train for moving into Lebanon as far as the outskirts of Beirut and in Syria to a depth of ten miles or more. Government leaders must resolve to fight this two-front war without allowing the terrible cost of casualties to tempt restraint. Seventh, because the IDF will be unable to initiate ground attacks with massed units until sometime after mobilized troops reach the borders, ground units and special forces already in the region must be prepared to block Radwan's activities and take on important but dangerous missions inside Lebanon without immediate support. Eighth, because the destruction of Hezbollah's threat is a vital national goal, Israel must steel itself to the likelihood that there will be many Lebanese casualties. Therefore, Israel must make clear to Israelis and the world ahead of time that it won't be swayed by Hezbollah's callous use of civilians to shield missiles and fighters. Ninth, where possible, I disagree with many who advocate wantonly destroying Lebanese infrastructure. Israel's goal in this war is the destruction of Hezbollah's capability to inflict immense harm. It should not be, where possible to avoid it while still destroying Hezbollah and minimizing its ability to resist, the destruction of Lebanon, despite its potential deterrent value. Plenty of infrastructure will be destroyed anyway. There is no need to manufacture more hatred than necessary by doing more than is needed to fulfill the mission. Planning for the war should reflect that. Item ten is more of a postscript. Going into the war, Israel must be determined to never revert to the Rules of the Game as they're presently understood. Any future attempts by Hezbollah to rearm must be met with overwhelming force inside Lebanon, Syria, or Iraq as necessary.

These ten prerequisites apply whether the war is preemptive or preventative.

But there is one more prerequisite for Israel to launch a preventative war that is a highly desirable but not necessary requirement for a preemptive war. America must at least covertly acquiesce, if not support a preventative strike. Without that, no matter how righteous the decision, how real the potential threat, world opinion and actions will swamp Israel, invariably causing it to constrain its forces, leaving Israeli citizens dismayed and Iran and its proxies empowered. To achieve that, Israel must share intelligence and knowledge with humility while acting as best it can to further America's policy agenda with the understanding that America will support Israel if Israel needs to launch a preventative or presumptive war. America is Israel's indispensable ally. Without it, Israel should think doubly hard about launching a preventative war, even though it may have no choice but to embark on a preemptive war in the direst circumstances.

Will Israel one day launch a preventative or preemptive war? Jonathan Schanzer told me:

> I have been arguing that every day the status quo continues with PGMs, the greater danger Israel faces. But…I can't say this is Israel's red line and therefore they need to go to war. What I am saying is the dangers look greater than they ever have and every day that passes those dangers mount. So, what are the Israelis waiting for? I don't know.

When I told Schanzer that I thought the odds were one out of four that Israel would strike first, he was reluctant to give his opinion regarding the odds of Israel doing that. However, he said, "Given Israel's history and given Israel's security needs, it stands to reason that they're going to need to do something at some point, right?" And then, he added ominously, "The system's blinking red."

Whatever the actual odds that Israel may initiate an attack, they are certainly high enough that it is quite possible. Unfortunately, I doubt that possibility will motivate Israel to fulfill many of the prerequisite actions I call for as long as Israel's governing process remains as unstable as it has been for the last several years. That is a recipe for potential disaster if the need to strike has not been matched by setting the conditions for ensuring success.

Sadly, I believe it is at least equally likely that Israel will eventually face a devastating first strike in which Hezbollah will play a large part. Hezbollah is becoming too strong, and too many advantages accrue to the side that attacks first for that not to be so. And even if neither side attacks first, then at some point both may blunder into an unintended war. Tensions run too high too often and there is too much rhetoric and present conflict for that not to be more than hypothetical musing. Unfortunately, both of these scenarios, a first strike by Hezbollah or an accidental war, have likely outcomes less favorable to Israel that an Israeli first strike.

Meanwhile, Iran, Hezbollah, Hamas, and others march forward. They want to destroy Israel. They have implemented a multi-decade plan for doing so that steadily increases their strength and radicalizes the populations they control. From their perspective, it is not if they destroy Israel, but when. The day may already be here that Israel's enemies have the capacity to inflict unacceptable harm on it. If not, it's coming soon. And if so, there might only be one answer to that threat—Israel must strike first while there is still time for it to have a meaningful impact. Israel delaying the attack to the point it won't matter is relying on hope and, as I wrote earlier, that is a slim reed on which to base the survival of a nation and its people.

Call me concerned. Very concerned.

Chapter Twenty-Six

What Might Israel Consider Doing Now?

We have traveled a long road together. Beginning with the 4th Century AD, we worked through Lebanon's formative years, its demographics, its statehood in 1943, and the arrival of the Palestine Liberation Organization's headquarters in 1970. Then, we examined Lebanon's civil war and the sectarian hatred that drove it, followed by Israel's incursions into Lebanon to squelch the PLO's ongoing terror campaign against targets in Israel. Next came the rise of Hezbollah in the early 1980s and Iran's pivotal role in the organization's development. Following that, we traced Hezbollah's path to dominance in Lebanon, its criminal and terrorist activities abroad, Israel's retreat in 2000, the war in 2006, and Hezbollah's involvement in Syria's civil war. Reaching more modern times, we looked at Hezbollah's current arsenal for war, Hezbollah's malign activities worldwide, politics and economics in Lebanon, and Iran's influence on Hezbollah and its other proxies. That led to chapters about UNIFIL's failure, Israel's defensive and offensive capabilities, Home Front Command, deterrence, and the Campaign Between Wars. We concluded by delving deeply into the use and misuse of information as a weapon, Israel's will to fight, what a war between Israel and Hezbollah might look like, and whether Israel should consider launching a preemptive or preventative war. Throughout, my purpose was to explain how Hezbollah evolved, its goals, the environment it operates in today, and its capability and methods coupled with Israel's response to the danger Hezbollah presents and considerations for the future. However, we spent little time on solutions.

Until now.

A boulder is rolling downhill toward Israel. If Hezbollah's boulder strikes Israel, it could cause unacceptable, even existential, harm. Now, it is picking up speed and becoming more dangerous the closer it gets, but it has yet to reach the bottom of the hill. Israel could stop it today by good fortune or by using the structures it now has in place. However, "could" suggests the laws of probability will come into play—which they do. Today, the odds of Israel achieving an acceptable outcome in a war with Hezbollah are unclear. Whether they are 50-50 or something better or worse is not certain. This is unacceptable and dangerous. Deterrence requires clarity. Hezbollah must know that, in a war with Israel, Israel would destroy it before it could achieve its goals. Mutual assured destruction is not good enough. How then, can Israel improve its chances of success in a manner that sends the appropriate message to Hezbollah? That requires increasing its strength, improving its resilience, highlighting northern Israel, and gaining more freedom of action by increasing the public's support at home and abroad. After studying the problem, I have nine suggestions on how Israel might address it.

Military Capability

Offense

The IDF has already intensified its training for a future war with Hezbollah and other Iranian proxies. In 2022, the IDF engaged in multiple training exercises for such a war, the largest being *Chariots of Fire*, a four-week-long exercise beginning in May 2022 that drew personnel from most IDF units—including the air force, navy, army, and cyber warriors—to simulate a multi-front war with Hezbollah,

Iran, and Iranian proxies. Its goal was to improve the readiness of all military and civilian arms that would have to cooperate and engage in such a war. On the home front, the exercise focused on finding alternative ways to bring troops north and supplying them while overcoming civilian injuries and disasters caused by incoming missiles and Radwan forces. To simulate decision-making, the exercise created a mock "cabinet." To my surprise and delight, that cabinet included Maj. Gen. (ret.) Gershon Hacohen, whom I interviewed a month earlier in his home at Nimrod in the Golan Heights. The drill was "unprecedented in scope" and the IDF's largest in decades. It even included landing thousands of troops on Cyprus, where they simulated long-range air and naval operations on terrain like what the IDF would find in southern Lebanon.

This is all good, and I'm sure it's instrumental in preparing the IDF for war. However, in the many articles I read on the subject and the interviews I conducted, there was a conspicuous absence. I found no mention of training exercises that would prepare the IDF for a preemptive or preventative war with Hezbollah. Israel must fill this gap in its training. Not only must the IDF prepare for such a scenario, but it must also publicize its readiness. If Israel hopes to establish a sufficient level of deterrence to prevent war, then it must be able to cripple Hezbollah by striking without warning and without suffering unacceptable damage on its home front. It's equally important that Hezbollah understands that Israel has that capability so that it will avoid actions that might prompt Israel to react. The Israeli people and the international community also need to be aware of Israel's capability to preempt. That capability will incentivize nations that value peace over bias to help constrain Hezbollah and it will jump-start the process of doing a better job informing Israeli citizens of the dangers Hezbollah poses and the solutions required to mitigate them.

I also argue that transparent actions are better than empty words. Repeating the time-honored phrase "nothing is off the table" is meaningless, as the past has proven in endless confrontations. Instead, Israel should overtly train for a preventative attack on Hezbollah. Since Nasrallah constantly reiterates that Hezbollah wants to destroy Israel, nobody should complain if Israel demonstrates that it can destroy Hezbollah. To do that, IAF planes would have to simulate a first strike by periodically taking off in mass throughout the country as it did at the outbreak of the Six-Day War. Regular ground units would need to practice flowing north in conjunction with large numbers of mobilized reservists. Troops stationed in the north would have to practice heading towards prearranged points to simulate protecting border communities (without, of course, duplicating war plans and tipping off Hezbollah); and special forces would have to travel by helicopters and ships to locations that would mimic where they would go in a first strike. These announced training exercises, which should be done frequently, would assure Israelis that their nation is not only capable of protecting them, but is also proactively addressing the threat of Hezbollah; in addition, the exercises will also expose any deficiencies that require correction. The public display would also send a message to Israel's enemies that they need to be careful—and peaceful. While the IDF is already doing some of this, it needs to do more.

Once the international community accepts that Israel may strike first, Israel should have even more leeway to conduct a more aggressive CBW wherever it wishes, which will be seen internationally as the lesser of the two evils. Meanwhile, Hezbollah's private recognition of Israel's capability and willfulness may hand Israel the additional deterrence it needs to start tilting the Rules of the Game more in its favor. Israel should use that tilt to strike the most critical targets in Lebanon without fear of a devastating Hezbollah response.

If Israel can tailor a newfound aggressiveness towards targets inside Lebanon that avoids killing civilians and damaging crucial infrastructure, the Lebanese people will see Hezbollah as a paper tiger that's afraid the IDF might render it toothless. This would weaken Hezbollah's argument that it needs arms to defend Lebanon. I'm not saying it would be the end of Hezbollah, and I am aware that Hezbollah would attempt to cling to its relevance by finding creative ways to hurt Israel. But there is hope that if Israel gains the capacity to defeat Hezbollah in detail without suffering too much damage at home, that will cow Hezbollah leading to diminished support for it in Lebanon. And then, you never know, good things can happen. That is when "hope" might have time to work—if buttressed by a power imbalance favoring Israel that creates the space for hope to turn into hard facts on the ground.

Defense

Reports are that an Iron Dome battery costs about one hundred million dollars. That's a lot of money. But so is the cost of multiple missiles pounding critical infrastructure and killing civilians. For years, Israel's goal, now achieved, was to have ten Iron Dome batteries. But the nature of the threat has changed. Hezbollah has far more missiles than before, too many of which are PGMs, and the number of increasingly capable UAV's in Hezbollah's hands are rising.

Rather than build more Iron Dome batteries, Israel's present response to the growing threat is to increase the capability of each battery by adding the number of launchers its radar and battle management systems can handle. That's all good. But it puts a lot of eggs in only a few places that could be subject to sabotage, overwhelming drone or missile attacks, and even run-of-the mill catastrophic breakdowns. Remember, the minimal effective range of Iron Dome is 2.5 miles and swarms of UAVs can penetrate well defended targets. Therefore, despite the cost, and the fact that buying more of one thing means less of another, I see no alternative but for Israel to purchase more Iron Dome systems—if not for anything else than to provide fast plug-and-play replacements for Iron Dome batteries that become inoperable, for whatever reason.

Syria

Should Israel continue its Campaign Between Wars? Of course. But Israel also needs to campaign for the hearts and minds of the Syrian public.

I heard Jonathan Spyer, whom I interviewed in April 2022, speak about this matter further in November of the same year. Spyer contends that the CBW addresses munitions but not the Iranian project that transforms large swaths of Syria. "There is a great deal of depth not being addressed [by Israel]," he explained, and that it cannot be done by airpower.

Much of the "depth" that Spyer refers to involves towns and villages previously occupied by Sunnis and people from other sects, who left during the Syrian civil war for safer pastures. Now the Syrian government will not let them return. Instead, it permits Iran to import Shiites from Iraq and Iran to replace those who left. In addition, Iran is co-opting elements of the Syrian armed forces. Combined, Spyer says this Iranian plan amounts to "a comprehensive structure for taking over the Syrian government."

What does all this have to do with Hezbollah in Lebanon? First, Hezbollah is a major player in helping develop a new Iranian proxy in Syria, which would go to war in lockstep with Hezbollah should there be a need. Second, a social and military structure parallel to what Israel faces in southern Lebanon would welcome Hezbollah's operations emanating from Syria with open arms. Third, Syria's servile and beholden government, coupled with the reformation of the population in strategic areas into a Shiite majority, will facilitate the movement of arms and manpower to Lebanon. None of this Israel can afford.

Therefore, Israel must take steps to fight the encroachment of Shiite doctrine and the control of the Syrian people. But, Spyer told me, Israel cannot do this alone. It needs help from the Sunni powers that have signed the Abraham Accords (like the UAE) or tacit support from nations that did not (like Saudi Arabia), and that share Israel's interest in reining in Hezbollah. Help can come in the form of financial resources, political pressure on Assad, and even agents on the ground coupled with social media and other information outlets. Israel can also weigh in with money, medical care, and even judicious use of its military to target those that present a threat to civilian populations. Would it be difficult to achieve measurable change? Yes. But a multi-level battle in Syria for hearts and minds for those that want to remain independent of outside influence (hoping to gain a love for or allegiance to Israel would be too ambitious) would fill a void that Iran and Hezbollah are taking full advantage of. Same with Assad. I doubt he enjoys being Iran's and Russia's vassal. I doubt he is happy that Israel is conducting the CBW on Syrian soil with relative impunity. Some experts I spoke with share my doubt. And I am certain some Sunni nations hold cards that could change how Assad is playing his hand—cards worth giving up in return for weakening Iran.

Would a concerted attempt to wean Syrians from Iran work? Maybe. But even if Israel challenging Iran for the allegiance of the Syrian people eventually fails, trying would at least make it more difficult and expensive for Iran and Hezbollah to place an armed Shiite militia on Israel's borders, which, if unchallenged, will grow in potency. Because Iran's resources are not infinite, that would be a victory of sorts anyway.

Home Front Command

It is the solemn duty of Israel's government and the IDF to safeguard Israel's home front as best they can during times of war. Doing this not only protects lives and infrastructure but also enables the IDF to fight Hezbollah for as long as it takes to reach its goals. If the IDF lacks freedom of action, the likelihood that the public would perceive Hezbollah as the victor in a future war would increase. That perception need not be true for it to harm the nation's morale and be dangerous for Israel's future.

Unfortunately, I am not confident that Home Front Command (HFC) is presently capable of performing its mission—not because it lacks dedication, but because it lacks the resources, planning, and support it needs to do its job. What follows is my prescription for change.

First, and foremost, HFC is currently steeped in confusion and ambiguity. That must be cleaned up. I spent hours researching the organization. I have learned far more about it than many people who have an interest and expertise in Israel's security seem to know, some of whom I found clueless. The average Israeli doesn't know much about HFC, either. Most had difficulty expressing HFC's specific role and how it will impact them. This is dangerous.

War is awash with uncertainty, and the lack of a clear organizational plan to protect the homeland only amplifies that uncertainty. This lack of clarity will cost lives. Who will coordinate the needs of HFC with the needs of the various civilian agencies operating in Israel? The National Emergency Management Agency? I think not. Will the IDF seamlessly consult with HFC and prioritize its operations while Hezbollah is filling the sky with rockets and UAVs, soldiers are dying, and military supplies and reinforcements must be brought to the front? I doubt it. Will generals focused on completing missions and preserving soldiers' lives care that fires are burning in civilian towns and foodstuffs are running out? Sure, but perhaps not so much while battles are raging. How will that general reconcile his mission with HFC's needs? Who will be evacuated? When and how will that be done? Where will evacuees go? Who will feed and shelter them? Why don't evacuees know the plan now? If fuel supplies become scarce, who will address the issue and how? The same applies to power, water, and medicine—who is responsible for getting those resources to the people and places that need them the most? While I am sure someone has a half-baked answer for most of these questions, I am equally sure that those answers are not known to those who will be most impacted. Nor have those answers been adequately tested.

The situation cries out for new legislation that would create an unambiguous organizational responsibility chart. Who decides where milk from a kibbutz cow near Gaza should be sent in an emergency? Who controls the means for transporting emergency supplies for citizens and where will they go? What comes first on a road leading north, the tank or the milk truck? This situation cries out for rectification. One entity, whether civilian or military, must take control. And everybody needs to know now who that is. Depending on military and civilian structures working together as needed is not a solution—it is an abdication of responsibility.

Next, as Shay Shemesh told me, HFC needs more manpower—in both the reserves and the regular army. To attract quality members, it must become "cool" to join the HFC so that enough people with local knowledge become part of the organization. Should Arab communities in northern Israel and elsewhere rebel, members of HFC, with their knowledge of the region, will need to swiftly stop marauding, free up the roads, and safeguard both Arab and Jewish communities. Israel will call on HFC to save townspeople trapped in homes or suffering from injuries and to distribute needed supplies. This requires manpower, which is not redirected elsewhere, and that's dedicated to the mission and familiar with the area.

Also, people in the north must know their evacuation plans and practice them and know when to shelter in place. Will they go or stay? If they stay, are they prepared to do that, and do they know why it is important that they sit out the war in their homes? Do they have enough emergency supplies, including food, water, and medicine? If not, HFC must correct those shortages now, before an emergency. And it also must monitor those levels continuously.

Which leads me to shelters. It was a brilliant idea to require shelters in all new construction. Unfortunately, because so many are living in housing more than thirty years old, many homes still lack shelters. Therefore, Israel needs to extend this program to older housing stock on an emergency basis wherever possible, despite the cost. And it needs to include Arab villages. There simply is no excuse, outside of politics perhaps, for why leadership does not enforce housing codes for new construction there. But since more needs to be done and it will take time, money, and political willpower, there will continue to be a need for public shelters for the foreseeable future. These shelters must be well maintained and ready to use at a moment's notice. And they must have the equipment and supplies needed to house people for lengthy periods because I do not for a moment think that large-scale evacuations under heavy missile fire will be possible. When a missile is falling from the sky, nobody will hesitate to dive into a damp, dirty shelter without basic items. But will they remain inside those shelters for days on end? Therefore, since Iron Dome will prioritize protecting military assets and crucial economic and infrastructure centers before protecting citizens, Israel must make a concerted effort to maintain a well-stocked public shelter program.

And then there is the issue of border settlements. They need their guns back. Storing semi-automatic weapons in central repositories miles away from the settlements will not help residents to stop terrorists who have crossed fences or popped out of undiscovered tunnels. Give these communities a chance. Give them their guns back! And make sure they have the supplies they need to remain in place. While prudence and plan might call for evacuating them on the first day of the war, events may not permit it. Give these places the capability to hold out until help arrives—and do not count on that help coming so soon.

UNIFIL

Recently, I read a book by Sean McFate titled *The New Rules of War*. When it comes to war, McFate delights in challenging prevailing wisdom. While I did not always agree with him, he did alert me to an unusual solution for fixing UNIFIL and other UN peacekeeping missions—one that makes sense.

Why does UNIFIL need fixing?

Because UNIFIL in its present form will never fulfill the mandate of the UN resolution that created it. Think about it. Why should soldiers from foreign lands go the extra yard in Lebanon to risk dying for causes that aren't theirs? UNIFIL might be a cash cow for nations that exchange their soldiers' services for UN payments, but for the soldier on the ground, it is just a dangerous post far from home. The governments that sent them are happy to gobble up the money, yet they don't want to pay a price in blood that would upset their constituents. Knowing this, Hezbollah exacerbates the problem by intimidating UNIFIL. The result? A neutered UNIFIL that coordinates its activities with Hezbollah's lapdog, the Lebanese Armed Forces (LAF), and sometimes with Hezbollah operatives, too.

But there is another option—hire mercenaries rather than nations. Or if you would rather use a more politically correct term—hire contractors to accomplish UNIFIL's lofty but glaringly unfulfilled goals.

"Wait a minute," you might say. The mere thought of an organization that promotes peace using mercenaries runs afoul of… runs afoul of what? Do you think mercenaries are inherently evil? Are you thinking that Russia's callous use of "little green men" in Ukraine in 2014 and its hiring of the vicious Wagner Group, run by a Russian oligarch, to participate in many conflicts—including the war Russia started in Ukraine in 2022—proves the point? But do you know that the United States has used contractors? It uses them for many operations, including security. Some NGOs also reportedly use them. Wealthier Arab nations have used contractors as well, as did Nigeria to fight Boko Haram, the terrorist group that kidnapped hundreds of schoolgirls to keep as "wives." Other countries have, too. And so does the UN!

A paper written by Åse Gilje Østensen in 2011 highlighted the UN's many agreements with private military and security contractors to provide support for security, logistics, policing at times, and other services for many UN-sponsored activities including peacekeeping and political missions. While not used in a leading role as peacekeepers, contractors (or would you rather me call them mercenaries) are often present.

In Lebanon, experienced, contract-soldier-peacekeepers might be more effective than often inexperienced and/or unmotivated soldiers arriving from a collection of frequently third-world nations who speak different languages and come from different cultures. If these contractors had clearly defined objectives and limitations, they could become a potent force for good. And this process would model for the world how to hire and employ contractors (it's okay if you want to call them mercenaries) successfully and ethically. This could help regulate an industry plagued by a history of abuse and misinformation and allow nations to use contract soldiers to stomp out evil. Sort of the beginning of international regulation of the contract-soldier industry!

Additionally, advocating for replacing national forces with contractors would give Israel a forum for highlighting UNIFIL's failure while simultaneously offering a solution.

But if UNIFIL is not replaced by a contractor force, and Israel cannot pull enough diplomatic strings to get the UN to force UNIFIL to perform its mission (as I suspect), Israel should lobby to terminate

UNIFIL and have it replaced with something better suited to address the complex problems of today. That would be a small group of civilians dedicated to providing a forum for informal dialogue between Hezbollah and Israel and mediation of their inevitable disputes. Since neither Hezbollah nor Lebanon will talk directly to Israel, that role is vitally important in helping to prevent the outbreak of an accidental war.

But let's stop kidding ourselves about UNIFIL's present value and lift the veil of naïve ignorance that presently exists—UNIFIL has made little effort to fully fulfill its mandate and has failed to prevent Hezbollah from strengthening its armed fortress that covers all southern Lebanon. Very few people know about UNIFIL's failure. By loudly and constantly agitating for change, Israel will shine a light on UNIFIL's incompetence and explain why the IDF may have to do far more than the world would otherwise accept.

How might Israel highlight UNIFIL's malfeasance? We will explore that in greater detail in the media and outreach sections of this chapter.

Intelligence

On the second day of the Six-Day War, King Hussein of Jordan and President Gamal Abdel Nasser of Egypt had a deceitful phone conversation. Twenty-four hours earlier, Israel's air force had obliterated the air forces of Egypt, Jordan, and Syria. Hoping to manufacture an excuse, Nasser called Hussein with a shady scheme. He asked the king to join him in charging the United States and Britain with attacking their airfields. Desperate, Hussein agreed. He believed that the "big lie," as U.S. President Lyndon Johnson called it, would help him preserve his throne.

Except there was a problem. Israel's intelligence service had recorded their call. Two days later, they publicized a transcript of the conversation. It was a classic example of a nation using information gathered by clandestine means to support its foreign policy. Years later, Israel released a recording of a phone call between the hijackers of the Achille Lauro and the PLO, proving the link between the two parties. Prime Minister Netanyahu did the same decades later by divulging Iranian nuclear secrets purloined by Israel's intelligence service. And in a separate revelation, Netanyahu identified the locations of hundreds of civilian sites in Lebanon where Hezbollah stored its missiles.

But Israel does not do this enough. Jonathan Conricus, the IDF's former spokesperson, told me that he would urge Israel's intelligence services to "collect intelligence for the purpose of media operations." He should know. On many occasions, Conricus and his predecessors were sent by the IDF "empty-handed" to brief the foreign press. That, Jonathan told me, all too often left Israel in a bad light. "We have," he said, "a rich arsenal of intelligence that simply isn't used as such." Failure to use it contributes to Israel frequently losing battles in the ongoing information war.

The United States practiced what Conricus preaches in the lead-up to Russia's invasion of Ukraine and still does. By publicly disclosing information gained surreptitiously, President Biden ably built a vast coalition within and without NATO. He hoped that the coalition would convince Putin not to attack. That failed, but the coalition has proved determined to help Ukraine defend itself after Russian boots crossed into its territory. Those ongoing public intelligence releases have frustrated many Russian false flag operations designed to break the coalition. It is an important lesson for Israel to learn.

Of course, intelligence professionals often oppose releasing information. It's in their nature to argue that doing so puts their sources and methods of collecting intelligence at risk. Furthermore, they contend that the information, if kept secret, might prove valuable on the battlefield. But operatives and analysts collect and analyze intelligence to serve the needs of the state—not the reverse. And intelligence can be used in multiple ways and for various reasons; sometimes in war, other times to prevent a war or to improve the likelihood of winning a war, or to stop a terrorist attack. But it also should be used to shape international and domestic opinion. That might prevent a war too. While Israel does that, it needs to do far more.

One example of Israel doing more of what I'm suggesting involves the CBW. In its early years, for good reason, Israel did not publicize its activity. As a result, Iran and Hezbollah rarely responded to CBW raids. But now the cat is out of the bag. Perhaps that is why Israel reveals more today—though still not enough. Israel must repeatedly remind the world what Iran and Hezbollah are doing in Lebanon and Syria and, very importantly, why that puts Israel at even greater risk. Therefore, even if Israel refrains from bombing certain locations, it should frequently—yet selectively—reveal where Hezbollah and Iran are storing and transporting weapons in Lebanon and Syria. When it does, Israel should routinely release before-and-after video footage if that target is destroyed. That would keep Hezbollah's and Iran's perfidy front and center—including the harsh reality that Hezbollah continues to callously use humans as shields to protect its missiles, which violates international law, and that Iran continues to shovel more dangerous weaponry into the hands of Hezbollah and its proxies in Syria. It would also leave Hezbollah and Iran guessing what else Israel knows, pressuring them to expend resources on correcting their failures to conceal weapons and causing them to doubt their successes. It would also have a salutary impact if Israel continued to release videos of Hezbollah operatives carrying guns and conducting training in areas where the UN has prohibited those activities. And why shouldn't Israel publicly expose Hezbollah every time it cracks down on civilians in ways that would make human rights advocates cringe? Show, don't tell, what life is like under Hezbollah's domination. Why not shout that out so loud that even those whose ears are closed will hear it? All this information is probably available to Israeli intelligence. Use it!

The goal is for Israel to reshape its global image through a constant flood of disclosures. Intelligence revelations are an important tool for doing so. More of the international community, and the public at large, should viscerally revile Hezbollah just as it does Putin, ISIS, and Al Qaeda. To accomplish that, Israel cannot wait for sensational revelations, and it should refrain from divulging everything at once. Instead, Israel should steadily leak morsels of information to the public. Rather than show 950 Hezbollah facilities at one time, Israel should highlight many sites all at once followed by a few sites every week for an extended period. Daily, it should provide information to favored journalists who will appreciate and treat the exclusives they get fairly, and then sprinkle in bigger reveals. Repetition may not be as appealing as sensationalism, but it is often far more effective. This is especially true when the revelations lead to a blockbuster, discovered, perhaps, by a mobilized force of independent journalists rather than Israeli intelligence services.

An article I read coined the phrase "coercive disclosure." That phrase perfectly describes what Israel must do—use the information it gathers to manage the world's opinion so that the IDF has the freedom of action to prevent a war and, should one break out, the freedom to win it.

Media, Entertainment and Outreach

While coercive disclosure is a powerful concept, it is just one of the many tools Israel should use to cultivate support throughout the world. Other tools include the sophisticated use of media, entertainment, and outreach. If Israel uses them properly, it will create an army of informed, supportive people who can influence their governments and will be motivated to ratchet up their assistance in trying times.

Media

Israel is loaded with journalists. Many advance their bias against Israel while happily availing themselves of Israel's comforts and free society. They paradoxically prefer the lifestyle Israel affords them to living amid squalor and fearing repression in the lands where Iran's proxies roam. Others, however, are professional reporters determined to report what they learn—wherever the truth takes them. Why doesn't Israel make their job easier? And consider exposing the hypocrisy of those that deserve it.

While conducting interviews in the northern Israel town of Kiryat Shmona for my 2019 book, *Living in Heaven, Coping with Hell,* I had the good fortune to talk with Shlomi Afrayat. Afrayat had established an impressive television news production empire from scratch, with headquarters built on a hilltop overlooking the town. I was impressed by Afrayat's foresight to design the building's rooftop as a perch from which reporters can watch when Hezbollah fires missiles at the region. He also has facilitated those same reporters' ability to broadcast timely news by renting them studios downstairs. It is the perfect marriage of profit motive with public good.

I am also aware of a private party's attempt to create something like Afrayat's rooftop in western Galilee. One of its goals was to help reporters contact local Israeli citizens during emergencies to get their side of the story. The organization also wanted to help reporters transmit news. To date, that effort is on hold. But why doesn't the Israeli government make similar efforts? Or for that matter, why doesn't the IDF allow foreign correspondents to embed with Israeli forces? The American military has done that repeatedly to great effect. Sharing dangers creates a dynamic that promotes sympathetic reporting.

Israel's public diplomacy arms should also match reporters with people who have truthful, interesting stories to tell and can articulate them—that's how you capture the hearts and minds of the public. The government must be proactive in nurturing this process; it shouldn't be aimlessly reacting to requests. I remember hearing an anecdote about Israel failing to make English speakers with diplomatic training available at important moments to brief reporters who only spoke English. There was another incident in which one arm of the Israeli government gathered a group of reporters to view locations of interest, only for a different arm of the government to bar the group from doing so. This sounds more like a communication error than a security concern. If I've heard of two such incidents, I'm certain there have been more.

If Israel could woo reporters with stories and access while frequently releasing intelligence reports, both broadly and selectively to individuals—it would be a powerful combination. It would also make reporters' jobs easier and their work product more informative.

It would also be powerful if Israel used social media creatively and intentionally, always mindful of how the public consumes information on different apps. To that end, Israel should identify relevant influencers with large or growing followings and bring them on trips to Israel designed to show them the issues in the north. This would be like the AIPAC-related entity that sends congressional staffers to Israel; or *Birthright* which sponsors free trips to Israel for young adult Jews. On Instagram, Facebook, TikTok, or whatever the rage of the day is, Israel and supportive media personalities and influencers should use coordinated professional videos and pictures to promote northern Israel, where the danger is perhaps the greatest, and highlight the issues it faces.

Combined, between traditional press and social media, Israel needs to make a relentless effort to juxtapose the hatred Israel's northern neighbors have for Israel and Jews in general with the desire northern Israelis have for peace and normality. Here, it is all about Hezbollah's and Iran's desire to destroy Israel—and how they're building the means to do it. Nothing more. To combat that, Israel should not just be vociferously spouting facts, but also humanizing the conflict's danger to Israeli citizens, every day, every hour, from every media hilltop. And making clear that today's conflict with Hezbollah is quite different from issues regarding the West Bank.

Entertainment

In a 2012 article for the *Jerusalem Post,* Abe Novick wrote that the movie *Exodus* "did more to shore up support for Israel and bolster positive feelings towards Zionism than any op-ed, letter-campaign or factual white paper ever could…[and that] the ability of a major motion picture to impact real politics can't be challenged."

Experts I interviewed for this book agreed with Novick. But something else that Novick wrote in that article was even more striking:

> What Israel needs, is to find and align with a major studio and Hollywood director who will make it their mission to tell the story of Israel. The ultimate goal should be more than just one movie, but a remake of "Exodus" would be a great start. Ultimately, it should be a series of epic blockbusters over a 10-year period. They could be stories from the bible. They could be movies that tell the world about modern-day Israel.

I could not agree more.

Israel has the stories. Hollywood has the movie magic. If Israel has a friend in the U.S., stories on film should be one of the most powerful ways to creatively connect and strengthen that bond.

Stories are powerful, and there is no shortage of dramatic ones set against the backdrop of northern Israel's breathtaking scenery. From biblical times to today, true encounters of war, revival, and resurrection dot the landscape. Themes of heroism and desperation interlaced with God and country are suffused throughout the lives of the people who have lived there. These are histories begging to be told; they could shine a light on the struggle Israelis are engaged in between life and death. Therefore, the government should prioritize creating a profitable economic environment for making compelling films about northern Israel by offering subsidies, access, and anything else that would attract filmmakers to the region. Through stories, and the emotions they might evoke, Israel can better win the battle for hearts and minds worldwide.

And entertainment, of course, extends beyond film. Books and podcasts are as educational as they are entertaining; and they have the power to transform people into more self-aware, empathetic citizens of the world. I've always been disappointed to find that the books in the Israel sections of bookshops often take a predominantly anti-Israel slant. That requires correction. Aso needing attention, is the dearth of editorials and investigative reporting about northern Israel and Hezbollah in newspapers worldwide. To change that, Israel's government must prioritize providing access to creators interested in telling the rich stories Israel has to offer. Writing is hard and securing interviews for books and guests for podcasts is challenging and time-consuming. Israel's government can make that easier by designing a streamlined process for doing so. Israel is not just engaged in a kinetic war with Hezbollah; it's also engaged in a war of words. Israel could just field its own army of storytellers but, in conjunction with that, mobilizing a global community of authors and creators willing to join the fray would be far more effective in disseminating the true, essential narrative of Israel's struggle with Hezbollah.

Films, books, podcasts, investigative reporting, and editorials are traditional tools that can illuminate political problems hidden from the public. But for those willing to think outside of the box, there are even more formats that combine entertainment with education. Two that come to mind are computer games and video games. In 2003, Hezbollah produced a video game that portrayed one of its operatives fighting the IDF. In 2018, it produced another first-person shooter game simulating fighting in Syria. It's not a bad idea—to use a game to introduce young people to geopolitical issues they can sympathize with. Israel could do the same, and more.

Already, in northern Israel, *Alma* has created a security crisis simulator that puts participants in the role of Israeli cabinet members and then feeds them simulated news and secret intelligence reports for them to react to. By now, more than a thousand people have participated in the simulation. But why should that be the only simulation of Israel's security challenges in northern Israel available to the public? Why not create computer war games and first-person shooter games involving IDF soldiers facing Hezbollah and other Iranian proxies? Why not develop computer games like SimCity that are centered around the development and challenges of a kibbutz? Or else computer games that address the geopolitical issues in the region. The possibilities are endless and the talent to execute these ideas is available. All that is lacking is money and will—and the government could use subsidies to stimulate both.

The point of this section is that Israel needs worldwide support, and especially American support, to maintain its freedom of action in fighting against Hezbollah's growing threat. But Israel will never "sell" its story to enough people if it just relies on solemn, formal announcements. There are too many crucial constituencies that this approach will not reach—especially younger generations. Instead, Israel must think multi-dimensional and reiterative. Not every path Israel takes will end with success. But the more paths it covers, the more likely it will find success. And the more often stories portray Israel in a favorable light when contrasted with Hezbollah, the more likely Israel will garner support. Which leads directly to the next subsection—outreach.

Outreach

There is much low-hanging fruit in the pro-Israel and neutral-Israel world. You can find it in synagogues, churches, political and community groups, and elsewhere. Most of those entities scramble to find people willing to talk to them on subjects of interest. Many would be happy to host speakers knowledgeable about Hezbollah and its threat to Israel. But few will think of the topic on their own, let alone find a qualified speaker. If Israel wants to effectively engage in public diplomacy, then it must identify those organizations that might be interested in learning more and then push information to them consistently. Nothing is better than personal contact.

A partial model for this already exists. My quick search of the internet uncovered multiple sites offering speakers about the Holocaust. The same could be the case regarding Hezbollah and northern Israel security issues or even just tourist information for visiting the north—one central location that lists individuals willing to speak to groups of any size. This would be perfect for smaller, distant organizations that might not attract speakers from large think tanks or official Israeli government outlets. In the United States, there are thousands of synagogues, community centers, and the like (3,700, according to a count done two decades ago) let alone churches and other community groups that number in the six figures. The goal here is to create a wave of knowledge, empathy, and political support from a multitude of ripples—a true grassroots effort.

Representatives

Israel needs to be very careful whom it selects to represent it worldwide—especially in the United States. America is Israel's crucial ally. Simply put, Israel would be in jeopardy if it lost America's support. That support must be bipartisan. Anything short of that and

Israel risks losing America's help because, while political parties in the United States ebb and flow, Israel's enemies do not. That's why the selection of Israel's ambassador to the United States is crucial. For four years, Michael Oren was its ambassador to the United States. Ron Dermer served the next eight years, with his term ending in 2021. What I am about to say has nothing to do with the quality of all other recent Israeli ambassadors. I am sure that they were, or are, highly competent, and I am equally sure that they had or have strengths that enhance the Israeli-US relationship. In fact, Yitzhak Rabin was an outstanding ambassador. But he lacked, as others have, the ability to speak English without a heavy accent; Oren and Dermer did not have that problem.

The position of ambassador requires two things. First, an ambassador must be able to communicate Israeli policy clearly and persuasively to the American government and relay America's views back to Israel without spin or prejudice. In addition, the Israeli ambassador must be able to positively influence U.S. policy, often at lower levels of government, while also looking for opportunities to create partnerships with other countries. Dermer did that effectively with the ambassador from the United Arab Emirates. This doesn't require the ambassador to speak English as fluently as an American-born speaker would. But the job also requires a second thing—communicating with the American people. Meeting with pro-Israeli organizations is low-hanging fruit. An ambassador doesn't need to speak perfect English to do that. But the Israeli ambassador will also appear on television news shows, interviews, and other news outlets in addition to his or her other speaking opportunities. To do this effectively, the ambassador should be a comfortable public speaker able to communicate clearly and persuasively without a difficult to understand heavy accent.

Therefore, if Israel hopes to win the battle of public opinion in the United States, it must think carefully about whom it selects as an ambassador or as an assistant to the ambassador, who will be the resident face of Israel to the American people. Although unaccented English should not be a prerequisite for the post, the person must be able to speak in public in an engaging manner that enhances communication with the American public. In short, they must be the welcomed, honored face of Israel, appearing on all the communication devices Americans use. The same is true for the selection of Israeli ambassadors to other countries. All must possess the language skills necessary to address the public wherever they are stationed.

And, also important, vitally so, the people who speaks to the world from Israel on behalf of the Israeli government must also be able to speak English, or any other applicable language, in a manner that is easily understood on television. For English speakers, Jonathan Conricus, the former IDF international spokesperson, fit that bill. Unfortunately, in the past, there have been times when I felt the person whose job it was to communicate lacked that talent. That can't be the case going forward. This is a necessity, not a luxury.

Get the Money

As described in Chapter Thirteen, Hezbollah's criminal enterprise earns hundreds of millions of dollars annually—if not more. But I have not found evidence that Israel does much to reduce that number. Israel needs to do something about that. The CBW targets weapons that make Hezbollah stronger. Why not target the money that procures them?

Unfortunately, Israel has not diminished Hezbollah's increasing influence on Shiite communities around the world and narcotic production closer to home. That influence generates money through ongoing criminal enterprises based in or facilitated by those communities. Those enterprises then funnel that money to Hezbollah in Lebanon which is then used for weapons purchases or channeled to social programs that strengthens Hezbollah's political support among Shiites there and elsewhere. No different than weapons sent from Iran, the ill-gotten money strengthens Hezbollah, too.

It's time to starve the beast.

Although Iran supplies Hezbollah with much of its budget, the funds garnered from its criminal enterprises are significant. While I imagine Israel's intelligence community passes actionable intelligence to foreign nations, the money keeps flowing. If Israel's CBW can stop weapons, it seems logical that Israeli special operators or the CBW could put a dent in Hezbollah's criminal activities. Even though some countries, such as the United States, would be off limits for political reasons, many that have weak governments and corrupt police would not be, and they might even welcome the help.

As for specifics, Matthew Zweig (an expert on sanctions and finance involving Hezbollah) directed me to some low hanging fruit— the narcotics trade. Not cocaine, but methamphetamine production. Matthew alerted me to the fact that within northern Lebanon and Syria, drug lords are ramping up the production of Captagon, a form of speed. According to a Dec 2021 *New York Times* article, major players include people with close ties to Hezbollah. A supposition that Nasrallah denies. However, according to the *Times*, some of the production facilities are in Syria and others in areas controlled by Hezbollah. Furthermore, some of the distribution networks run through areas under Hezbollah's influence in Lebanon to the nation's ports and international airport near Beirut. Therefore, it stands to reason that one way or the other, Hezbollah derives a financial benefit from the production of Captagon in the region. Why not, then, destroy the production facilities in Syria as part of the CBW? Since Israeli intelligence is so effective determining where Hezbollah and Iran store weapons in Syria, it shouldn't be too hard to locate Captagon production facilities in Syria and destroy them.

Israel taking action in Syria and worldwide to interdict the flow of money would not turn off the cash faucet altogether, but surely it would lower its pressure—a worthy endeavor indeed. While I hope it is happening undercover, and Jonathan Schanzer believes it likely is to some extent, I still believe that Israel could and should do more.

Promote Northern Israel

Northern Israel is a beautiful, historic, and romantic place and is home to many religious sites significant to Jews, Christians, and other faiths. The Golan Heights has an ancient and well-preserved synagogue at Ein Keshatot; great hiking trails, including the one that leads to the ancient Jewish fortress of Gamla, which was destroyed by the Romans; a huge crusader fort; and modern battlefields from the Six-Day and Yom Kippur Wars—plus wineries, cherry picking, and so much more. The northern Galilee, especially around the Sea of Galilee, has many locations significant to Christians, and it is there, at Degania, where the establishment of kibbutzim and early achievements of the Zionist dream can be best understood. But religion and history are not all that visitors will find. Archeological wonders are also present. And tourists can bask in a beautiful lake, enjoy the cultural center of Rosh Pina, the beauty of Metula, or just stroll through the towns. In Western Galilee, there is a plethora of hiking trails, more forts, and beautiful beaches, plus a center for Kabbalah at Safed. In addition, visitors can immerse themselves in Druze culture and a historic synagogue up close along the cobbled lanes of Pekiin and explore hints of the ancient Arab world in Acre's markets hidden behind the walls of an old crusader fortress. And anyone who appreciates seeing examples of Arab and Jewish cooperation can visit the merged city of Ma'alot-Tarshiha.

In short, northern Israel has much to offer; however, it rarely occupies more than a couple of days on the itineraries of first and even second-time visitors to Israel. Nor is it on the radar screen of governments and people around the globe. The areas of controversy that occupy the international community are in the center of Israel. There the insolvable issues of the West Bank and Gaza permeate the region. But in the north the issues are simple, and the need is great. Because familiarity breeds love and caring, Israel should promote visitation and even consider subsidizing travel to the north. A subsidy that would benefit the region's economy as well. Even if a person visited the area for just several days, they would leave with a memorable experience and intimate understanding of the dangers the north faces.

To further promote the region, Israel's government should create high-quality videos highlighting attractions in the north and emphasizing why visiting is important for both tourists and for the people who call the north home. One non-profit research and education center that creates content and furthers understanding is *Alma*. I am certain that anyone who spends time on a security tour with *Alma's* guides along the northern borders; who reviews the plethora of reports, videos, and podcasts it produces; or who participates in *Alma's* geopolitical simulation game will never forget the experience.

In short, it should be the government's policy to proactively promote the region and the threats it endures. By doing so, it would enlarge, invigorate, and motivate those who oppose Hezbollah.

Israel cannot win the battle for hearts and minds from afar. It must also fight the battle up close. Israel can and should do more.

But so can we. That is the subject of the final chapter of this book.

Chapter Twenty-Seven

What Can You Do to Make a Difference?

First, I want to thank you for reading this book. I am in your debt.

And even though I salute you for all that may you already do for Israel, I humbly ask that you endeavor to accomplish even more.

Israel needs your help and, most particularly, your efforts could help Israelis living in northern Israel. Their families are most threatened, their property is most endangered, and their way of life is most at risk. They endure all of this because an implacable foe with malicious intent sits just across the border—within eyesight, sometimes only yards away from their communities. But we can stand collectively against this implacable foe by boosting the lives of Israelis in times of peace and by bettering their prospects in times of war.

You might ask, "What can I do?" But it is not what "I" can do. Rather, it is the sum of what "all of us" can do together. Throughout history, the dramatic actions of a few brave souls, amplified by the smaller actions of countless supporters, have shaped history in extraordinary ways. The Israeli people are doing the heavy lifting, fighting Hezbollah at every step. However, our ripples of support can collectively create a wave of political, economic, and informational power that will help frustrate Hezbollah's plans. But that takes each of us to do whatever we are comfortable with, no matter how slight.

What exactly might we do? I have some suggestions.

Stay Informed

"Knowledge is power." This oft-quoted phrase has many fathers, including Thomas Jefferson. Likewise, I found several definitions for the term. The definition found on Dictionary.com resonated with me the most. It says, "The more one knows, the more one will be able to control events." That's especially true regarding Hezbollah. However, Hezbollah's malevolence—short of war or an unspeakable tragedy—is a topic that mainstream media seldom covers. But if we are to make a difference in the fight, no matter how small, then we must always be aware of what is happening in the region. Here are some suggestions for further reading that will help you do that:

1) Alma's Newsletter and website - Based near the Lebanese border, this research and education center is the go-to source for current information on Hezbollah and the threat it poses to Israel. Every week, *Alma* publishes in-depth reports on its website along with a newsletter that highlights revelations and provides expert analysis. In addition, *Alma* regularly produces informative podcasts featuring qualified guests who delve deeply into a myriad of issues affecting the region. At the very least, sign up for *Alma's* newsletter.

Consider signing up for *Alma's* newsletter at http://israel-alma.org

2) My Biweekly Newsletter, *Israel's Northern Borders* - This newsletter features links to at least three pertinent news articles or reports that will keep you informed on developments in northern Israel. In addition, in each issue I provide a short, convenient summary of events over the prior two weeks.

Consider signing up for my newsletter at http://CliffordSobin.com

3) Endowment for Middle East Truth (EMET) newsletter - This Washington, D.C.-based think tank produces a detailed newsletter as well as podcasts that, while devoted to all things Israel, frequently cover Hezbollah and other items of interest.

Consider signing up for EMET's newsletter at http://emetonline.org

4)   Lebanese Hezbollah Interactive Map, Produced by The Washington Institute for Near East Policy

Be sure to explore Matthew Levitt's interactive map and timeline of Hezbollah's activities around the world, from its foundation in the early 1980s until today.

Visit:

https://www.washingtoninstitute.org/hezbollahinteractivemap/

Support

Every dollar you donate or spend—and every minute you volunteer your efforts to support those who are devoted to exposing and/or counteracting Hezbollah's perfidy—is a dollar or minute well spent. Although it might not seem that your actions would matter, collectively they make a world of difference. It is those small individual efforts, in mass, that allow others to devote their full-time efforts to helping Israel prevail against the threat posed by Hezbollah and its patron Iran. Below are some things you can do to add your strength to the fight:

1)   *Buy books by authors who cover Israel's conflict with Hezbollah, Iran, and other Iranian proxies.* Not only will you learn much by reading their work, but you'll also be supporting their

efforts and will influence them, and others, to write more about those subjects. And your purchases will cause those books to be more visible on Amazon and increase the likelihood that bookstores and libraries will stock them which will broaden their reach. Culled from many worthy candidates, here is a list of four easy-to-read books I recommend, along with two other titles that offer extensive details, plus a volume that provides important background information and a feel for what life in northern Israel is like.

- *The Transforming Fire: The Rise of the Israel-Islamist Conflict by Jonathan Spyer:* This Israeli author sneaked into Lebanon and lived to write about it. His enlightening and well-written book is about that experience and the overall rise of Israel's conflict with Islam.
- *The Road to Fatima Gate* by Michael Totten: A somewhat dated reporter's view from inside Lebanon. A fascinating read.
- *Gaza Conflict 2021: Hamas, Israel and Eleven Days of War* by Jonathan Schanzer: This easy-to-read book about the war in Gaza contains information relevant to Israel's confrontation with Hezbollah.
- *Israeli National Security Strategy: A New Strategy for an Era of Change* by Charles D. Freilich: This one-of-a-kind book offers comprehensive insight into Israel's present challenges and suggests a long-term strategy for meeting them.
- *Israel's Long War with Hezbollah: Military Innovation and Adaption Under Fire* by Raphael Marcus: This detailed book contains much military information with a focus on

how the IDF's approach to fighting Hezbollah has changed over the decades.

- *Hezbollah: The Global Footprint of Lebanon's Party of God* by Matthew Levitt: A detailed look at Hezbollah's nefarious criminal activities worldwide.
- *Living in Heaven, Coping with Hell: Israel's Northern Borders—Where Zionism Triumphed, the Kibbutz Evolves, and the Pioneering Spirit Prevails* by Clifford Sobin (Yes, that is me!): Based on my extensive research, travels, and interviews, this book explores settlement in northern Israel, the people who live there, and the problems the region faces today. It is, I dare say, a joy to read.

2) Financially support *Alma.*

In full disclosure, I serve on *Alma*'s Board and *Alma's* president, Sarit Zehavi, has helped me significantly with her insights and gaining access to experts interviewed for this book. But I am not the only one who thinks highly of Sarit and her work. In 2021, the *Jerusalem Post* named her one of the fifty most influential Jews of the year, and she is frequently quoted in a variety of publications. Therefore, I strongly suggest you peruse *Alma's* website (www.Israel-Alma.org), especially its research section. I also suggest listening to her talk on AIPAC's center stage, in 2018, before 18,000 people. You can find it easily by Googling "Sarit Zehavi AIPAC." Then, decide whether you wish to donate.

3) *Join AIPAC*

Simply put, you should consider joining this organization and attending regional meetings. Consider going to the annual national meeting, should post COVID, AIPAC start up those annual meetings again. You will learn a lot. If the format remains the same, on the last day of meetings you will have an opportunity to meet with your local congressional delegation to advocate for Israel. Belonging to AIPAC will keep you aware of Israel's current geopolitical situation and expose you to a plethora of cultural offerings and other items of interest. And if you have more time, energy, and motivation, consider getting involved with AIPAC's National Council, which has in the past held two yearly meetings with your state's congressional leaders—often in their conference rooms with just a limited number of attendees.

4) If your politics or beliefs take you elsewhere than *AIPAC*, that's okay, too. Join the organizations that best express your views while also supporting Israel. There are plenty of them.

Speak Out

Meeting people individually or in small groups is the best way to inform others and yourself. Decades ago, my father told me the only way to fully understand an issue is to write about it or teach it. So true.

If you have access to men's or women's clubs, synagogues, churches, community centers, and the like, ask them if you could speak to their members about Israel's struggle with Hezbollah. If you are uncomfortable speaking in small groups or do not yet feel knowledgeable enough to speak about Hezbollah, then ask the leaders of those groups to bring in speakers on the subject. And, if you are financially able, you can sponsor those speakers yourself. Or consider speaking to groups you create composed of friends, family, and acquaintances. While it would be great if several people attended, just one person is enough. While fulfilling my responsibilities as managing partner of a law firm, I learned that marketing requires trying many things, most of which will fail, to find the one or few people who will make a difference. It is no different in Israel's battle for support, which is essential for Israel's success in any future confrontation with Hezbollah.

Which leads me to family. Speaking does not require talking to strangers. Your spouses, children, grandchildren, parents, brothers and sisters, uncles and aunts, and cousins, are important for ensuring Israel's future. They are, if you pardon the expression, your low-hanging fruit. Try to expose them to your passions and concerns. Of course, they can be your most difficult customers, too. There is a delicate balance between preaching and avoidance.

I leave you with this thought; if we want to make an impact on the world, we might choose to tread different paths, but I suggest trying to walk at least one that is comfortable.

<u>Travel</u>

There is no substitute for seeing things for yourself. And nothing is more likely to inspire your family and friends to learn more about Israel and its struggles than seeing it for themselves. Unfortunately, most people who visit Israel spend little time in northern Israel, except for those who are interested in the Sea of Galilee for religious or other reasons. That is a shame. Northern Israel is a fascinating, beautiful, and multicultural place—easily capable of supporting a visit for several days or more.

Why else should you bother going? Because visiting the region will allow you to see firsthand how Hezbollah's proximity to the border poses such a threat to Israel. By stopping at the following seven locations presented below from east to west, you will get the picture.

First, drive to the top of Mount Bental on the Golan Heights. There, you will find an abandoned IDF military position, a coffee shop, and an incredible view of the Syrian plain below. By gazing down on the valley below, you will appreciate the dangers Israel faced from Syria in 1973 and still faces today from Iranian and Hezbollah operatives embedded in nearby towns.

Second, go to Ghajar, the town that Hezbollah contends is a part of Lebanon but whose residents want to remain a part of Israel. This peninsula of habitation, bordered on three sides by Lebanon and populated mostly by residents of the Alawite faith, was Syrian until 1967. Now, its Arab inhabitants are Israeli citizens and wish to remain so. Hezbollah wants to force them to live under its control as Lebanese citizens. Walk the town's perimeter. The border fence is a visual reminder of the danger nearby.

Third, visit Metula. Another peninsula sticking into Lebanon, this Jewish town, founded in 1896, is home to verdant agricultural fields, a now struggling community seeking to return to its former vibrancy, and multiple reminders of the danger Hezbollah presents. On three sides, hills and flatlands Hezbollah displays its flag. These flags are often joined by signs and billboards featuring messages designed to frighten and dispirit Metula's inhabitants. A hike down a gorge on the eastern side of town leads to two waterfalls. It also passes a hilltop. On the day I took that walk, three young men lounged at the top of the hill doing nothing but watching and maybe photographing. Likely, they were Hezbollah operatives keeping track of what was happening in the town.

Fourth, stop by Misgav Am, on a hilltop overlooking the Lebanese town of Odaisseh. Make reservations ahead of time for a conversation with a guide from *Fortress of the People*, a glass-walled structure with an incredible view of Metula and the surrounding border.

Fifth, if you're traveling in a group, be sure to stop by *Alma* in Tefen to play their geopolitical simulation. Also, whether you are alone or with a group, arrange for an *Alma* guide to accompany you on a security tour to one of the places I list here, or elsewhere.

Sixth, head for Kibbutz Hanita, a storied kibbutz high on the mountains separating Lebanon and Israel. Here, you can visit its museum, which highlights the kibbutz's origin as one of the tower and stockade settlements built in the 1930s to hold critical land. Also, walk the perimeter road to appreciate how close to Hezbollah its residents live. Finish with a bite at its cafe or by buying a bottle of gin at the Julius distillery there.

Your final stop should be at Rosh Hanikra along the coast. There, you will see Lebanon on the other side of a fence, a security wall at the top of an adjoining hill, and the buoys stretching out beyond the horizon that mark part of Israel's boundary at sea. You will also note the Israeli naval vessel on constant patrol to the south.

If you do all that I suggest, or even just a part of it, you will see for yourself what Israel faces. But out of all my suggestions, there is one you should certainly do—schedule a security tour with *Alma*. Through their eyes and words, you will learn much about Israel's tenuous hold on its land and its struggle with Hezbollah.

<u>Vote</u>

We all should support candidates for office who care about the threats Israel faces. I'm not asking you to be a single-issue voter, but I am asking you to ensure that those you vote for do not have a track record by word, or deed, of undercutting Israel's security. One litmus test for that is where the candidate stands on the Memorandum of Understanding (MOU).

Every ten years, Israel and the U.S. president negotiate a new MOU. The MOU constitutes America's promise to ensure that Israel has the military capability to defend itself by itself. Israel uses the money to procure arms—many from the United States—that are fundamental to its security. However, Congress is responsible for funding that promise. Therefore, the House and Senate must vote every year to fulfill the MOU's terms. Overwhelmingly, representatives from both houses of government, whether from the right or the left, vote in favor of it. We cannot count on the few congressional members who vote against the MOU or abstain from voting on the matter to support Israel in a conflict with Hezbollah. You should take that into account when you vote.

You can do this comfortably regardless of whether your political views range from liberal to conservative, libertarian to independent. I am fully aware that readers of this book may have differing perspectives regarding Palestinians and the West Bank. But defending Israel from Hezbollah has nothing to do with that. As such, I only ask you to consider one thing dipositive for your vote—would the candidate you lean toward support Israel's continued existence in a time of great need?

Recognize the Danger of Unilateral Withdrawals

Jonathan Conricus put it succinctly in a Podcast interview in 2022, "There is this thing with unilateral withdrawals without a security agreement in place that provides for the day after. I don't think trying to end the conflict unilaterally without having the other side sign on to what the situation will be the day after is a wise thing."

Twice, Israel has withdrawn its forces without obtaining written agreements signed by the opposing side: Once from Lebanon in May 2000 and again from Gaza in 2005. Both times, Israel's attempts to create conditions for peace were met with more missiles and more terror. Why? Because in each case the other side retained its agenda without having to agree to any limitations and end to their physical attacks. And in each case, it was a recipe for more war and more devastation.

It is our responsibility to advocate for peace, but only peace acknowledged by both sides of the conflict. Not a peace imposed on one side and rejected by the other. There will be future confrontations with Hezbollah. There will be moments during those confrontations when the international community will attempt to impose a ceasefire on Israel or a withdrawal. The litmus test for determining whether these attempts are based on bias or fairness must be whether Hezbollah is named and specifically agrees to the terms of an agreement that ends the conflict. If not, then it is our job to explain to friends, family, and those with political influence why Israel would be ill-served by the deal.

Economic Sanctions—Advocate for Them and the Means to Implement Them

First, let's make sure we understand what economic sanctions are. Essentially, they are commercial and financial penalties imposed by a nation in furtherance of its political, military, or social purposes against another state, or against a group or individual. Since the United States has branded Hezbollah a Foreign Terrorist Organization in 1997, and because it threatens American interests in a variety of ways, Hezbollah, and anyone who helps it, is fair game for sanctions.

So far, the United States has enacted two rounds of sanctions that are aimed directly at Hezbollah and those that support it. The first sanction bill, enacted in 2015, had the fancy title *Hezbollah International Financing Prevention Act of 2015*. The second sanction bill, which greatly expanded the reach of the first bill, was signed by President Trump in 2018. Combined, they allow the U.S. government to deny access to the U.S. financial system by any foreign bank that is involved with significant financial transactions with Hezbollah or its affiliates or partners.

Denying access to the U.S. financial system might not sound like much, but it really is! Since the dollar is the world's reserve currency, access to American banks is necessary for much international commerce. It is hard to imagine that any bank which wants to do business outside of its country of origin can thrive without access to the dollar and the ability to exchange foreign currency for dollars. In addition, the United States is the world's largest market. Few financial institutions would willingly give up the ability to do business with entities based in the United States. In short, to be denied access to the United States is a near-death blow for most foreign financial institutions.

An example of how this works happened recently. In December 2022, the United States slapped terrorist sanctions on two companies and two accountants that provided financial services to Hezbollah. A third person was sanctioned for assisting Hezbollah with purchasing weaponry. As a result, any bank that allows these entities to keep accounts with them, or helps them with any financial transactions, will be barred from participating in the U.S. financial system. Therefore, no bank will work with these designated individuals and companies, which will complicate their ability to benefit Hezbollah, make them less profitable, and disincentivize others from doing so.

In theory powerful stuff. In practice, that is not always the case.

One major problem is the delay between enactment and enforcement.

Matthew Zweig, an expert on sanction legislation who has worked for many years in various positions in government, including the State Department and for seventeen years for the House Foreign Affairs Committee, before becoming a senior fellow at FDD, patiently explained the problem to me. First, the path from when a sanctions bill becomes law to when the U.S. government will act on it can be long and tortured. A major sticking point is regulations. The sanction bills provide a framework. Regulations provide the rules of the road. Until they are thrashed out, the Office of Foreign Assets Control (OFAC), which is the office charged by the Treasury Department to administer and enforce economic sanctions, will do little or nothing because it won't know what to do. In needs the guidelines regulations provide. Regulations are promulgated by the Treasury Department in most cases, or sometimes by Executive Order of the President. Generally, the process takes months. Matthew told me that when he wrote and negotiated sanction legislation, he would try to include within it that regulations would be written within 180 days of enactment of the statute. However, he admitted that the inclusion of that provision is more of an aspiration than a mandate.

However, as frustrating as regulatory delays might be, at least that problem has an endpoint when the regulations are written. Forever lasting is the question of enforcement. Enforcement requires political will, often dependent on the whims of the White House. And, also, resources. Matthew called it "absorptive capacity." Bottom line, that asks: Are there enough people to do the work? OFAC employs a finite number of people with the skills needed to ferret out those who should be sanctioned. There are many, many sanctions enacted for many worthwhile purposes and many, many worthy targets for each sanction bill. Simply put, there are not enough people to go around. So, sanction legislation gets prioritized by OFAC. Sometimes, Hezbollah might be a high priority, but sometimes not. Over the last year, sanctions targeting Russia have received the highest priority. All other meritorious sanction bill enforcement suffers as a result—quite likely those targeting Hezbollah too.

Is there a solution to this problem? Perhaps. But solutions can get caught up in politics. A sanction bill targeting Hezbollah could include a provision that would fund enforcement. For example, ten million dollars. But that can get caught up in funding philosophy differences between democrats and republicans. Matthew told me that the most effective funding would mandate a fixed amount for specific purposes for a certain number of years. But there are strong political currents against that form of funding unless a specific program is identified from which an identical sum can be reduced. As a result, it is easier not to specify an amount in the legislation. This, of course, waters down its impact.

Having supplied you with the theoretical, let's look at an example of how good legislative intentions alone are not enough to make an impact. In December 2018, the Human Shields Prevention Act became law. Several months before that, an IDF spokesperson said that "One in every three or four houses in southern Lebanon is a headquarters, post, weapons depot, or a Hezbollah hideout." In part to counter that, as well as similar conduct by Hamas in Gaza, Congress passed the human shields law, which includes a request that the President enact sanctions against those who perpetrate such behavior that endangers civilians. The administration of President Trump did nothing to enforce the law. Neither has President Biden.

Therefore, as you can see, sanction laws are important. But they are a starting point, not an endpoint. That's where we come in. It is up to us to advocate, not just for their enactment, but for their enforcement. You can keep current regarding impending sanctions by regularly checking AIPAC's website.

A Final Word

Israel faces a growing danger that presents an existential threat to its way of life, its ability to thrive, and even its very existence. While in some ways that is old news, the threat Israel faces today is radically different. It is not the threat of invasion. It is the very real threat of societal destruction. None of Israel's enemies can presently send hordes of tanks and soldiers to invade the country. But Hezbollah and Iran's other proxies possess the means to fire throngs of missiles with one purpose—devastate the nation, especially northern Israel. This fight might not change borders, but it could ruin vast swaths inside the country. Israel is trying mightily to mitigate that danger. But Israel could use help.

Our help.

We are not mere bystanders in this ongoing saga. We are players with roles, large or small. From our tiny ripples of action can come waves that push back hard on the enemy's designs.

By reading this book you have already come a long way. You now understand the environment in which Hezbollah developed and currently thrives, what Israel has already faced, the challenges that still exist, and what Israel is, and might consider, doing about it.

I hope you are now convinced that we must stand up collectively to Hezbollah's challenge because Israel needs all of us to join in this fight.

Acknowledgments

This book could not have been written without the assistance of *Alma*, the northern Israel research and education center than specializes in Israel's security challenges. Its president and founder, Lt. Col. (res.) Sarit Zehavi, has been my guide, friend, and mentor over the last six years. I owe her a debt of gratitude, as I do to Alma's CEO, David Ur, who accompanied me to many interviews, and Avraham Levine with whom I have spent hours talking politics, history, and life.

I also am indebted to Jonathan Schanzer. Jonathan is the senior vice president for research at the Foundation for Defense of Democracies (FDD). His advice and willingness to put me in touch with relevant experts added greatly to this book.

Also, a thanks to my editor, Craig Dowd, who put up with my mangled syntax and navigated the transcript to a cohesive whole.

And most of all, a huge thank you to my wife, Julie, who put up with my trips to Israel to obtain in-person interviews, my many hours of writing and researching, and my often-vacant stares as I thought through the issues raised in this book.

Sources and Background

<u>Interviews in Alphabetic Order</u>

Col (Res.) Boaz Amidror – Experienced warrior and commander in Lebanon at all levels up to Brigade and author of the groundbreaking book, *Cease Fire, Friendlies!: Practical Insights from the Battlefield to Mitigate Friendly Fire.*

Lilach Ashtar – Served in multiple command, intelligence, and liaison positions with the IDF.

Dr. Eitan Azani – Now Director of Research at the International Institute for Counterterrorism, he had much IDF operational experience with Counterterrorism and the author of, *Hezbollah: The Story of the Party of God – From Revolution to Institutionalization.*

David Azulay – Mayor of Metula.

Tal Beeri – Director Research at *Alma* and former officer in the IDF.

Lt. Col. Jonathan Conricus - Led the IDF's International Media Branch for four years before retiring in 2021. Also held numerous liaison positions with the IDF in northern Israel, including interfacing with UN forces in Lebanon and on the Golan and was as an IDF representative at the UN. Earlier, he served as an infantry combat platoon and company commander.

Jonathan Davis - Now Vice President for External Relations at Reichman University in Israel, Davis served in a paratrooper reconnaissance unit that performed many behind-the-lines missions in Syria and Iraq during the 1973 war. Then, as a reservist paratrooper, he fought in the 1982 Lebanon war, and was an IDF spokesperson during the intifada and the 2006 Lebanon War.

Seth Frantzman - Senior correspondent for the *Jerusalem Post* who writes about military affairs and the author of the book *Drone Wars.*

Professor Chuck Freilich - Former member of Israel's National Security Agency and a prolific author, having penned two award-winning books on Israel's national security policy, a forthcoming book about the cyber threat to Israel, as well as numerous articles and podcasts related to Israel's security. Freilich teaches political science at NYU, Columbia and Tel Aviv universities.

Major General (Res.) Gershon HaCohen - Held various positions, including Commander of the Northern Corps of the IDF, Commander of the IDF Colleges, Head of Training & Doctrine Division in the General Staff, Reserve Division Commander of the Northern Command, and Commander of the 7th Brigade of the IDF Armor Division. In 2005, Major General Hacohen oversaw Israel's disengagement from the Gaza Strip.

Claude Ibrahim – Born in Marjayoun, Claude is the son of a SLA commander and is now integrally involved with the SLA community now living in Israel.

Brig. Gen. (Res.) Yossi Kuperman - Former Director General of the Israel Ministry of Strategic Affairs and an Israeli security expert.

Major (Res.) Avraham Levine – Speaker and Digital Content Manager at *Alma*. Levine served in command positions in Lebanon.

Brigadier General (Res.) Erez Maisel - Held leadership roles at northern command that included twenty years of creating and delivering actionable intelligence and a stint as commander of the IDF's International Cooperation Unit tasked with coordinating its efforts with the many other national militaries operating in the region.

Asma Maroun (pseudonym) – A former citizen of Lebanon who witnessed Lebanon's Civil War firsthand.

Professor Jacob Nagel - Headed the committee which was responsible for Israel's decision to develop the Iron Dome and held many high-level positions including head of Israel's National Security Council and acting national security advisor to the prime minister.

Yaron Ofek-Fuchs – Formerly served as an officer in the Givati Brigade, he now lives in northern Israel.

Uzi Rubin – Oversaw development of the Arrow anti-missile program, won the Israel Defense Prize in 1996, and today is a highly respected analyst of missile defense systems.

Lt. Col. (Res.) Teddy Sapir - Intelligence Analyst. Middle East expert. Specializes in modern history of Hezbollah, Lebanon and Syria. Research fellow at the *Alma*.

Dr. Jonathan Schanzer - Author of *Gaza Conflict 2021*, two other books about Middle East issues and countless other articles and reports. Schanzer is now the senior vice president for research at the Federated Defense of Democracies (FDD). Formerly, he worked as a terrorism finance analyst at the U.S. Department of the Treasury.

Yoram Schweitzer – Now head of the INSS Program on Terrorism and Low Intensity Conflict, following a distinguished career in the Israeli intelligence community as well as in the academic world. Among other positions, he served as a consultant on counter-terror strategies to the prime minister's office and the Ministry of Defense, and head of the Counter International Terror Section in the IDF.

Colonel (Res.) Shay Shemesh - Served as an outpost commander in the late 1990s in Lebanon and now is a reserve brigade commander and has a leadership role with Home Front Command in northern Israel.

Jonathan Spyer - Author of *Days of the Fall*, based on his undercover journalist trips to Syria and Iraq, and *The Transforming Fire*, based, in part, on his undercover journey to Lebanon. Spyer is now a much-sought expert on Middle East geopolitical issues.

Lt. Col. (Res.) Sarit Zehavi - Founder and president of *Alma* – a nonprofit and independent research and education center focusing on Israel's security challenges on its northern border. Zehavi served for fifteen years in the IDF, specializing in Military Intelligence.

Mathew Zweig – Now a senior fellow at FDD. Prior work has included senior sanctions advisor in the Office of the Special Representative for Syria Engagement, and seventeen years' service with the House Foreign Affairs Committee where he was responsible for various aspects of sanctions and illicit finance policy.

David Ur – CEO of *Alma*.

A Brief Listing of Informative Books

- *34 Days: Israel, Hezbollah, and the War in Lebanon*, Amos Harel (Palgrave Macmillan, 2008)
- *A House Divided*, Sandra Mackey (W.W. Norton & Company, 2006)
- *A Table Against Mine Enemies – Israel and the Lawfare Front*, Larry M. Goldstein. (Gefen Publishing House, 2017)
- *Assad: The Struggle for the Middle East*, Patrick Seale (University of California Press, 1989)
- *Assad or We Burn the Country*, Sam Dagher (Back Bay Books, Reprint 2020)
- *Defensive Shield*, Gal Hirsch (Gefen Books, 2016)
- *From Beirut to Jerusalem*, Thomas L. Friedman (Picador, Revised Edition, 2012)
- *From Prague to Jerusalem: An Uncommon Journey of a Journalist*, Milan Kubic (Northern Illinois University Press, 2017)
- *Gaza Conflict 2021*, Jonathan Schanzer (Foundation for Defense of Democracies, 2021)
- *Hezbollah – A Short History*, Augustus Richard Norton (Princeton University Press, 2018)

- *Hezbollah: Between Iran and Lebanon*, Shimon Shapira (Moshe Dayan Center for Middle Eastern and African Studies, 2021)
- *Hezbollah, The Global Footprint of Lebanon's Party of God*, Matthew Levitt (Georgetown University Press, Revised ed. 2015)
- *Hezbollah: The Story of the party to God*, Dr. Eitan Azani (Palgrave Macmillan, 2011)
- *High Price: The Triumphs and Failures of Israeli Counterterrorism*, Daniel Byman (Oxford University Press, 2011)
- *Israel and the Cyber Threat*, Charles D. Freilich (Oxford University Press, 2023)
- *Israel's Long War with Hezbollah,* Raphael D. Marcus (Georgetown University Press, 2018
- *Israeli National Security Strategy: A New Strategy for an Era of Change*, Charles D. Freilich (Oxford University Press, 2018)
- *Living in Heaven, Coping with Hell—Where Zionism Triumphed, the Kibbutz Evolves, and the Pioneering Spirit Prevails,* Clifford Sobin (Lean Forward Publishing, 2019)
- *Making David into Goliath*, Joshua Muravchik (Encounter Books, 2014)
- *Preemption: A Knife that Cuts Both Ways*, Alan M. Dershowitz (W.W. Norton & Company, 2006)
- *Pumpkin Flowers*, Matti Friedman (Algonquin Books, 2016)
- *Rise and Kill First*, Ronen Bergman (Random House, 2018)
- *Six Days of War,* Michael Oren (Presidio Press Kindle, 2017)
- *The Road to Fatima Gate*, Michael Totten (Belmont Estate Books, 2015)

- *The New Rules of War* by Sean McFate, (Avon, Reprint 2019)
- *The Pivotal Years*, Clifford Sobin (Clifford Sobin, 2017)
- *The Transforming Fire: The Rise of the Israel-Islamist Conflict,* Jonathan Spyer (Continuim, 2010)
- *Warriors of God*, Nicholas Blanford (Random House, 2011)
- *Window to the Backyard* – Yair Ravid (Ofir Bikurim, 2016)

Comprehensive Bibliography

A more comprehensive bibliography, broken down by chapter, can be found at www.CliffordSobin.com

My Request for a Review

If you enjoyed this book, and think it is worth recommending to others, please consider taking the time to write a short review on whichever platform you purchased it. I would greatly appreciate it.

About the Author

Cliff Sobin is a writer with a special interest in northern Israel. Cliff has spoken to numerous groups regarding his mother's Holocaust experience, his books regarding Israel, and workers' compensation. He also was the managing partner of his law firm from its inception in 1991 until he retired. His written work includes books, articles, and blogs concerning Israel, Maryland Workers' Compensation, Jackson Hole, and database application design. He now serves on the international advisory board for *Alma* and on AIPAC's National Council.

You can check out Cliff Sobin's new projects, thoughts, and ideas at www.CliffordSobin.com, as well as sign up for his newsletter there regarding northern Israel.

www.ingramcontent.com/pod-product-compliance
Lightning Source LLC
Chambersburg PA
CBHW070741030726
47601CB00001B/97